Public Records Law

FOR NORTH CAROLINA LOCAL GOVERNMENTS

SECOND EDITION 2009

David M. Lawrence

UNC
SCHOOL OF
GOVERNMENT

The School of Government at the University of North Carolina at Chapel Hill works to improve the lives of North Carolinians by engaging in practical scholarship that helps public officials and citizens understand and improve state and local government. Established in 1931 as the Institute of Government, the School provides educational, advisory, and research services for state and local governments. The School of Government is also home to a nationally ranked graduate program in public administration and specialized centers focused on information technology, environmental finance, and civic education for youth.

As the largest university-based local government training, advisory, and research organization in the United States, the School of Government offers up to 200 courses, seminars, and specialized conferences for more than 12,000 public officials each year. In addition, faculty members annually publish approximately fifty books, book chapters, bulletins, and other reference works related to state and local government. Each day that the General Assembly is in session, the School produces the *Daily Bulletin*, which reports on the day's activities for members of the legislature and others who need to follow the course of legislation.

The Master of Public Administration Program is a full-time, two-year program that serves up to sixty students annually. It consistently ranks among the best public administration graduate programs in the country, particularly in city management. With courses ranging from public policy analysis to ethics and management, the program educates leaders for local, state, and federal governments and nonprofit organizations.

Operating support for the School of Government's programs and activities comes from many sources, including state appropriations, local government membership dues, private contributions, publication sales, course fees, and service contracts. Visit www.sog.unc.edu or call 919.966.5381 for more information on the School's courses, publications, programs, and services.

First edition 1997. Second edition 2009.

Printed in the United States of America

21 20 19 18 17 3 4 5 6 7

ISBN 978-1-56011-614-1

Contents

Preface

Governments constantly generate records. Accounting records track the financial position of the government. Leases, insurance policies, and other contracts evidence and govern a wide variety of business relationships. Personnel files reflect the qualifications, performance, and evaluations of public employees. Employees and consultants produce reports on a myriad of matters of interest to government officials and often develop large banks of raw data in the process of doing so. Employees write memoranda to each other. Clerks prepare minutes of meetings. Law enforcement agencies and regulatory agencies compile extensive investigatory files in the process of doing their work. In generating all these forms of records, governments are no different than large private organizations. Business needs require records. But because these records are generated by public organizations, the law has, since at least the nineteenth century, imposed a special burden on *public* records. They are, in general, open to the public for both inspection and for copying. This book is about the contours of the public's right of access to public records held by North Carolina local governments. (A short chapter also summarizes the law on managing and disposing of public records.)

This is the second edition of a book first published in 1997 and twice supplemented since then. This edition expands upon the original in two ways. First, the passage of a dozen years has brought many new issues to the fore, and therefore the book addresses a goodly number of issues not covered in the first edition. Second, the General Assembly has continued to add exceptions to the right of access, and therefore the book addresses those new statutes as well.

Like the earlier version, the book is in two parts. The first part discusses public records in general and seeks to understand what records are public, what agencies are subject to the public records law, and what the right of public access means in detail. There are also short chapters on the impact of federal law on access to public records and on the special qualities of electronic records. The second part of the book begins with a general discussion of exceptions to the right of public access and then proceeds to look at a number of the statutes that exempt, or that might exempt, categories of records from the right of public access. For each such statute, the book summarizes the exemption and then discusses a variety of legal issues pertinent to each statute. I have not attempted to discuss every statute that creates an exemption, but I have covered those of the broadest application within local government. (The book is directed at *local* government, but much of it will also be of use to officials in *state* government in North Carolina.)

The North Carolina appellate courts have had only a few occasions to address public records issues in the seventy-five years since the current public records statute was first enacted. North Carolina's statute, however, shares many characteristics with the statutes of other states, and I have not hesitated to turn to cases decided in other states to help understand and answer questions about our statutes. These out-of-state cases have been one source of the issues that I address in the book. The other sources have been my own reading of the statutes and the countless questions that have been addressed to me by state and local government officials, and by reporters and citizens, in the thirty-plus years I have been working on public records issues. I hope these sources will, in combination, lead to a book that will be of significant practical use to local government officials and their attorneys and to the state's news media and the public at large.

A number of my colleagues at the School of Government have helped with the book by reading one or more chapters involving their areas of work: Mark Botts, Bob Joyce, Diane Juffras, Tyler Mulligan, and Aimee Wall. The book is much better for their help. In addition, I owe an enormous debt to Kathy Burke, who did a detailed cite check of each of the chapters. Kathy's work saved me from far more errors than I care to admit. I thank them all.

I am finishing this book with just a few months to go before I retire, after more than forty-one years at the Institute and now the School of Government. It has been a wonderful place to work, especially because of the wonderful people with whom I have worked. In recognition of the friendship and gratitude I have to all of them, I dedicate this book to all who have worked at the Institute and School since I arrived in the summer of 1968.

David M. Lawrence
William Rand Kenan Jr. Professor
of Public Law and Government

Chapel Hill
December 2009

PART I—Public Records Generally

Chapter 1—Basic Principles: What Is a Public Record?

Introduction

The Term "Public Record"

Under the North Carolina General Statutes as interpreted by the appellate courts, there are at least three separate and somewhat distinct usages of the term "public record." This section reviews those three usages.

G.S. Chapter 121

The first usage, and the broadest, is found in Chapter 121 of the North Carolina General Statutes [hereinafter G.S.], especially G.S. 121-5. That section designates the Department of Cultural Resources as the official archival agency of the state and empowers the department to regulate the retention, preservation, and destruction of public records. The department has used this power to prepare and disseminate a variety of record retention and destruction schedules applicable to different sorts of governments and agencies. The department's powers apply to public records as defined in G.S. 121-2(8), as follows:

> "Public record" or "public records" shall mean all documents, papers, letters, maps, books, photographs, films, sound recordings, magnetic or other tapes, electronic data processing records, artifacts, or other documentary material, regardless of physical form or characteristics, made or received pursuant to law or ordinance *or* in connection with the transaction of official business by any agency.

G.S. Chapter 132

The second usage, a little narrower than the first, is found in G.S. Chapter 132, which is the Public Records chapter of the General Statutes. The chapter regulates custody of public records, provides for public inspection and copying of records, and references the powers of the Department of Cultural Resources under G.S. Chapter 121. The chapter applies to public records as defined in G.S. 132-1, which contains the same definition as set out in G.S. 121-2(8), with one noteworthy exception. The "or" (which is italicized in the Chapter 121 definition set out above) is missing from the definition in G.S. 132-1.[1] Although deletion of the "or" might be thought to narrow the definition, it has not done so in practice, and the appellate courts have drawn no attention to the difference. Despite the almost identical definitions of public record in Chapters 121 and 132, the practical coverage of Chapter 132—except as noted in the next paragraphs—is somewhat narrower. This is because a number of statutes that seem primarily intended to exempt certain classes of records from public inspection do so by providing that the subject classes are not public records under G.S. 132-1, thereby exempting the records from the entire chapter. An example of such an exemption is G.S. 132-1.4, which provides that criminal investigation and criminal intelligence records "are not public records as defined by G.S. 132-1."

The Right of Public Access

The third usage refers to those records that members of the public are entitled to inspect and to copy. This is a narrower usage than the first two because a great many statutes exempt described classes of records from public access. The greater part of this book discusses the statutes of this sort that are most important to local governments.

In this book the first and second usages will be the focus of chapter 3. Otherwise, the book will focus on the third usage, either directly, in chapters 1, 2, and 4, or indirectly, in the chapters that discuss statutory exemptions from the right of public access.

An Initial Summary of Public Records Law

North Carolina law defines the term public record very broadly, and the state supreme court has held that "in the absence of clear statutory exemption or exception, documents falling within the definition of 'public records' in the Public Records Act must be made available for public inspection."[2] Therefore, if an item meets the definition of public record,

---

1. The statutes are set out in appendix 1A at the end of this chapter.
2. News & Observer Publ'g Co. v. Poole, 330 N.C. 465, 486, 412 S.E.2d 7, 19 (1992).

the custodian must allow public inspection unless the custodian can point to some North Carolina (or federal) statute that permits or requires denial of public access.[3] A number of those statutes are the subject of Part II of this book, but in general the great bulk of material held by local governments is public record and open to public access. This point is elaborated in the remainder of this chapter.

The basic right of public access is set out in G.S. 132-6 and is two-fold. First, a person enjoys a right of inspection—that is, the right to read or otherwise examine the public record. Second, a person enjoys a right to make or have made a copy of the record. A government may charge the person for the direct cost of making a copy, but there is no charge authorized for the simple right of inspection or for the cost of locating the record preparatory to making the copy. Chapter 2 of this book discusses in detail the rights of inspection and copying.

Agencies Subject to the Public Records Law

In General

G.S. 132-1 extends the reach of the public records law to every agency of state or local government in North Carolina. The section defines the covered agencies to include "every public office, public officer or official (State or local, elected or appointed), institution, board, commission, bureau, council, department, authority or other unit of government of the State or of any county, unit, special district or other political subdivision of government." Thus, at the local level, the law extends to counties, cities, school administrative units, community colleges, special districts such as sanitary districts or metropolitan sewerage districts, and public authorities such as water and sewer authorities, hospital authorities, and regional public transportation authorities. It also extends to joint entities such as councils of government, district health departments, area mental health authorities, regional libraries, and joint agencies established by contracts between local governments. In *News & Observer Publishing Co. v. Poole*, the defendants argued that an agency that was exempt from the state's open meetings law should, for that reason, also be exempt from the state's public records law, but the court rejected the argument summarily.[4] Therefore, for example, even though a particular board might not be subject to the open meetings law, the minutes of its meetings would still be a public record.

Nonprofit Corporations and Other Private Entities

G.S. 132-1 also reaches some agencies that are not formal parts of local government. Usually these are nonprofit corporations, and for that reason most of the discussion in this section focuses on this sort of entity. Some of the cases from other states, however, even

3. The possible impact of federal legislation on records held by North Carolina local governments is discussed *infra* in chapter 4.

4. 330 N.C. 465, 412 S.E.2d 7 (1992). The court wrote: "The Public Records Act and the Open Meetings Law are discrete statutes, each designed to promote in a different way openness in government. There is no suggestion in either statute that an agency not subject to one is, *ipso facto*, exempt from the other." *Id.* at 478, 412 S.E.2d at 15 (emphasis in original).

subject for-profit entities to public records statutes, and that possibility should not be overlooked.

Local governments frequently contract with and appropriate money to nonprofit organizations in order for the nonprofit entity to carry on some activity on behalf of the local government. In many cases the nonprofit organization is clearly separate from the local government, and its relationship to the local government is that of independent contractor. In such a case the nonprofit organization is not an agency under the public records law, and its records are not subject to that law. This is true even when all or nearly all of the revenues of the nonprofit entity come from one or more governmental contracts. A good, common example of such a nonprofit is a volunteer fire department.[5] But sometimes the nonprofit organization has ties to the local government beyond those of the usual independent contractor. The local government may appoint some or all of the members of the organization's board of directors; the local government may possess power to approve the organization's budget or the sale of the organization's assets; employees of the local government may serve as staff to the organization; the local government may own the facilities that are operated by the organization; and so on. In the case of such a nonprofit organization, its private form of organization does not automatically exempt the organization from the public records law. Rather, at some point its ties to local government become so numerous and the activities of the organization so intertwined with the local government that the organization becomes an agency of the government for purposes of the public records law.[6] There are at least three different approaches by which the facts concerning a particular organization might be analyzed and lead to a conclusion that the nonprofit organization is a public agency for purposes of public record access.

The first approach focuses on the degree of supervision or control that one or more clearly governmental entities have over the nonprofit organization and is illustrated by the North Carolina Court of Appeals decision in *News & Observer Publishing Co. v. Wake County Hospital System, Inc.*[7] In that case, the newspaper sought records of the nonprofit corporation that operated hospital facilities owned by Wake County. The court reviewed the entire relationship between the county and the corporation, as demonstrated in three documents: the corporation's articles of incorporation, a lease agreement between the county and the corporation, and an operating agreement between the county and the corporation. It found that the county had clear supervisory responsibilities and control over the corporation, as indicated by the following factors: (1) upon its dissolution, all of the corporation's assets would vest in the county; (2) the filling of all vacancies on the board of directors of the corporation had to be approved by the county; (3) county facilities were leased to the corporation for one dollar a year; (4) the board of county commissioners was empowered to review and approve the corporation's annual budget; (5) the county was entitled to conduct

---

5. Although it is virtually certain that a volunteer fire department in North Carolina is not subject to the public records law simply because it contracts with a county or city to provide fire protection, at least one state court has reached a contrary conclusion under that state's public records statute. *See* Yantic Volunteer Fire Co. v. Freedom of Info. Comm'n, 679 A.2d 989 (Conn. 1996).

6. A nonprofit corporation can also become subject to the public records law by specific statutory direction. See N.C. Gen. Stat. [hereinafter G.S.] § 55A-3-07, which makes two sorts of nonprofit corporations, both serving state government, subject to the public records law.

7. 55 N.C. App. 1, 284 S.E.2d 542 (1981).

a supervisory audit of the corporation; (6) the corporation was required to report its rates and charges to the county; (7) county revenue bonds financed improvements to the facilities operated by the corporation; (8) revenues collected by the corporation were county revenues for purposes of revenue bond repayment; and (9) the corporation could not change its corporate existence or amend its articles of incorporation without county consent. The court found the pattern of supervision and control sufficient to hold that the corporation was an agency of the county for purposes of the public records law.[8]

A second case stands in helpful contrast to the *Wake County Hospital System* case. In *Chatfield v. Wilmington Housing Finance & Development, Inc.*,[9] the plaintiffs sought access to the meetings and records of the defendant nonprofit corporation. At various times in the past, the defendant or a predecessor corporation had been subject to a variety of controls exercised by the county, the city, and the local housing authority, as follows: (1) the original stated purpose of the corporation was to assist the Wilmington Housing Authority in its operations, and the incorporator was the authority's executive director; (2) the corporation's accounting practices and finances were subject to annual review by the authority; (3) the corporation's net earnings were to accrue to the authority, and the authority was to get the corporation's assets upon dissolution; (4) the authority had to approve any changes in the corporation's articles of incorporation; and (5) a majority of the corporation's board of directors were appointed by the county, city, and authority. By the time the trial court finally ruled on the plaintiff's suit, however, each of these controls had been removed, and the trial court granted summary judgment to the corporation. The court of appeals noted that none of the nine factors listed in the *Wake County Hospital System* case were any longer applicable in *Chatfield* and affirmed the trial court.

The *Wake County Hospital System* case is notable for the extensive degree of control and supervision that the county retained over the nonprofit corporation. Unfortunately, it is not greatly helpful in determining whether other nonprofit agencies, with somewhat different relationships to other local governments, are agencies of those local governments for public records purposes. The court acknowledged that each relationship of this type must be looked at individually, in its own context, and that point was repeated in *Chatfield*. Two other North Carolina hospital cases, though, decided in other contexts, suggest three factors that can be especially important—the power of one or more local governments to control the board of directors of the nonprofit corporation; the regular or eventual transfer of assets to one or more governments; and the power of one or more local governments to exercise significant control over the corporation's fiscal affairs. In *Coats v. Sampson County Memorial Hospital, Inc.*,[10] the defendant was a nonprofit corporation that operated a county-owned hospital under a ten-year lease. The county commissioners appointed the

---

8. The attorney general's office relied directly upon the *Wake County Hospital System* case in concluding that the Northeast Partnership, a nonprofit corporation, was an "agency" within the meaning of the public records act. The partnership had been established by the Northeastern North Carolina Regional Economic Development Commission, a statutorily created agency; the commission's board members were automatically the board members of the partnership; and the commission had handed over to the partnership its responsibilities and resources. Letter to Melanie Thompson, 9 March 1999, Advisory Opinion No. 414, *available at* www.ncdoj.gov/About-DOJ/Legal-Services/Legal-Opinions.aspx.

9. 166 N.C. App. 703, 603 S.E.2d 837 (2004).

10. 264 N.C. 332, 141 S.E.2d 490 (1965).

corporation's board of directors, and the corporation's charter provided that the county would succeed to all of the corporation's assets should it be dissolved. The suit was brought in Harnett County, where the plaintiff electrical contractors resided. G.S. 1-77, however, requires that suits against public officers and agencies be brought in the county where the cause of action arose, and the North Carolina Supreme Court held that the hospital corporation was a county agency for purposes of this venue statute. In *Sides v. Cabarrus Memorial Hospital, Inc.*,[11] the hospital corporation had been established pursuant to a special act of the General Assembly. Although the corporation was legally separate from the county, the county commissioners appointed the board of trustees, the county treasurer served as the corporation's treasurer, and the corporation was directed to submit an annual financial report to the county commissioners. On these facts the North Carolina Supreme Court held that the corporation was a county agency for purposes of liability insurance coverage.[12]

The second approach looks not so much at government control over the nonprofit but at whether the nonprofit is acting in the government's stead and as its agent (rather than as a truly independent contractor). This approach is best exemplified by the case of *Memphis Publishing Co. v. Cherokee Children & Family Services, Inc.*,[13] in which the Tennessee Supreme Court applied a test of "functional equivalency" to a company hired by the state

---

11. 287 N.C. 14, 213 S.E.2d 197 (1975).

12. Some cases from other states that that have used this approach to hold that nonprofit corporations are subject to public records laws include *Denver Post Corp. v. Stapleton Development Corp.*, 19 P.3d 36 (Colo. App. 2000), in which the defendant corporation was held subject to the state's public records law in part because it had been created by Denver's urban renewal agency and all members of the corporation's board of directors were appointed by the mayor or the urban renewal agency and confirmed by the city council; *Andy's Ice Cream, Inc. v. City of Salisbury*, 724 A.2d 717 (Md. Ct. Spec. App. 1999), in which the Salisbury Zoo Commission, a nonprofit corporation, was held to be a city agency for public records purposes because the mayor and city council appointed the corporation's board of directors, the city council had to approve the corporation's budget, the mayor and council could unilaterally change the corporation's bylaws although the corporation itself could not, and the mayor and council could dissolve the corporation; and *Professional Firefighters of New Hampshire v. Healthtrust, Inc.*, 861 A.2d 789 (N.H. 2004), in which the defendant, which writes health insurance coverage for New Hampshire local governments, was held to be subject to the public records law in part because all its members were local governments and its governing board was composed entirely of public officials and employees. But see *State ex rel. Stys v. Parma Community General Hospital*, 755 N.E.2d 874 (Ohio 2001), in which the court held that the hospital corporation was not subject to the state's public records law even though sixteen of eighteen directors were appointed by the mayors of the six municipalities that had established the corporation.

A number of other cases have used the same approach to conclude that certain nonprofit corporations are not subject to the state's public records law, namely, *Dow v. Caribou Chamber of Commerce & Industry*, 884 A.2d 667 (Me. 2005), in which the corporation got 60 percent of its budget from grants from the city but only two of eleven board members represented the city; *Ervin v. Southern Tier Economic Development, Inc.*, 809 N.Y.S.2d 268 (App. Div. 2006), in which six of the corporation's nine members were private individuals not appointed by or controlled by the city or county; *Rumore v. Board of Education*, 826 N.Y.S.2d 545 (App. Div. 2006), *leave to appeal denied*, 866 N.E.2d 454 (N.Y. 2007), in which the corporation's budget was not approved by any public agency and its board was self-selected; and *Spokane Research & Defense Fund v. West Central Community Development Ass'n*, 137 P.3d 120 (Wash. Ct. App. 2006), *review denied*, 158 P.3d 614 (Wash. 2007), in which the association, which operates a community center located in a city park, was governed by a board of directors with no connection to the city.

13. 87 S.W.3d 67 (Tenn. 2002).

to help poor families find subsidized day care. Because the company had taken over a function theretofore performed by the state, received almost 100 percent of its funding from public sources, and was subject to significant state control in its operations, it was subject to the Tennessee public records statute. The court summarized its approach as follows:

> As the facts of these cases [from other states] demonstrate, private entities that perform public services on behalf of a government often do so as independent contractors. Nonetheless, the public's fundamental right to scrutinize the performance of public services and the expenditure of public funds should not be subverted by government or by private entity merely because public duties have been delegated to an independent contractor. When a private entity's relationship with the government is so extensive that the entity serves as the functional equivalent of a governmental agency, the accountability created by public oversight should be preserved.[14]

Interestingly, the Tennessee court cited the *Wake County Hospital System* case as an example of this same approach from another state.

The *Memphis Publishing* case involved the nature of an agency as a whole (as did the *Wake County Hospital System* case). This approach, however, has also been used to support public access to selected records of an otherwise apparently private organization, often a for-profit organization. Two cases illustrate this possibility.

First, in *Stanfield v. Salvation Army*,[15] the Florida District Court of Appeals examined the relationship between a county and the Salvation Army. Under a contract between the two parties, the Salvation Army undertook the county's statutory responsibility for the six-month period of supervision imposed on all misdemeanants placed on probation. It was responsible for job placement and for monitoring compliance with the conditions of probation, reporting probation violations, and collecting supervision fees. Under the contract, the Salvation Army was required to maintain a record on each person subject to supervision. The appellate court held that because the Salvation Army was providing probationary services on the county's behalf, it was the county's agent and, therefore, the probation records kept by the Salvation Army were subject to the public records law.[16]

Second, in *State ex rel. Gannett Satellite Information Network v. Shirey*,[17] the Ohio Supreme Court considered a contract under which a private consultant assisted a city in

---

14. *Id.* at 78–79. A later Tennessee case that also illustrates this approach is *Allen v. Day*, 213 S.W.3d 244 (Tenn. Ct. App. 2006), in which the court held that records generated and held by a for-profit private management company that managed Nashville's hockey arena were public records.

15. 695 So. 2d 501 (Fla. Dist. Ct. App. 1997).

16. Another Florida case is *Prison Health Services, Inc. v. Lakeland Ledger Publishing Co.*, 718 So. 2d 204 (Fla. Dist. Ct. App. 1998). In that case a county sheriff contracted with a private company to provide total health care services to the inmates and detainees in the county jail, and the court held that because the company was acting on behalf of the sheriff, its records with respect to the jail would be public records to the same extent as if the sheriff had generated them. *See also* Booksmart Enters., Inc. v. Barnes & Noble College Bookstores, Inc., 718 So. 2d 227 (Fla. Dist. Ct. App. 1998) (textbook request forms provided by public college faculty to private company operating on-campus book store; held, public records); Burkett v. UDS Mgmt. Corp., 741 So. 2d 838 (La. Ct. App. 1999) (records relating to publicly owned utility system held by private company managing utility system; held, public records).

17. 678 N.E.2d 557 (Ohio 1997).

hiring a department head. The court held that the consultant, by receiving and evaluating applications and presenting the city with a short list of finalists for the position, was carrying on the city's business; thus the city could not escape the public records law by entering into such a contract.[18]

The third approach focuses on the creation of the nonprofit corporation and on daily operating connections between government and the corporation. For example, if a government agency was instrumental in creating the nonprofit corporation, the corporation is housed in a government building, and the corporation is staffed by government employees, these ties might well be sufficient to cause a court to label the corporation a public agency for public records purposes. For example, in *Macon Telegraph Publishing Co. v. Board of Regents*,[19] the plaintiff newspaper sought the records of the University of Georgia Athletic Association, a private corporation that was the apparent employer of the university's football coach and other athletic personnel. The court noted that the university's president was head of the association, the university's vice president of business and finance was treasurer of the association, and state statutes imposed on the university president the responsibility of supervising intercollegiate athletics, which he did through the association. It concluded that the association's records were therefore subject to the state's public records law.[20]

---

18. The Ohio courts have explicitly accepted the functional equivalency test as the most appropriate approach to these sorts of cases. *See* State *ex rel.* Oriana House, Inc. v. Montgomery, 854 N.E.2d 193 (Ohio 2006), and State *ex rel.* Repository v. Nova Behavioral Health, Inc., 859 N.E.2d 936 (Ohio 2006). In the Ohio cases, the court sets out four factors that should be considered in a functional equivalency test: (1) whether the private entity performs a governmental function, (2) whether the level of government funding is significant, (3) the extent of government involvement in or regulation of the private entity's operations, and (4) whether the entity was created by the government.

In *Durham Herald Co. v. North Carolina Low-Level Radioactive Waste Management Authority*, 110 N.C. App. 607, 430 S.E.2d 441 (1993), the court held that material gathered by a contractor for the authority was not a public record until turned over to the authority. This decision, however, depended on the particular language of the statute under which the authority operated and did not establish a more general rule applicable to all contractors for public agencies in North Carolina.

An interesting question raised by this line of reasoning is the status of the records of a North Carolina political party's county executive committee when it is exercising its statutory right to, as a practical matter, appoint replacements to certain vacant positions in county government. Under G.S. 153A-27.1, the appropriate county executive committee in some forty-two counties is authorized to nominate a person to fill a vacancy in the board of county commissioners, and the board of commissioners is directed by statute to appoint the person so nominated. Under G.S. 162-5.1, the appropriate county executive committee in some forty-five counties is given the same power with respect to vacancies in the sheriff's office. The cases discussed in this section certainly lend weight to the conclusion that a committee's records in fulfilling these responsibilities are public records.

19. 350 S.E.2d 23 (Ga. 1986).

20. *State ex rel. Toledo Blade Co. v. University of Toledo Foundation*, 602 N.E.2d 1159 (Ohio 1992), might be thought to combine the second and third approaches. Predecessor foundations to the defendant had been housed in university buildings without paying rent, and university employees served as staff to these earlier foundations. The earlier foundations had complied with the public records law. The current foundation, however, paid rent for its office space, and its employees were no longer university employees. The court noted, however, that the university continued to pay state retirement system benefits for the employees and that the foundation's role was to accept all donations made to the university. On that basis the court held that the foundation continued to be subject to the state's public records law.

What Documents and Other Items Are Included within the Meaning of "Public Record"?

In General

G.S. 132-1 establishes a very broad definition of "public record," generally unlimited by the form of the material in question or by the circumstances under which it was received or created. The statute begins by including within the definition not only documents and other papers but also "maps, books, photographs, films, sound recordings, magnetic or other tapes, electronic data-processing records, [and] artifacts, . . . regardless of physical form or characteristics." The statute then goes on to state that public record means the listed items "made or received pursuant to law or ordinance in connection with the transaction of public business."[21]

Litigants have sometimes argued that the latter part of the definition—"made or received pursuant to law or ordinance"—contains words of limitation and that only those records whose receipt is specifically required by statute or local ordinance are public records. The court of appeals rejected such a limiting reading in *News & Observer Publishing Co. v. Wake County Hospital System, Inc.*[22] Among the records sought in that case were expense account records submitted to the agency by members of its staff and governing board. In holding that these were public records, the court stated that "[t]he phrase in G.S. 132-1, 'pursuant to law or ordinance in connection with the transaction of public business,' should include, in addition to those records required by law, those records that are kept in carrying out lawful duties."[23] The North Carolina Supreme Court did not specifically address the definition of public record in *News & Observer Publishing Co. v. Poole*,[24] its leading discussion of the public records statute. But the court obviously accepted a broad reading of the statutory language, consistent with the statement by the court of appeals. A number of the documents involved in *Poole* were not required by any law,[25] yet the court held they were public records.

---

21. A few states have narrower definitions of public records, and the difference in definition can lead to a difference in outcome. For example, in *State ex rel. Dispatch Printing Co. v. Johnson*, 833 N.E.2d 274 (Ohio 2005), the newspaper was seeking the home addresses of employees. The court noted that the Ohio statute defines a record as any document "which serves to document the organization, functions, policies, decisions, procedures, operations, or other activities of the office," and then held that the employee addresses, collected for payroll purposes, did not meet the definition. The addresses would clearly meet the North Carolina definition of public record, although they would be shielded from public access as part of the employees' personnel files. Similarly, in *Argus Leader v. Hagen*, 739 N.W.2d 475 (S.D. 2007), the South Dakota Supreme Court read that state's statute to restrict the right of access to records whose maintenance or retention is required by law; therefore, an invitation list to a gubernatorial function was held not to be a public record, because it was not required by law to be maintained. Such a list would be open to public access in North Carolina. The larger point, however, is that someone relying on cases from other jurisdictions must be sure that the other jurisdiction's definition of public record is comparable to North Carolina's.

22. 55 N.C. App. 1, 284 S.E.2d 542 (1981).

23. *Id.* at 13, 284 S.E.2d at 549.

24. 330 N.C. 465, 412 S.E.2d 7 (1992).

25. For example, the plaintiffs sought minutes of the Poole Commission, a body established and appointed by the president of the university system, and copies of draft reports written by two commission members at the conclusion of its work. The commission was a nonstatutory body, not subject to the state's

It may sometimes be that a record has not been received by a public agency, or perhaps not received quite yet. In *Salt River Pima-Maricopa Indian Community v. Rogers*,[26] the court held that a document that belonged to a private bank but that was found, for unexplained reasons, in the office of the state treasurer, was not a public record. The document had not been used by the treasurer's office, nor had it been generated for any responsibility of the office; it seems, rather, simply to have been inadvertently left in the office. The court held that a document's mere presence in a public office, without anything more, is insufficient to make the document a public record. A number of North Carolina cities accept payment for private utility bills, collecting on behalf of the private company. This case suggests that the records associated with such an arrangement are not public, despite their presence in the city's offices and the city's involvement in the collection process. The records were not received for any public business of the public agency. In a related vein, local governments sometimes begin contracting processes by issuing a request for proposals. Typically the proposals are submitted in a sealed form, to be opened only after the deadline for submissions. It seems reasonable to conclude that the proposals have not been "received" and therefore are not open to the public until at least the envelope or other enclosure has been opened.

Sometimes public officials and private parties seek to avoid a document's becoming a public record by attempting to keep the document always in private possession. For example, a private person or entity might bring a document along to a meeting with a public official or agency, and the document might be used during the meeting, but the private person or entity would then take it away after the meeting so that the public official or agency had no copy of the document. This probably would not serve to prevent the document from becoming a public record. In *Times Publishing Co. v. City of St. Petersburg*,[27] for instance, the city was in discussion with the Chicago White Sox about a possible move by the team to the Florida city. To avoid disclosure of the negotiations, or even of the existence of the talks, the baseball team claimed ownership of all documents, such as draft leases, and retained sole possession of them. The team retained Florida counsel and sent copies of documents to that private attorney. The city officials could inspect the documents only at the lawyer's office and were not permitted to make copies, but the documents evolved as a result of the meetings between the team and city officials. In a suit by the newspaper for copies of the documents, the Florida court held that once a document had been presented to the city and revised during meetings between the city and the team, it was a public record, and the arrangements made by the team and the city were to no avail. It seems likely a North Carolina court would agree.[28]

---

open meetings law, and therefore there was no law that required that it keep minutes nor any law that required it to make a report.

26. 815 P.2d 900 (Ariz. 1991).

27. 558 So. 2d 487 (Fla. Dist. Ct. App. 1990).

28. *Accord* Journal/Sentinel, Inc. v. School Bd., 521 N.W.2d 165 (Wis. Ct. App. 1994). The school superintendent sued the district and the school board and the suit was settled, with the settlement memorialized by a memorandum of understanding. A draft of the memorandum had been passed out to school board members but then retrieved and retained by the attorney representing the district. The court held that the memorandum was a public record. *But see* State *ex rel.* Cincinnati Enquirer v. Cincinnati Bd. of Educ., 788 N.E.2d 629 (Ohio 2003). The school board was interviewing finalists for superintendent and informed the applicants that they could bring application materials with them to the interview and then take those materials away with them. The court held that the materials that were taken away were

In summary, then, the definition of a public record is quite broad. Here is an informal and incomplete listing of some of the many sorts of documents that are clearly public records under the statutory language:

- Animal adoption records
- Bank statements and other financial records[29]
- Citizen complaints about services
- Contracts[30]
- Correspondence between a government agency and others—private citizens, contractors, other governments, and so on
- Documents from private contractors showing compliance with contract terms[31]
- Documents obtained through discovery in litigation[32]
- Donation records, including the names and addresses of donors
- Electronic mail
- Grant applications
- Inspection reports and supporting materials
- Insurance policies purchased by the government and related materials
- Leases
- License and permit applications and copies of issued licenses and permits[33]
- Names of persons participating in recreational leagues and other activities
- Property transaction documents, including deeds, land-sale contracts, and appraisals
- Video tapes[34]
- Voice mail[35]

---

not public records. It relied, however, on language in the Ohio statute that applied the public records law to documents "kept by any public office," holding that the school board had not *kept* these application materials. The North Carolina statute applies to documents that have been "received" by the public agency, and a North Carolina court might easily distinguish the Ohio case by holding that comparable documents had in fact been received by the interviewing agency.

29. Bank account numbers, however, are not public records. G.S. 132-1.10.

30. *See, e.g.*, Lakewood Residents Ass'n. v. Lakewood Hous. Auth., 682 A.2d 1201 (N.J. Super. Ct. App. Div. 1996) (housing assistance contracts between housing authority and Section 8 landlords).

31. *See, e.g.*, Sapp Roofing Co., Inc. v. Sheet Metal Workers' Int'l Ass'n, Local Union No. 12, 713 A.2d 627 (Pa. 1998) (roofing contractor payroll records, submitted to public agency to demonstrate compliance with prevailing wage statute, are public records).

32. Hill v. Prudential Ins. Co., 701 So. 2d 1218 (Fla. Dist. Ct. App. 1997); Memphis Pub. Co. v. City of Memphis, 871 S.W.2d 681 (Tenn. 1994). If a party litigating against a government wishes to protect its discovered documents from becoming public records, it needs to obtain a protective order. *Cf.* Star Tribune v. Minnesota Twins P'ship , 659 N.W.2d 287 (Minn. Ct. App. 2003).

33. In Letter to W.A. "Doc" Hoggard III, 15 August 1997, Advisory Opinion No. 319, *available at* www.ncdoj.gov/About-DOJ/Legal-Services/Legal-Opinions.aspx, the attorney general's office concluded that in general an application for a license issued by a state licensing board was a public record, as were supporting materials.

34. *See, e.g.*, Hemeyer v. KRCG-TV, 6 S.W.3d 880 (Mo. 1999) (video tapes made of various locations in sheriff's office).

35. In Letter to Ann W. Spragens, 18 April 1996, Advisory Opinion No. 255, *available at* www.ncdoj.gov/About-DOJ/Legal-Services/Legal-Opinions.aspx, the attorney general's office opined that in general voice mail records are public records.

Preliminary Drafts

Public officials sometimes argue that although a specific document will be a public record once it is finished, it is not a public record until that point is reached. They contend that early versions of the document, still being worked on by its author or perhaps being circulated to others for comment, need not be made available to the public for inspection or copying. How have courts, in North Carolina and elsewhere, responded to this argument?

A version of the argument was made to the North Carolina Supreme Court in the *News & Observer Publishing Co. vs. Poole* decision. Two members of the Poole Commission drafted reports on the commission's work, and versions of these reports were submitted to the president of the university system. The court held that the reports, in this form, were public records and available to the public, rejecting the defendants' argument that preliminary drafts should be excepted from the access provisions of the law.[36] It is possible to argue that the "draft" reports in question were not really preliminary drafts, inasmuch as it does not appear that the commission or its members ever submitted final versions of the reports to the president. Other courts, when faced with such an apparent attempt at subterfuge, have had no problem characterizing the reports in question as actually final and therefore open to public access.[37] It would be possible, therefore, to attempt to distinguish *Poole* on its facts if a records request involved a draft that was legitimately still in the preliminary stage. Unfortunately for such an argument, the court's language in *Poole* is broad and makes no distinction between real and sham drafts.

Much of the case law from other states also mandates access to preliminary material. In *Missouri Protection & Advocacy Services v. Allen*,[38] the plaintiffs sought a copy of a preliminary draft report sent by a federal agency to a state agency for the latter's review and comment. The court ruled for the plaintiffs, holding that a report need not be in final form to be a public record. In *Times Publishing Co. v. City of St. Petersburg*,[39] the plaintiff sought a copy of drafts of leases still being negotiated between the city and another party. There, too, the court ruled for the plaintiffs.[40] And in *MacEwan v. Holm*,[41] the court held that data collected by a state agency in order to prepare a report were public records, "irrespective of [the data's] tentative or preliminary character."[42]

The *Poole* decision and the Missouri and Florida cases cited above each involved documents that were in printed form, even if the form was not yet the final form. The Oregon case involved raw data, but the data could be made available to the public without that interfering with the preparation of the report for which it was collected. There do not appear to be any reported decisions in which plaintiffs sought records in the midst of their preparation, before any draft had been circulated to others and at a time at which

---

36. 330 N.C. 465, 412 S.E.2d 7 (1992).

37. *E.g.*, Fox v. Bock, 438 N.W.2d 589 (Wis. 1989).

38. 787 S.W.2d 291 (Mo. Ct. App. 1990).

39. 558 So. 2d 487 (Fla. Dist. Ct. App. 1990).

40. It should be noted, however, that the Florida Supreme Court in *Shevin v. Byron, Harless, Schaffer, Reid & Associates, Inc.*, 379 So. 2d 633 (Fla. 1980), wrote that "rough drafts" "obviously would not be public records." *Id.* at 640. That case involved handwritten notes rather than rough drafts, however, and so the quoted language is perhaps dicta.

41. 359 P.2d 413 (Or. 1961).

42. *Id.* at 420.

the content of the draft might be changing daily or even more often. It remains possible that a court might exclude such a draft from the definition of public record, at least until the authority begins to circulate it to others, but there appears to be little other room for excluding from public access documents that are closer to completion.[43] Thus, for example, it is virtually certain that the public has a right of access to such documents as a board's draft minutes or departmental budget requests made to the manager or budget officer.

It also should be noted that a draft remains public record even after the final version has been prepared. Although it is permitted to destroy such drafts once there is a final version,[44] if a draft has not been destroyed it retains its character as a public record even though there is a final version.

Records That Could Have Been Disposed Of

Chapter 3 discusses the rules that govern retention and disposition of public records. Many local governments retain various sorts of records well past the time that they are permitted to dispose of the records. A city clerk, for example, might retain several years' worth of audio tapes of council meetings, even though the tapes can be erased or written over as soon as the council approves the minutes of the taped meeting. That the records could have been disposed of, but have not been, has no effect on whether they are open to public access. As long as the records remain in existence, they remain public records and open to public inspection and copying.

Data, Surveys, and Other Source Materials

As they do with preliminary drafts, public officials sometimes argue that the source materials upon which completed reports or other records are based are not themselves public records. Source materials include items such as scientific or economic data, surveys or questionnaires, interview summaries, and audit working papers. In general the courts have rejected such arguments.[45]

---

43. In an opinion letter written in 1994, after the *Poole* decision, the attorney general's office suggested that a court might hold that documents in an earlier stage of preparation than had been the case in *Poole* were not yet public records. Letter to Deborah Crane, 29 August 1994, Advisory Opinion No. 140, *available at* www.ncdoj.gov/About-DOJ/Legal-Services/Legal-Opinions.aspx. In *Smith v. Elliott*, 305 N.Y.S.2d 94 (N.Y. Sup. Ct. 1969), the court ordered access to the city's master plan, even though city officials argued that it was not yet complete. The court rejected the defendants' argument on the facts of the case, but because the plan was in a "finalized state" and was scheduled for publication in a few weeks, the court did indicate that access would have been denied had the plan been in a significantly earlier stage of preparation. It should be repeated that in *Shevin v. Byron, Harless, Schaffer, Reid & Associates, Inc.*, 379 So. 2d 633 (Fla. 1980), the Florida Supreme Court emphatically stated that rough drafts were not public records under the test developed by that court; there were no rough drafts at issue in the case, however.

44. *See* Government Records Branch, N.C. Dep't of Cultural Resources, Public Records with Short-Term Value, *available at* www.records.ncdcr.gov/guidelines.htm#short.

45. The North Carolina attorney general's office has also concluded that such materials are public records. *See* Letter to R. Glen Peterson, 12 January 1999, Advisory Opinion No. 403, *available at* www.ncdoj.gov/About-DOJ/Legal-Services/Legal-Opinions.aspx. The department concluded that questionnaires and answer sheets circulated to and filled out by employees of the department of administration were public records and therefore, except as they might involve specific employees, were open to the public.

MacEwan v. Holm,[46] which was briefly mentioned in the discussion of preliminary drafts, is a leading case on this question. The Oregon State Board of Health collected a variety of data on the amounts of radioactive substances in the air and in rainwater, which the board then used to prepare summary reports. In *MacEwan* the Oregon Supreme Court held that the foundation data were public records as well, and that they were public records from the time they were collected. The court rejected arguments that premature release of the data might be misleading. In the years since *MacEwan* was decided, other courts have followed the Oregon court's lead. In *Legislative Joint Auditing Committee v. Woolsey*,[47] the Arkansas Supreme Court held that the working papers of a government audit were public records. In *Laplante v. Stewart*,[48] the Louisiana Court of Appeal held that the foundation data for a state study comparing student performance at individual schools were public records. In *Moser v. Kanekoa*,[49] and *Yacobellis v. City of Bellingham*,[50] the Washington Court of Appeals held that summaries of interviews conducted as part of a jail administration study and individual questionnaires received as part of a golf course administration study were all public records. And in *Veltri v. Charleston Urban Renewal Authority*,[51] the West Virginia Supreme Court held that the meeting tapes from which the authority's clerk prepared minutes were public records.[52]

Can Access to Preliminary Drafts or Backup Material Be Delayed?

In some instances public officials have acknowledged that early drafts and various forms of backup material are public records, but they have argued that custodians should not have to open such records to public inspection until the final draft or report is completed or until the transaction for which the materials were prepared has occurred. For example, a county might argue that departmental budget requests need not be made public until the manager has presented a budget to the board of commissioners, or a city might argue that consulting proposals received in response to a request for proposals need not be made public until they have been analyzed by staff and presented to (and perhaps acted upon by) the governing board.

By and large these sorts of arguments have not succeeded when made to courts in other states. For example, in *Gannett Co. v. Goldtrap*,[53] the Florida Court of Appeals held that written appraisal reports, prepared for a county in the midst of land negotiations, were public when received by the county; public access did not have to await completion of the

---

46. 359 P.2d 413 (Or. 1961).
47. 722 S.W.2d 581 (Ark. 1987).
48. 470 So. 2d 1018 (La. Ct. App. 1985).
49. 744 P.2d 364 (Wash. Ct. App. 1987).
50. 780 P.2d 272 (Wash. Ct. App. 1989).
51. 363 S.E.2d 746 (W. Va. 1987).
52. See also *Atlantic City Convention Center Authority v. South Jersey Publishing Co.*, 637 A.2d 1261 (N.J. 1994), which held that such tapes were public records under the common law. Two cases held that field record cards produced during the process of property tax appraisal and on which notes about individual properties were entered were not public records: *Dunn v. Board of Assessors*, 282 N.E.2d 385 (Mass. 1972), and *Kottschade v. Lundberg*, 160 N.W.2d 135 (Minn. 1968). In both cases, however, the courts were interpreting a statutory definition of public record much narrower than North Carolina's.
53. 302 So. 2d 174 (Fla. Dist. Ct. App. 1974).

negotiations. In *Bartels v. Rousell*,[54] the Louisiana Court of Appeals held that departmental budget requests in the mayor's office were public at that time, and public access did not have to await adoption of the parish's annual budget. And in *Conover v. Board of Education*,[55] the Utah Supreme Court held that a board's minutes were public records from the time the clerk finished preparing them, and public access need not await approval by the board itself.[56]

Internal Communications

The federal Freedom of Information Act (FOIA) exempts from public access communications within and among federal agencies. In the absence of such an express statutory provision, however, there is no ground for arguing that intraoffice and interoffice communications are anything but public records in North Carolina. What small amount of case law there is in other states regarding such communications consistently holds that they are public records.[57]

Personal E-Mail, Personal Notes, and Other Personal Material

A number of cases throughout the country have held that a variety of materials, even though kept or found in government offices or stored on government equipment, are not public records because they involve the private affairs of officials or employees rather than government or agency business. The *Salt River* case, discussed above in the context of the meaning of the word "received" in the definition of public records, is an example of this line of cases; it involved a private document that appeared to have been left inadvertently in a governmental office. The two most common sorts of records illustrating this principle, however, are personal e-mail and personal notes.

Personal E-Mail

A number of cases have held that personal e-mail messages on the government-owned computer of a government employee are not public records, despite their location. The Ohio case of *State ex rel. Wilson-Simmons v. Lake County Sheriff's Department*[58] is a good example of this group of cases. The petitioner in that case was a corrections officer with the sheriff's department who had allegedly been the victim of racist e-mails sent by other departmental employees. She sued for copies of the e-mails under the Ohio public records statute. The Ohio Supreme Court rejected her suit, holding that the e-mails were not public records because they had nothing to do with the operation of the sheriff's department.

---

54. 303 So. 2d 833 (La. Ct. App. 1974).

55. 267 P.2d 768 (Utah 1954).

56. See also *State ex rel. Halloran v. McGrath*, 67 P.2d 838 (Mont. 1937), in which the court held that referendum petitions were public in the hands of the county clerk and that a citizen did not have to wait until the clerk had certified the signatures and sent the petitions on to the secretary of state to gain access to the petitions.

57. Coleman v. Austin, 521 So. 2d 247 (Fla. Dist. Ct. App. 1988) (intra- and interoffice memoranda, "which formalized knowledge and communicated information between public employees," are public records); City of Topeka v. Stauffer Commc'ns, Inc., 642 P.2d 120 (Kan. Ct. App. 1982) (internal memoranda in fire department regarding fire inspections are public records). See also *Shevin v. Byron, Harless, Schaffer, Reid & Associates, Inc.*, 379 So. 2d 633 (Fla. 1980), in which the court gave interoffice and intraoffice memoranda as examples of documents that clearly are public records.

58. 693 N.E.2d 789 (Ohio 1998).

The court wrote that "although the alleged racist e-mail was created by public employees via a public office's e-mail system, it was never used to conduct the business of the public office and [therefore] did not constitute records" subject to the public records law.[59] A comparable case is *Griffis v. Pinal County*,[60] which began when a newspaper sought all the e-mail messages to and from the county manager over a specific period of time. Originally the county and the manager agreed that many of the e-mails were personal in nature, but once the newspaper threatened suit, the county was prepared to turn over even the personal e-mails. The manager thereupon brought suit to enjoin the release, and eventually the Arizona Supreme Court held that personal e-mail messages, even on a government-owned computer, were not subject to the public records law. In supporting its conclusion, the court wrote:

> To hold otherwise would create an absurd result: Every note made on government-owned paper, located in a government office, written with a government-owned pen, or composed on a government-owned computer would presumably be a public record. Under that analysis, a grocery list written by a government employee while at work, a communication to schedule a family dinner, or a child's report card stored in a desk drawer in a government employee's office would be subject to disclosure. The public records law was never intended to encompass such documents; the purpose of the law is to open *government* activity to public scrutiny, not to disclose information about private citizens.[61]

The outcome in these two cases and other, comparable cases conforms with the guidelines of the North Carolina Department of Cultural Resources, which is charged by statute with the responsibility for supervising public records practices by state and local governments. The department's guidelines for retaining and disposing of e-mail note that "[p]ersonal e-mail is not a public record."[62]

If personal records do not become public records simply because they are found in a governmental office or on a government-owned computer, it logically follows that material that is otherwise a public record because of its substance does not lose that status simply because it is found in a private home or office or on a privately owned computer. It is not location but rather content that is dispositive. Thus, for example, official e-mail sent or

---

59. *Id.* at 793.

See also Denver Publ'g Co. v. Bd. of County Comm'rs, 121 P.3d 190 (Colo. 2005) (romantic e-mails between public employees on government-owned computer not public records); State v. City of Clearwater, 863 So. 2d 149 (Fla. 2003) (private e-mail on government-owned computer not public record). *Contra* Capital Newspapers v. Whalen, 505 N.E.2d 932 (N.Y. 1987) (personal and party documents found in public official's office after his death are public records because found in public office). *See* Cowles Publ'g Co. v. Kootenai County Bd. of County Comm'rs, 159 P.3d 896 (Idaho 2007) (court held that personal e-mails between two county employees were public records because it had become a public issue as to whether one of the employees defended the performance of the other on merit or because of their relationship; in other circumstances, such e-mails might not be public records).

60. 156 P.3d 418 (Ariz. 2007).

61. *Id.* at 421 (emphasis in original).

62. Archives & Records Section, N.C. Dep't of Cultural Resources, E-Mail as a Public Record in North Carolina: Guidelines for Its Retention and Disposition 3 (Aug. 2002), *available at* www.ah.dcr.state.nc.us/records/e_records/Email_8_02.pdf.

received by a county manager would be a public record even if sent to a computer owned by the manager and kept at his or her home.[63]

Personal Notes

One category of documents that has frequently, though not always, been held not to be public record is rough notes written and kept by a public employee or officer—notes made at an interview with a prospective employee or during a telephone call, notes made at a meeting and retained to help the note taker recollect what happened there, notes jotted down by a police officer investigating a crime or by an assessor appraising a lot, notes made in preparation for a presentation, or notes made by the clerk or secretary of a board and used to prepare the formal minutes. An illustrative case is *Shevin v. Byron, Harless, Schaffer, Reid & Associates, Inc.*,[64] in which the Florida Supreme Court held that the rough notes made at interviews of prospective public employees were not public records. Interpreting a statutory definition of public records almost identical to North Carolina's, the Florida court stated that records were only those materials "intended to perpetuate, communicate, or formalize knowledge of some type," and that rough notes did not meet that standard.[65] Rough notes, in effect, were not records.[66] Similarly, in *Conover v. Board of Education*,[67] the Utah Supreme Court held that notes made by the clerk to a board of education at board meetings, to be used to prepare the board's minutes, were not public records. To hold otherwise would, in the court's phrase, "deify doodling."[68]

---

63. See *Media General Operation, Inc. v. Feeney*, 849 So. 2d 3 (Fla. Dist. Ct. App. 2003), which involved records of telephone conversations by public officials involving public business but on private telephones. The court ordered that the records be produced; but because the private provider of the phones voluntarily produced the records the court did not reach the issue of whether it was required to do so.

64. 379 So. 2d 633 (Fla. 1980).

65. *Id.* at 640.

66. In *Coleman v. Austin*, 521 So. 2d 247 (Fla. Dist. Ct. App. 1988), the court held that preliminary notes written by a state's attorney, to himself and for his personal use, were not public records.

67. 267 P.2d 768 (Utah 1954).

68. *Id.* at 770. An appellate court in New Jersey reached the same conclusion about the clerk's handwritten notes, taken to help prepare minutes. O'Shea v. West Milford Bd. of Educ., 918 A.2d 735 (N.J. Super. Ct. App. Div. 2007), *certif. denied*, 927 A.2d 1291 (N.J. 2007). In supporting its conclusion, the court wrote:

> We reject O'Shea's contention that the Secretary's handwritten notes, jotted down as a memory aid to assist in preparing the formal minutes, are a public record merely because they were "made" by a government official. Under that rationale any Board member's personal handwritten notes, taken during a meeting to assist the member to recall what occurred, would be a public record because the member might arguably refer to them later in reviewing the Secretary's draft of the formal minutes. Taken further, every yellow-sticky note penned by a government official to help him or her remember a work-related task would be a public record. Such absurd results were not contemplated or required by OPRA.

Id. at 738.

The Ohio courts have also held that rough notes and other personal papers are not public records. State *ex rel.* Cranford v. Cleveland, 814 N.E.2d 1218 (Ohio 2004) (handwritten notes of city department head, made during hearing before civil service commission); State *ex rel.* Steffen v. Kraft, 619 N.E.2d 688 (Ohio 1993) (trial judge's handwritten notes, made during trial); UAW v. Voinovich, 654 N.E.2d 139 (Ohio 1995) (governor's personal calendar and appointment books). In *Wick Communications Co. v. Montrose County Board of County Commissioners*, 81 P.3d 360 (Colo. 2003), the court held that a county manager's personal diary was not a public record. See also *Asbury Park Press, Inc. v. State*, 558 A.2d 1363 (N.J. Super. Ct. App. Div. 1989), in which the court analogized a spreadsheet used to help prepare a presentation to rough notes

The federal courts have taken a similar position in interpreting the federal Freedom of Information Act. In *Sibille v. Federal Reserve Bank of New York*,[69] the plaintiff sought handwritten notes of meetings and telephone calls. The notes were made for the use of the employee making them and were never used by other employees. In these circumstances the court held that the notes were not agency records and therefore not subject to FOIA. The court stated that in determining the status of other handwritten notes, one should look at the purpose for which the notes were made, whether they were circulated to others, and whether they were stored in a way that was conducive to use by others. Other federal courts reached the same result in *Porter County Chapter, Izaak Walton League of America, Inc. v. United States Atomic Energy Commission*[70] and in *British Airports Authority v. Civil Aeronautics Board*.[71]

Not all courts agree with this characterization of rough notes, however. In *Fox v. Estep*,[72] the Idaho Supreme Court refused to hold, as a matter of law, that the notes of a clerk, used to help prepare minutes, were not a public record. The court argued that because the notes were taken in order to allow the clerk to fulfill her statutory duty of preparing minutes, they could not be characterized as personal. In *People v. Pearson*,[73] the California appellate court held that notes prepared by a police officer to assist in testifying in cases were a public record for purposes of a criminal statute that prohibited removing public records from public offices.[74] In *Oregon School Employees Association v. Lake County School District*,[75] a school principal had kept notes on the performance of two employees for several months, which he retained in a "problem file" in his office. Eventually the school district discharged the two employees, using material in the notes as partial support for the personnel action. Under the school district's collective bargaining agreement the union was granted access to personnel records, and the union brought suit to inspect the notes in question. The Oregon court held that because the notes were used in evaluating the employees they were therefore

---

and refused to require access to it. The Montana Supreme Court reached a different, but distinguishable, result in *Bryan v. Yellowstone County Elementary School District No. 2*, 60 P.3d 381 (Mont. 2002). There the school board established a committee to assist in determining which elementary schools to close. A member of the committee prepared a spreadsheet that compared various characteristics of schools in the district and assigned ratings to each school. Because the person who created the spreadsheet with the ratings did so in his capacity as a committee member and because the spreadsheet was generated to help the committee fulfill its duties, it was a document subject to public inspection.

69. 770 F. Supp. 134 (S.D.N.Y. 1991).

70. 380 F. Supp. 630 (N.D. Ind. 1974).

71. 531 F. Supp. 408 (D. D.C. 1982). In *Bureau of National Affairs, Inc. v. United States Department of Justice*, 742 F.2d 1484 (D.C. Cir. 1984), the court held that the appointment calendars of agency officials and telephone message slips given to an agency official were not agency records and therefore were not subject to FOIA. The court emphasized that both the calendars and the message slips were created for the convenience of the officials in question and were not generally distributed to others within the agency. By contrast, the same court later held that certain electronic calendars that were used by other persons to schedule meetings were agency records and therefore subject to FOIA. Consumer Fed'n of Am. v. Dep't of Agric., 455 F.3d 283 (D.C. Cir. 2006).

72. 797 P.2d 854 (Idaho 1990).

73. 244 P.2d 35 (Cal. Ct. App. 1952).

74. In North Carolina the same General Statutes chapter that governs access to public records prohibits unlawful removal of such records from public offices, and the same definition of public record applies in both contexts. *See* G.S. 132-3.

75. 726 P.2d 955 (Or. Ct. App. 1986).

personnel records subject to the agreement. Because these handwritten notes were used to inform official action, they differed from the notes at issue in the other cases discussed in this section.

In summary, there is significant support in decisions from other jurisdictions, including some with statutory language quite similar to North Carolina's, for concluding that rough personal notes are not public records for purposes of G.S. Chapter 132, even though an employee prepared them to assist in his or her work. There is also case law support, however, for a contrary position, although probably a minority of cases. To the extent that personal notes are placed in a common file and used by others or are the basis for official action, these contrary cases are more likely to predict the outcome in North Carolina.[76]

Correspondence and Other Material Held by or about Elected Officials

Local elected officials send and receive a variety of communications—to or from constituents, local government staff, other elected officials, state or national organizations, and so on. Sometimes they receive or send these communications through the facilities of the local government; at other times they do so at or from their homes or private offices. Increasingly, these kinds of communications are made by electronic mail and may be routed through the local government's server or stored on a computer provided by the local government. In addition, elected officials also sometimes generate materials in the process of preparing proposals for the boards on which they serve. This section discusses which of these communications and materials are public records. It should be noted that the North Carolina public records statute does not address these issues directly, nor have the state's appellate courts considered them. Indeed, there is almost no case law on these issues from any U.S. jurisdiction. As a result, the following discussion is inevitably somewhat speculative.

As a way of framing the discussion, it is important to recall the lesson set out in the section just above: material that is personal in nature does not become a public record simply because it is found in a public facility or on a government-owned computer, but material that involves public business does not lose its public record status simply because it is found in a private facility or on a privately owned computer. Clearly, at least some of the communications to or from an elected official or some of the materials prepared by an elected official are personal in nature and therefore not public records. The difficulty lies in determining where to place the line between public and personal records. The following paragraphs delineate a variety of communications or other materials and offer my suggestions on whether they are public records.

---

76. Some of the personnel privacy statutes (e.g., G.S. 153A-98 and 160A-168) contain a specific provision concerning notes. These provisions state that even if part of a personnel file, "notes" are not open to inspection even by the employee, unless they are the basis of a personnel action. G.S. 153A-98(c1)(4); G.S. 160A-168(c1)(4). This language might be understood to imply that in its absence such notes are public record, but it might also be understood as nothing more than a clarification; that is, that notes used as a basis for a personnel action are part of the personnel file and, like almost all else in the file, are open to the employee.

Communications with Local Government Staff

E-mail and other communications between local government staff and an elected official are almost always public record. (An elected official could, of course, have a personal relationship with a staff member, and some of their communications could therefore be personal in nature, but that would be relatively unusual.) Presumably, communications in this category relate to local government business and therefore are public records for both the official and the staff member.

Communications with State or National Organizations

Some elected officials are active in state or national organizations representing local governments, such as the North Carolina Association of County Commissioners or the National League of Cities. Although they become involved in such organizations because of their elected positions, their activities within the organizations are personal to them and are not part of their official responsibilities. Therefore, any communications with or about these kinds of organizations and any materials associated with these organizations presumably are personal rather than public records.

Communications with Constituents

It is much more difficult to be categorical about this set of communications. At one end, many are clearly public in nature—a citizen may be seeking help with respect to a local government service, petitioning for some governing board action, and so on. Although probably not conclusive, the fact that such constituent communications are routed through a local government's mailroom or through an e-mail address belonging to the local government strongly suggests that these are public rather than personal records.[77] But messages to or from constituents can also be political in nature, particularly if the constituent is personally acquainted with the elected official or the communication is sent to the official's home or private e-mail address. And if they are political, the messages are probably per-

---

77. The North Carolina attorney general's office has advised the General Assembly that communications between a legislator and a member of the public on the issue of legislative redistricting appear to be public records. Although the opinion does not make this explicit, it appears that the communications in question were made through the General Assembly's mail facility or its e-mail server. Letter to Terrence D. Sullivan, 14 February 2002, Advisory Opinion No. 529, *available at* www.ncdoj.gov/About-DOJ/Legal-Services/Legal-Opinions.aspx.

On the other hand, a superior court judge has ruled that constituent letters sent to a member of a board of county commissioners are not public records. Boney Publishers, Inc. v. Sharpe, No. 00 CVS 569 (N.C. Super. Ct., Alamance County, Mar. 20, 2000). The complaint and briefs in the case do not make clear whether the correspondence was received through the county's facilities or at the commissioner's home, and it may not have made any difference to the court. The decision was not appealed.

In *State ex rel. Glasgow v. Jones*, 894 N.E.2d 686 (Ohio 2008), a retired state employee sought copies of a state legislator's e-mails to and from constituents about legislation that would have affected investments in the state's pension fund. The Ohio court held that in general e-mail exchanges with a legislator's constituents were public records. The legislator had conceded that such messages on her home computer were no different than those on the state's computer system, but the court cautioned that because of the concession, "we need not address the issue whether an e-mail message sent from or to a private account can be a public record." *Id.* at 691.

sonal to the officeholder. It might be necessary to judge each such message individually to determine from its content whether it is public or personal.[78]

Communications with Other Elected Officials

Again, there may be distinctions among these messages based on such factors as the number of officials involved and whether they might be considered a caucus of the entire governing board. For example, if a city council member sends an e-mail message to each of the other members of the council making a proposal about an upcoming agenda item, the message is probably a public record. But if the communication is only between two minority party members of a board of county commissioners, it might be more about the fortunes of their party than about county business and therefore a personal rather than a public record. Here again, categorical assertions are impossible.

Materials Associated with a Proposal Still in the Planning or Draft Stage

If an elected official is working with local government staff in preparing a proposal for eventual presentation to the governing board, materials associated with that effort are clearly public records. But if, instead, the elected official is working with a community group or a set of political advisers, any materials associated with that effort are probably personal in nature and therefore not public records. In this latter case, the materials might be considered comparable to personal notes prepared by a public employee to assist in his or her job; or they might be considered political in nature. Either way, they would not be public records unless they were included in the official's eventual presentation of the proposal to the governing board.

Elected Officials' Telephone Numbers

Sometimes elected officials will give their unlisted home telephone numbers or their private cell phone numbers to the government to assist in reaching. Once the government has this information, there is no exception that keeps it from being a public record.[79]

Computer Programs

Government agencies sometimes develop computer software programs that might be useful to other governments or might have commercial value. Is the source coding for such a program subject to the public records law, or may the government agency that developed the software retain control over its distribution and use? A relatively recent federal decision and an opinion from the North Carolina Attorney General both held that such

---

78. In *Tribune-Review Publishing Co. v. Bodack*, 961 A.2d 110 (Pa. 2008), the newspaper sought the cell phone records of council member cell phones paid for by the city. The court held that the bills were presumptively open to the public but then held that the phone numbers of persons called by or calling the council members should be redacted before the bills were open to public access. The court relied, however, on specific provisions of the Pennsylvania statute that favored private security and privacy interests and cited the privacy of individuals who might have called or been called by the council members. There are no comparable provisions in the North Carolina statute, so the case is not particularly relevant to this state.

79. In this respect, information about elected officials is different than information about employees. The same information from a public employee is probably part of that person's personnel file and therefore not open to the public. See chapter 7.

software is not subject to access under public records statutes. In *Gilmore v. U.S. Department of Energy*,[80] a citizen invoked the federal Freedom of Information Act to seek a copy of software held by the department. The software had been developed by a private company that operated a federally owned research laboratory, and the copyright was nominally in the company's name. The court held, however, that even if the software were owned and controlled by the federal government, it would not be an agency record because it did not "illuminate the structure, operation, or decision-making structure" of the federal agency.[81] Similarly, in a 1998 advisory opinion involving software developed by the state Division of Motor Vehicles, the attorney general's office argued that the North Carolina public records law distinguishes between, on the one hand, software and computer systems and, on the other, the records generated by those systems.[82] The opinion concluded that software standing alone is not a public record.[83]

Records in Private Hands

Local governments make frequent use of private contractors in carrying out their public responsibilities. They retain attorneys in private practice, engage consultants to assist in studying public operations, hire firms to manage public property, and so on. When, if ever, are records held by these private contractors subject to the public records law and therefore open to public inspection? Although these questions have not been extensively litigated in North Carolina, courts in other states have decided a significant number of cases, and two consistent principles emerge from those cases.

First, and perhaps most importantly, if the arrangements between the local government and the private contractor provide that the records developed during the contract work belong to the local government, or if they provide that the local government has essentially complete access to the records, or if a court finds that the government in effect owns the records, then the courts have uniformly determined that the records in question are public records and therefore open to public access. Two cases illustrate these principles. In *Pathmanathan v. St. Cloud State University*,[84] the plaintiff was appointed to an administrative position with the university, subject to a background investigation. The university employed a private investigator to conduct the background check, and as a result of the investigation the university revoked the appointment. The plaintiff then sought access to all the documents collected by the investigator, including tape recordings and field notes. Although these documents were held by the investigator, his contract with the university gave the university ownership of all the materials he collected. On that basis the court held

---

80. 4 F. Supp. 2d 912 (N.D. Cal. 1998).

81. *Id.* at 920.

82. Letter to Janice Faulkner, 28 May 1998, Advisory Opinion No. 366, *available at* www.ncdoj.gov/About-DOJ/Legal-Services/Legal-Opinions.aspx.

83. *Rogers v. Hood*, 906 So. 2d 1220 (Fla. Dist. Ct. App. 2005), is perhaps comparable. The plaintiffs wanted to take possession of unused ballots from the 2000 presidential election, but the court held that they were no more than boxes of blank paper held in a public office and did not become public records until used. The same logic would extend to stationery.

84. 461 N.W.2d 726 (Minn. Ct. App. 1990).

that the records were subject to the state's public records law.[85] And in *Daily Gazette Co. v. Withrow*,[86] the plaintiff newspaper sought a copy of a settlement of a Section 1983 lawsuit between a former sheriff's deputy and the county. The county's retained attorney held possession of the settlement, but the court found that fact irrelevant. It held that the settlement was a public record, which the county could reclaim from the attorney at any time, and that the county could not avoid its obligations to permit access simply by moving possession of the record to a private actor.[87]

---

85. *Accord* State *ex rel.* Cincinnati Enquirer v. Krings, 758 N.E.2d 1135 (Ohio 2001) (construction records in hands of private project manager under contract with county were public records because county had full access to the records); State *ex rel.* Medina County Gazette v. City of Brunswick, 672 N.E.2d 1070 (Ohio Ct. App. 1996) (city council employed private consultant to help evaluate manager, and as part of the process the consultant collected questionnaires from each council member in which the members gave individual evaluations; because questionnaires were prepared for city to carry out public responsibility and because city had full access to the questionnaires, they were public records); Baytown Sun v. City of Mont Belvieu, 145 S.W.3d 268 (Tex. App. 2004) (contract under which private company manages city recreation complex gave city right to inspect books and records of the complex; therefore those books and records were public records).

By contrast, the American Institute of Architects' model contract between owner and architect provides that all drawings and specifications remain the property of the architect and gives the owner only a limited right to copies. The American Institute of Architects, *AIA Document B101-2007, Standard Form of Agreement Between Owner and Architect, in* The Architect's Handbook of Professional Practice app. D at 973, art. 7 (Joseph A. Demkin, executive ed. 14th ed. 2008). "The Architect and the Architect's consultants shall be deemed the authors and owners of their respective Instruments of Service, including the Drawings and Specifications, and shall retain all common law, statutory and other reserved rights, including copyrights. Submission or distribution of Instruments of Service to meet official regulatory requirements or for similar purposes in connection with the Project is not to be construed as publication in derogation of the reserved rights of the Architect and the Architect's consultants." *Id.* § 7.2. "[T]he Architect grants to the Owner a nonexclusive license to use the Architect's Instruments of Service solely and exclusively for purposes of constructing, using, maintaining, altering and adding to the Project . . . . The license granted under this section permits the Owner to authorize the Contractor . . . to reproduce applicable portions of the Instruments of Service solely and exclusively for use in performing services or construction for the Project." *Id.* § 7.3. This language may limit public records access to the drawings and specifications.

See also the rules on professional ethics and conduct adopted by the North Carolina Board of Certified Public Accountant Examiners, which make clear that client records belong to the client. 21 N.C. Admin. Code § 8N .0305 (2008).

The federal position may be somewhat different. In *Forsham v. Harris*, 445 U.S. 169 (1980), the U.S. Supreme Court held that records generated by a federal grantee as part of its grant-supported work were not "agency records" with the Freedom of Information Act, even though the granting agency did have a right of access to the records and a contractual right (which had not been exercised) to acquire the records in its sole discretion. Perhaps this case can be distinguished because the records were those of a *grantee* studying a matter that the government thought worthwhile, as opposed to a *contractor* studying actual government operations.

86. 350 S.E.2d 738 (W. Va. 1986).

87. In *Journal/Sentinel, Inc. v. School Board*, 521 N.W.2d 165 (Wis. Ct. App. 1994), which involved a copy of a memorandum of settlement of a lawsuit that was in the possession of the school board's law firm, the court stated: "The school board appellants' argument thus resolves to whether a public body may avoid the public access mandated by the public-records law by delegating both the record's creation and custody to an agent. Posing this question provides its answer: it may not." *Id.* at 170. Other cases reaching similar conclusions include *International Brotherhood of Electrical Workers Local 68 v. Denver Metropolitan Major League Baseball Stadium District*, 880 P.2d 160 (Colo. App. 1994) (prequalification documents and a bid proposal from an electrical subcontractor, in hands of general contractor, held to be public records because district had full access to the documents and used them in deciding whether to approve the subcontractor);

Local Government Attorneys

A specific application of this first principle has been established by the court of appeals for attorneys who represent local governments and their agencies. In *Womack Newspapers, Inc. v. Town of Kitty Hawk*,[88] the newspaper sought a variety of records associated with oceanfront condemnations undertaken by the town; these included records related to engineering, surveying, and other professional services rendered in connection with the condemnation litigation. The town argued that these were not public records because they were in the possession of the town's attorney, a law firm engaged in private practice, and therefore were not subject to the public records law. The court rejected the argument, setting out three alternative rationales for its decision.

First, the court reiterated earlier holdings that a city attorney is a public officer, because the position is created by statute. (G.S. 160A-173 provides that the city council "shall appoint a city attorney to serve at its pleasure and to be its legal adviser.") Because the public records law extends to records in the possession of any public officer, these records were therefore public records. This specific rationale would reach records held in the private law offices of persons or firms designated as city or county attorneys,[89] but attorneys who represent school boards and other local government entities are not mentioned by statute and therefore do not appear to be public officers. Therefore, this first rationale would not reach these other attorneys.

Second, the court looked to the rules of professional conduct applicable to an attorney's files, which the court summarized by saying that "[i]n North Carolina, anything in a client's file, which is in the hands of the client's attorney, belongs to the client, with the exception only of the attorney's notes or work product."[90] Therefore, the court went on, the client

---

Wisner v. City of Tampa Police Department, 601 So. 2d 296 (Fla. Dist. Ct. App. 1992) (documentation of polygraph test, conducted by private company for police department and in hands of private company, was public record); *Times Publishing Co. v. City of St. Petersburg*, 558 So. 2d 487 (Fla. Dist. Ct. App. 1990) (drafts of leases between city and baseball company, kept exclusively in offices of baseball company's attorney, still public records); *State ex rel. Mazzaro v. Ferguson*, 550 N.E.2d 464 (Ohio 1990) (working papers of CPA firm auditing local government are public records when such a firm is hired only when state auditor certifies his or her office is unable to conduct the audit); *Carbondale Township v. Murray*, 440 A.2d 1273 (Pa. Commw. Ct. 1982) (cancelled checks of township, in possession of bank, are public records subject to inspection because township has control over the checks); *Creative Restaurants, Inc. v. City of Memphis*, 795 S.W.2d 672 (Tenn. Ct. App. 1990) (leases of space in city-owned property, entered into by and in possession of private management company acting as city's agent, are public records; such leases in possession of private attorney retained by city to review lease terms also public records). *See also* MacKenzie v. Wales Twp., 635 N.W.2d 335 (Mich. Ct. App. 2001) (township contracted with nearby city for latter to convert township's paper tax records into electronic records; when citizen sought a copy of the tapes, in the possession of the city, the court held that the township must either direct the city to give a copy to the citizen or procure a copy from the city and provide it to the citizen).

In some very small towns in North Carolina, the town does not have its own offices and records are kept in the homes of one or more town officials. In such a situation there is no room to argue that the records are not public; the records' custodian clearly must allow public access to them.

88. 181 N.C. App. 1, 639 S.E.2d 96, *petition for review withdrawn*, 361 N.C. 370, 644 S.E.2d 564 (2007).

89. G.S. 153A-114 provides that the "board of commissioners shall appoint a county attorney to serve at its pleasure and to be its legal adviser."

90. 181 N.C. App. at 13, 639 S.E.2d at 104. The court mentions that the attorney's notes and work product do not belong to the client and therefore are not public records. The same would presumably apply to an attorney's trust account records, which also do not belong to the client.

town, not the law firm town attorney, owned the contested documents. Obviously, this rationale reaches beyond city and county attorneys to reach any attorney who represents a local government entity in a specific transaction or specific litigation.[91]

Third, the court pointed out the policy implications of a contrary result:

> Allowing defendants to prevail on their argument that these documents were the private property of the Town Attorney, and not property of the Town itself, would be permitting the Town to place documents such as these in the hands of a so-called independent contractor in order to escape the public records disclosure requirements. If an argument such as this were to prevail there would be nothing to prevent municipalities and other governmental agencies from skirting the public records disclosure requirements simply by hiring independent contractors to perform governmental tasks and to have them retain all documents in conjunction with the performance of those tasks that municipalities and agencies chose to shield from public scrutiny.[92]

This third rationale might easily be extended beyond attorneys to other professionals performing work for local governments; how far it can be extended may have to await future litigation, but the general principle set out at the beginning of this section is probably relevant.

The second principle that emerges from the national case law, in contrast to the first, is that if the conditions of ownership or access set out above do not apply, the private records of private contractors are generally not subject to the public records law. For example, in *News & Sun-Sentinel Co. v. Schwab, Twitty & Hanser Architectural Group, Inc.*,[93] a school board employed an architectural firm to design a public school. The Florida Supreme Court held that the firm was not acting on behalf of the school system but rather was an independent actor. Its records were therefore not subject to the Florida public records law. A similar result was reached in *State ex rel. Tindel v. Sharp*,[94] which involved the files of a personnel consultant who had been employed to assist a school board in selecting a new superintendent of schools. The consultant had developed an extensive file of various professional educators through his work for other counties, and the court held that these files were not public records.[95]

---

91. A number of cases in other states have dealt with records held by an attorney retained by an insurance company to handle matters pursuant to an insurance policy issued to a local government. By and large the cases held that the attorney is, as a practical matter, representing the insured (the local government) and not the insurer (the insurance company), even though he or she was actually retained by the company. Therefore, the records have been held to belong to the government insured and to be public records. *E.g.*, Knightstown Banner, LLC v. Town of Knightstown, 838 N.E.2d 1127 (Ind. Ct. App. 2005), *transfer denied*, 860 N.E.2d 585 (Ind. 2006); Tribune-Review Publ'g Co. v. Westmoreland County Hous. Auth., 833 A.2d 112 (2003). In the latter case the insurance company retained complete control of the defense of an action and did not communicate with the insured, and the settlement documents were retained by the insurance company; nevertheless the court held that the settlement documents were public records.

92. 181 N.C. App. at 14, 639 S.E.2d at 105.

93. 596 So. 2d 1029 (Fla. 1992).

94. 300 So. 2d 750 (Fla. Dist. Ct. App. 1974).

95. The outcome might be different if the consultant's files are developed solely for the current public contract and there is significant government involvement in the process of developing the records. In

This second principle probably holds true even if the government has some ability to gain access to or have a copy made of these private records. For example, both the telephone company and a local government customer of the company will have records of each call made from phone numbers assigned to the local government. If the local government appropriately disposes of its copy, the telephone company will probably be willing to provide another copy, as it would to any customer—but the records in such a case are clearly those of the telephone company. Although the local government can receive records on request, if it has no need to do so it probably cannot be forced to seek the records simply because a citizen would like to review them.[96] After all, the basic premise of the public records law is that public access rights attach to those records that the government has, because of its own needs, generated or collected. With one important exception, the law does not require the government to generate or collect records that the government has no independent need for simply because a citizen wishes to have access to those records.[97]

Forum Publishing Co. v. City of Fargo, 391 N.W.2d 169 (N.D. 1986), the city contracted with a private executive search firm to assist in the selection of a new police chief. Applications were distributed by the city's personnel office but submitted to the firm, which was to reduce the number of applicants to six. The court noted the city's involvement in the application process and held that the applications were public records, even in the hands of the firm. (In North Carolina such applications are exempt from public access, even in the hands of a public agency. Elkin Tribune, Inc. v. Yadkin County Bd. of County Comm'rs, 331 N.C. 735, 417 S.E.2d 465 (1992).) Another case with a comparable outcome is *State ex rel. Gannett Satellite Information Network v. Shirey*, 678 N.E.2d 557 (Ohio 1997), discussed in the text at notes 17 and 18.

96. *See, e.g.*, Affiliated Constr. Trades Found. v. Reg'l Jail & Corr. Facility Auth., 490 S.E.2d 708 (W. Va. 1997) (although authority had right to receive payroll records from subcontractor on construction project, it had not done so, and the court held that a citizen could not demand that it do so); Forsham v. Harris, 445 U.S. 169 (1980) (The federal "FOIA applies to records which have been *in fact* obtained, and not to records which merely *could have been* obtained." *Id.* at 186 (emphasis in original).). In *Kissinger v. Reporters Committee for Freedom of the Press*, 445 U.S. 136 (1980), the committee sought records that Kissinger had generated as secretary of state and, toward the end of his term, had deeded to the Library of Congress as his private papers. (The library is not subject to the federal FOIA.) One argument the committee made was that the State Department was obliged to demand the return of the papers from the library. The Court rejected the argument, writing:

> If the agency is not required to create or to retain records under the FOIA, it is somewhat difficult to determine why the agency is nevertheless required to retrieve documents which have escaped its possession, but which it has not endeavored to recover. If the document is of so little interest to the agency that it does not believe the retrieval effort to be justified, the effect of this judgment on an FOIA request seems little different from the effect of an agency determination that a record should never be created, or should be discarded.

Id. at 152–53.

The Idaho Supreme Court took a different position, however. In *Idaho Conservation League v. Idaho State Department of Agriculture*, 146 P.3d 632 (Idaho 2006), the league sought certain plans that cattle feedlot operators were required to submit to the department for approval; once the plans were approved they were returned to the feedlot operators, although the plans were to be available to the department upon its request. On that set of facts the court held that the plans were public records and that the department was required to retrieve them from the operators and provide them to the league.

97. The exception involves indexes of computer databases, discussed in chapter 5.

Appendix 1A—Statutes

G.S. 121-2(8)

§ 121-2. Definitions.

For the purposes of this Article:

. . .

(8) "Public record" or "public records" shall mean all documents, papers, letters, maps, books, photographs, films, sound recordings, magnetic or other tapes, electronic data processing records, artifacts, or other documentary material, regardless of physical form or characteristics, made or received pursuant to law or ordinance or in connection with the transaction of official business by any agency.

G.S. 132-1

§ 132-1. "Public records" defined.

(a) "Public record" or "public records" shall mean all documents, papers, letters, maps, books, photographs, films, sound recordings, magnetic or other tapes, electronic data-processing records, artifacts, or other documentary material, regardless of physical form or characteristics, made or received pursuant to law or ordinance in connection with the transaction of public business by any agency of North Carolina government or its subdivisions. Agency of North Carolina government or its subdivisions shall mean and include every public office, public officer or official (State or local, elected or appointed), institution, board, commission, bureau, council, department, authority or other unit of government of the State or of any county, unit, special district or other political subdivision of government.

(b) The public records and public information compiled by the agencies of North Carolina government or its subdivisions are the property of the people. Therefore, it is the policy of this State that the people may obtain copies of their public records and public information free or at minimal cost unless otherwise specifically provided by law. As used herein, "minimal cost" shall mean the actual cost of reproducing the public record or public information.

Chapter 2—The Right of Access

The public's right to inspect and copy public records is set out in the first sentence of Section 132-6 of the North Carolina General Statutes [hereinafter G.S.], which reads:

> Every custodian of public records shall permit any record in the custodian's custody to be inspected and examined at reasonable times and under reasonable supervision by any person, and shall, as promptly as possible, furnish copies thereof upon payment of any fees as may be prescribed by law.[1]

Although other sections of G.S. Chapter 132 elaborate upon this sentence, the statute leaves a number of questions unanswered. In addition, there are only a few decisions from the state's appellate courts interpreting these sections of the statute. Therefore, this chapter's discussion of the meaning of the right of access draws heavily on court decisions interpreting public records laws in other states and the federal Freedom of Information Act (FOIA). The chapter covers five topics:

1. The distinction between public records and the information in those records
2. The limits, if any, on inspection and access rights that depend on who is seeking access and for what purpose
3. The right of inspection
4. The right to a copy of public records and whether and what amount of fees may be charged for that service
5. The remedies that are available to a citizen who believes his or her request for access to or copies of a public record have been improperly denied

The Distinction between Records and Information

Governments Need Not Create New Records

The theory of the public records law is that when a government creates or maintains records for its own business reasons, the public enjoys a general right to inspect and copy those records. But, subject to the exception noted below, the public has no right to demand that a government create or maintain records that the government has no need for itself, nor does the public have the right to demand that a government maintain records in a way that facilitates use of the records by others if that use is unimportant to the government. Courts usually express this principle through the statement that the public records law does not require governments to create new records, and the General Assembly has affirmed the principle in the public records statute as well.[2]

For example, governments need not compile information from their records for the benefit of a member of the public if the government has no need for the compilation. In a Pennsylvania case the plaintiff sought a list of the names and addresses of retired Pennsylvania

---

1. The statute is set out in appendix 2A at the end of this chapter.

2. N.C. GEN. STAT. [hereinafter G.S.] § 132-6.2(e) states that "[n]othing in this section shall be construed to require a public agency to respond to a request for a copy of a public record by creating or compiling a record that does not exist."

state employees. The retirement board did not maintain such a list, however, and the court held that it could not be made to do so for the plaintiff's benefit. The plaintiff would have to develop his own list by plowing through the records on his own.[3] In another Pennsylvania case a newspaper requested that the city tax office provide a list of local businesses that had not paid various local taxes. The office refused, because it had no such list, and the appellate court upheld the refusal, making the following point:

> If we were to decide [that the office must prepare the list], because no reason ever has to be given to examine the record, anyone could come to a public agency and ask for preparation of lists for any reason, e.g., a credit card company could request a list of taxpayers whose public assessments were over a certain amount, or direct marketers could ask for a list of all people who applied for building permits to see if they needed a second mortgage. As a result, public employees would, in effect, become the "agents" of individuals seeking to "slice and dice" information for commercial purposes, taking them away from the jobs that they were hired to perform. This is not the intent of the [public records] Act.[4]

This principle has had important implications as government records have increasingly been kept in electronic form. Governments frequently maintain very large amounts of data in electronic records and access and use that data through specialized software. Private individuals or organizations have sometimes seen that a governmental database contains information of special usefulness to them but have found that the government's computer programs do not generate the information in the form desired by the individual or organization. Relying on the principle that a government need not create new records, the courts have refused to order governments to write new programs that access and manipulate the data in the manner desired by the individual or organization.[5] (Chapter 5 contains a

---

3. Mergenthaler v. Commonwealth State Employees' Ret. Bd., 372 A.2d 944 (Pa. Commw. Ct. 1977), *aff'd on reconsideration*, 381 A.2d 1032 (Pa. Commw. Ct. 1978), *questioned in part on other grounds by* Hartman v. Dep't of Conservation & Natural Res., 892 A.2d 897 (Pa. Commw. Ct. 2006).

4. Scranton Times, L.P. v. Scranton Single Tax Office, 736 A.2d 711, 713 (Pa. Commw. Ct. 1999), *order aff'd*, 764 A.2d 17 (Pa. 2000). Other examples of this principle include *Kenyon v. Garrels*, 540 N.E.2d 11 (Ill App. Ct. 1989) (township not required to answer questions posed by plaintiff; it is enough to provide copies of the records to him); *Jones v. Jackson County Circuit Court*, 162 S.W.3d 53 (Mo. Ct. App. 2005) (plaintiff made request for set of specific items of information about all cases filed in court in certain areas of law; there was no record with the requested information, and the court was not required to create it); *Winston v. Mangan*, 338 N.Y.S.2d 654 (Sup. Ct. 1972) (park district not required to make list and records summaries solely for purpose of public inspection); *State ex rel. Zauderer v. Joseph*, 577 N.E.2d 444 (Ohio Ct. App. 1989) (agency maintains traffic accident reports alphabetically rather than chronologically and therefore need not respond to request for all reports for a given day); and *Borom v. Crawford*, 651 F.2d 500, 501 (7th Cir. 1981) (court rejected plaintiff's argument that federal agencies "cannot avoid disclosure merely because their record-keeping systems do not compile and store the information in the precise form in which plaintiff has requested it.").

5. *E.g.*, State *ex rel.* Scanlon v. Deters, 544 N.E.2d 680 (Ohio 1989) (a requested computer search would require an inquiry of a public database in ways not used by the public agency; the court held for the agency, stating that it could not be required to create a new document), *overruled on other grounds by* State *ex rel* Steckman v. Jackson, 639 N.E.2d 83 (Ohio 1994). In *Seigle v. Barry*, 422 So. 2d 63 (Fla. Dist. Ct. App. 1982), the court refused to order the agency to run a program designed by the private entity seeking access without a showing of extraordinary circumstances warranting such action. One exception to this line of cases is *Board of Education v. New Jersey Department of Treasury*, 653 A.2d 589 (N.J. Super. Ct. App. Div.

somewhat fuller discussion of the cases involving requests for information in governmental databases.)

Records That Contain Both Confidential and Public Information

One important possible exception to the principle that governments need not create new records arises when a government record contains both public information and information to which the public is not entitled to access. Personnel records are a common example of such combined records. There is no doubt that a government may combine public and confidential records in such a way if doing so best meets its business needs,[6] but it cannot use the combining as an excuse to deny public access to the public portions of the records. Rather, the government must in some fashion permit access to the public portions, either by extracting the public parts from the whole or by excising the confidential parts. When governments have argued that such requirements amount to creation of new records, the courts have consistently denied the analogy,[7] and North Carolina's statute now explicitly requires public access to the public portions of such combined records.[8] It should be noted that the statute also requires that the government—and not the requester of the record—bear any cost incurred by separating confidential from public material in order to allow access to the public material.[9]

Stopping Record Maintenance

Courts have also relied on the basic principle that agencies need not create records they have no need for themselves to allow governments to stop generating or maintaining records that they no longer need, even though those records may be particularly useful to a private individual or entity who has been using them. In *State ex rel. Kavanaugh v. Henderson*,[10] for example, the Missouri state liquor supervisor had been keeping records showing liquor sales in the state by brand name. A new supervisor proposed to stop keep-

---

1995), *aff'd*, 678 A.2d 660 (N.J. 1996), in which a state agency was ordered to retrieve information in its records even though it had no use for the information itself and did not retrieve it for its own uses; the plaintiff was required to pay for the cost of the retrieval, however.

6. Griffin-Spalding County Hosp. Auth. v. Radio Station WKEU, 241 S.E.2d 196 (Ga. 1978) (error for trial court to order hospital authority to maintain separate record systems for the public and medically confidential records associated with its ambulance service; the authority could combine the records).

7. *E.g.*, Family Life League v. Dep't of Pub. Aid, 493 N.E.2d 1054 (Ill. 1986) (medically confidential material must be excised); State *ex rel.* Stephan v. Harder, 641 P.2d 366 (Kan. 1982) (medically confidential material must be excised). *See also* Northwest Publ'ns, Inc. v. City of Bloomington, 499 N.W.2d 509 (Minn. Ct. App. 1993); Gordon v. Sandoval County Assessor, 28 P.3d 1114 (N.M. Ct. App. 2001) (confidential information must be excised from property tax valuation cards).

8. See G.S. 132-6(c), which reads: "No request to inspect, examine, or obtain copies of public records shall be denied on the grounds that confidential information is commingled with the requested nonconfidential information. If it is necessary to separate confidential from nonconfidential information in order to permit the inspection, examination, or copying of the public records, the public agency shall bear the cost of such separation . . . ."

9. It should be noted that some of the statutes that exempt categories of records from public access exempt those records from the public records law entirely. *E.g.*, G.S. 131E-97 (medical records maintained by a health care facility are "not public records as defined by Chapter 132"). Presumably, no part of such a record is subject to the access provisions of G.S. 132-6(c).

10. 169 S.W.2d 389 (Mo. 1943).

ing the brand-name information, and the petitioner in the case sought to require that the records continue to be maintained. The court refused, holding that the brand-name records were public for as long as they were maintained, but no statute required that they be maintained and the supervisor was free to stop doing so.[11]

No Requirement to Reveal Information

The distinction between records and information also means that simply because a public employee knows a specific piece of information, he or she has no obligation to reveal that information to anyone who requests it. For example, if a public employee has been told of a developer's plan for a tract of land but the information was given orally rather than in writing, the employee has no obligation under the public records law to pass that information along to individuals or entities who request it.

Who and Why

Who May Inspect and Copy

The statute accords the rights of inspection and copying to "any person," and there is no reason to think the quoted words are limiting in any way. The rights extend both to natural persons and to corporations and other artificial persons; they extend to residents and nonresidents; they extend to citizens and noncitizens.[12] Nor can the right of inspection be denied to someone simply because he or she has made numerous public records requests.[13]

The Purpose of Inspection or Use of the Record

Sometimes records custodians attempt to deny access because of the purpose for which the person seeking access intends to use the records. Some custodians have argued, for example, that the purpose of the right of access is to permit monitoring of government operations and therefore records need not be made available to persons who intend to use them for commercial purposes. Courts have consistently rejected this argument,[14] even when the

---

11. In *Clark v. Banks*, 515 N.W.2d 5 (Iowa 1994), a sheriff returned firearms permit applications to applicants once he had approved them. Because no statute required that the sheriff retain such documents, the court held that they were no longer public records once the sheriff had released them.

12. In *Lee v. Minner*, 458 F.3d 194 (3d Cir. 2006), a federal court of appeals held that a Delaware statute that limited access to public records in that state to Delaware citizens violated the Privileges and Immunities Clause of the federal constitution. In *Los Angeles Unified School District v. Superior Court*, 60 Cal. Rptr. 3d 445 (Ct. App. 2007), the court held that both a city and an elected official were entitled to assert the right to obtain copies of public records maintained by another government. In *City of Elkhart v. Agenda: Open Government, Inc.*, 683 N.E.2d 622 (Ind. Ct. App. 1997), the court held that the alleged misuse of records obtained from an earlier request was not a reason to deny a later, legitimate request for records from the same entity. There is no reason to believe that a North Carolina court would decide any of these cases differently.

13. Zink v. City of Mesa, 166 P.3d 738 (Wash. Ct. App. 2007) (the citizens in question had made 172 requests over a thirty-month period).

14. *E.g.*, Data Tree, LLC v. Romaine, 880 N.E.2d 10 (N.Y. 2007) (company sought land records to sell through Internet). *See also* Associated Tax Serv., Inc. v. Fitzpatrick, 372 S.E.2d 625 (Va. 1988) (company

commercial operation in question was one that would compete with the government or official holding the records.[15] In general, a person's intended use of the records is irrelevant to his or her right of access, and the custodian may not deny access simply because of the nature of that purpose.[16] Indeed, since 1995 G.S. 132-6(b) has prohibited custodians from requiring that a person requesting access to or a copy of a public record disclose his or her purpose or motives in seeking access or the copy.

The requester's motive remains legally irrelevant even if the intended use is one that the custodian and many citizens might disapprove of. Alarm system salespeople sometimes seek police incident reports in order to solicit the victims of break-ins; Bible salespeople sometimes seek death records in order to visit and sell specially inscribed Bibles to the relatives of the recently dead; estranged husbands might seek utility department records in order to locate their wives. That the custodian believes the intended use of the records will take advantage of people or even *suspects* they might be used to bring physical harm to someone does not justify refusing access.[17] (A few older cases suggest that access may be denied if it is clear that the records will be used for an unlawful purpose,[18] but such a

---

sought tax list held by city treasurer in order to prepare list of mortgagor's taxes for bank—"the purpose or motivation behind a request is irrelevant to a citizen's entitlement to requested information," 372 S.E.2d at 629.).

15. *E.g.*, Lieber v. Bd. of Trs., 680 N.E.2d 374 (Ill. 1997) (operator of private housing facility given access to university records concerning students desiring housing, even though operator in competition with university in providing housing); Techniscan Corp. v. Passaic Valley Water Comm'n, 549 A.2d 1249 (N.J. 1988) (plaintiff searched public records for title insurance company seeking liens for unpaid water bills; access allowed, even though defendant custodian charged fee for the same service); Rock County v. Weirick, 128 N.W. 94 (Wis. 1910) (county sought to enjoin retiring register of deeds from copying deed abstract books in order to go into business in competition with county upon retirement; court upheld access and right to copy). See also *Warden v. Bennett*, 340 So. 2d 977 (Fla. Dist. Ct. App. 1976), in which the court upheld the right of access of a labor organizer to the names and addresses of the public agency's employees.

16. *E.g.*, Harrison v. Powers, 127 P. 818 (Cal. Dist. Ct. App. 1912); Union Leader Corp. v. City of Nashua, 686 A.2d 310 (N.H. 1996) (use of record by requester irrelevant to statutory balancing test in determining whether to release record); State *ex rel.* Fant v. Enright, 610 N.E.2d 997 (Ohio 1993).

Sometimes legislation denies access to some persons, depending on the use to which those persons intend to put the records. G.S. 132-10 permits counties and cities to deny copies in magnetic media of geographic information system database records to persons who would put the records to commercial use, and G.S. 130A-189 provides that the copy of a rabies vaccination certificate held by a county animal control agency "shall not be used for commercial purposes." A number of other states have enacted legislation that denies access to criminal justice records to persons who would use the records for commercial use, such as lawyers who might solicit business from those charged with crimes. A number of federal courts held these sorts of statutes unconstitutional as violations of the First Amendment's protection of commercial speech, *e.g.*, Innovative Database Sys. v. Morales, 990 F.2d 217 (5th Cir. 1993), but the United States Supreme Court later held that such a statute did not in fact violate the First Amendment, Los Angeles Police Dep't v. United Reporting Publ'g Corp., 528 U.S. 32 (1999), and therefore these sorts of restrictions appear to be constitutional.

17. In *State ex rel. Thomas v. Ohio State University*, 643 N.E.2d 126 (Ohio 1994), the defending university sought to deny access to the names and addresses of animal researchers because release might jeopardize their safety. The court's response was that "criminal conduct should be punished by criminal sanctions" and not by new interpretations of the public records statute. 643 N.E.2d at 130 (internal quotation marks omitted).

18. For example, *Harrison v. Powers*, 127 P. 818 (Cal. Dist. Ct. App. 1912), states that "where the statute expressly confers the right upon the citizen to inspect or to copy a public record, and *he seeks to exercise such right for no unlawful or scandalous purpose*, . . . the statutory right may not be denied." 127 P. at 818 (emphasis added).

use should be clear rather than merely suspected.) Custodians sometimes worry that if the records are misused and someone is harmed the custodian might be held liable to the victim because of the release of the records. The chance of any such liability is remote at most and probably nonexistent. The custodian who releases records is simply carrying out a statutory mandate, and it is the recipient who is legally responsible for the uses he or she makes of records legally received.[19] The better course for custodians is to not even ask why someone is requesting the records in question.

The Right of Inspection

The public's right to inspect public records imposes a corresponding duty on the custodian of those records to permit such inspections. This section discusses various elements of the right of inspection and the duty to permit inspections.

The Custodian

G.S. 132-6 directs that the *custodian* of public records is to permit inspection and copying of records in his or her custody. Who is the custodian?[20] G.S. 132-2 specifies that "[t]he public official in charge of an office having public records shall be the custodian thereof."[21] Sometimes local governments seek to centralize public records requests made to agencies of the government by requiring that all requests be made to the manager or perhaps to the public information or public affairs officer. Such a requirement appears to conflict with the statutory definition of "custodian," inasmuch as the manager or the public information or public affairs officer is clearly not the official in charge of every office of county or city government. At least one superior court judge so interpreted the statute, ruling that a county's attempt to require that all records requests go through the manager violated the

---

19. In *Carlson v. Pima County*, 687 P.2d 1242 (Ariz. 1984), a jail inmate brought suit against the sheriff, alleging that the newspaper publication of a jail "offense report" involving the plaintiff had defamed him. The court held that the report was a public record and therefore the sheriff was privileged and could not be held liable. In *Zientara v. Long Creek Township*, 569 N.E.2d 1299 (Ill. App. Ct. 1991), a township employee was discharged, allegedly because of statements he made at public meetings. He argued that his statements were based on public records and therefore somehow privileged. The court disagreed, holding that the public records law entitles a person to copies of the records but has no concern with what the person does with the copies once received. He or she must bear whatever burden that use imposes. See also *Williams v. City of Minneola*, 575 So. 2d 683 (Fla. Dist. Ct. App. 1991), in which the court stated that the public records laws do not "give license to individuals . . . to do whatever they please with public records with immunity from all the safeguards for individual rights which the common law has painstakingly developed over the centuries." *Id.* at 687.

In *Williams* the court was willing to hold records custodians liable in tort because of the release of records *when the records in question were not open to public access.* Police officers had showed to friends a videotape and photographs made at an autopsy, and survivors of the deceased brought suit for intentional infliction of emotional damage. The videotape and the photographs were not open to public access, but neither were the custodians under any statutory duty to maintain the confidentiality of the records. In that limited circumstance the court was willing to impose some responsibility on the custodians for their release of the records.

20. Chapter 3 includes a more detailed discussion of the identity and duties of a records custodian.

21. The statute is set out in appendix 2A at the end of this chapter.

public records law.[22] Even though a local government cannot require all requests to be made through the manager, it certainly has the power to require all custodians within the local government to report any requests that have been made to the manager (or some other central administrator), simply in order to keep track of requests.

When Inspection Is Allowed

The statute directs custodians of public records to permit inspection of the records "at reasonable times."[23] The most likely meaning of this language is during the regular office hours of the agency holding the records. The agency need not extend its regular hours for the sole purpose of permitting inspections,[24] but neither may it refuse to permit inspections for extended periods during its regular hours.[25] In special cases, of course, the phrase may mean something other than regular office hours. A very small town, for example, may not even have an office, keeping the records in the home of the town clerk; clearly, such a town would still have to provide some opportunities for inspection of its records. Similarly, records custodians probably may limit records requests to a period of time slightly shorter than regular office hours, providing, for example, that no request will be received during the last fifteen or thirty minutes of the day.

---

22. Dawes v. Buncombe County Bd. of Comm'rs, No. 99 CVS 03497 (N.C. Super. Ct., Buncombe County, Sept. 1, 1999).

23. G.S. 132-6(a).

24. G.S. 132-6.2(d) provides that "[n]othing in this section shall be construed to require a public agency to respond to requests for copies of public records outside of its usual business hours."

25. In *Zink v. City of Mesa*, 166 P.3d 738 (Wash. Ct. App. 2007), the court invalidated an attempt to limit inspection of records by a couple who had made numerous requests for records to one hour per day; the statute required that records be available during business hours. There are a number of other cases that generally support the statement in the text, but they are not directly on point. Most of them interpret statutes that specify that records are to be available during the agency's office hours, and the North Carolina statute has no specific reference to office hours. There do not seem to be any cases interpreting statutes comparable to the more general requirement of the North Carolina statute. The relevant cases include *Bruce v. Gregory*, 423 P.2d 193 (Cal. 1967) (tax collector ought not to deny inspection during the first half hour and last half hour of the business day); *Chambers v. Kent*, 201 N.Y.S.2d 439 (Sup. Ct. 1960) (records must be made available during all office hours); *State ex rel. Butler County Bar Ass'n v. Robb*, 575 N.E.2d 497 (Ohio Ct. App. 1990) (county clerk shortened office hours because of budget cutbacks, thus limiting time during which records were available; court held that the statutory requirement that records be available during "regular business hours" means the hours of the office itself and not some general standard). A case taking a different view is *State ex rel. Cartwright v. Oklahoma Industries Authority*, 629 P.2d 1244 (Okla. 1981). There the public agency had but one employee, who opened the office only three or four days a week and was in and out of the office a great deal. The court held that the statutory requirement that records be available during "regular business hours" referred to a general community standard and not to the hours of each agency. Therefore, the office was required to be open to permit records inspection for eight hours a day, Monday through Friday.

The Arkansas public records statute permits records inspection during the "regular business hours of the custodian." In *Hengel v. City of Pine Bluff*, 821 S.W.2d 761 (Ark. 1991), the court applied this standard to a city police department that was open twenty-four hours a day and held that records inspection must therefore be permitted twenty-four hours a day. More recently, however, the Ohio Supreme Court refused to impose a similar requirement, holding that a police department that is open twenty-four hours a day still need only respond to public records requests between 8:00 A.M. and 4:00 P.M. State *ex rel.* Warren Newspapers, Inc. v. Hutson, 640 N.E.2d 174 (Ohio 1994).

Interference with Other Office Duties and Other Record Uses

Records custodians often have other responsibilities and are tempted to place requests to inspect (or receive copies of) public records behind those other responsibilities, giving such requests a lower priority. By and large the courts have rejected the propriety of such policies. For example, during World War II one county clerk argued that her office was shorthanded due to the war and therefore could not respond promptly to a request to inspect one month's worth of expenditures of a county department. The Oklahoma Supreme Court rejected the clerk's argument, holding that her duties relating to public records had the same priority as other duties and could not, as a matter of policy, be subordinated to the other duties.[26] Obviously, a custodian need not drop whatever he or she is doing to respond to a request to inspect records, but neither may a custodian put off a request with a statement that he or she "will get to it when I've finished everything else I've got to do."[27]

Custodians have also sought to deny inspection on the ground that it interfered with the custodian's (or other public officials') own use of the records, which, after all, is normally the reason the records have been established and maintained. When the argument is made generally, with the purpose of denying all access to the records, the courts have rejected it.[28] But when made more selectively, as a justification for temporary limitations on the right of inspection, the argument has been more successful. For example, courts have upheld temporary denials of inspection when the records are actually being used by public officials; those officials do not have to interrupt their use of the records in order to permit inspection.[29] Courts have also upheld regulations that respond to one person's repeated and heavy demands on a records custodian—demands much greater than those of other members of the public. In one Ohio case, for example, a company's employees were in a public office every day, making constant use of a particular record. The company's demand for that record was so heavy that it regularly interfered with the ability of public employees in that office to use the same record. Under those circumstances, the Ohio Supreme Court upheld restrictions on the public's right to freely inspect the record in question.[30]

---

26. State *ex rel.* Research Inst. v. Nix, 155 P.2d 983 (Okla. 1944).

27. *See also* North v. Foley, 265 N.Y.S. 780 (App. Div. 1933) (even though records examination necessarily interferes with the normal operation of the custodian's office, the custodian has a duty to permit inspections); Welt v. Bd. of Educ., 328 N.Y.S.2d 930 (Sup. Ct.), *aff'd*, 334 N.Y.S.2d 369 (App. Div. 1972) (inspection cannot be denied on the ground of inconvenience).

28. *E.g.*, State *ex rel.* Wogan v. Clements, 195 So. 1 (La. 1940).

29. *E.g.*, Bruce v. Gregory, 423 P.2d 193, 197 (Cal. 1967) ("We cannot construe the statutes to give a member of the public priority over county officers in the use of official records."); Gallagher v. Town of Windham, 427 A.2d 37 (N.H. 1981) (records being used, in the field, by chairman of planning commission, and therefore need not be provided to plaintiff); State *ex rel.* Higgins v. Lockwood, 64 A. 184 (N.J. 1906) (registration books did not have to be available for inspection during times board of elections was in session and using them).

30. State *ex rel.* Louisville Title Ins. Co. v. Brewer, 70 N.E.2d 265 (Ohio 1946). The record in question was an index to probate records; the court upheld a regulation that use of the index was to be rendered through the custodian's employees. See also *Bruce v. Gregory*, 423 P.2d 193 (Cal. 1967), which explained that access could be restricted when one person is "monopolizing certain records to the detriment of other members of the public who wish to inspect them." *Id.* at 201.

The Specificity of the Request

Sometimes records custodians suggest that a particular request is too broad and for that reason need not be responded to. It may be that a request to inspect (or obtain copies of) every record held by a local government is too broad,[31] but courts have upheld requests to inspect every record within a particular office or department.[32] The key matter appears to be whether the request is sufficiently specific so that the records custodian knows what he or she is looking for.[33] If there is no issue about what records are being sought, that a great number is being sought is probably of no legal importance. It would simply increase the amount of time it might take to locate the records and thereby respond to the request.

The Custodian's Response Time

North Carolina's statute directs custodians to provide copies of public records "as promptly as possible,"[34] and a court would probably attach that same standard to a request to inspect records. It should certainly take no longer to produce records for inspection than to provide copies of those same records. Even so, this statutory standard does not indicate whether a custodian must respond immediately, within an hour or day, or within some longer period. Although the cases from other states do not speak with one voice, they suggest that in most cases a response within a few days, or even shorter, is required. The Ohio public records law also requires that records be made available "promptly," and the case of *State ex rel. Consumer News Services, Inc. v. Worthington City Board of Education* is typical of the Ohio courts' interpretation of the requirement. The petitioner newspaper had sought the names of five finalists for the position of school system treasurer, a public record in Ohio. It eventually took the system six days to produce the names and resumes of all five, and the Ohio Supreme Court held that, because the request was not large and it was reasonably clear what records were requested, the six days exceeded what the statute required.[35] In Florida the

---

31. In *Hangartner v. City of Seattle*, 90 P.3d 26 (Wash. 2006), a citizens' group sought "the opportunity to inspect all books, records, documents of every kind and the physical properties of the Elevated Transportation Company," which was the city's public transportation agency. The Washington statute requires public agencies to produce "identifiable public records," and the court held that this request was inconsistent with the statute's implicit requirement that the records sought be identified. It should be noted that there is not comparable language in G.S. 132-6(a). In *Rosenthal v. Hansen*, 110 Cal. Rptr. 257 (Ct. App. 1973), the plaintiff had sought copies of documents originally totaling some 80,000 to 85,000 pages and later reduced, and the court rejected his request as too voluminous.

32. In *North v. Foley*, 265 N.Y.S. 780 (App. Div. 1933), the petitioners sought access to all the records in the city's water department in order to allow an accountant engaged by petitioners to conduct an audit of the records; the petition was granted. In *Welt v. Board of Education*, 328 N.Y.S.2d 930 (Sup. Ct.), *aff'd*, 334 N.Y.S.2d 369 (App. Div. 1972), the court upheld a request to inspect all the school board's purchase records for student desks, chairs, and replacement parts for the preceding two years.

33. *E.g.*, State *ex rel.* Morgan v. City of New Lexington, 857 N.E.2d 1208 (Ohio 2006) (city knew which records requester sought and knew where they were and therefore was required to respond to the request). In contrast, in *Anderson v. Village of Jacksonville*, 103 S.W.3d 190 (Mo. Ct. App. 2003), the requester sought title documents held by the village to "property that was previously leased by Mr. Anderson from the Railroad," without further identifying the property in question. The court held that as so stated the request was insufficiently specific.

34. G.S. 132-6(a).

35. 776 N.E.2d 82 (Ohio 2002). *See also* State *ex rel.* Wadd v. City of Cleveland, 689 N.E.2d 25 (1998) (petitioner sought order requiring police department to make accident reports available within eight days after accident; court grants mandamus, noting that whatever "promptly" may mean, it certainly means

statutory standard is that the custodian provide access to the records within a reasonable time. In *Tribune Co. v. Cannella*, the Florida Supreme Court held that the only justifications for delaying a response (which in the case amounted to two days) were retrieving the record and checking for any material in the record that was exempt from public access.[36] (The requester had sought a personnel record, and the custodian had delayed her response in order to inform the employee whose record was being sought and to allow that employee to be present. The court held that these were inappropriate reasons for delay.)

The most likely interpretation of North Carolina's law is that a records custodian should respond to a fairly simple records request either immediately, within a few hours, or perhaps in a day or two. As the request becomes more substantial, however, and the burden on the custodian becomes correspondingly greater, it seems reasonable to allow the custodian somewhat more time to locate and deliver the records that are wanted. Among factors that might appropriately delay granting access are the number of records requested, whether they are scattered in several sites, how large the public agency is, and whether any part of the records must be redacted.[37] Unless a request is extraordinary, though, a custodian should always respond within a week or so at most.

Original Records versus Copies

The general rule is that the right of inspection applies to the originals of the records and not to copies that have been made of those originals.[38] This applies not only to paper records but also to tapes. In *State ex rel. Swigart v. Barber*,[39] the custodian of a tape recording refused to allow the requester to listen to the tape, instead insisting that he pay to have the tape transcribed. The appellate court held that the requester had a right of access to the tape itself and need not settle for a transcript. This rule may not extend in full force, however, to electronic records. As is elaborated more fully in chapter 5, it is unlikely that a court would require a government to allow a citizen to sit at a government computer and enter the government's computer system, or even require that the government set aside a dummy terminal to permit public access to that system.

Extracting Specific Records from a Larger Group

Sometimes a citizen will seek records about a specific subject, and in order to meet the request it might be necessary for the custodian to spend a good bit of time going through a group of associated records looking for those concerned with the specific subject. As a general rule, the custodian need not undertake this work. Rather, it is sufficient to give the citizen access to the larger group of records and expect that person to do the more detailed

---

within eight days); Specht v. Finnegan, 776 N.E.2d 564 (Ohio Ct. App. 2002) (delaying up to two months in providing copies does not meet statutory requirement of promptness).

36. 458 So. 2d 1075 (Fla. 1984).

37. In WIREDATA, Inc. v. Village of Sussex, 751 N.W.2d 736 (Wis. 2008), the court quoted with approval from an amicus brief that a reasonable response time "depends on the nature of the request, the staff and other resources available to the authority to process the request, the extent of the request, and other related considerations." *Id.* at 753.

38. *E.g.*, Hubka v. Pennfield Twp., 504 N.W.2d 183 (Mich. 1993); Florence Morning News, Inc. v. Bldg. Comm'n, 218 S.E.2d 881 (S.C. 1975).

39. 692 N.E.2d 639 (Ohio Ct. App. 1997).

searching himself. (Of course, if the custodian has an index or other finding aid, that index or finding aid should be made available to the citizen.) For example, if a citizen asked for all references to annexation in a city council's minutes over a ten-year period, it would be sufficient for the city to provide the citizen with access to the minute books. Or, if a citizen asked for all correspondence dealing with one aspect of a large project, the government could provide the citizen with the entire correspondence file for the project and expect the citizen to locate the specific letters desired.

Records in Multiple Locations

Many government records can be found in more than one location. If one public official sends a letter to a second, both the sender and the receiver may retain a copy of the letter. If a local government makes a report to a state agency, both the local government and the agency will probably have a copy of the report. Occasionally, records custodians have argued that a citizen seeking a copy of such a record should go to the other location and seek it there. The courts have rejected these arguments. For example, in *Keddie v. Rutgers, the State University*,[40] a professor sought from the university copies of pleadings, briefs, affidavits, and other documents filed with courts, agencies, and arbitrators. The university refused to provide the copies, arguing that he should instead go to the locations at which the records were filed, such as the local courthouse. The New Jersey Supreme Court held that simply because a record is available in more than one location does not diminish a person's right to access to the record in any one of those locations.[41]

Protecting the Integrity of the Records

The custodian not only must allow access to public records, he or she must also protect the integrity of those records while they are being inspected or copied. Therefore, the custodian is under no obligation to let outsiders into the file system; a local government may limit access to records storage locations to its own employees, who will retrieve records for requesters.[42] The custodian should also oversee any inspection of the records to assure that no records are lost, damaged, or modified.[43] This responsibility may necessitate detailing an employee to sit with someone working with public records to assure the safety of the records. Finally, the custodian should not permit records to be taken from the public premises unless under the supervision of a public employee.[44]

No Inspection Fees

G.S. 132-6 and G.S. 132-6.2 expressly permit fees for *copies* of public records, but neither section makes mention of any fees for the right of *inspection* only. G.S. 132-6.2(b) includes language permitting special service charges when "requests" involve extensive use of human

---

40. 689 A.2d 702 (N.J. 1997).

41. *Accord* Wichita Eagle & Beacon Publ'g Co. v. Simmons, 50 P.3d 66 (Kan. 2002).

42. *See* Gorton v. Dow, 282 N.Y.S.2d 841 (Sup. Ct. 1967).

43. *E.g.*, Bruce v. Gregory, 423 P.2d 193 (Cal. 1967); Direct Mail Serv., Inc. v. Registrar of Motor Vehicles, 5 N.E.2d 545 (Mass. 1937).

44. Gorton v. Dow, 282 N.Y.S.2d 841 (Sup. Ct. 1967). G.S. 132-7 admonishes records custodians that "public records should be kept in the buildings in which they are ordinarily used."

or technological resources, but the context clearly indicates that this authorization is limited to copy charges and does not include charges associated solely with inspection. The section is entitled "Provisions for copies of public records; fees," and the earlier use of the word requests in the subsection clearly concerns copies only. This silence as to inspection fees is the common statutory pattern around the country, and as a result there have been a number of court decisions concerning whether fees may be charged for inspection only. Although a few very early cases were decided in favor of such fees (possibly because the public officers with custody of the records were compensated by fees), the modern decisions generally hold that custodians may not, without statutory authority, charge fees for mere inspection, when the custodian does no more than locate and retrieve the record and no copy is provided.[45] Nor may a local government require a person who simply wants to inspect a record to purchase a copy;[46] a person is entitled to inspect the record and make his or her own notes or own hand copy. Some local governments have made arrangements to store older records off-site, in private storage facilities, and sometimes there is a charge, even to the government, when a record is retrieved from the storage site. The principles discussed in this paragraph seem to bar a government from passing such a charge along to someone seeking to inspect a record kept in such a storage facility.

Some courts have made exceptions to this rule when extraordinary services are provided as part of the inspection. In one Michigan case, for example, the records custodian believed it was necessary, to protect the integrity of the records, for an employee to sit with the requester while the records were being inspected. The court agreed with that judgment and permitted the custodian to charge for the employee's time if (but only if) the inspection continued for more than two weeks.[47]

Requests Received by Telephone, Fax Machine, or Mail

Requests for a Record

A records custodian's obligation is to permit inspection and copying of public records by members of the public. That usually means that a person is entitled to visit the office in which the record is kept, inspect it at that location, and receive a copy at that location. Sometimes, however, a person might request a copy of a record from a remote location, by telephone, facsimile machine, surface mail, or e-mail. If the requester states that he or she will visit the office to pick up the copies, there is no question that such a request must be complied with. It is not as clear, however, when the requester asks that the copies be sent

---

45. *E.g.*, McFrugal Rental of Riverdale, Inc. v. Garr, 418 S.E.2d 60 (Ga. 1992) (fees may be charged only when inspection imposes an unusual administrative cost or burden); Thornton v. Dep't of Pub. Safety, 536 So. 2d 595 (La. Ct. App. 1988) (no fees for inspection); State *ex rel.* Patterson v. Ayers, 171 N.E.2d 508 (Ohio 1960) (records may be examined free of charge); York Newspapers, Inc. v. City of York, 826 A.2d 41 (Pa. Commw. Ct. 2003). *See* Black v. Sw. Water Conservation Dist., 74 P.3d 462 (Colo. App. 2003) (statutory authority to make regulations "reasonably necessary for the protection of such records and the prevention of unnecessary interference with the regular discharge of the duties of the custodian or the custodian's office" permits imposing research and retrieval fee of $15 per hour and $20 per hour in exceptionally voluminous requests).

46.Despain v. City of Collinsville, 888 N.E.2d 163 (Ill. Ct. App. 2008); Dooley v. Luzerne County Bd. of Assessment Appeals, 649 A.2d 728 (Pa. Commw. Ct. 1994).

47. Cashel v. Regents of the Univ. of Mich., 367 N.W.2d 841 (Mich. Ct. App. 1985).

to him or her by mail or facsimile machine. G.S. 132-6 directs that custodians permit any record in their custody "to be inspected and examined at reasonable times . . . and furnish copies thereof." This language clearly establishes a duty to allow inspection at the place where the record is kept, but it is possible to further understand the language to mean that the duty to provide a copy is limited to that location only. A number of courts have interpreted their states' public records laws in that way, holding that custodians had no duty to provide copies by mail.[48] It is also possible, however, to read the two duties as independent: the duty to permit inspection at the office at which the record is located, and the duty to provide a copy without regard to the presence or absence of the requester at the office where the record is located. Other courts have reached that conclusion.[49] Given North Carolina's strong statutory policy favoring access, it seems more likely that our courts would follow the second group of cases than the first, but the matter remains unresolved.[50]

Requests for Information

Citizens who cannot visit a government office sometimes ask the records custodian to provide information that is contained in public records by telephone, facsimile machine, or mail. Many custodians are happy to comply with such a request, but the statute does not require them to do so. The custodian's duties are to permit inspection of records and provide copies of records; the statute does not require a custodian to act as a reference desk.

Adoption of Regulations

Numerous cases acknowledge that records custodians may adopt regulations detailing the right of access, and no doubt North Carolina custodians may do so as well. G.S. 132-6(a) imposes the duty of permitting inspections on the person with custody of the records; therefore, it follows that the custodian has independent authority to adopt such regulations. Most custodians, however, are part of a larger government structure and report directly or indirectly to an elected official or an elected board. If the official or board adopts regulations applicable to all the public offices under the official's or board's control, those regulations should prevail over any contrary regulations adopted by a particular custodian for the records in his or her office.

Among the matters often included in regulations are (1) the hours during which inspection is allowed, (2) the form that requests must take, (3) how records are removed from files, (4) spaces in the office available to persons inspecting records, (5) whether inspections must be supervised, and (6) how copies are to be made and at what price.

---

48. *E.g.*, *Ex parte* Gill, 841 So. 2d 1231 (Ala. 2002); State *ex rel.* Fenley v. Ohio Historical Soc'y, 597 N.E.2d 120 (Ohio 1992). *See also* Conely v. Peck, 929 S.W.2d 630 (Tex. App. 1996) (no duty to produce public records outside of government office where they are located).

49. *E.g.*, Wootton v. Cook, 590 So. 2d 1039 (Fla. Dist. Ct. App. 1991); Elliott v. District Attorney of Baton Rouge, 664 So. 2d 122 (La. Ct. App. 1995); Waller v. Bryan, 16 S.W.3d 770 (Tenn. Ct. App. 1999).

50. In *O'Bradovich v. Village of Tuckahoe*, 325 F. Supp. 2d 413 (S.D.N.Y. 2004), the village had had a policy of responding to public records requests that were sent by U.S. mail, e-mail, or facsimile. When the village began receiving a very large number of requests, it responded by stating that it would answer only those coming by U.S. mail or overnight delivery; it would no longer respond to those coming by e-mail or facsimile. The federal court held that this change was a rational response to a volume problem and therefore violated neither procedural nor substantive due process.

Custodians sometimes ask if they may require that requests be in writing, and the answer is uncertain. Requiring written requests seems reasonable; it facilitates locating the specific record or records wanted by the inspector. The public records statute, however, expressly permits custodians to require written requests for copies of computer databases[51] and is silent about written requests for access to or copies of other kinds of records. The express statutory authorization for written requests for one kind of record might suggest that a local government may not require written requests for other sorts of records. Nevertheless, if an agency receives a large volume of requests and if a requirement of a written request is not imposed or implemented in order to impede the right of inspection, courts would probably sustain such a requirement.[52]

Not so, though, with requirements that persons requesting access to or copies of public records identify themselves. It would almost certainly be found unreasonable to condition a person's right of access to public records upon a requirement that the person give his or her name or other identifying information.

The Right to a Copy

The requester's right of access under the public records law is two-fold: a right to inspect the record and a right to make or have made a copy of the record. This section discusses some of the issues that arise concerning the right to a copy.

Standing Requests

A number of local governments have received requests to receive all e-mails or correspondence to or from selected officials. A city, for example, might have received such a request for its mayor, its council members, and its manager. One issue that such requests have triggered is basic—whether the public records law permits a standing records request, that is, a request for future records that have not yet been created. There is nothing particular to the North Carolina statutes that provides an answer to the question, but courts in at least two other states appear to have upheld the legitimacy of such requests, at least in certain situations. The more direct case is *West Valley View, Inc. v. Maricopa County Sheriff's Office.*[53] In that case the sheriff's office discontinued sending a copy of each press release by e-mail to a newspaper because of dissatisfaction with the newspaper's uses of the press releases. (It routinely sent the press releases by e-mail to other newspapers in the county.) When the sheriff's office refused to recommence e-mailing the releases, the newspaper sued and won in the trial court. A major issue before the Arizona court of appeals was the propriety of the newspaper's standing request. The sheriff argued that the law did not require a response to requests for future records; rather, the argument ran, a custodian need only respond to

51. G.S. 132-6.2(c).

52. In *Citizens Progressive Alliance v. Southwestern Water Conservation District*, 97 P.3d 308 (Colo. App. 2004), the court approved a number of public records regulations established by the district, including a requirement that requests be in writing.

53. 165 P.3d 203 (Ariz. Ct. App. 2007).

requests made after creation of a record. The court disagreed and upheld the enforceability of a standing request:

> In view of the presumption requiring disclosure that guides our application of Arizona's public records laws, we do not construe [the statute] to require the submission of separate *seriatim* requests for copies of each successive record when what the requester wants is every record within a clearly articulated and defined category of records that a public agency creates over time.[54]

It should be noted that the court emphasized that the request being litigated involved press releases, and all of them. The court exhibited some sympathy with the notion that it might be too cumbersome to make the office filter the press releases for only those covering the paper's circulation area or filter a different kind of record for those that are public and those that are not. Such a need to filter could quickly become particularly onerous if a growing number of people made the request.[55]

The second case is *Howard v. Sumter Free Press, Inc.*,[56] which also involved a sheriff's office that had stopped providing access to records to a newspaper with which it disagreed. The newspaper had a standing request for certain sorts of records, and the sheriff pointed out that the public records law does not require creation of records. Here was the court's response:

> It is true, as Howard maintains, that the Act applies to existing records in that no public officer or agency is required to prepare reports, summaries, or compilations not in existence at the time of the open records request. But, the evidence in this case was that the documents at issue were generated on an ongoing basis and that the newspaper's requests for access to the documents were continuing.[57]

The response seems to indicate that an ongoing request for regularly generated documents is legitimate under a public records statute. The court's language appears to be consistent with the direction suggested by the *West Valley View* case—that such requests may become illegitimate if they require much in the way of filtering by the public agency in order to fulfill them. An ongoing request for all e-mails sent or received by a public official may be close to the line under these cases, inasmuch as responding to such a request would usually require filtering out e-mails that are not open to immediate public access.[58]

---

54. *Id.* at 206 (citation omitted).

55. Thus, this case does not present more difficult questions that might be implicated by a request, for example, for documents received or created in the future relating to any crime occurring at a particular address or involving any one of a number of specified individuals. To the contrary, the newspaper's request for press releases only seeks copies of a single easily defined and identifiable category of documents that the public agency admittedly regularly generates.

Id. at 208.

56. 531 S.E.2d 698 (Ga. 2000).

57. *Id.* at 699 (citation omitted).

58. In *Cape Publications v. City of Louisville*, 147 S.W.3d 731 (Ky. Ct. App. 2003), the newspaper was challenging a decision by the state's attorney general concerning access to certain information in police incident reports. In a footnote the court of appeals noted that the newspaper had alleged that it had made a "continuing open records request" for these reports and that the attorney general had "explained that

The Custodian Must Provide a Copy

G.S. 132-6 and G.S. 132-6.2 impose on the custodian a duty to provide copies of public records to persons who request them. Under the latter statute, the copy may be certified or uncertified, at the option of the person making the request.

Use of Copying Equipment

As noted above, the statute requires custodians to provide a copy of a public record upon request. Sometimes, though, the requester would rather make his or her own copies. The requestor might, for example, want copies of a large number of records and be able to provide them more cheaply with his or her own photocopying machine or scanner. In such a situation, does the requester have the right to bring to the record location and use his or her own copying equipment, or does the custodian have a right to insist on providing the copies using the government's machine?

This question has been litigated a number of times in other states, and the courts have decided the issue both ways.[59] The cases cannot be reconciled, but a couple of suggestions may be hazarded. If the custodian insists on using his or her own equipment because of a legitimate concern about possible damage to the records from using outside equipment, a court will probably support the custodian in that policy. G.S. 132-6(f) provides that the "inspection or copying of any public record which, because of its age or condition could be damaged during inspection or copying, may be made subject to reasonable restrictions intended to preserve the particular record."[60] If the custodian's preference is based on other grounds, however, such as a desire to collect fees for making the copies, it is probably more vulnerable to challenge.

Copy Format

Once computers became commonplace in government workplaces and many records were created in electronic formats, a new question arose about copies of public records: does a citizen's right to a copy of an electronic record include a right to an electronic copy, or may a government instead insist on providing only a printout of the electronic information? The question has been litigated in a number of states and under the federal Freedom of

---

ongoing or continuing requests are not proper under the law." *Id.* at 732. The court did not reach that question.

59. Cases that uphold a requirement that copies be made on the custodian's equipment are *Adams County Abstract Co. v. Fisk*, 788 P.2d 1336 (Idaho Ct. App. 1990) (microfilm machine) and *Moore v. Board of Chosen Freeholders*, 186 A.2d 676 (N.J. 1962) (photocopy machine). Cases that allow citizens to use their own equipment are *Title Research Corp. v. Rausch*, 450 So. 2d 933 (La. 1984) (microfilm machine); *First Commerce Title Co. v. Martin*, 887 So. 2d 716 (La. Ct. App. 2004) (portable scanner); *Land Title Guarantee & Trust Co. v. Essex*, 368 N.E.2d 326 (Ohio Ct. App. 1977) (camera equipment); and *State ex rel. Milwaukee Police Ass'n v. Jones*, 615 N.W.2d 190 (Wis. Ct. App. 2000) (tape recording machine).

In *Permian Report v. Lacy*, 817 S.W.2d 175 (Tex. App. 1991), the plaintiff wished to microfilm, on its own equipment, land records in the clerk's office. The clerk sought to require the plaintiff to pay the cost of public employees to supervise the copying and to require the plaintiff to post a bond providing indemnification against possible damage to the records. The court invalidated both regulations.

60. In *Adams County Abstract Co. v. Fisk*, 788 P.2d 1336 (Idaho Ct. App. 1990), the court expressed concern about the integrity of the records if a citizen were allowed to use his or her own microfilm machine. In *Moore v. Board of Chosen Freeholders*, 186 A.2d 676 (N.J. 1962), the court expressed concern about damage to the originals if a variety of copying machines were used.

Information Act, with decisions going both ways, but it has been settled in North Carolina by statute. G.S. 132-6.2(a) provides that persons requesting copies of public records

> may elect to obtain [the records] in any and all media in which the public agency is capable of providing them. No request for copies of public records in a particular medium shall be denied on the grounds that the custodian has made or prefers to make the public records available in another medium.

The statute was enacted with electronic records in mind, so that someone requesting a copy of an electronic record could receive it in paper form or as an electronic file, but it is not limited to electronic records and therefore affects other sorts of records as well. For example, if a local government has a printed document and a citizen makes a request for a copy of the document in PDF form, the government is required to produce the document in that form if it has the equipment and software necessary to do so. Similarly, if a local government owns a photograph that a citizen requests a digitized copy of, the local government is required to provide the digitized copy if it has the necessary scanning equipment.

A couple of points should be made about the need for the government to have the capability of making a copy in the preferred format. First, if a requester were to make the request for a PDF version of a document set out above, and a small local government did not have a scanner and so could not produce a PDF version of the record, it would not have to do so. It could provide a photocopy of the document and thereby meet its statutory obligation. Second, the government is always under the obligation to provide some sort of copy of a public record. Say, for example, that a local government tape records its council meetings to help in preparation of the minutes, it has a machine that allows the clerk to listen to the tape, but it does not have a machine that would copy the tape. If someone requested a copy of the tape, the government would have to make arrangements for producing the copy, probably commercially, if the requester was unable or unwilling to bring in his or her own copying equipment. (Of course, as discussed in the next section, the government could pass along the cost of making such a copy to the person making the request.)

Copying Fees

Introduction

It was noted above that custodians generally may not charge fees to persons who simply wish to inspect public records. If a person wishes to obtain a copy, however, and if the custodian makes or provides the copy, the statute does permit the custodian to charge a fee for doing so. (If a member of the public makes his or her own copy of a record, the custodian may not charge a fee for that copy.) [61] The statute does not set the fees that may be charged but rather sets a standard for establishing such fees.

---

61. Cummings v. Kempf, 570 So. 2d 133 (La. Ct. App. 1990) (custodian sought to charge person with own copying machine a fee of 25 cents per page for supervision of copying); Permian Report v. Lacy, 817 S.W.2d 175 (Tex. App. 1991) (custodian sought to charge person with own microfilm machine the cost of using a public employee to supervise copying).

The General Rule

G.S. 132-6.2 directs that a fee for copies be based on the actual cost of making the copy. The statute limits "actual cost" to

> direct, chargeable costs related to the reproduction of a public record as determined by generally accepted accounting principles [not including] costs that would have been incurred by the public agency if a request to reproduce a public record had not been made.

Three elements of the quoted provision are important.

First, a local government may determine actual cost pursuant to generally accepted accounting principles. That means that a local government may establish a cost accounting system associated with providing copies of public records and use that system as the basis for the fees charged for such copies. Most local governments, of course, do not have such cost accounting systems in place, and it is unlikely that the demand for copies of public records will justify establishing such a system. As long as a government's fees for copies are nominal—perhaps up to as much as 25 cents per page for photocopies of paper records[62] or the cost of materials for copies of electronic records—the lack of any accounting support for fees should not be a problem. Should a government attempt to impose fees that significantly exceed these nominal levels, however, the statutory language suggests that the government must be able to support the higher fees by a developed cost accounting system.

Such a system is most likely with electronic records. Many larger local governments account for their information technology operations through internal service funds. By using such a fund, the government can bill the full cost of information technology to the various departments that use that service. If the only reference in the statute were to generally accepted accounting principles, a local government that accounted for its information technology operations through an internal service fund would be able to charge citizens for copies of electronic records on the same basis that it charged internal departmental users of the system. But the second and third important elements of the provision quoted above usually require some modification of departmental charges before the fees that may be charged to the public are determined.

The first of these other two noteworthy elements is the limitation of actual costs to direct costs. This seems intended to prohibit seeking return of indirect costs as part of the system of fees for copies of public records. That is, the cost accounting system may include only the costs directly incurred by the information technology system itself and not such indirect costs as a pro rata share of the costs of the manager's office, the finance department, the human resources department, and so on.

The final noteworthy element prohibits including in the fee for a copy costs that would have been incurred whether the copy request was made or not. Two important cost elements that this provision may exclude from the calculation of the fee are personnel costs and equipment depreciation costs. In general employees will be paid whether or not a request is made for a copy of a record. Only if overtime is necessary to provide a copy

62. In *Specht v. Finnegan*, 776 N.E.2d 564 (Ohio Ct. App. 2002), the court held that a charge of 25 cents per page was excessive, when actual cost was about 10 cents.

promptly does it seem possible to charge for employee time, and then only for the overtime.[63] With regard to depreciation, the method of depreciation will determine the legality of recovering that cost through a fee. If a local government depreciates equipment by the straight-line method, making a copy of a public record imposes no new cost on the government. But if the local government depreciates equipment on a unit-cost basis, expensing depreciation only as equipment is used, making a copy does impose new costs and the government may include depreciation in determining the fee.[64]

If the local government does not own or have available the equipment necessary to meet a request for copies of public records and therefore arranges for the records to be copied commercially, the charges imposed by the commercial copier would be direct costs incurred by the government in providing the copy and could be passed along to the records requester.[65]

Other Statutes

The general rule discussed in the preceding paragraphs applies "[e]xcept as otherwise provided by law."[66] There are a few statutes that specify other fees for copies of public records, although most of those statutes apply only to state agencies. The principal exception at the local government level is the statute setting fees for copies from the register of deeds, G.S. 161-10.[67]

Certified Copies

The general rule applies to uncertified copies. If a citizen wishes a certified copy of a public record, G.S. 132-6.2 states that the custodian is to charge the "fees . . . as provided by law."

---

63. If a local government agency receives such a consistent level of requests for copies of public records that a single employee (or the full-time equivalent of a single employee) is needed simply to provide copies of public records, that agency can argue that, absent the requests for copies, that employee's position would not have been necessary at all. Perhaps in that situation, which is probably quite rare, the employee's time can be included in the costs recovered by the fee for copies.

64. Other statutes sometimes permit specific public offices to charge fees for copies that reflect costs not permitted under G.S. 132-6.2. For example, G.S. 161-10(a)(11) permits registers of deeds to recover the "cost of purchasing and maintaining copying and/or computer equipment" when setting fees for uncertified copies.

65. In *State ex rel. Gibbs v. Concord Township Trustees*, 787 N.E.2d 1248 (Ohio Ct. App. 2003), the citizen asked for copies of some 10,000 pages of public records associated with a lengthy ongoing construction project. The township's costs were 5 cents a page, but it determined that the request was too large to be handled by staff and therefore it proposed to have the work done commercially at a cost of 6 cents a page. When the citizen refused to pay the extra penny per copy, a lawsuit ensued. The Ohio court of appeals held that the township was entitled to pass along to the citizen the full costs of the commercial copying, but it should be noted that there was support for doing so in the language of the Ohio statute. The court, however, made several other decisions that could be useful in other states: (1) it was reasonable to employ an outside firm to make copies when the volume of a request would tax the capacity of the governmental entity; (2) it would be reasonable to pass along the costs of rented office equipment if it would be unsafe to allow records to leave the public building in which they are housed; and (3) it would be reasonable to give a citizen the choice between getting records quickly, through a commercial copy firm, or more slowly and at a lower cost, from the government directly.

66. G.S. 132-6.2(b).

67. G.S. 90-411 provides a statutory fee for copies of medical records in certain circumstances, and sometimes this statute may apply to a health care facility that is subject to the public records laws.

The difficulty is that there is no generally applicable statute that sets the amount of such fees. G.S. 161-10(a)(9) sets certified copy fees for the register of deeds, perhaps the local official most likely to be asked to provide such copies, at $5 for the first page and $2 for each additional page. That is probably an acceptable standard for copies certified by other custodians.

Records Held by Agents

Sometimes local governments contract for outside entities to maintain custody of public records. If a citizen seeks a copy of a record subject to such an arrangement, what sort of fee can be charged to the citizen? It seems clear that the local government cannot leave the matter to be negotiated between the citizen and the private entity. The records belong to the government, and it cannot avoid its responsibilities under the public records law by placing those records in the possession of a private entity. The better answer appears to be that the government should procure a copy of the record from the private entity, as if it were doing so for its own purposes, and pass along to the citizen whatever fee the private entity charges the government, assuming it is reasonable.[68] The fee is, after all, the actual cost to the government in providing a copy of the record, and no part of the fee represents money the government would have expended without the records request having been made. It would be wise for a government to anticipate such requests and make provisions in the contract with the private entity for meeting public records requests at a reasonable cost.

Extraordinary Copying Requests

G.S. 132-6.2(b) also allows a local government to charge a somewhat higher fee for a copy than is otherwise permitted when "the request is such as to require extensive use of information technology resources or extensive clerical or supervisory assistance by personnel of the agency involved." This provision seems to allow charging for equipment use when it takes extraordinary use to make the copy or charging for employee time when that time is also quite out of the ordinary. If the person seeking the copy believes a fee is unreasonable, the statute permits that person to ask the State Chief Information Officer or his or her designee to mediate the dispute with the local government. The State Chief Information Officer has no authority, however, to order the government to reduce the fee.

---

68. See *Sierra Club v. Pennsylvania Public Utility Commission*, 702 A.2d 1131 (Pa. Commw. Ct. 1997), *order aff'd*, 731 A.2d 133 (Pa. 1999), in which the court approved a charge of almost $6,000 for a transcript of a hearing before the state utilities commission. The commission contracted with a private court reporting firm for such transcripts and required parties to a proceeding to obtain copies of the transcript; the firm charged $2.45 a page. The court made clear that it approved the charge only because it arose in the context of litigation before the utilities commission. It probably would not have approved such a charge for a more standard public records request, and three of the seven judges would not have approved it even in this case.

One North Carolina county stored electronic copies of land records with a private company, and the company proposed to charge the county more than $5,000 for a copy of a set of the records stored on a computer disk—a charge that the county proposed to pass on to the newspaper requesting the records. When the newspaper sued, the county settled the suit and agreed to provide the records at a nominal cost; the trial judge, in approving the settlement, emphasized that public records should be available at an inexpensive cost.

The Cost of Creating the Record—GIS Records

Sometimes records custodians wish to include in the fee for copies some element reflecting the government's cost in creating the record. This might be particularly true if the record was expensive to create and the requester of the copy is likely to make commercial use of the record. In general the public records law does not permit including such a cost in a fee for copies,[69] but the General Assembly has created a special rule for electronic copies of GIS records. G.S. 132-10 permits a local government providing an electronic copy of a GIS database to condition doing so on the requester's agreement not to use the copy for commercial purposes. If the requester wants to use the database in that way, the local government is free to negotiate whatever fee the parties can agree to as a condition of providing the copy.[70]

Enforcing Payment

In *Fenstermaker v. Edgemont Union Free School District*, the school district refused to respond to a request for copies of public records until the requester had paid for earlier requests; and the appellate court upheld the district's practice.[71] This seems a reasonable outcome—a public agency ought not to have to throw further good money after bad—and it is likely a North Carolina court would agree.

Records Subject to Copyright

Some documents and other materials that meet the statutory definition of public record are protected by copyright. In some instances the government receives or purchases the copyrighted documents or materials; in that situation the copyright is held by some person or entity other than the government. In other instances the government produces the documents or materials itself and asserts its own copyright interests in them. When documents or other materials are protected by copyright, the copyright owner generally enjoys the right to control reproduction of the documents or materials.[72] How does that right comport with the public's right to make copies of public records? (In general a copyright owner does not have the right to deny inspection of copyrighted material, and so there is no inconsistency between copyright and the right of inspection of public records.)

Neither the federal copyright statutes nor the North Carolina public records statutes make any reference to the other, but it should be recalled that the copyright statutes, as federal enactments, preempt inconsistent state laws. Therefore, to the extent that there is irreconcilable conflict between the two statutory systems, the copyright rules must be followed even if that means the public records rules are not followed. The discussion below looks first at records that have been copyrighted by some person or entity other than the government and then at records for which the government itself owns the copyright.

---

69. For recognition of this point in another state, see *Granger v. Litchfield*, 645 So. 2d 1262 (La. Ct. App. 1994) (fee for copy of computer tape may not include cost of generating the information on the tape), *reversed in part on other grounds*, 649 So. 2d 397 (La. 1995).

70. G.S. 132-10 is discussed in more detail *infra* in chapter 21.

71. 856 N.Y.S.2d 115 (N.Y. Sup. Ct. App. Div. 2008).

72. 17 U.S.C. § 106(1) (2006).

The Copyright Is Held by Others

There are a variety of circumstances in which a government may purchase or receive materials that are protected by copyright and the copyright owner is not the government. Here is a list of examples:

- Architectural or engineering drawings submitted to the government as part of a permitting process
- Architectural or engineering drawings prepared for one of the government's own construction projects
- Instructional materials purchased by the government for its employee training programs
- Photographs or art work purchased by the government for its facilities
- Reports from consultants under contract with the government[73]

For some of these materials, there is no question about the legitimacy of the copyright or the government's acquisition of the materials subject to copyright. That buildings must be permitted or subdivisions approved does not destroy the copyright of the designer who prepared the plans. Nor does the purchase by a government of copyrighted training materials change the copyrighted status of those materials. It might be that when a government enters into a contract to acquire materials that are subject to copyright—such as a consultant's report or design plans for a government construction project—the demands of the public records law require the government to insist, in the contract, that the other party relinquish any copyright claims it might otherwise have. That point is uncertain, however, and it does not seem to have been litigated anywhere. The remainder of this discussion assumes that the government that has received copyrighted materials has neither an obligation nor leverage to seek relinquishment of the copyright owner's rights.

As noted in the introduction to this discussion, a copyright owner is generally entitled to control reproduction of copyrighted materials, an entitlement that is inconsistent with the public's normal right to copy a public record. One important exception to the owner's right to control reproduction is the doctrine of "fair use." Under the copyright statutes, fair use of copyrighted materials, including their reproduction, "for purposes such as criticism, comment, news reporting, teaching (including multiple copies for classroom use), scholarship, or research, is not an infringement of copyright."[74] Therefore, if a person wishes to make a copy of a copyrighted public record—such as a set of drawings submitted to the inspections department—and intends to make only fair use of the record, the person is entitled to do so under the copyright statutes and therefore also entitled to do so under the public records statutes. If the person's intended use, however, is not fair use, then making the copy would be copyright infringement and a violation of the copyright statutes.

---

73. There are two other large categories of materials that governments acquire that are protected by copyright: (1) books purchased for a public library system and (2) computer software. While library books technically meet the definition of public records—they have been received by the government in the course of its business—no one seriously argues that they are subject to the general right of copying applicable to public records. And, as noted *supra* in chapter 1, in the text accompanying notes 80 through 83, computer software does not appear to be a record at all.

74. 17 U.S.C. § 107 (2006).

Unfortunately, this is not a matter simply between the copyright owner and the member of the public who makes or receives the copy. The copyright statutes provide that if a library or archive provides unsupervised photocopying equipment for its patrons, and sets out a warning that making a copy might be subject to the copyright statutes, the library or archive is not liable for copyright infringement, regardless of what the person who makes a copy does with it.[75] Unfortunately, the statute does not define what qualifies as a library or archive—but even if a government office holding public records might be considered an archive, the fact is that many public record copies are not made on unsupervised copying equipment but rather by public employees. It is possible that by making the copy the government's employee might be infringing on the copyright, regardless of what use is made of the copied records by the ultimate user.[76] Therefore, the government holding a copyrighted record will often be at risk of liability if it makes a copy of the record for a citizen or otherwise participates in the making of the copy. There will certainly be situations in which a proposed use of a copy is fair use,[77] but the copyright statute does not establish a bright line between fair use and inappropriate use, leaving that determination to a court should there be litigation. Therefore, unless a government is quite certain that the use that will be made of a copyrighted document is fair use, the better course appears to be to refuse to make a copy of the document despite its status under the North Carolina public records law.

The Government Holds the Copyright

The situation discussed above, in which the copyright on a public record is held by a person or entity other than the government, has generated almost no case law. By contrast, there is case law that addresses the situation in which the government itself holds the copyright to a public record. In these cases, the courts have attempted to reconcile the demands of both the copyright statutes and the public records statutes.

First, as a matter of federal law a state or local government may hold a copyright on material that it generates. The copyright statutes prohibit the federal government from holding copyrights in its own work,[78] but they say nothing about the capacity of state or local governments to do so. As a consequence, the courts have held that the federal statutes permit state and local governments to obtain and assert copyrights in their own work.[79]

Second, there does not appear to be anything in North Carolina law that prohibits the state or its local governments from obtaining or asserting copyright protections for mate-

---

75. 17 U.S.C. § 108(f)(1) (2006).

76. Princeton Univ. Press v. Michigan Document Servs., Inc., 99 F.3d 1381 (6th Cir. 1996); Basic Books, Inc. v. Kinko's Graphics Corp., 758 F. Supp. 1522 (S.D.N.Y. 1991).

77. In *Lindberg v. County of Kitsap*, 948 P.2d 805 (Wash. 1997), the plaintiffs wanted to provide comments on proposed residential developments at public hearings. To prepare for their presentations, they sought to make copies of the drainage and other engineering plans for the proposed developments that had been submitted to the planning department, but the department refused on the ground that the plans were protected by copyright. The Washington Supreme Court agreed that the plans were protected by copyright but allowed the copies to be made as fair use of the copyrighted materials. The court noted that the plaintiffs wished to use the copies in a public proceeding and not for any commercial purpose.

78. 17 U.S.C. § 105 (2006).

79. National Conference of Bar Exam'rs v. Multistate Legal Studies, Inc., 495 F. Supp. 34 (N.D. Ill. 1980), *aff'd*, 692 F.2d 478 (7th Cir. 1982).

rials they generate.[80] Therefore, it appears that a North Carolina local government may obtain copyright protection for appropriate materials that are public records.

Third, the two courts that have addressed the issue of the effect of such a copyright on the public's rights under a state public records law have reached the following conclusion: a member of the public retains the right, under the public records law, to inspect and make a copy of copyrighted material when the government owns the copyright, but the government may assert its rights as copyright owner and restrict the uses that may be made of a copy of the copyrighted material. The more recent case is *Seago v. Horry County*, a 2008 decision by the South Carolina Supreme Court.[81] The county had developed a GIS database at an initial cost of $7.5 million and was spending about $1 million annually to maintain the database. It had applied for and received copyrights in the database. Seago owns a company that collects electronic mapping data and posts it to a subscriber-only database. When he sought copies of Horry County's GIS database under the South Carolina public records law, the county refused to produce them unless the company signed an agreement licensing the data and restricting commercial use without the county's consent. The county was prepared to charge a fairly nominal fee for the copy but substantially more for the licensing agreement. Seago refused to sign the agreement and instead brought suit under the state's public records statute. The South Carolina Supreme Court first held that the county was entitled to obtain the copyright and then turned to the reconciliation of the public records statute and the copyright statutes. It noted that the public records law entitled anyone to make a copy of a public record and that the county was willing to allow that. But it was not, the court held, inconsistent with the public records law to allow federal copyright law to govern the use of that copy by the recipient. Therefore, it was appropriate for the county to require the licensing agreement as a condition of providing the record.[82]

The South Carolina case described just above involved GIS databases, which are the subject of a special public records statute in North Carolina, G.S. 132-10.[83] The North Carolina statute specifically permits a local government to refuse to make an electronic copy of a GIS database if the requester plans to use the database for "trade or commercial purposes." That is very akin to the rights of a copyright owner and raises the question of whether this statute implies that the state or a local government *does not* have comparable rights with respect to other public records for which it might own the copyright. Such a conclusion probably reads too much into the statute. The statute itself makes no mention of copyright, and therefore there is no evidence that the General Assembly was consciously protecting the rights of a copyright owner. The statute was enacted in 1995, and it was not necessarily

---

80. In *Microdecisions, Inc. v. Skinner*, 889 So. 2d 871 (Fla. Dist. Ct. App. 2004), the question was whether a county could assert copyright protection of GIS maps created by the county. The court pointed out that the Florida legislature had explicitly authorized certain state agencies to obtain copyright protection of certain sorts of documents and specifically permitted certain categories of public records, such as software, to be copyrighted. The court held that copyright was not available for agencies and records not covered by specific legislation. There is no comparable pattern of piecemeal legislation in North Carolina.

81. 663 S.E.2d 38 (S.C. 2008).

82. In reaching its decision, the South Carolina court relied on *County of Suffolk v. First American Real Estate Solutions*, 261 F.3d 179 (2d Cir. 2001), which determined that a county could restrict a requester's further distribution of its copyrighted documents in a case involving copyrighted county tax maps.

83. This statute is the subject of chapter 21, *infra*.

clear at that time that GIS databases were even capable of being copyrighted. For those reasons, it is likely that G.S. 132-10 does not restrict a local government's ability to assert rights as copyright owner with respect to categories of public records besides GIS databases.

Remedies for Failure to Provide Access to a Record

If a records custodian refuses to allow inspection of a record, or refuses to provide a copy of a record, G.S. 132-9 permits the person who has been denied inspection or a copy to "apply to the appropriate division of the General Court of Justice for an order compelling disclosure or copying, and the court shall have jurisdiction to issue such orders."[84]

The Nature of the Proceeding

In the 1980s and 1990s, a number of lawsuits seeking access to records under G.S. 132-9 were begun with the filing of a document titled something like "Application for Order Compelling Disclosure of Public Records." At the same time, the party filing the application, usually denominated "petitioner," sought an *ex parte* order from the trial court, directing the public agency with the contested record to either make the record public or show cause why the court should not enter an order directing it to do so. Typically, the show-cause hearing was a month or so after the filing of the application. The apparent justification for this procedure was the statutory direction, noted below, to set public records suits down for immediate hearing.[85] For a time no agency objected to this procedure, but in *Charns v. Brown*, the agency did object.[86] In the case, a person unhappy with the City of Durham's response to his request for public records brought an action under G.S. 132-9 using the procedure just described. The trial judge entered the show-cause order before any service of process on the city, and in fact no summons was ever issued in the action. Rather, as had become common, the city was served with a copy of the petitioner's application and a copy of the court's *ex parte* order. Instead of responding substantively to the application and order, however, the city filed motions to dismiss the action for insufficiency of process, insufficiency of service of process, and lack of personal jurisdiction. Another superior court judge granted those motions. On appeal the court of appeals affirmed, holding that an action under G.S. 132-9 is a standard civil action (and not a special proceeding) and that the usual rules of civil procedure apply to such an action. Since then suits for access to public records have been initiated with complaints and have followed the usual course of civil lawsuits.

Who May Bring an Action

G.S. 132-9 provides that an action to compel disclosure or copying might be brought by "[a]ny person who is denied access . . . or who is denied copies." What does this provision mean when the person who actually made the request was acting for some sort of artificial

---

84. The statute is set out in appendix 2A at the end of this chapter.

85. Cases in which this sort of procedure was followed include *S.E.T.A. UNC-CH, Inc. v. Huffines*, 101 N.C. App. 292, 399 S.E.2d 340 (1991), and *Wilmington Star-News, Inc. v. New Hanover Regional Medical Center, Inc.*, 125 N.C. App. 174, 480 S.E.2d 53 (1997).

86. 129 N.C. App. 635, 502 S.E.2d 7 (1998).

entity, such as a corporation or partnership? In *Advance Publications, Inc. v. City of Elizabeth City*,[87] the plaintiff was a newspaper whose employees had made the public records request, and the defendant city argued that only a natural person could bring an action under the statute. The court had no difficulty in rejecting the argument, holding that the phrase "any person" extended as much to an artificial person as to a natural one. A different twist was attempted in *Womack Newspapers, Inc. v. Town of Kitty Hawk*.[88] In that case the town accepted that a corporate entity, the newspaper, could bring the action, but it also argued that because the actual requests had been made by a reporter and the editor of the newspaper, those two individuals were also necessary parties. The court of appeals rejected this argument as well, holding that when individuals are acting on behalf of their employer, the employer may bring suit to compel disclosure without having to join the employees who made the actual requests.

In *McCormick v. Hanson Aggregates Southeast, Inc.*,[89] the corporation had been seeking certain records from the city attorney's office. In order to settle the matter, the city attorney brought a declaratory judgment action against the corporation, seeking a judgment that the records in question were not subject to public access. The court of appeals held that the public records statute did not permit such an action, pointing out that allowing a records custodian to force a citizen into court might very well discourage citizens from requesting public records. Therefore, under the statute, only a person denied inspection or a copy could bring an action, and not the records custodian.[90]

Intervention in Order to Assert Rights to Access Records

In *Bangor Publishing Co. v. Town of Bucksport*, a business taxpayer in the midst of a tax dispute with the town was required to submit what it considered proprietary business information to the town in order to maintain its position in the tax dispute.[91] As a result, the taxpayer brought an action against the town seeking a protective order regarding the information; and the trial court granted the protective order. The newspaper learned of the order some two weeks after it was entered, waited about two more months, and then brought an action seeking the records under the public records law. The Maine Supreme Court held that the protective order overrode the public records law and that the newspaper could not bring a collateral action challenging its validity. Rather, the court held, the newspaper should have intervened in the original action and sought to challenge the order in that action. The court remarked that the newspaper would have been an intervenor as of right in the earlier action, inasmuch as it was seeking to assert rights under the public records law. That is, because the newspaper had a right to bring an action to seek access to public records, it had a right to intervene in an action in which a party was seeking to close access to what were claimed to be records open to the public. This seems a sensible outcome, and therefore it is likely the North Carolina courts would reach a similar conclusion.

---

87. 53 N.C. App. 504, 281 S.E.2d 69 (1981).

88. 181 N.C. App. 1, 639 S.E.2d 96 (2007).

89. 164 N.C. App. 459, 596 S.E.2d 431 (2004).

90. The court reiterated this holding in *City of Burlington v. Boney Publishers, Inc.*, 166 N.C. App. 186, 600 S.E.2d 872 (2004).

91. 682 A.2d 227 (Me. 1996).

Who Must Be Joined as Defendant

In the *Kitty Hawk* case, the newspaper plaintiff sued the town, the elected town officials, the town manager, and the town attorney. (The attorney was sued because some of the records sought were in the attorney's possession, and one category of record sought was the attorney's bills submitted to the town.) The town sought to have the suit dismissed because the town clerk, who is the statutory custodian of town records, was not joined in the suit. The court held that it was not necessary to join the statutory custodian, inasmuch as the town's claim was that the records in question were not open to public access. It was the more senior town officials who were resisting release of the records, and therefore, the court held, it was sufficient to join only those more senior officials.

As a matter of practice, probably a majority of cases do not name the record custodian as defendant but rather name the corporate entity whose records are at issue.

Timing

G.S. 132-9(a) provides that "[a]ctions brought pursuant to this section shall be set down for immediate hearing, and subsequent proceedings in such actions shall be accorded priority by the trial and appellate courts." Despite this injunction for speed, it should be noted that these disclosure actions are subject to the usual rules of civil procedure, so that the defendants or respondents have the usual time to file motions to dismiss or an answer or other motions in the cause.

Attorneys' Fees

In the normal civil action, each party is responsible for paying its own attorneys, regardless of who wins the lawsuit. G.S. 132-9(c) provides a different rule in actions seeking access to public records.

If the Plaintiff Prevails

If the plaintiff "successfully compels the disclosure of public records, the court *shall* allow the prevailing party to recover its reasonable attorneys' fees if attributed to those public records." Thus, the statute directs the court to award attorneys' fees to a prevailing plaintiff in the usual case. This basic direction is subject to only two exceptions:

1. "[T]he agency acted with substantial justification in denying access to the public records;" or
2. "[T]he court finds circumstances that would make the award of attorneys' fees unjust."

Although there has been no interpretation of these specific provisions by the appellate courts, a predecessor statute was the subject of their attention and those cases are helpful in understanding the provisions of G.S. 132-9(c).

The earlier statute was G.S. 6-19.2, which provided for the possibility of an award of attorneys' fees to persons who had successfully sued to open public records; it was repealed when attorneys' fees provisions were added to G.S. 132-9. The earlier statute was differently structured than the current statute. It permitted a trial court to award attorneys' fees, rather than directing that it do so, and before making such an award the court had to find that the agency had acted “without substantial justification in denying access” to the records and that “there are no special circumstances that would make the award of attorney’s fees unjust.” Thus, the earlier statute used language that was comparable to the current statute but inverted the usage of that language. Nevertheless, the cases decided under the earlier statute are helpful in interpreting the current one.

Is the plaintiff the prevailing party? In *North Carolina Press Association, Inc. v. Spangler*,[92] the plaintiffs had requested access to written reports concerning intercollegiate athletics prepared by the chancellors of the various University of North Carolina campuses and submitted to the University’s president. When the president denied access, the plaintiffs brought suit and won at trial and, after appeal, sought attorneys’ fees. While the first appeal was pending the president had released the reports, and he argued in the attorneys’ fee segment of the case that the plaintiffs had not been the prevailing party. Rather, he argued, he had always intended to release the reports eventually, once he had had a chance to reflect on them, and it was this original intention rather than the lawsuit that led to the reports’ release. The court of appeals rejected this reasoning:

> To strike the trial court’s award of attorney’s fees simply because respondents claim the records were released pursuant to a decision made prior to suit would condone and reward their withholding of requested public records. Which party has prevailed is determined by an examination of the trial court’s order. The fact that the respondent, after entry of the order, elects to make the disclosure ordered does not affect the issue of who prevailed in the proceeding to compel disclosure. . . . That respondents were able to obtain a stay of the trial court’s order pending appeal does not alter the fact that petitioners were the prevailing party in their action.[93]

What is substantial justification? Under the earlier statute the trial could award attorneys’ fees if the agency, in denying access, acted “without substantial justification,” and under the current statute the trial court must award such fees unless the agency acted “with substantial justification.” In *S.E.T.A. UNC-CH, Inc. v. Huffines*, the court noted that former G.S. 6-19.2 used the same standards as G.S. 6-19.1, which provides for attorneys’ fee awards in actions against state agencies, and relied on cases decided under the latter statute in interpreting the former.[94] In *Crowell Constructors, Inc. v. State ex rel. Cobey*, the North Carolina Supreme Court interpreted G.S. 6-19.1 and its requirement of substantial justification and reached this conclusion:

> This standard should not be so strictly interpreted as to require the agency to demonstrate the infallibility of each suit it initiates. Similarly, this standard should not be so loosely interpreted as to require the agency to demonstrate only that the suit is not frivolous, for “that is assuredly not the standard for Government litigation of which a reasonable person would approve.” Rather, we adopt a middle-ground objective standard to require the agency to demonstrate that

92. 94 N.C. App. 694, 381 S.E.2d 187 (1989).
93. *Id.* at 697, 381 S.E.2d at 190.
94. 107 N.C. App. 440, 420 S.E.2d 674 (1992).

its position, at and from the time of its initial action, was rational and legitimate to such degree that a reasonable person *could* find it satisfactory or justifiable in light of the circumstances then known to the agency.[95]

Although they both predate the *Crowell* decision, the two court of appeals decisions that interpreted G.S. 6-19.2 seem consistent with the standard articulated in *Crowell* and flesh out what might constitute a substantial justification. In *Spangler,* the University argued that it had acted in good faith in denying access and therefore had had substantial justification. The court rejected that standard: "We . . . do not accept respondents' contention that bad faith is the standard to be used by the trial court in determining whether the withholding of public records was without substantial justification."[96]

As a second argument in *Spangler,* the University argued that it believed there should be an exception to the right of access for preliminary, interoffice communications and that these reports would be covered by such an exception. The litigation thus gave the University an opportunity to seek judicial recognition of the exception, and for that reason there was substantial justification for refusing access. The court agreed that these were relevant factors that a trial court could consider but noted that the trial court did in fact consider them and still awarded the attorneys' fees; the appellate court refused to characterize the trial court's decision as an abuse of discretion. This approach was also supported in *Huffines*, in which the court set out the arguments against access that the defendant agency had made during the substantive portion of the case and concluded that they were justified to a degree that would satisfy a reasonable person and therefore constituted substantial justification.[97]

What are circumstances that would make an award unjust? There has been much less interpretation of the provision involving circumstances that would make an award of attorneys' fees unjust. The only case to address the issue directly is *Spangler,* in which the University argued that the special circumstances in that case were that the president would have released the contested documents in a few days in any event and therefore the litigation was unnecessary. The court rejected the argument, noting that the "fact that a governmental agency chooses to chart its own course regarding the timing of the requested release of public documents does not make an award of attorney's fees against it 'unjust.'"[98]

The statute also directs that normally any award of attorneys' fees is to be "charged against the operating expenses of the agency." That is, the public is to pay the attorneys' fees. If the court finds, however, that a public employee or official "knowingly or intentionally committed, caused, permitted, suborned, or participated in a violation" of the statute,[99] the court may (but need not) direct that the employee or official pay personally some or all of the attorneys' fees awarded to the plaintiff or petitioner. Such an award may not be

---

95. 342 N.C. 838, 844, 467 S.E.2d 675, 679 (1996).

96. *Id.* at 697, 381 S.E.2d at 190.

97. See also *N.C. Div. of Sons of Confederate Veterans v. Faulkner,* 131 N.C. App. 775, 509 S.E.2d 207 (1998), another case interpreting substantial justification under G.S. 6-19.1.

98. 94 N.C. App. at 698, 381 S.E.2d at 191.

99. The statute actually reads "committed . . . or participated in a violation of this *Article,*" although Chapter 132 is not divided into articles.

made, though, if the employee or official had sought the advice of an attorney and had followed that advice.

If the Defendant Prevails

If a government or agency convinces the court that there is no right of access to the records, that does not mean that it is entitled to attorneys' fees. Rather, G.S. 132-9 permits an award against an unsuccessful plaintiff only if the court determines that the suit was brought in bad faith or was frivolous.

Appendix 2A—Statutes

G.S. 132-2

§ 132-2. Custodian designated.

The public official in charge of an office having public records shall be the custodian thereof.

G.S. 132-6

§ 132-6. Inspection and examination of records.

(a) Every custodian of public records shall permit any record in the custodian's custody to be inspected and examined at reasonable times and under reasonable supervision by any person, and shall, as promptly as possible, furnish copies thereof upon payment of any fees as may be prescribed by law. As used herein, "custodian" does not mean an agency that holds the public records of other agencies solely for purposes of storage or safekeeping or solely to provide data processing.

(b) No person requesting to inspect and examine public records, or to obtain copies thereof, shall be required to disclose the purpose or motive for the request.

(c) No request to inspect, examine, or obtain copies of public records shall be denied on the grounds that confidential information is commingled with the requested nonconfidential information. If it is necessary to separate confidential from nonconfidential information in order to permit the inspection, examination, or copying of the public records, the public agency shall bear the cost of such separation on the following schedule:

State agencies after June 30, 1996;

Municipalities with populations of 10,000 or more, counties with populations of 25,000 or more, as determined by the 1990 U.S. Census, and public hospitals in those counties, after June 30, 1997;

Municipalities with populations of less than 10,000, counties with populations of less than 25,000, as determined by the 1990 U.S. Census, and public hospitals in those counties, after June 30, 1998;

Political subdivisions and their agencies that are not otherwise covered by this schedule, after June 30, 1998.

(d) [*Special provision for economic development records. See chapter 12, "Economic Development Records."*]

(e) The application of this Chapter is subject to the provisions of Article 1 of Chapter 121 of the General Statutes, the North Carolina Archives and History Act.

(f) Notwithstanding the provisions of subsection (a) of this section, the inspection or copying of any public record which, because of its age or condition could be damaged during inspection or copying, may be made subject to reasonable restrictions intended to preserve the particular record.

G.S. 132-9

§ 132-9. Access to records.

(a) Any person who is denied access to public records for purposes of inspection and examination, or who is denied copies of public records, may apply to the appropriate division of the General Court of Justice for an order compelling disclosure or copying, and the court shall have jurisdiction to issue such orders. Actions brought pursuant to this section shall be set down for immediate hearing, and subsequent proceedings in such actions shall be accorded priority by the trial and appellate courts.

(b) In an action to compel disclosure of public records which have been withheld pursuant to the provisions of G.S. 132-6 concerning public records relating to the proposed expansion or location of particular businesses and industrial projects, the burden shall be on the custodian withholding the records to show that disclosure would frustrate the purpose of attracting that particular business or industrial project.

(c) In any action brought pursuant to this section in which a party successfully compels the disclosure of public records, the court shall allow the prevailing party to recover its reasonable attorneys' fees if attributed to those public records, unless the court finds the agency acted with substantial justification in denying access to the public records or the court finds circumstances that would make the award of attorneys' fees unjust.

Any attorneys' fees assessed against a public agency under this section shall be charged against the operating expenses of the agency; provided, however, that the court may order that all or any portion of any attorneys' fees so assessed be paid personally by any public employee or public official found by the court to have knowingly or intentionally committed, caused, permitted, suborned, or participated in a violation of this Article. No order against any public employee or public official shall issue in any case where the public employee or public official seeks the advice of an attorney and such advice is followed.

(d) If the court determines that an action brought pursuant to this section was filed in bad faith or was frivolous, the court shall assess a reasonable attorney's fee against the person or persons instituting the action and award it to the public agency as part of the costs.

Chapter 3—Records Management

Chapter 132 of the North Carolina General Statutes [hereinafter G.S.] and G.S. 121-5[1] establish responsibilities for records management for two sorts of actors: (1) each custodian of one or more public records, and (2) the state Department of Cultural Resources. Together, the custodians and the department are responsible for maintaining the integrity of public records and for developing a plan for management of records in every public office and agency. In addition, G.S. Chapter 132 incorporates a number of provisions that directly protect the integrity of records and fix legal custody of records.

1. The relevant statutes are set out in appendix 3A at the end of this chapter.

Protecting Records' Integrity

Records Subject to Protection under G.S. Chapter 132

Chapter 1 noted and discussed briefly the different meanings of the term "public records." One of those meanings applies to records subject to G.S. Chapter 132. As discussed in the first two chapters of this book, G.S. Chapter 132 establishes the basic right of public access to public records. It also defines the custodian of different categories of public records and sets out a number of provisions intended to protect the integrity of public records. Some of the statutes, however, that exclude certain categories of public records from the right of public access are drafted so that those records are also excluded from the provisions in G.S. Chapter 132 that protect records and provide for their management. The basic right of public access is set out in G.S. 132-6, and many of the statutes that create exceptions to that right are couched as exceptions to that specific section. For example, most of the personnel privacy statutes begin "[n]otwithstanding the provisions of G.S. 132-6 . . . ."[2] Some of the statutes that create exceptions to access, however, are couched as exceptions to G.S. 132-1, the section defining public records for Chapter 132, or as exceptions to Chapter 132 itself. For example, G.S. 132-1.4 states that most law enforcement records "are not public records as defined by G.S. 132-1,"[3] while G.S. 131E-97 states that medical records held by health care facilities "are not public records as defined by Chapter 132 of the General Statutes."[4] While this result may or may not be unintended, if a category of records are not public records as defined in G.S. 132-1 or within the meaning of G.S. Chapter 132, then the provisions of that chapter that protect records from abuse and neglect and that provide for their management and protection do not apply to that category.[5] That does not mean, however, that the records in question are not subject to the supervisory jurisdiction of the Department of Cultural Resources, because the department's authority issues from G.S. 121-5 and the definition of public records in G.S. 121-2.

The Custodian

G.S. Chapter 132 imposes a number of responsibilities on the custodian of public records. This official maintains public records, may bring actions to recover records held improperly by others, and is required to permit public inspection of records and provide copies of records to those who request them. G.S. 132-2 defines the "custodian" as the official in charge of the office in which the records are held. Thus, the register of deeds is the custo-

---

2. *E.g.*, N.C. Gen. Stat. [hereinafter G.S.] § 122C-158 (area authorities); G.S. 153A-98 (counties); and G.S. 160A-168 (cities).

3. Other statutes that follow this convention include G.S. 132-1.1 (attorney communications to clients); G.S. 8-53 (records within the physician–patient privilege); G.S. 130A-12 (confidential medical records held by public health departments); G.S. 143-518 (medical records held by EMS agencies); G.S. 132-1.7 (public security information); and G.S. 115C-402 (student records held by public school administrative units).

4. Other statutes that follow this convention include G.S. 131E-97.1 (personnel records of public hospitals); G.S. 153A-148.1 and 160A-208.1 (certain local tax records); and G.S. 131E-97.3 (competitive health care information held by public hospitals).

5. This consequence is recognized in G.S. 122C-52(a). That subsection states that confidential information about clients of area authorities is not a public record under Chapter 132 of the General Statutes, "[e]xcept as provided in G.S. 132-5" (which allows the proper custodian of records to demand their custody).

dian of records in his or her office, the sheriff is the custodian of records held by the sheriff's department, the county tax administrator is the custodian of the records in the tax department, and so on. The statute uses the term "office," and it is not clear whether it intends the word in a physical sense or an organizational one. The latter seems more sensible and ties the legal responsibility for records to organizational decisions about agency structure and personnel decisions about supervisory responsibility. For instance, it seems likely that the head of the utility department would be the custodian of records held at a water treatment plant, rather than the on-site plant operator. Another ambiguity is whether office is synonymous with department, or whether it refers to lower-level classifications such as divisions. For example, is the county health director the custodian of all records within the health department, or are his or her subordinates who are heads of divisions or other agencies within the health department the custodians of the records within their divisions or agencies? Given the statutory provisions concerning the rights and obligations of custodians, it seems sensible to have fewer rather than more custodians, which argues for recognizing the department head as custodian of all records within his or her department. Given the ambiguity, however, it is probably open to a government's or agency's governing board to designate the organizational level for public records custodians within the government or agency.

G.S. 132-6(a) also makes clear that the legal custodian of a record may be separate from the agency with physical possession of the record. It provides that the term custodian "does not mean an agency that holds the public records of other agencies solely for purposes of storage or safekeeping or solely to provide data processing." Thus, the Department of Cultural Resources is not the custodian of those records that it holds for state agencies or local governments, nor is an information technology department the custodian of the various electronic records that are on a local government's server (except for those generated by the department for its own business uses).

G.S. 160A-171 provides that the city clerk is the custodian of all city records. (There is no comparable provision with respect to the clerk to the board of county commissioners.) There is some ambiguity about the meaning and effect of this provision. One possible meaning is that the clerk is custodian of all public records held by a city government. While this reading of the statute would make the clerk the proper party to exercise the powers of protecting and managing records set out in G.S. Chapter 132, it makes little sense to impose on the clerk the responsibility of responding to every request to inspect or copy a public record held by a city—particularly a large city—or to require citizens to go through the clerk's office each time they wish to inspect or copy a city record. The better understanding of this provision is that the clerk has a supervisory responsibility over records management practices throughout city government, but the head of each city department is responsible for complying with the public access requirements of G.S. 132-6.

Custody and Transfer of Records

G.S. 132-4 directs custodians, when their term of office or period of employment ends, to deliver the records of their office to their successors. A refusal or failure to do so constitutes a misdemeanor. Similarly, G.S. 132-5 directs new custodians of records to demand custody of any records subject to their control when the records are not where they should be. If the person with illegal custody of the records refuses to turn them over, that person has committed a misdemeanor. Finally, G.S. 132-5.1 establishes a civil action that a custodian (or the secretary of cultural resources) may bring against anyone with unauthorized possession of public records and permits the petitioner in such an action to seek immediate protection of the records until the suit is concluded.

Preservation of Records

G.S. 132-7 sets out a number of hortatory directives intended to safeguard public records yet permit their use. Custodians must "[i]nsofar as possible" keep records in fireproof safes or vaults or rooms fitted with noncombustible materials. If records books become worn, damaged, or difficult to read, the custodian "should" have them copied, rebound, repaired, or renovated, as appropriate.[6] Custodians "should" maintain records in the buildings in which they are ordinarily used and store them so that they are "easily accessible for convenient use." To some extent these provisions concern a narrower group of records than the public records defined in G.S. 132-1. A city's minute books and bond documentation may well be placed in the city's vault, but there will remain vast numbers of records that are scattered throughout the city's departments, in file cabinets and desks and on desktop computers.

Records Retention and Disposition

G.S. 132-3 prohibits any public official from destroying, selling, loaning, or otherwise disposing of any public record, except in accordance with G.S. 121-5. That statute, in turn, declares that the Department of Cultural Resources is the "official archival agency" of North Carolina and empowers the department to decide how long different categories of records are kept and whether they may be destroyed. It goes on to prohibit the destruction of public records except with the consent of the department.[7]

In furtherance of its responsibility to decide how long various records are retained, the Department of Cultural Resources has promulgated a series of *records retention and disposition schedules* for almost all forms of records held by counties, cities, and other sorts of local governments. (The current versions of these schedules may be found on the department's website.)[8] Once agreed to by the officials of a particular local government, these schedules, which are quite detailed, govern whether various categories of records may be disposed of and when that may occur. The schedules reflect two fundamental premises

---

6. If copying a record is necessary, the public official who causes the copy to be made is to attest it and certify on oath that the copy is accurate. Once that is done, the copy has the force of the original.

7. G.S. 132-3 and 121-5 each include an exception for records destroyed pursuant to G.S. 13-A-99. G.S. 130A-99 permits county registers of deeds to destroy copies of birth and death certificates if the certificates are for individuals who were born or who died in other counties and if the registers first confirm that copies of those certificates are kept by the state registrar or state archives.

8. Schedules for records held by counties; municipalities; regional councils; county and municipal boards of elections; county departments of social services, health, and veterans services; registers of deeds; sheriff's offices; local education agencies; public hospitals; public transportation systems; tax administration authorities; mental health facilities; and water and sewer authorities and sanitary districts are located at www.records.ncdcr.gov/local/default.htm.

of the department's work in this area. First, the department has made its own informed decisions about what kinds of records are of such historical value that they should be kept permanently (that is, forever). Second, for other records without long-term historical value, the department works with state agencies and local governments to determine how long records must be kept to serve the business needs of the agencies and governments. Once those needs have been met, the schedules permit destruction of the records.

Some examples will illustrate how the schedules work. The original of all minutes of a city or county governing board must be retained permanently.[9] Contracts may be destroyed three years after their termination if there is no outstanding litigation.[10] Records evidencing routine maintenance of government vehicles may be destroyed after one year, while records of other sorts of maintenance must be kept for the life of the vehicle.[11] Tape recordings of meetings, made to assist in preparing the minutes, may be destroyed once the minutes are approved.[12] Administrative correspondence without historical value may be destroyed once its administrative value has ended.[13]

G.S. 132-8.2 directs the Department of Cultural Resources to establish a program for making and safeguarding "preservation duplicates" of those public records "considered essential to the operation of government and to the protection of the rights and interests of persons."[14] The department has determined that all records that, pursuant to the schedules noted above, are to be kept permanently will be part of this program.[15] The department suggests that preservation duplicates be either in paper or microfilm format and requires such "human-readable" formats for permanent records that affect many people, have long-term significance, document governance or citizenship, or are used for routine public inspection.[16] If the record is microfilmed, the department also offers to store the original version of the microfilm in the state archives.[17] There are a substantial number of records that the

---

9. Record Services Branch, N.C. Dep't of Cultural Resources, Municipal Records Retention and Disposition Schedule 7 (May 19, 2009), *available at* www.records.ncdcr.gov/local/municipal_2009.pdf [hereinafter Municipal Records Schedule]; Government Records Branch, N.C. Dep't of Cultural Resources, Records Retention and Disposition Schedule, County Management 7 (April 1, 2006), *available at* www.records.ncdcr.gov/local/countyManagement_2006.pdf [hereinafter County Management Schedule].

10. *E.g.*, Municipal Records Schedule, *supra* note 9, at 85; County Management Schedule, *supra* note 9, at 44.

11. *E.g.*, County Management Schedule, *supra* note 9, at 11.

12. *E.g.*, Municipal Records Schedule, *supra* note 9, at 2; County Management Schedule, *supra* note 9, at 2.

13. *E.g.*, County Management Schedule, *supra* note 9, at 3.

14. Because this directive is in Chapter 132, presumably it does not apply to those records that have been excepted from the definition of public records in G.S. 132-1 or that have been excluded entirely from Chapter 132.

15. *See* Government Records Branch, N.C. Dep't of Cultural Resources, Public Records Requiring Human-Readable Preservation Duplicates, *available at* www.records.ncdcr.gov/guides/Humreadabledupspolicy050217.pdf.

16. *Id.*

17. *E.g.*, Municipal Records Schedule, *supra* note 9, at viii; County Management Schedule, *supra* note 9, at iv.

retention schedules require to be kept permanently,[18] so this requirement of making preservation duplicates is significant.

To be able to dispose of records pursuant to a schedule, a local government's governing board must agree to the schedule and its chief officers must sign an agreement to that effect with the Department of Cultural Resources.[19] If no agreement is signed, the local government has no continuing authority to dispose of any records.[20] If, having signed an agreement, a local government develops a new record that does not appear to fall within any of the categories included within the existing schedules, it may apply to the department for an amendment to the schedule to include the new record.[21] Similarly, if a local government discovers old records that are not listed and that it no longer needs, it may apply to the department for permission to dispose of the records.[22]

When a local government exercises its authority under a schedule to destroy records, departmental rules permit it to do so by

- burning the records;
- shredding the records so that their content is destroyed;
- placing the records in an acid vat, thereby reducing them to pulp;
- burying the records so that their content becomes indecipherable; or
- selling the records as waste paper if the purchaser gives written assurance that the records will not be resold as documents or records.[23]

In addition, certain sorts of records can be, and occasionally are, disposed of by turning them over to local historical societies or museums. These are records that have ceased having administrative value to the government itself and that do not have state-recognized historical value and so need not be kept permanently. If a local government receives a request to dispose of unneeded records in this fashion, the Department of Cultural Resources urges it to obtain governing board approval for the transfer so that there is some official and permanent record of the transfer.

---

18. A few of the kinds of records that must be retained permanently are charters, deeds, legal opinions, legal case files, official policies, minutes, ordinances and resolutions, annual budgets, annual reports, park maps, performance audits, building codes, rezoning applications, and subdivision records.

19. *See* G.S. 121-5(c). *See also, e.g.*, MUNICIPAL RECORDS SCHEDULE, *supra* note 9, at iii; RECORD SERVICES BRANCH, N.C. DEP'T OF CULTURAL RESOURCES, REGISTER OF DEEDS SCHEDULE ii (AUGUST 15, 2003), *available at* www.records.ncdcr.gov/local/ROD/RoDfinal.pdf.

20. *E.g.*, COUNTY MANAGEMENT SCHEDULE, *supra* note 9, at iii ("Without approving this schedule, your county is obligated to obtain permission to destroy *any* record, no matter how insignificant.")

21. *E.g.*, COUNTY MANAGEMENT SCHEDULE, *supra* note 9, at vi.

22. *E.g.*, *id.*

23. 7 N.C.A.C. 4M .0510 (2009).

Appendix 3A—Statutes

G.S. 132-3

§ 132-3. Destruction of records regulated.

(a) Prohibition—No public official may destroy, sell, loan, or otherwise dispose of any public record, except in accordance with G.S. 121-5 and G.S. 130A-99, without the consent of the Department of Cultural Resources. Whoever unlawfully removes a public record from the office where it is usually kept, or alters, defaces, mutilates or destroys it shall be guilty of a Class 3 misdemeanor and upon conviction only fined not less than ten dollars ($10.00) nor more than five hundred dollars ($500.00).

(b) Revenue Records.—Notwithstanding subsection (a) of this section and G.S. 121-5, when a record of the Department of Revenue has been copied in any manner, the original record may be destroyed upon the order of the Secretary of Revenue. If a record of the Department of Revenue has not been copied, the original record shall be preserved for at least three years. After three years the original record may be destroyed upon the order of the Secretary of Revenue.

(c) Employment Security Commission Records.—Notwithstanding subsection (a) of this section and G.S. 121-5, when a record of the Employment Security Commission has been copied in any manner, the original record may be destroyed upon the order of the Chairman of the Employment Security Commission. If a record of the Commission has not been copied, the original record shall be preserved for at least three years. After three years the original record may be destroyed upon the order of the Chairman of the Employment Security Commission.

G.S. 132-4

§ 132-4. Disposition of records at end of official's term.

Whoever has the custody of any public records shall, at the expiration of his term of office, deliver to his successor, or, if there be none, to the Department of Cultural Resources, all records, books, writings, letters and documents kept or received by him in the transaction of his official business; and any such person who shall refuse or neglect for the space of 10 days after request made in writing by any citizen of the State to deliver as herein required such public records to the person authorized to receive them shall be guilty of a Class 1 misdemeanor.

G.S. 132-5

§ 132-5. Demanding custody.

Whoever is entitled to the custody of public records shall demand them from any person having illegal possession of them, who shall forthwith deliver the same to him. If the person who unlawfully possesses public records shall without just cause refuse or neglect for 10 days after a request made in writing by any citizen of the State to deliver such records to their lawful custodian, he shall be guilty of a Class 1 misdemeanor.

G.S. 132-5.1

§ 132-5.1. Regaining custody; civil remedies.

(a) The Secretary of the Department of Cultural Resources or his designated representative or any public official who is the custodian of public records which are in the possession of a person or agency not authorized by the custodian or by law to possess such public records may petition the superior court in the county in which the person holding such records resides or in which the materials in issue, or any part thereof, are located for the return of such public records. The court may order such public records to be delivered to the petitioner upon finding that the materials in issue are public records and that such public records are in the possession of a person not authorized by the custodian of the public records or by law to possess such public records. If the order of delivery does not receive compliance, the petitioner may request that the court enforce such order through its contempt power and procedures.

(b) At any time after the filing of the petition set out in subsection (a) or contemporaneous with such filing, the public official seeking the return of the public records may by ex parte petition request the judge or the court in which the action was filed to grant one of the following provisional remedies:

(1) An order directed at the sheriff commanding him to seize the materials which are the subject of the action and deliver the same to the court under the circumstances hereinafter set forth; or

(2) A preliminary injunction preventing the sale, removal, disposal or destruction of or damage to such public records pending a final judgment by the court.

(c) The judge or court aforesaid shall issue an order of seizure or grant a preliminary injunction upon receipt of an affidavit from the petitioner which alleges that the materials at issue are public records and that unless one of said provisional remedies is granted, there is a danger that such materials shall be sold, secreted, removed out of the State or otherwise disposed of so as not to be forthcoming to answer the final judgment of the court respecting the same; or that such property may be destroyed or materially damaged or injured if not seized or if injunctive relief is not granted.

(d) The aforementioned order of seizure or preliminary injunction shall issue without notice to the respondent and without the posting of any bond or other security by the petitioner.

G.S. 132-6.2

§ 132-6.2. Provisions for copies of public records; fees.

(a) Persons requesting copies of public records may elect to obtain them in any and all media in which the public agency is capable of providing them. No request for copies of public records in a particular medium shall be denied on the grounds that the custodian has made or prefers to make the public records available in another medium. The public agency may assess different fees for different media as prescribed by law.

(b) Persons requesting copies of public records may request that the copies be certified or uncertified. The fees for certifying copies of public records shall be as provided by law. Except as otherwise provided by law, no public agency shall charge a fee for an uncertified copy of a public record that exceeds the actual cost to the public agency of making the copy.

For purposes of this subsection, "actual cost" is limited to direct, chargeable costs related to the reproduction of a public record as determined by generally accepted accounting principles and does not include costs that would have been incurred by the public agency if a request to reproduce a public record had not been made. Notwithstanding the provisions of this subsection, if the request is such as to require extensive use of information technology resources or extensive clerical or supervisory assistance by personnel of the agency involved, or if producing the record in the medium requested results in a greater use of information technology resources than that established by the agency for reproduction of the volume of information requested, then the agency may charge, in addition to the actual cost of duplication, a special service charge, which shall be reasonable and shall be based on the actual cost incurred for such extensive use of information technology resources or the labor costs of the personnel providing the services, or for a greater use of information technology resources that is actually incurred by the agency or attributable to the agency. If anyone requesting public information from any public agency is charged a fee that the requester believes to be unfair or unreasonable, the requester may ask the State Chief Information Officer or his designee to mediate the dispute.

(c) Persons requesting copies of computer databases may be required to make or submit such requests in writing. Custodians of public records shall respond to all such requests as promptly as possible. If the request is granted, the copies shall be provided as soon as reasonably possible. If the request is denied, the denial shall be accompanied by an explanation of the basis for the denial. If asked to do so, the person denying the request shall, as promptly as possible, reduce the explanation for the denial to writing.

(d) Nothing in this section shall be construed to require a public agency to respond to requests for copies of public records outside of its usual business hours.

(e) Nothing in this section shall be construed to require a public agency to respond to a request for a copy of a public record by creating or compiling a record that does not exist. If a public agency, as a service to the requester, voluntarily elects to create or compile a record, it may negotiate a reasonable charge for the service with the requester. Nothing in this section shall be construed to require a public agency to put into electronic medium a record that is not kept in electronic medium.

G.S. 132-7

§ 132-7. Keeping records in safe places; copying or repairing; certified copies.

Insofar as possible, custodians of public records shall keep them in fireproof safes, vaults, or rooms fitted with noncombustible materials and in such arrangement as to be easily accessible for convenient use. All public records should be kept in the buildings in which they are ordinarily used. Record books should be copied or repaired, renovated or rebound if worn, mutilated, damaged or difficult to read. Whenever any State, county, or municipal records are in need of repair, restoration, or rebinding, the head of such State agency, department, board, or commission, the board of county commissioners of such county, or the governing body of such municipality may authorize that the records in need of repair, restoration, or rebinding be removed from the building or office in which such records are ordinarily kept, for the length of time required to repair, restore, or rebind them. Any public official who causes a record book to be copied shall attest it and shall certify on oath that it is an accurate copy of the original book. The copy shall then have the force of the original.

G.S. 132-8

§ 132-8. Assistance by and to Department of Cultural Resources.
The Department of Cultural Resources shall have the right to examine into the condition of public records and shall give advice and assistance to public officials in the solution of their problems of preserving, filing and making available the public records in their custody. When requested by the Department of Cultural Resources, public officials shall assist the Department in the preparation of an inclusive inventory of records in their custody, to which shall be attached a schedule, approved by the head of the governmental unit or agency having custody of the records and the Secretary of Cultural Resources, establishing a time period for the retention or disposal of each series of records. Upon the completion of the inventory and schedule, the Department of Cultural Resources shall (subject to the availability of necessary space, staff, and other facilities for such purposes) make available space in its Records Center for the filing of semicurrent records so scheduled and in its archives for noncurrent records of permanent value, and shall render such other assistance as needed, including the microfilming of records so scheduled.

G.S. 132-8.1

§ 132-8.1. Records management program administered by Department of Cultural Resources; establishment of standards, procedures, etc.; surveys.
A records management program for the application of efficient and economical management methods to the creation, utilization, maintenance, retention, preservation, and disposal of official records shall be administered by the Department of Cultural Resources. It shall be the duty of that Department, in cooperation with and with the approval of the Department of Administration, to establish standards, procedures, and techniques for effective management of public records, to make continuing surveys of paper work operations, and to recommend improvements in current records management practices including the use of space, equipment, and supplies employed in creating, maintaining, and servicing records. It shall be the duty of the head of each State agency and the governing body of each county, municipality and other subdivision of government to cooperate with the Department of Cultural Resources in conducting surveys and to establish and maintain an active, continuing program for the economical and efficient management of the records of said agency, county, municipality, or other subdivision of government.

G.S. 132-8.2

§ 132-8.2. Selection and preservation of records considered essential; making or designation of preservation duplicates; force and effect of duplicates or copies thereof.
In cooperation with the head of each State agency and the governing body of each county, municipality, and other subdivision of government, the Department of Cultural Resources shall establish and maintain a program for the selection and preservation of public records considered essential to the operation of government and to the protection of the rights and interests of persons, and, within the limitations of funds available for the purpose, shall

make or cause to be made preservation duplicates or designate as preservation duplicates existing copies of such essential public records. Preservation duplicates shall be durable, accurate, complete and clear, and such duplicates made by a photographic, photostatic, microfilm, micro card, miniature photographic, or other process which accurately reproduces and forms a durable medium for so reproducing the original shall have the same force and effect for all purposes as the original record whether the original record is in existence or not. A transcript, exemplification, or certified copy of such preservation duplicate shall be deemed for all purposes to be a transcript, exemplification, or certified copy of the original record. Such preservation duplicates shall be preserved in the place and manner of safekeeping prescribed by the Department of Cultural Resources.

G.S. 121-5

§ 121-5. Public records and archives.

(a) State Archival Agency Designated.—The Department of Cultural Resources shall be the official archival agency of the State of North Carolina with authority as provided throughout this Chapter and Chapter 132 of the General Statutes of North Carolina in relation to the public records of the State, counties, municipalities, and other subdivisions of government.

(b) Destruction of Records Regulated.—No person may destroy, sell, loan, or otherwise dispose of any public record without the consent of the Department of Cultural Resources, except as provided in G.S. 130A-99. Whoever unlawfully removes a public record from the office where it is usually kept, or alters, mutilates, or destroys it shall be guilty of a Class 3 misdemeanor and upon conviction only fined at the discretion of the court.

When the custodian of any official State records certifies to the Department of Cultural Resources that such records have no further use or value for official and administrative purposes and when the Department certifies that such records appear to have no further use or value for research or reference, then such records may be destroyed or otherwise disposed of by the agency having custody of them.

When the custodian of any official records of any county, city, municipality, or other subdivision of government certifies to the Department that such records have no further use or value for official business and when the Department certifies that such records appear to have no further use or value for research or reference, then such records may be authorized by the governing body of said county, city, municipality, or other subdivision of government to be destroyed or otherwise disposed of by the agency having custody of them. A record of such certification and authorization shall be entered in the minutes of the governing body granting the authority.

The North Carolina Historical Commission is hereby authorized and empowered to make such orders, rules, and regulations as may be necessary and proper to carry into effect the provisions of this section. When any State, county, municipal, or other governmental records shall have been destroyed or otherwise disposed of in accordance with the procedure authorized in this subsection, any liability that the custodian of such records might incur for such destruction or other disposal shall cease and determine.

(c) Assistance to Public Officers.—The Department of Cultural Resources shall have the right to examine into the condition of public records and shall, subject to the availability of staff and funds, give advice and assistance to public officials and agencies in regard to preserving or disposing of the public records in their custody. When requested by the Department of Cultural Resources, public officials shall assist the Department in the preparation of an inclusive inventory of records in their custody, to which inventory shall be attached a schedule, approved by the head of the governmental unit or agency having custody of the records and the Department of Cultural Resources, establishing a time period for the retention or disposal of each series of records. So long as such approved schedule remains in effect, destruction or disposal of records in accordance with its provisions shall be deemed to have met the requirements of G.S. 121-5(b).

The Department of Cultural Resources is hereby authorized and directed to conduct a program of inventorying, repairing, and microfilming in the counties for security purposes those official records of the several counties which the Department determines have permanent value, and of providing safe storage for microfilm copies of such records. Subject to the availability of funds, such program shall be extended to the records of permanent value of the cities, municipalities, and other subdivisions of government.

(d) Preservation of Permanently Valuable Records.—Public records certified by the Department of Cultural Resources as being of permanent value shall be preserved in the custody of the agency in which the records are normally kept or of the North Carolina State Archives. Any State, county, municipal, or other public official is hereby authorized and empowered to turn over to the Department of Cultural Resources any State, county, municipal, or other public records no longer in current official use, and the Department of Cultural Resources is authorized in its discretion to accept such records, and having done so shall provide for their administration and preservation in the North Carolina State Archives. When such records have been thus surrendered, photocopies, microfilms, typescripts, or other copies of them shall be made and certified under seal of the Department, upon application of any person, which certification shall have the same force and effect as if made by the official or agency by which the records were transferred to the Department of Cultural Resources; and the Department may charge reasonable fees for these copies. The Department may answer written inquiries for nonresidents of the State and for this service may charge a search and handling fee not to exceed twenty-five dollars ($25.00). The receipts from this fee shall be used to defray the cost of providing this service.

Chapter 4—The Role and Effect of Federal Law

Public records law, as it applies to state and local governments, is primarily a matter of state law. There is no federal constitutional right of access to public records held by state or local governments. Litigants have sometimes sought such a right in the First Amendment's protection of the rights of free speech or the press, but a significant majority of courts, including the North Carolina Supreme Court, have refused to find such a right within the amendment.[1] In addition, the federal Freedom of Information Act (FOIA) governs access only to records held by federal agencies; it does not extend to records held by state or local government agencies, even when such a government is expending federal grant funds.[2] There are two areas, however, in which federal law might affect access to public records held by a North Carolina local government:

1. An occasional federal statute might preempt state law with respect to a particular sort of record.
2. The federal (or state) constitutional right of privacy might occasionally limit public access to a particular sort of record.

---

1. The North Carolina case is *News & Observer Publishing Co. v. State ex rel. Starling*, 312 N.C. 276, 322 S.E.2d 133 (1984). Other cases finding no constitutional right under the First Amendment include *Trimble v. Johnson*, 173 F. Supp. 651 (D.D.C. 1959); *Herald Co. v. McNeal*, 511 F. Supp. 269 (E.D. Mo. 1981); *Schuloff v. Fields*, 950 F. Supp. 66 (E.D.N.Y. 1997); *C. v. C.*, 320 A.2d 717 (Del. 1974); and *McMullan v. Wohlgemuth*, 308 A.2d 888 (Pa. 1973). In *Houchins v. KQED, Inc.*, 438 U.S. 1 (1978), the U.S. Supreme Court, in a 4-3 decision with two justices not participating, held that a broadcasting company did not have a First Amendment right of access to a county jail; the four justices in the majority agreed that the media did not enjoy "an implied special right of access to government-controlled sources of information." *Id.* at 7–8, 16. Two cases finding a constitutional right of access to government information are *Houston Chronicle Publishing Co. v. City of Houston*, 531 S.W.2d 177 (Tex. Civ. App. 1975), *writ ref'd n.r.e.*, 536 S.W.2d 559 (Tex. 1976), and *Sheridan Newspapers, Inc. v. City of Sheridan*, 660 P.2d 785 (Wyo. 1983). In each of the latter two cases, the court held that any constitutional right of access was not absolute and that legislatures had some authority to limit access based on their perceptions of the public good.

2. St. Michael's Convalescent Hosp. v. California, 643 F.2d 1369 (9th Cir. 1981) (state agency not subject to federal Freedom of Information Act (FOIA), even though it received significant federal funding). *Accord* State *ex rel.* Findlay Publ'g Co. v. Schroeder, 669 N.E.2d 835 (Ohio 1996).

The remainder of this chapter explores these two possible areas of federal influence on public records law.

The Possibility of Federal Preemption

Occasionally a specific federal statute or regulation, dealing with a specific sort of record, may appear to apply to state or local records. If the federal statute or regulation prohibits public access to the record in question,[3] even though the record would be public under state law, the supremacy of federal law requires that the federal statute or regulation prevail: the record would not be open to public access. This section explores the contours of such federal preemption. The conclusion is that this is but a narrow exception to the primacy of state law.

First, the fact that federal law prohibits a federal agency from releasing a certain type of record to the public does not mean that the prohibition also applies to any state or local agency with possession of the same or a similar record. A Colorado case decided in 1986 illustrates this principle.[4] A railroad had contracted to deliver coal to a Colorado public utility district, a public agency subject to that state's public records law. When a newspaper sought a copy of the contract, the railroad resisted on the ground that the contract included proprietary rate information. Federal law required that such contracts be submitted to the Interstate Commerce Commission (I.C.C.) for approval and restricted the release of the contracts by the I.C.C. The Colorado court held that the federal statute was irrelevant to the question of access to the district's copy of the contract; rather, state law controlled that question, and the court held for the newspaper.[5]

Second, the preferences of federal officials about release of records held by state or local government officials are irrelevant to questions of access under state law. In *Treadway v. Jones*,[6] for example, a reporter sought access to several proposals by private companies to manage the New Orleans housing authority. Officials at the federal Department of Housing and Urban Development had recommended that the proposals be kept confidential, but

3. I know of no example of the opposite—a federal statute or regulation that requires public access to a record that is closed to public access under state law.

4. Freedom Newspapers, Inc. v. Denver & Rio Grande W.R.R., 731 P.2d 740 (Colo. App. 1986).

5. Another example is *Newsday, Inc. v. State Department of Transportation*, 833 N.E.2d 210 (N.Y. 2005). In that case the state DOT argued that because certain records were not subject to discovery under the federal rules of civil procedure, therefore they should not be open to public access under the state's public records statute. The New York court rejected the argument, noting that if the records were obtained under the state statute, they still would not be admissible in any federal litigation. Two other cases dealing with this issue are *Wallace v. Guzman*, 687 So. 2d 1351 (Fla. Dist. Ct. App. 1997), and *Ostric v. Board of Appeal on Motor Vehicle Liability Policies & Bonds*, 280 N.E.2d 692 (Mass. 1972). In *Wallace*, a local agency, as part of its application to seek approval from a state agency to establish a savings bank, submitted individuals' financial and other personal records to a federal agency for review; the court held that the federal law, which may have kept the records confidential in the hands of the federal agency, did not extend to the records in the hands of the local agency, and that the documents were open to the public under the state's public records law. In *Ostric*, the court upheld a state requirement that driver's license applicants include their Social Security numbers on their applications, rejecting as irrelevant the then-current federal rule against release of such numbers by federal agencies.

6. 583 So. 2d 119 (La. Ct. App. 1991).

neither federal law nor federal regulation required such confidentiality. In those circumstances, the court held that state law prevailed and that the proposals were open to public access.[7]

Third, if a local or state agency submits a document to a federal agency, that document becomes subject to federal law *in the hands of the federal agency.* But that federal status is not exclusive and does not extend to any copy retained by the submitting state or local agency. As long as the state or local agency retains a copy of the document in its own files, that retained copy remains a state or local record, and access to it is regulated exclusively by the state's public records law.[8]

Fourth, and most starkly, at least one state court has held that a federal law that threatens a state or local agency with a loss of federal funding if specific records are made public does not create an automatic exception to the state's public records law. In *Troutt Brothers, Inc. v. Emison*,[9] a newspaper sought records giving the names of three juveniles who had escaped from detention and the reasons for their initial arrest. One argument against disclosure made by the defendant sheriff's department was that a federal statute conditioned grant funds for juvenile justice improvements on the recipient's keeping confidential the names of juveniles charged with crimes. The Arkansas Supreme Court rejected the argument, holding that such a threat of loss of funds did not create an exception to the state's public records law. The lesson of this case is that if state and local agencies are to be protected against such a loss of federal funding because of a federal condition of confidentiality, the relevant state statutes must be amended to restrict access to the records in question.[10]

Fifth, and moving in the other direction from the above discussion, occasionally courts have held that agencies established under state law are directly subject to federal regulation. A Florida court, for example, held that a municipal port agency was authorized by state law to operate as a common carrier under federal law and therefore was subject to federal restrictions on access to records of common carriers.[11] This is an unusual circumstance, however, and state courts are more likely to deny federal status to government agencies created by state law. A much more recent Florida case rejected an argument from a

---

7. *See also* Missouri Prot. & Advocacy Servs. v. Allan, 787 S.W.2d 291 (Mo. Ct. App. 1990). A federal agency monitoring state compliance with a federal education act sent a draft copy of its report to the state agency for its comments. The final report would be released only after the federal agency reviewed any comments on the draft by the state agency being monitored. The Missouri court held that the draft report was a public record in the hands of the state agency and therefore open to public access.

8. Epps v. Simms, 598 A.2d 756 (Md. Ct. Spec. App. 1991). The defendant state's attorney pointed out that the public records in question had been turned over to the federal government for use in prosecuting the plaintiff and therefore were no longer in the exclusive possession of the defendant; for that reason, argued the defendant, they need not be made public. The court rejected the argument. It held that if records began life as state records, turning copies over to the federal government did not cause them to lose that status.

9. 841 S.W.2d 604 (Ark. 1992).

10. Perhaps the most prominent example of such a condition on federal grants is the so-called Buckley Amendment, which conditions the continued receipt of federal education funding on the confidentiality of student records. 20 U.S.C. § 1232g(b) (2000 & Supp. V 2005). The North Carolina General Assembly has recognized the need for state action to meet the federal requirement by enactment of N.C. Gen. Stat. [hereinafter G.S.] § 115C-402, which declares that student records are not public records subject to G.S. Chapter 132. Thus, federal funding to North Carolina public schools is protected.

11. State *ex rel.* Cummer v. Pace, 164 So. 723 (Fla. 1935).

municipal housing authority that it was a federal agency for purposes of the federal Privacy Act. Even the extensive federal oversight that accompanies federal assistance to such authorities was insufficient to make the housing authority into a federal agency for public records purposes.[12]

Generally, then, if federal law is to preempt a state's public records law and govern access to records in the hands of state or local agencies, the federal law must do so explicitly. Such explicit provisions are relatively unusual in federal law, but here is a list of four kinds of records for which there is some express federal preemption:

1. *Social Security numbers.* Federal law explicitly regulates collection by a state or local agency of a person's Social Security number from that person. In addition, a second federal statute may restrict release of such numbers to the public by state or local officials. These federal statutes, as well as the North Carolina statutes on Social Security numbers, are discussed in chapter 15.
2. *Medical records.* The federal Health Insurance Portability and Accountability Act of 1996 (HIPAA) regulates release of medical records in certain circumstances. This statute, along with the North Carolina statutes dealing with medical records, is discussed in chapter 14.
3. *Motor vehicle records.* The federal Driver's Privacy Protection Act regulates the release by state departments of motor vehicles (DMVs) of "personal information . . . about any individual obtained by the department in connection with a motor vehicle record." In addition, if the state DMV discloses protected information to another governmental agency, such as a local government, that second agency is also prohibited from releasing the information. This statute and the implementing state legislation is discussed in chapter 17.
4. *Homeland security information.* The federal Homeland Security Act provides that if a federal agency shares *critical infrastructure information*, as defined in the act, with a state or local agency, the latter is prohibited from releasing the information pursuant to a state public records law. North Carolina's statutes on comparable information are discussed in chapter 20.

Unless a federal provision such as those just listed can be found or is pointed out to a local government with custody of a public record, though, federal law does not preempt the rules established by the North Carolina public records statutes.

The Constitutional Right of Privacy

Many records held by governments contain information about specific individuals that many of those individuals and others would consider private. Public hospitals, health departments, and mental health clinics maintain medical records of specific patients. Tax records include detailed information about the income and wealth of specific tax-

12. Housing Auth. v. Gomillion, 639 So. 2d 117 (Fla. Dist. Ct. App. 1994).

payers. Law enforcement records include detailed investigations of individuals suspected, and cleared, of crime. Social services departments and public housing agencies maintain records detailing the financial condition of persons receiving public assistance and living in public housing. And the list goes on. The General Assembly has recognized that public access to many such records would invade the privacy of the individuals covered and has excluded those records from public access.[13] But unlike the federal FOIA and some state public records laws, the North Carolina public records law does not include a general exemption from access for such records, even when their release would constitute an invasion of privacy. Therefore, if no specific statute limits access to a category of record, even though access might be considered invasive of individual privacy, access must be allowed unless doing so would somehow be unconstitutional.

Both the North Carolina and United States constitutions appear to recognize and protect some sort of right of individual privacy, shielding that right against governmental intrusion,[14] and many other state constitutions explicitly recognize this right. As a result, persons seeking to deny public access to public records, whether custodians of the records or subjects of the records, often argue that allowing access would intrude upon this constitutional right of privacy. In general, however, the courts have rejected the argument—and it is unlikely, though not impossible, that the constitutional right of privacy, whether state or federal, extends beyond the statutory exemptions already enacted by the General Assembly.

In the large majority of cases in which privacy arguments have been made, the courts have rejected the arguments. Among the many sorts of records that courts have held to be open to public access, over arguments that allowing such access would unconstitutionally invade personal privacy, are

- Applications of persons seeking to rent public housing, when the applications include personal financial statements, details of family histories, and medical histories[15]
- Lists of persons living in public housing whose rent is overdue and the income of such persons[16]
- Records showing the amounts of subsidies received by landlords in Section 8 housing and the addresses of their projects[17]

---

13. The General Assembly has recognized the privacy interest in each of the sorts of records listed in this paragraph, except for records that include financial information about public housing tenants. The statutes excluding the relevant records from public access are discussed in several of the chapters in Part II of this book.

14. For the federal right, see JOHN E. NOWAK & RONALD D. ROTUNDA, CONSTITUTIONAL LAW § 14.30(a) (7th ed. 2004). As for the state right, in *Treants Enterprises, Inc. v. Onslow County*, 83 N.C. App. 345, 350 S.E.2d 365 (1986), *aff'd*, 320 N.C. 776, 360 S.E.2d 783 (1987), the court of appeals held that an ordinance provision violated "the right to privacy of patrons of companionship businesses under both the federal and state constitutions." *Id.* at 359, 350 S.E.2d at 374. The court did not offer a citation to this state constitutional right, however, and the supreme court did not address the issue in its opinion in the case.

15. Forsberg v. Hous. Auth., 455 So. 2d 373 (Fla. 1984).

16. Doe v. Sears, 263 S.E.2d 119 (Ga. 1980).

17. Mid-America Television Co. v. Peoria Hous. Auth., 417 N.E.2d 210 (Ill. App. Ct. 1981).

- Lists of physicians performing publicly funded abortions and showing the amounts received by each physician for such services[18]
- Records showing the names and addresses of various volunteers or private citizens[19]
- Coroner's records showing the names of persons who committed suicide[20]
- Records containing complete appraisal and other descriptive information about individual properties subject to taxation[21]
- Tax records showing the amount of tax paid by each taxpayer under a hotel-motel occupancy tax measured by gross receipts[22]
- Personnel records showing the names of job applicants[23]
- Workers' compensation records showing the names of persons filing claims, amounts of claims, and in some cases the nature of injuries[24]

In general the courts have argued that there can be no privacy rights that prohibit public review of the basis for decisions to spend public money or of the government's administration of programs.[25] They have also noted that persons who work for or hold office in government must expect and tolerate a lesser right of privacy than persons outside of government.[26]

A few courts, though, in narrow circumstances, have denied access to records because access would invade individual privacy. Most of these cases have involved records that under North Carolina statute are not open to the public in any event. For example, a court in Louisiana included certain public personnel records within a constitutional zone of privacy;[27] and a Texas court included criminal investigation records within a zone of pri-

---

18. Minnesota Med. Ass'n v. State, 274 N.W.2d 84 (Minn. 1978).

19. Cape Cod Times v. Sheriff of Barnstable County, 823 N.E.2d 375 (Mass. 2005) (volunteer reserve deputies); Local 100, Serv. Employees' Int'l Union v. Forrest, 675 So. 2d 1153 (La. Ct. App. 1996) (nurses' aides listed on a state registry).

20. *Cf.* State *ex rel.* Findlay Publ'g Co. v. Schroeder, 669 N.E.2d 835 (Ohio 1996).

21. Pensyl v. Peach County, 314 S.E.2d 434 (Ga. 1984).

22. *Cf.* Booth Newspapers, Inc. v. Kent County Treasurer, 438 N.W.2d 317 (Mich. Ct. App. 1989).

23. Capital City Press v. E. Baton Rouge Parish Metro. Council, 696 So. 2d 562 (La. 1997).

24. Indus. Found. of the South v. Tex. Indus. Accident Bd., 540 S.W.2d 668 (Tex. 1976) (names of claimants); Pisciotti v. County of Wayne, 76 F. Supp. 2d 307 (W.D.N.Y. 1999) (name of claimant, amount of payment, and nature of injury).

25. *E.g.*, Forsberg v. Hous. Auth., 455 So. 2d 373 (Fla. 1984), and Booth Newspapers, Inc. v. Kent County Treasurer, 438 N.W.2d 317 (Mich. Ct. App. 1989).

26. *E.g.*, Citizens to Recall Mayor James Whitlock v. Whitlock, 844 P.2d 74 (Mont. 1992).

27. Trahan v. Larivee, 365 So. 2d 294 (La. Ct. App. 1978) (denial of access explicitly based on state constitutional provision protecting individual privacy). *But see* Hilbun v. State *ex rel.* Div. of Admin., 745 So. 2d 1189 (La. Ct. App. 1999) (release of summaries of interviews of public employees, undertaken as part of a personnel investigation, not unconstitutionally invasive of personal privacy).

Other courts have rejected arguments that a right of privacy shields various personnel records from public access. *E.g.*, Int'l Ass'n of Fire Fighters, Local 1264 v. Mun. of Anchorage, 973 P.2d 1132 (Alaska 1999) (state constitutional right of privacy does not protect names or compensation of public employees); Shevin v. Byron, Harless, Schaffer, Reid & Assocs., Inc., 379 So. 2d 633 (Fla. 1980) (applications for public employment not protected by federal constitutional right of privacy); Fincher v. State, 497 S.E.2d 632 (Ga.

vacy.[28] A few cases, however, have found constitutional protection for records that would be open to the public under North Carolina statutes, and so there remains a small chance that such a constitutional argument might succeed. There is no particular thread that unites these cases, and so they are simply set out here as examples of information that one court or another has found protected against access by a constitutional right of privacy:

- The federal Court of Appeals for the Second Circuit suggested that it might be an unconstitutional invasion of privacy to permit access to personal financial statements that taxicab owners filed with New York City's Taxi and Limousine Commission.[29]
- The federal Court of Appeals for the Sixth Circuit held that it would be unconstitutional to release personal information that a local government held about persons owning or working in sexually oriented businesses.[30]
- The Ohio Supreme Court held that it would be an unconstitutional invasion of privacy to release information required of children wishing to use a city's recreational facilities.[31] The information included names, home addresses, family information, emergency contact information, and the children's medical histories.
- The Louisiana Court of Appeals held that the state constitution's protection of individual privacy barred release of the payroll records of a company constructing a project for the state, to the extent that those records associated the names and addresses of company employees with their compensation.[32]

Ct. App. 1998) (release of report of investigation of sexual harassment claim, which supports claim, not unconstitutionally invasive of privacy).

28. *Cf.* Houston Chronicle Publ'g Co. v. City of Houston, 531 S.W.2d 177 (Tex. Civ. App. 1975) (release of an individual's arrest record would be an unwarranted invasion of personal privacy), *writ ref'd n.r.e.*, 536 S.W.2d 559 (Tex. 1976).

29. Statharos v. New York City Taxi & Limousine Comm'n, 198 F.3d 317 (2d Cir. 1999).

30. Deja Vu of Nashville, Inc. v. Metro. Gov't of Nashville & Davidson County, Tenn., 274 F.3d 377 (6th Cir. 2001).

31. State *ex rel.* McCleary v. Roberts, 725 N.E.2d 1144 (Ohio 2000).

32. Angelo Iafrate Constr., L.L.C. v. State *ex rel.* Dep't of Transp. & Dev., 879 So. 2d 250 (La. Ct. App. 2004).

Chapter 5—Electronic Records

Section 132-1 of the North Carolina General Statutes [hereinafter G.S.] defines "public records" to explicitly include "magnetic or other tapes [and] electronic data-processing records." It is important to recognize that electronic records are not a separate category of public records but rather simply records that are created, transmitted, and stored through electronic methods. As with any document created or received by a government, the status of an electronic record under the public records laws depends entirely on the content of the record. Nevertheless, there are issues in public records law that are unique to electronic records or that are intensified with electronic records. This book makes reference to electronic records in several different chapters when the context makes such a reference appropriate. Still, there is value in consolidating into a single chapter a discussion of issues that are unique to electronic records or that raise special concerns, even if the discussion is somewhat redundant to short portions of other chapters. That is the purpose of this chapter.

Defining Electronic Records as Public Records

Mandatory Database Indexing

G.S. 132-6.1(b), enacted in 1995, requires each public agency that compiles or creates a computer database after a specified date to concurrently create an index for the database.[1] This index must include "a list of the data fields; a description of the format or record layout; information as to the frequency with which the database is updated; a list of any data fields to which public access is restricted; a description of each form in which the database can be copied or reproduced using the [unit's] computer facilities; and a schedule of fees for . . . copies in each available form." The statute was to be implemented over several years, based on the size of the government maintaining the database. Although the deadline for full implementation passed more than a decade ago, the subsection provides that it is optional for a unit to create an index for any database "compiled or created" before the deadline, and the Department of Cultural Resources has therefore advised governments that the indexing requirement applies only to databases created, significantly changed, or merged with other databases after the statutory deadlines, and not to those to which new data merely is added after those dates.[2] Therefore, the deadlines retain some importance. They were as follows:

- *July 1, 1997.* Cities of 10,000 or more, counties of 25,000 or more, and public hospitals in those counties.
- *July 1, 1998.* All other local governments.

The requirement applies only to databases that are compiled or created pursuant to action of the agency itself and that are maintained for agency purposes.[3] If an employee creates a database for his or her own purposes—such as an electronic list of telephone numbers maintained on a desktop computer—that database has not been created by the agency for which the employee works and the employee need not create the statutory index.

Many agency databases are part of software packages purchased by local governments from private vendors. It seems reasonable to expect such a vendor to prepare the necessary index as part of its installation of the software.

Is Software a Public Record?

Software Created by a Local Government

Chapter 1 includes a paragraph discussing whether software created by a local government is a public record, such that anyone would have a right to copy the source code for the software.[4] The discussion cites a federal case and a North Carolina attorney general's opinion,

---

1. The statute is set out in appendix 5A at the end of this chapter.

2. The department's position is found in State Public Records Cataloging Services, N.C. Dep't of Cultural Resources, Public Database Indexing: Guidelines and Recommendations 3 (Release 1.1, Sept. 1996), *available at* www.records.ncdcr.gov/erecords/pubdata/pdata1-1.pdf. It was based on legal advice from the attorney general's office. *See* Letter to Elizabeth F. Buford, 26 February 1996, Advisory Opinion No. 239, *available at* www.ncdoj.gov/About-DOJ/Legal-Services/Legal-Opinions.aspx.

3. *See* State Public Records Cataloging Services, N.C. Dep't of Cultural Resources, Public Database Indexing: Guidelines and Recommendations 3–5 (Release 1.1, Sept. 1996), *available at* www.records.ncdcr.gov/erecords/pubdata/pdata1-1.pdf.

4. *See supra* text in chapter 1 accompanying notes 80 through 83.

both concluding that such software is not a public record and therefore there is no right to a copy of the source code.

Software Purchased by a Local Government

If software created by a government is not a public record, the logic of that position applies equally to software purchased by a government from a commercial vendor. Therefore, any software program that a government might be using is not itself a public record.

Computer Storage Media

In early 2008 a citizen requested, pursuant to the public records law, that a North Carolina local government allow him to copy the desktop computer hard drives of several of the local government's officials. Obviously, most of the files on such a hard drive would be public record, but the hard drive itself almost certainly is not—it is not a record itself but simply the medium upon which a number of records are stored. Furthermore, allowing such a request raises security issues that may be insurmountable. Even if various records that are not open to the public are "deleted" from the hard drive, those records do not in fact disappear from the hard drive and may in many cases be retrievable from the hard drive with appropriate software.

Metadata

A very recent emerging issue has been whether electronic metadata associated with a record is itself part of the record and therefore subject to the various rules applicable to public records. Metadata has been described as follows:

> Metadata is sometimes referred to as "data about data." Metadata can come from a variety of sources: created automatically by a computer, supplied by a user, or inferred through a relationship to another document. Some metadata, such as file dates and sizes, can easily be seen by users; other metadata may be hidden or embedded and unavailable to computer users who are not technically adept.[5]

It may be useful to set out some of the common examples of metadata:

- File names associated with files created within computer software applications
- Information associated with computer files that show when the information was created and on whose computer
- Information associated with computer files that permits those files to be searched electronically
- Formulas in a spreadsheet by which the numbers that actually appear are calculated
- So-called track changes that show the evolution of a document over time
- Header and thread information associated with e-mail, including addressee and addressor, reception date, and blind copy recipients

---

5. The Sedona Conference, The Sedona Guidelines: Best Practice Guidelines & Commentary for Managing Information & Records in the Electronic Age 28 (2d ed. 2007) (footnote omitted), *available at* www.thesedonaconference.org/content/miscFiles/publications_html.

Thus, metadata, as understood by information technology professionals, includes an array of information. Some of it is created by the computer user; much is not. Some of it is visible (or can be made visible to a computer user); some is not. Examples of visible metadata include the formulas in a spreadsheet or the addressor and addressee in an e-mail message. To some extent, the judicial treatment of metadata as a general category under public records laws may depend on the type of metadata in question. It may be easier to treat metadata that is visible to a user as a public record than it is metadata that the user is not even aware exists.

By the fall of 2009 there had been two appellate cases that considered the status of metadata under a state's public records laws. The two cases involved different sorts of metadata but reached the same conclusion—the metadata at issue was a record open to the public. The first case is *O'Neill v. City of Shoreline*, a 2008 decision by the Washington Court of Appeals.[6] At a city council meeting in Shoreline, the city's deputy mayor stated that she had received an e-mail that alleged improper influence by council members over a zoning issue and that the message had come from two specific persons. (The message had been forwarded to the deputy mayor by someone other than the persons she named.) The case involved the efforts of one of the named persons to obtain copies, both printed and electronic, of the e-mail mentioned by the deputy mayor. O'Neill, the person in question, ultimately made clear to the city that she wanted not only the text of the e-mail but also the metadata associated with it. This metadata included the header information—whom the e-mail was from, and the name, e-mail address, and Internet protocol address of the recipient. The Washington statute defines a public record as "any writing containing information relating to the conduct of government or the performance of any governmental or proprietary function prepared, owned, used, or retained by any state or local agency regardless of physical form or characteristics." The court first determined that the e-mail itself was a public record because it was a writing, it related to city business, and it had been used by the deputy mayor at a council meeting. The court then went on to hold that at least some of the metadata associated with the e-mail was also public record. It too qualified as a writing, it was owned by the deputy mayor in her official capacity, and it contained information that related to city business: "[f]or example, it shows the e-mail addresses of persons who may have knowledge of alleged government improprieties in dealing with a zoning matter."[7] The court's decision left open the possibility that some portions of the metadata, however, might not relate to city business and therefore might not be part of the public record. (In this instance, it is important that the e-mail was sent to the deputy mayor's home e-mail account; under the court's analysis, it is likely that all the metadata associated with an e-mail sent through the city's server would be public record.)

The second case is *Lake v. City of Phoenix*, a 2009 decision of the Arizona Supreme Court.[8] Lake, a city police officer, had made a public records request to the city for notes kept by seven named police lieutenants over a one-year period. Upon receiving the notes, Lake suspected that those from one of the lieutenants had been back-dated; therefore, he

---

6. 187 P.3d 822 (Wash. Ct. App. 2008).

7. *Id.* at 827.

8. 218 P.3d 1004 (Ariz. 2009).

requested the metadata associated with the notes. He expected to be able to determine from the metadata when the notes had actually been made. When the city denied the request, he brought suit. In a 2-1 decision, the Arizona Court of Appeals held that the metadata was not a public record,[9] but the Arizona Supreme Court reversed. The appeals court held that metadata should be considered separately from the document for which it was created (an approach that seems also to have been taken by the Washington appellate court), and as such the metadata did not meet the Arizona definition of public record. The dissenter disagreed with that approach, arguing that the metadata was part of that primary record and should be treated accordingly, and the Arizona Supreme Court agreed:

> The metadata in an electronic document is part of the underlying document; it does not stand on its own. When a public officer uses a computer to make a public record, the metadata forms part of the document as much as the words on the page.[10]

Therefore, because the underlying record was available to the public, so too should be the associated metadata.

If there is to be a single public records status for metadata, it seems to me the Arizona Supreme Court has the better argument. An e-mail is inescapably incomplete without the names of the sender and recipient; a spreadsheet may be meaningless without the formulas associated with it. Even if the underlying record is meaningful without the metadata—as were the notes at issue in the Arizona case—verification is not possible without it.

It is possible, of course, that courts might decide not to accord all metadata the same status. Rather, they might determine that some metadata is public record and some is not. Here are some ideas about treatment of various forms of metadata should that approach be taken:

- Some records are not fully comprehensible without their associated metadata. An e-mail separated from the names of the sender and the recipient is like a letter without the salutation; a spreadsheet without the underlying formulas may not be understandable. Metadata that is necessary in order for a record to be fully comprehensible probably represents the strongest case for metadata being part of a public record.
- Other metadata is useful in demonstrating the integrity of the electronic record.[11] The properties of an electronic file show when it was first created and last modified, and that information may be important in determining whether the record is what it is represented as being.
- One characteristic of the two sorts of metadata discussed above is that they are easily made visible by anyone with an electronic copy of an electronic file. If a court wanted to give public records status to some metadata but not all, that characteristic would be one possible basis for a distinction. It is reinforced by the language of G.S. 132-6.2(a), which provides that a person requesting a copy of a

---

9. 207 P.3d 725 (Ariz. Ct. App. 2009).
10. *Lake*, 218 P.3d at 1007.
11. Metadata of this sort can, however, be unreliable; it can also be manipulated.

public record "may elect to obtain [it] in any and all media in which the public agency is capable of providing [it]." If a requester seeks an electronic copy of an electronic record and asks for it in the application within which it is created, this sort of metadata will be included automatically in the record.

- Other metadata is part of the electronic file but is embedded so that it is not readily visible.[12] In particular, embedded metadata includes track changes or comments in a word processing document. Government agencies are allowed to destroy drafts of documents as later drafts, and then the final version, are created, and so it might be thought that track changes and comments, which reveal earlier drafts, ought not to be automatically open to public inspection. On the other hand, embedded metadata also includes that metadata that allows a document to be electronically searched, and large documents are much more useful to recipients with that capability. The statutory policy set out above that entitles a recipient of a copy of a public record to specify the format in which the copy is to be provided was intended to allow requesters to insist upon electronic copies in order to take advantage of such a copy's unique characteristics. That policy is advanced by providing copies of electronic records that are searchable, and that fact argues for including embedded metadata as part of the record that is subject to public access.
- Still other metadata is part of the computer system but is not part of the underlying electronic file.[13] This category of metadata perhaps offers the strongest argument for differential treatment, inasmuch as it is not part of the file.[14]

Cookies

"Cookies" are very small text files that are placed on computer hard drives by websites visited by that computer. These files have a unique ID tag and may store some small amount of additional data associated with that ID tag. If that computer later revisits the website, the website can recognize it by matching the cookie with a counterpart in its own database. By examining the cookies on a computer, a knowledgeable person can determine what websites have been visited by the computer. Occasionally local governments have received requests for the cookies on a particular computer, and therefore the question arises as to whether cookies are public records and open to public inspection.

There is no settled answer, but my best guess is that they are not. It might be thought that cookies are similar to metadata and should be treated the same way, but there are differences between metadata and cookies that might be significant. First, metadata is part of the

---

12. The Sedona Conference Glossary defines "Embedded Metadata" as "Generally hidden, but an integral part of ESI [electronically stored information], such as 'track changes' or 'comments' in a word processing file or 'notes' in a presentation file." THE SEDONA CONFERENCE, THE SEDONA CONFERENCE GLOSSARY: E-DISCOVERY & DIGITAL INFORMATION MANAGEMENT 19 (2d ed. 2007), *available at* www.thesedonaconference.org/content/miscFiles/publications_html.]

13. The Sedona Conference Glossary defines "File System Metadata" as "Metadata generated by the system to track the demographics (name, size, location, usage, etc.) of the ESI [electronically stored information] and, not embedded within, but stored externally from the ESI." *Id.* at 22.

14. The Arizona Supreme Court explicitly limited its holding to metadata that is embedded in the file and moves with the file when it is moved or copied.

underlying electronic record, but a cookie is not part of any record created by the computer user: a cookie is inserted on a user's hard drive independently of any record created and stored on that hard drive. There is no association between a record and a cookie; rather, a cookie simply records an action taken by a person using the computer. Second, metadata is made within and by the computer of a person creating an underlying record, and it is a direct result of actions taken by that person. A cookie, on the other hand, is made by an outside actor, the Internet website visited by a computer user. Metadata is automatically created when the underlying record is created, but a cookie is not; it depends upon the action of an outside entity, the operator of the visited website.

Even if we accept that some cookies might be public records, many would not be. To the extent that cookies reflect nonbusiness use of a computer by a government employee or official, the usual principle that one looks to the content of records to determine their character would cause those cookies to be excluded because of that personal use, just as personal e-mail is not public record even if on a government-owned computer. Finally, the one use a government is most likely to make of cookies is to monitor employees' Internet use, and cookies gathered for that purpose would be part of an employee's personnel file and not open to the public in any event.

Personal E-Mail and Comparable Electronic Files

Chapter 1 discussed the numerous cases from around the country that have held that personal e-mail is not a public record, even when found on a government-owned computer.[15] These cases demonstrate that it is the content of a record that determines its character under the public records law, rather than its location. This same principle would apply to other electronic records that might be found on a government-owned computer. If a government employee, for example, used his or her employer's computer to type a personal letter or create a spreadsheet for a civic club the employee belonged to, neither the letter nor the spreadsheet would be a public record because each is personal in nature. (It is, of course, a separate issue as to whether such use of a government-owned computer is permissible; that differs from one government employer to another.)

Although personal e-mail and other files generated from personal use of a government-owned computer are not public records, and therefore there is no automatic right of public access to them, that does not necessarily preclude the government from releasing such e-mails or files if it wishes to. An employee enjoys privacy rights in such material on his or her employer's computer only to the extent that he or she has a reasonable expectation of such privacy.[16] There is some question about whether an employee might ever reasonably have such an expectation, particularly as to e-mail found on a government server, but the issue can be best resolved by the government's developing and disseminating to its employees a computer use policy that makes clear that the government retains full authority to

15. See *supra* text in chapter 1 accompanying notes 58 through 63.

16. The basic rules in this area were set in *O'Connor v. Ortega*, 480 U.S. 709 (1987). The case involved a government employer's search of an employee's office, desk, and file cabinets, but its principles can be applied to computer systems as well. The principal reported case dealing with computer systems is *Smyth v. Pillsbury Co.*, 914 F. Supp. 97 (E.D. Pa. 1996), in which the court found no reasonable expectation in certain e-mail communications made by one employee to another, using the company's e-mail system.

monitor and inspect material on government-owned computers or storage devices. Here is an excellent example of such a policy, used by the City of Charlotte:

> Users should have no expectation of privacy regarding e-mail or anything else created, stored, sent or received using the City's Computer Network. The Computer Network is the property of City of Charlotte, and all e-mail messages and attachments created or transmitted on the City's Computer Network become the property of the City, regardless of the subject matter or purpose. The City reserves the right to access, review, copy and delete all materials created, stored, sent or received through the Computer Network or any City Internet connection. The City further reserves the right to disclose such materials to any party (inside or outside the City), as the City deems appropriate. This Policy applies to personal messages and documents as well as work-related messages and documents. The fact that the City's Computer Network may allow Users to designate messages as "confidential" or "private," or restrict access to documents with a password, does not alter this Policy or confer upon Users any right to privacy regarding such messages or documents.[17]

It should be noted that the principle that it is the content of a record that controls whether it is subject to the public records law works both ways. That is to say, if a public employee or official sends or receives e-mail relating to government business through a personal e-mail account, or drafts a government document on a privately owned computer, the e-mail or the document is still a public record. Just as being found on a government-owned computer does not cause personal e-mail or personal electronic records to become public records, so too the location of otherwise-public e-mail or electronic records on a privately owned computer does not cause the e-mail or other electronic record to lose its character as a public record. Location does not matter; content does.

Access to and Copies of Electronic Records

Who Is the Custodian of Electronic Records?

In many local governments various electronic records are in the physical custody of an information technology (IT) department, even though the records have been generated in some other department. In that situation, which department is the legal custodian of the records? (Recall that G.S. 132-2 specifies that the custodian is the "public official in charge of an office having public records.") The public records law makes clear that the custodian is the department that generated the records, not the IT department. G.S. 132-6(a) specifies that the custodian is not "an agency that holds the public records of other agencies solely

---

17. City of Charlotte, Computer Network and Internet Access Policy, paragraph 7, No Expectation of Privacy (Aug. 1, 2002) (on file with author). Governor Purdue has issued an Executive Order that specifies that all Executive Branch employees "shall assume that information on the State's e-mail system is subject to public review and to review by state officials." Exec. Order 18, E-Mail Retention and Archiving Policy, issued 7 July 2009, *available at* www.governor.state.nc.us/NewsItems/UploadedFiles/4980c704-1af0-41c4-9f30-98eb7d612c84.pdf.

for purposes of storage or safekeeping or solely to provide data processing." Therefore, any requests to inspect or obtain a copy of such electronic records should be made to the generating department rather than to the IT department.

Copy Format

It is worth repeating here that a person who has made a request for copies of one or more public records is entitled by G.S. 132-6.2(a) to receive those copies in any medium in which the government or agency is capable of providing them. Most importantly, this means that the requester is entitled to copies of electronic records in either electronic form or paper form, at the requester's discretion. Chapter 2 discusses this provision in more detail.

Records Requests That Require Programming

Chapter 2 makes the fundamental point that governments are not required to create new records in response to requests to inspect or make copies of public records and briefly discusses the application of this principle when a citizen makes a request for records that would necessitate some computer programming by the government in order to meet the request. In general, as the text in chapter 2 notes, the courts have refused to order governments to write new programs in order to access and manipulate electronic data in the manner desired by persons outside the government, when the government has no use itself for the data structured in that fashion.[18] Of course, if confidential information is included with nonconfidential information in a single electronic file, so that some programming is necessary to generate a record containing only the public information, the public records statute makes clear that the programming must be done, and done at the expense of the government.[19]

The writing of a new program must be distinguished from the use of a query feature in a database. Such a feature permits a user, with a few keystrokes, to ask questions about the information in one or more databases and thereby generate data in a form that is customized for a particular query. A number of courts have considered the issue of whether making such a query is enough like writing a new program to allow a government to refuse to make database queries on behalf of members of the public because the act of doing so constitutes creation of a new record. In general the answer has been no—using a query feature is not the same as writing a new program. The case of *Board of Education v. New Jersey Department of Treasury*,[20] decided by the New Jersey Supreme Court in 1996, is

---

18. In addition to the cases cited in chapter 2, note 5, the following cases have addressed the issue: *Schulten, Ward & Turner, LLP v. Fulton-DeKalb Hospital Authority*, 535 S.E.2d 243 (Ga. 2000) (need not reprogram computer system to generate requested records, nor allow computer technician provided by requesters to reprogram system), and *State ex rel. Kerner v. State Teachers Retirement Board*, 695 N.E.2d 256 (Ohio 1998) (need not reprogram computer system to generate requested records). *But see* Tennessean v. Elec. Power Bd., 979 S.W.2d 297 (Tenn. 1998) (if newspaper will pay reprogramming costs, must reprogram computer system to generate records requested by newspaper).

19. N.C. Gen. Stat. [hereinafter G.S.] § 132-6(c) provides that "[n]o request to inspect, examine, or obtain copies of public records shall be denied on the grounds that confidential information is commingled with the requested nonconfidential information. If it is necessary to separate confidential from nonconfidential information in order to permit the inspection, examination, or copying of the public records, the public agency shall bear the cost of such separation."

20. 678 A.2d 660 (N.J. 1996).

illustrative. The local school board sought information available from the state treasury in a departmental database; in order to generate the information, however, the state agency needed to initiate a query of the database, and the agency argued that doing so amounted to creation of a new record. The supreme court disagreed, holding that "the process of retrieving the [requested] information is better characterized as a selective copying from the [state agency's] existing data base" than as creation of a new record.[21] This is a sensible outcome, given the relative ease of making a query of a database, and it is likely that the New Jersey court's decision, and others similar to it, would be followed in North Carolina.[22]

Access to the Computer System

If a citizen wishes to examine an electronic record without having a copy made, he or she has no right to insist on doing so by entering the government's computer system, any more than someone can demand to be able to come into an official's or employee's office and go through a file cabinet in the corner. In *Tax Data Corp. v. Hutt*,[23] the plaintiff used city tax records in its business. The tax office employees accessed the records through eight terminals in the office, and the plaintiff sought the right to use those terminals as well. The court noted that these were not dumb terminals, and therefore, allowing the plaintiff, or any other citizen, to use the terminals would permit such an outside user to alter records within the system. The city had a legitimate concern with the security and integrity of the records. The court denied the plaintiff's attempt for direct access to the computer system.[24]

Computer System Security Features

In a slightly roundabout way, G.S. 132-6.1 denies public access to the security features of various information technology systems.[25] Subsection (c) of the section provides that

> [n]othing in this section requires a public agency to disclose security features of its electronic data processing systems, information technology systems, telecommunications networks, or electronic security systems, including hardware or software security, passwords, or security standards, procedures, processes, configurations, software, and codes.

Government Publication on the Internet

A growing number of local government agencies publish records on the Internet. This is perhaps most common with registers of deeds, many of whom have placed land records on the Internet, but government agencies have also posted property tax records, court records,

---

21. *Id.* at 666.

22. Comparable cases are *Williams Law Firm v. Board of Supervisors of Louisiana State University*, 878 So. 2d 557 (La. Ct. App. 2004), and *Locator Services Group, Ltd. v. Suffolk County Comptroller*, 836 N.Y.S.2d 223 (App. Div. 2007).

23. 826 P.2d 353 (Colo. App. 1991).

24. *Accord* WIREdata, Inc. v. Village of Sussex, 751 N.W.2d 736 (Wis. 2008). In *Sperr v. City of Spokane*, 96 P.3d 1012 (Wash. Ct. App. 2004), the plaintiff had requested all police records referring to him by name, and the city claimed to have responded fully. Because he had not found a record that he believed to exist, the plaintiff brought suit for the right to do his own search in the department's computer system. The Washington appellate court rejected his suit, holding that there was no right under the state's public records law to access an agency's computer system to search for a record.

25. This statute is discussed in slightly more detail in chapter 20, *infra*.

building permits, restaurant inspection records, and other categories of public records. This sort of publication has raised new questions about privacy. For example, some law enforcement officers object to their home addresses appearing on the Internet through either deed or tax records because of concerns over their and their families' safety. Even though the same record is available to the public in hard copy at the register of deed's or tax administrator's office, publication on the Internet makes the record much more accessible as a practical matter.

There is no general statutory regulation of this sort of publication as of yet in North Carolina, although, as noted below, there is some regulation of publication of certain records that might include Social Security numbers or other personal identifying information. In this circumstance, a couple of principles can be stated with some certainty. First, except for records with Social Security numbers and other specific identifying information, the public office with possession of the records has the clear right to publish them on the Internet, over the objections of persons whose personal information might be in the records.[26] After all, any citizen could come to the public office, request the electronic files with the records, and then publish them on the Internet. Second, when a public office publishes public records on the Internet, it does so as a public service and not from any legal obligation. For that reason, the custodian of the records may choose to delete some records or some information from the records before they are placed on the Internet. A tax office, for example, might choose not to include identifying information about law enforcement officers when it publishes tax records. Clearly the records will be less useful if the custodian chooses to edit them in some way, but the editing is a legitimate response to the privacy issues generated by Internet publication. It would be good practice, though, to make clear in some fashion at the Internet location that some records have been omitted and to include an explanation of the principles behind the omissions.

Land Records and Other Records with Social Security Numbers and Other Personal Identifying Information

G.S. 132-1.10 regulates government collection, use, and release of Social Security numbers and regulates release of certain other so-called identifying information.[27] (G.S. 132-1.10 is

---

26. In *Lambert v. Hartman*, 517 F.3d 433 (6th Cir. 2008), the plaintiff had received a speeding ticket, which included her driver's license number and Social Security number. The county clerk of court later posted the ticket, as a matter of course, on the court's website, and eventually there was evidence that the plaintiff's driver's license number and Social Security number had been used to steal her identity. She brought an action under 42 U.S.C. § 1983 seeking damages for the loss of constitutional privacy and consequent identity theft, but the federal court of appeals refused to allow the action. The court stated:

> Lambert has undoubtedly shown that, as a policy matter, the Clerk's decision to provide unfettered Internet access to people's Social Security numbers was unwise. This much is evidenced by the fact that Defendants have subsequently removed the citations in question from the website and changed the local rules to better protect sensitive personal information. But to constitutionalize a harm of the type Lambert has suffered would be to open a Pandora's box of claims under 42 U.S.C. § 1983, a step that we are unwilling to take.

Id. at 445. It should be noted that the court mentions that the Sixth Circuit's definition of "constitutional privacy" is narrower than that of some other circuits.

27. The full list of identifying information is set out in G.S. 14-113.20(b). The definition of "identifying information" found in G.S. 14-113.20(b) is used in G.S. 132-1.10 with the exceptions noted in G.S. 132-1.10(b)(5).

discussed in detail *infra* in chapter 15.) In the past, Social Security numbers frequently were included in land records, especially deeds of trust, and in a variety of court records. G.S. 132-1.10 now prohibits inclusion of these numbers in records filed with a register of deeds or a clerk of court. It also prohibits inclusion of the following personal identifying information: a person's employer taxpayer identification number, driver's license number, state identification number, passport number, checking account or savings account number, credit card or debit card account number, or any personal identification code or password. The statute, however, only became effective December 1, 2005, and these numbers remain in many older records. The General Assembly recognized that many of these records had been or would be published on the Internet by registers of deeds or clerks of court and sought to protect against this form of release of the numbers. Therefore, G.S. 132-1.10(f) now permits any person to demand that a register of deeds or a clerk of court remove the person's Social Security number or any of the other listed identifying information from any document that is or will be placed on the Internet by the register or clerk. The usual way of doing this is to delete the number or other identifying information from the online version of the record, leaving it on the original paper record in the public office. The statute, however, seems to recognize the possibility of deleting the number or information from the original, inasmuch as it states that the register or clerk has no duty to reinstate the number, if requested to do so, if reinstating is "impossible."

Retention and Disposition of Electronic Records

Chapter 3 describes the system under which the state Department of Cultural Resources controls retention and disposition of public records. In that system the content of a particular record determines how long the record must be retained and when it may be disposed of. So it is with electronic records: an electronic record is not a separate kind of record and therefore we look again to content to determine the record's place in the retention and disposition system. If a particular sort of paper record is to be retained for three years, an electronic record with the same content is also to be retained for three years.

It is worth saying something more about e-mail, though, because there is both confusion and a lack of knowledge about the retention and disposition rules applicable to this form of communication. It should be helpful at the outset to say something about how a typical e-mail system works.

When e-mail arrives at a government's or agency's e-mail system, it first moves to the server that supports that system. (The government or agency may have software in place that attempts to filter out spam or junk e-mail before it reaches the server.) Individual users of the system then access the e-mail addressed to them. In some small systems the e-mail is downloaded to the user's desktop computer; in larger ones it usually stays on the central server. In either case, the e-mail is managed by the employee. He or she analyzes the e-mail and answers it, forwards it, deletes it, or otherwise handles it, and the employee is responsible for assuring that the e-mail is retained appropriately under the retention and disposition system in place in that governmental unit or agency. If an employee deletes an e-mail, it typically is moved to a "Deleted Items" folder that is still easily accessible by the employee. It is only when the e-mail is deleted from this second folder that it has been purged from the system. At that point it is no longer on the employee's desktop computer nor on the server.

Typically the government or agency will back up the e-mail system at the end of each work day, in order to protect the system against some sort of catastrophic failure. Such a backup tape or other storage device is normally kept for a relatively short period of time—perhaps thirty or sixty days—and then it is recycled. A few local governments, however, have begun retaining these backup tapes for several years.

Basic Retention Rules for E-Mail

Although the Department of Cultural Resources stresses that electronic records are to be treated based on their content, it has recognized that the issues associated with e-mail are such that some separate attention to this form of electronic communication is warranted. For that reason, the department has produced a separate set of e-mail guidelines, dated July 2009 and entitled *E-Mail as a Public Record in North Carolina: A Policy for Its Retention and Disposition.*[28] The policy repeats the fundamental point that the treatment of e-mail, like the treatment of any other public record, depends on its content. The basic direction is, as noted above, to manage and retain e-mail in the same manner as a paper record with the same sort of content. It is crucial to understand that appropriate retention is the primary responsibility of each employee using the e-mail system; that person is the one who must decide whether a particular e-mail must be retained and for how long. It should be noted that the retention requirement can be met either by saving the e-mail in some sort of electronic form or by printing it out and saving it in paper form. For illustration, here are some retention periods for the sort of records that might be found in e-mail:[29]

- Administrative directives—Permanently
- Conference materials—One year
- Correspondence—One, three, or five years, depending on the subject matter
- Law enforcement case files—Five years for misdemeanors, twenty years for felonies
- Meeting agendas—One year
- Printing requests—Destroy when reference value ends
- Vehicle requests from employees—Two years

The policy includes an authorization for fairly immediate destruction of e-mail in certain circumstances. On page 8 of the policy, there are examples of e-mails that are short-term records, temporary in nature. These include e-mails from professional listservs or employee announcements. Such e-mails "have no significant value to an agency."

---

28. The guidelines can be viewed and downloaded from the Department of Cultural Resource's website at www.records.ncdcr.gov/erecords/Email_Policy.pdf.

29. These retention periods are taken from the *Municipal Records Retention and Disposition Schedule* issued by the Department of Cultural Resources on May 19, 2009, which can be viewed and downloaded at www.records.ncdcr.gov/local/municipal_2009.pdf.

Therefore, the user may delete such an e-mail when that user determines the e-mail's reference value has ended. In permitting this fairly immediate deletion of e-mail, the department is continuing to direct that e-mail be treated in the same way as a paper record with similar content. The department also has issued a more general set of guidelines, *Public Records with Short-Term Value*, which permits fairly immediate destruction of certain paper records as well.[30] This more general document is "intended to authorize the expeditious disposal of records possessing only brief administrative, fiscal, legal, research, or reference value, in order to enhance the efficient management of public records," and that is the apparent goal of the comparable authorization in the e-mail guidelines. But if the e-mail is of a more substantial nature, such that a paper record with the same content must be kept for some specified period, then the user must take steps to keep the e-mail for that same specified period. It should be stressed that the backup storage that is an integral part of managing an e-mail system does not substitute for appropriate retention under the applicable retention schedules. There are certain sorts of e-mails that must be kept for longer periods than even the longest period that backup storage is retained; furthermore, backup storage is rarely organized, and retained e-mail in a properly managed e-mail system will be archived in a way that facilitates access to the records, whether by the government or agency or by the public.

Public Access to Deleted E-Mail

As was noted above, when a user deletes an e-mail message from his or her inbox folder, the e-mail is transferred to the user's deleted items folder. If someone asks for a copy of the e-mail at that stage, is it still a public record, or has it now been disposed of? Neither the statute nor the guidelines give any sort of answer to this question, and no reported cases have been found that address it. It seems likely, though, that a court would conclude that such an e-mail is still in fact a public record and therefore subject to the rights of public access. It is simple for the user to recover such an e-mail, and as a practical matter users frequently do have occasion to go into their deleted items folder in order to do so. Given the ease with which such e-mails can be reached and the fact that users do access them from time to time, it makes sense to recognize that reality and consider them as still-existing records.

The situation might change, however, once the user has deleted a particular e-mail from the deleted items folder. The e-mail now has been purged from the system and is no longer easy for the employee to access. It may be possible for a short time, depending on the length of the backup cycle used in a particular government or agency, to recover the e-mail from a backup tape that was made before the final deletion was done, but it is unclear whether the deleted e-mail remains a public record when it exists solely on a backup tape. Certainly the backup tape itself meets the definition of a public record—it has been made in connection with the transaction of public business—but not all files on the tape are for that reason available to the public. Those that fit within various exceptions to public access certainly retain the exception, and those that are personal in nature would also not be available. It is also possible that a court would consider an e-mail message that has been appropriately deleted from the system, so that it is no longer a record within the system, no longer a

30. This document can be viewed and downloaded at www.records.ncdcr.gov/guidelines.htm#short.

public record on the backup tape either. That is, the record's presence on the backup tape should not change the status of the document.[31]

A recent Ohio case involved a different aspect of deleted e-mail. In *State ex rel. Toledo Blade Company v. Seneca County Board of Commissioners*,[32] the newspaper had made a public records request for a couple of years' worth of e-mails between county commissioners. The county's response made it clear, at least to the Ohio Supreme Court, that some of these e-mails had been deleted from the system in violation of the county's records retention requirements. After the newspaper presented an affidavit from a computer expert that at least some of the deleted e-mails could probably be recovered through a forensic analysis of the hard drives of computers used by the commissioners, the court ordered the county to undertake, at its own expense, the necessary analysis. The court emphasized that its holding only applied to e-mail (and presumably other sorts of electronic records) that had been unlawfully destroyed. There was no obligation to undertake the necessary analysis in order to recover e-mails that had been destroyed in conformity with the relevant retention schedule.

---

31. It should be noted, however, that Governor Purdue's Exec. Order No. 18, paragraph 8, *supra* note 17, concerning e-mail retention and archiving, requires that backup tapes be kept for ten years. The requirement seems based on the assumption that material on such tapes, even if it has been deleted, is a record open to public access.

32. 899 N.E.2d 961 (Ohio 2008).

Appendix 5A—Statute

G.S. 132-6.1

§ 132-6.1. Electronic data-processing records.

(a) After June 30, 1996, no public agency shall purchase, lease, create, or otherwise acquire any electronic data-processing system for the storage, manipulation, or retrieval of public records unless it first determines that the system will not impair or impede the agency's ability to permit the public inspection and examination, and to provide electronic copies of such records. Nothing in this subsection shall be construed to require the retention by the public agency of obsolete hardware or software.

(b) Every public agency shall create an index of computer databases compiled or created by a public agency on the following schedule:

State agencies by July 1, 1996;

Municipalities with populations of 10,000 or more, counties with populations of 25,000 or more, as determined by the 1990 U.S. Census, and public hospitals in those counties, by July 1, 1997;

Municipalities with populations of less than 10,000, counties with populations of less than 25,000, as determined by the 1990 U.S. Census, and public hospitals in those counties, by July 1, 1998;

Political subdivisions and their agencies that are not otherwise covered by this schedule, after June 30, 1998.

The index shall be a public record and shall include, at a minimum, the following information with respect to each database listed therein: a list of the data fields; a description of the format or record layout; information as to the frequency with which the database is updated; a list of any data fields to which public access is restricted; a description of each form in which the database can be copied or reproduced using the agency's computer facilities; and a schedule of fees for the production of copies in each available form. Electronic databases compiled or created prior to the date by which the index must be created in accordance with this subsection may be indexed at the public agency's option. The form, content, language, and guidelines for the index and the databases to be indexed shall be developed by the Office of Archives and History in consultation with officials at other public agencies.

(c) Nothing in this section shall require a public agency to create a computer database that the public agency has not otherwise created or is not otherwise required to be created. Nothing in this section requires a public agency to disclose security features of its electronic data processing systems, information technology systems, telecommunications networks, or electronic security systems, including hardware or software security, passwords, or security standards, procedures, processes, configurations, software, and codes.

(d) The following definitions apply in this section:

(1) Computer database.—A structured collection of data or documents residing in a database management program or spreadsheet software.

(2) Computer hardware.—Any tangible machine or device utilized for the electronic storage, manipulation, or retrieval of data.

(3) Computer program.—A series of instructions or statements that permit the storage, manipulation, and retrieval of data within an electronic data-processing system, together with any associated documentation. The term does not include the original data, or any analysis, compilation, or manipulated form of the original data produced by the use of the program or software.
(4) Computer software.—Any set or combination of computer programs. The term does not include the original data, or any analysis, compilation, or manipulated form of the original data produced by the use of the program or software.
(5) Electronic data-processing system.—Computer hardware, computer software, or computer programs or any combination thereof, regardless of kind or origin.

PART II—Specific Categories of Records Exempt from Public Access

Chapter 6—Records Not Open to the Public: General Principles

How Are Exceptions to the Right of Access Created?

A Legislative Responsibility

Chapter 1 noted that if an item meets the definition of "public record," the custodian must allow public inspection unless the custodian can point to some North Carolina (or federal) statute that permits or requires denial of public access. This statement makes the fundamental point that it is up to the legislature, not the judiciary or the executive, to decide what sorts of records will be closed to public access. The state supreme court emphasized the need for legislative action several times in its opinion in *News & Observer Publishing Co. v. Poole*,[1] still the fullest statement by the court on the state's public records law. For example, the defendants in the case argued that the minutes of the Poole Commission should not be subject to the public records law, because the commission was not subject to the open meetings law. The court rejected the argument, noting that "[w]e decline to create such a broad exception to the Public Records Act where the legislature has not elected to do so."[2] Later on the defendants argued that the court should recognize a "deliberative processes" exception to the right of public access, suggesting that in the absence of such an exception "knowledge by the agencies that public scrutiny may occur will chill free and frank decision-making."[3] The court admitted some weight to the argument but refused the invitation to recognize the exception because the General Assembly had not seen fit to create it.[4]

---

1. 330 N.C. 465, 412 S.E.2d 7 (1992).
2. *Id.* at 478, 412 S.E.2d at 15.
3. *Id.* at 481, 412 S.E.2d at 16.
4. "While we recognize this policy argument, we must yield to the decision of the General Assembly, which enacted several specific exceptions to the Public Records Act, none of which permanently protects a deliberative process like that of the Commission after the process has ceased." *Id.* at 481, 412 S.E.2d at 16.

Very occasionally, the state constitution can affect the public's right of access to records. In *News & Observer Publishing Co. v. Easley*, 182 N.C. App. 14, 641 S.E.2d 698 (2007), *review denied and review dismissed*, 361 N.C. 429, 648 S.E.2d 508 (2007), the court of appeals held that the state constitution's grant of power to the governor to grant clemency "subject to regulations prescribed by law" changed the usual

It should be noted that the various legislative exceptions that have been made are found throughout the North Carolina General Statutes [hereinafter G.S.], not just in G.S. Chapter 132, which is titled "Public Records." Indeed, although many important exceptions are in G.S. Chapter 132, the majority of the exceptions, including several of considerable importance, are elsewhere.

Evidentiary Privileges Do Not Create Exceptions to Public Access

At another point in the *Poole* litigation, the defendants sought to deny access to certain records because the records contained privileged attorney–client communications. The court refused the invitation to hold that material that was within this evidentiary privilege was therefore not subject to public access. Instead, the court noted that the General Assembly had enacted what is now G.S. 132-1.1(a), which denies public access for three years to certain communications from an attorney to a public body client, and it held that this statute—not the evidentiary privilege—determined what was public and what was not as far as attorney–client communications were concerned. Most of the other evidentiary privileges involve medical or mental health relationships, and the public records laws contain exceptions from public access that are probably at least coextensive with these other privileges. Therefore, as a practical matter, the holding in the *Poole* case is probably limited to records involving attorney–client communications.

Agency Promises of Confidentiality Do Not Create Exceptions

Occasionally a local government or other public agency will solicit information or documents from others and, in order to encourage a positive response, will promise that the information or documents will be held confidential. If, however, there is no statute that creates an exception to the right of public access with respect to the sort of information or document involved, such a promise is not enforceable against someone seeking the information or document as a public record. Local governments and other public agencies simply do not have the authority to create exceptions to the right of access in that way.[5]

Records That Might Be Both Open and Closed to the Public

Location Can Be Important

It may seem odd, but it is possible that a record that is confidential in one public office might be available to the public in another. Here are some examples:

- An individual's state income tax return in the hands of the Department of Revenue is closed to public access under G.S. 105-259, but if the taxpayer were to give a copy of the return to a local government in support of an application for a community development loan, that copy would be open to the public.

---

presumption that records were open. The court held that in the absence of such regulations, clemency-related records in the governor's office were not subject to the public records law.

5. *E.g.*, Kureczka v. Freedom of Info. Comm'n, 636 A.2d 777 (Conn. 1994); City of Newark v. Law Dep't, 760 N.Y.S.2d 431 (App. Div. 2003). *Contra* State *ex rel.* Newsome v. Alarid, 568 P.2d 1236 (N.M. 1977).

- The Department of Revenue certifies tax assessors and keeps records of their scores on examinations required for certification. No statute exempts the test scores from public access in the hands of the Department of Revenue, but if the department were to transmit the scores to a county, they would probably be part of the personnel files of the employees in question and therefore not open to public access.
- The Criminal Justice Education and Training Standards Commission certifies local police officers and occasionally has reason to issue letters of reprimand to them. These letters appear to be open to the public in the hands of the commission, but they would presumably be part of the officers' personnel files at the local government level.

The basic principle behind this sort of transfiguration was stated in the *Poole* decision. At the time of the decision, G.S. 114-15 provided that records and evidence compiled by the State Bureau of Investigation (SBI) were not to be considered public records under G.S. Chapter 132.[6] The SBI did a number of investigations on behalf of the Poole Commission, and the defendants in *Poole* argued that the resulting investigative reports were covered by G.S. 114-15. The supreme court disagreed and emphasized the importance of the location of a record to its availability to the public:

> Plaintiffs do not seek disclosure of investigative reports in the possession of the SBI. They seek disclosure of copies of such reports in the possession of the [Poole] Commission. The issue before us is whether these reports which have become Commission records continue to be exempt from the Public Records Act pursuant to section 114-15. We conclude that they do not.
>
> To extend the statutory exemption to SBI investigative reports which have been placed in the public domain is like unringing a bell—a practical impossibility. When such reports become part of the records of a public agency subject to the Public Records Act, they are protected only to the extent that agency's records are protected. When the SBI investigative reports here became Commission records, they, as Commission records, ceased to be protected by section 114-15. They became subject to disclosure under the Public Records Act to the same extent as other Commission records.[7]

Purpose Can Be Important

Occasionally the same record might be subject to an exception or not, depending on the purpose for which the record was created or by whom. A Texas case illustrates this possibility. The police department in *City of San Antonio v. San Antonio Express-News*[8] prepared a

---

6. That statute has been supplanted by N.C. Gen. Stat. [hereinafter G.S.] § 132-1.4.

7. 330 N.C. at 474, 412 S.E.2d at 12–13. An example of such a situation from another state is found in *Kyle v. Perrilloux*, 868 So. 2d 27 (La. Ct. App. 2003), in which a district attorney had obtained work papers of the legislative auditor as part of an investigation. When the investigation ended, the district attorney's files became public, including the work papers from the auditor, even though those same work papers were confidential in the hands of the auditor himself.

8. 47 S.W.3d 556 (Tex. App. 2000).

"use-of-force" report whenever an officer used force in making an arrest. The department used these reports to track trends in the use of force by the city's police department but not to evaluate individual officers. The court therefore held that the reports were not part of the officers' personnel files and not exempt from disclosure. On the other hand, if a department used such reports in evaluating and disciplining officers, it is likely the court would hold them to be part of the officers' personnel files and therefore not subject to disclosure. Similarly, if a law enforcement agency placed and maintained a video camera in a public office building, the primary purpose might be criminal intelligence, and the tapes would be subject to G.S. 132-1.4, which declares that records of criminal intelligence information made by law enforcement agencies are not public records. But if the same camera were placed and maintained by a department in charge of building maintenance rather than a law enforcement agency, the tapes would not be exempt from disclosure under G.S. 132-1.4.

Public Records Used in Creating a Confidential File

In creating a confidential file, a public officer or employee might include in the file documents that are public records in their original location. For example, a law enforcement agency might collect copies of various sorts of public records as part of an investigation. In the hands of the law enforcement agency, those copies would be part of a criminal investigation file and therefore not open to the public. But that confidential status would not apply to the documents in their original location. G.S. 132-1.4(f) states explicitly that "use of a public record in connection with a criminal investigation or the gathering of criminal intelligence shall not affect its status as a public record," but the statutory statement is almost certainly a statement of the law in any event.[9] There is no comparable provision in any of the personnel privacy statutes, but if a human resources department were to use public records as part of an internal investigation of an employee, that use should not change the character of those records in their original location. They would remain open to the public even if the copies used in the internal investigation were appropriately part of the employee's personnel file.

The last sentence makes a related point. Simply because the original record is open to the public does not change the character of the record in the confidential file. If a copy of a public record has been collected as part of a police investigation, it is as much a part of the criminal investigation file as any other document. If a copy of a public record has been collected as part of an internal employee investigation, it is as much a part of the personnel file as any other document. Similarly, if a police officer takes a set of public records, analyzes them, and produces a report as part of an investigation, that report is part of the criminal investigation file even though it was created in reliance on public records, and even though someone else could analyze the same records and produce a comparable report.

---

9. *See, e.g.*, Worcester Telegram & Gazette Corp. v. Chief of Police, 787 N.E.2d 602 (Mass. App. Ct. 2003). The police department had used police reports, incident reports, arrest logs, a commercial phone book listing, and a computer printout from an Internet website in conducting an internal affairs investigation. The court noted that these were all public documents, created for reasons other than the internal affairs investigation, and held that they could not become confidential simply because they were used in the investigation.

Two Types of Exceptions to the Right of Access

The Basic Distinction

In enacting exceptions to the right of access, the General Assembly has done so in two fundamentally different ways. The first, which we'll call Category 1, is simply to provide that there is no right of public access to a particular category of record. Such a removal of the public's right, however, does not automatically prohibit the government from deciding to release the record anyway, particularly if the custodian or the agency has a reasonable basis for doing so. The second legislative approach, which we'll call Category 2, is to prohibit the custodian from releasing the record except in specified circumstances. In some instances, the statutes even make unauthorized release a crime. Prominent examples of each of these two basic approaches to creating exceptions to the right of access are shown in tables 1 and 2.[10]

Possible Liability for Release of Category 1 Records—Rare

There may sometimes be occasions when a public agency wishes to release to the public a record that is excepted from the right of public access through a Category 1 exception. A common example occurs when a law enforcement agency releases information from an ongoing criminal investigation in hopes that doing so will help solve the crime. For instance, the agency might release video tapes that show a suspect or a photograph of someone sought for questioning. For the most part, a public agency is free to so release records in its own discretion, without concern for any liability for having done so. A trio of appellate cases from elsewhere, though, demonstrate that very occasionally there might be a risk of liability.

The first case arose from a 1985 incident in which two bombs exploded in Salt Lake City, killing two people, including the wife of a man named Sheets. As part of their investigation, the city police requested and received from Sheets his wife's diary. Sheets provided the diary under the belief that it would be kept confidential, and there was evidence that Sheets received assurance to that effect from at least one police officer. One of the investigators copied extracts from the diary for his own investigative file and included in the file thorough notes about the diary. Once the investigation was completed and convictions were obtained, that investigator allowed an author writing a book on the bombings to look through the case file. The resulting book included quotations from the diary. Thereupon Sheets brought an action in federal court, claiming an invasion of his constitutional right to privacy, and in *Sheets v. Salt Lake County*[11] the federal court of appeals upheld a jury verdict in Sheets's favor. The court found that Sheets had a legitimate expectation of privacy in the diary entries, he had not waived that expectation by cooperating with the police, and therefore the release of the diaries violated his constitutional rights.

The second case arose from Florida, where some police officers showed to friends a videotape and photographs made at an autopsy. Neither the tape nor the photographs were open to public access, but neither were the custodians under any statutory duty to maintain the confidentiality of the records. Nevertheless, when survivors of the deceased brought suit for

10. Each of the categories of records listed is discussed in detail in later chapters.
11. 45 F.3d 1383 (10th Cir. 1995).

Table 1. Category 1: Exceptions That Deny Public Access but Do Not Prohibit Release

Confidential legal communications	G.S. 132-1.1(a)
Public enterprise billing information	G.S. 132-1.1(c)
Criminal investigation and criminal intelligence information	G.S. 132-1.4
Emergency response plans	G.S. 132-1.6
Sensitive public security information	G. S. 132-1.7
Trial preparation material	G.S. 132-1.9
Economic development records	G.S. 132-6(d)
Minutes or general accounts of closed sessions	G.S. 143-318.10(e)
Informal bids	G. S. 143-131

intentional infliction of emotional damage, the Florida appellate court allowed the suit to go forward, noting that the public records laws do not "give license to individuals . . . to do whatever they please with public records with immunity from all the safeguards for individual rights which the common law has painstakingly developed over the centuries."[12]

The final case arose in Oklahoma,[13] where a woman was allegedly raped while unconscious and the rape was videotaped. The victim obtained a copy of the video and took it to her local police department. The detective to whom she gave the tape eventually turned it over to a local television reporter, and the reporter's station ultimately played the tape on the evening news (taking care to obscure the victim's identity). The woman brought suit against the detective, seeking damages for invasion of privacy, and the trial court denied the detective's motion to dismiss. The federal court of appeals affirmed the trial court's decision, noting that the detective would have an opportunity at trial to prove that there was a law enforcement purpose in releasing the tape to the reporter. If the detective proved unsuccessful, the plaintiff would be entitled to damages.

These cases illustrate the need to think carefully before releasing records that are not automatically open to public access, at least if the records contain information that most people would consider private or confidential.

Possible Liability for Release of Category 2 Records—from Rare to Likely

As noted above, a few of the Category 2 exceptions to the right of public access make it a crime to release the records in violation of the statute. Examples of such statutes are most of the personnel privacy statutes,[14] statutes prohibiting access to certain local tax records,[15] and statutes prohibiting release of public assistance records.[16] Most of the Category 2

12. Williams v. City of Minneola, 575 So. 2d 683, 687 (Fla. Dist. Ct. App. 1991).

13. Anderson v. Blake, 469 F.3d 910 (10th Cir. 2006).

14. G.S. 160A-168(e), for example, makes it a misdemeanor to "knowingly, willfully, and with malice permit[] any person to have access" to information in a protected personnel file.

15. G.S. 160A-208.1 and 153A-148.1 each make it a misdemeanor to release tax records protected by those sections.

16. G.S. 108A-80 prohibits release of "information concerning persons applying for or receiving public assistance or social services" and makes violation of the section a misdemeanor.

Table 2. Category 2: Exceptions That Prohibit Release of the Record to the General Public

Local tax records showing income or gross receipts	G.S. 132-1.1(b)
Trade secrets	G.S. 132-1.2(1)
Electronic payment account numbers	G.S. 132-1.2(2)
Social Security numbers and personal identifying information	G.S. 132-1.10
Personnel files	Various statutes
Medical and patient information	Various statutes

statutes, however, do not carry criminal penalties or, for that matter, any other penalties.[17] They provide no enforcement provisions at all. The question that then arises, and that is considered here, is whether there is any possibility of civil liability to the subject of a protected record or to the owner of information included in the record, if a record is released despite a statute prohibiting release. There can be no certain answer in North Carolina for most such records, but, except for trade secrets and medical records, the likelihood of such liability is not great.

Trade Secrets

One effect of the statute that excepts trade secrets from the right of public access appears to be to subject governments that hold private trade secrets to the Trade Secrets Protection Act, an act that provides a civil action in favor of the owners of trade secrets against persons or entities that misappropriate those secrets under the terms of the statute. If a local government releases a trade secret, in violation of G.S. 132-1.2(1), it may well be liable for doing so under G.S. 66-154. This possibility is discussed at greater length *infra* in chapter 11, "Trade Secrets," and the reader is referred to that discussion.[18]

Medical Records

The release of protected medical information might also lead to liability under state law or, possibly, federal law. A significant number of cases "hold that a healthcare provider is or may be liable for improper disclosure of medical information, that is, disclosure to which the patient objects."[19] Nationally, these cases base liability on a variety of grounds—invasion of privacy, breach of a professional duty to maintain confidentiality, defamation, or breach of contract.[20] The one North Carolina case in this line of cases asserts that improper release

17. A few of these statutes carry other sorts of remedies or consequences of violation. G.S. 114-19.3 permits the state Department of Justice to provide criminal records checks about prospective employees to public hospitals and directs that the information is to remain confidential. The statute provides that violation of confidentiality may cause a recipient hospital to lose its right to receive such information in the future. And G.S. 133-33, which permits public agencies to keep confidential certain contract bid information, provides that an employee who violates an agency's confidentiality rules is subject to discipline, although that seems an unnecessary provision.

18. The discussion is found in the last section of that chapter, "Release of Trade Secrets."

19. Anne M. Dellinger, *Medical Records, in* HEALTHCARE FACILITIES LAW § 8.12 (Anne M. Dellinger ed., 1991).

20. *Id.*

of medical information is a sort of medical malpractice.[21] None of these cases appear to distinguish between private and public health care providers, and so they might be extended as easily to a public hospital or health department as to a private hospital or physician. Therefore, if a case arose in North Carolina, the clear statutory policy of confidentiality of patient records held by public health care facilities would probably suggest strongly that any right of action that is recognized should apply as much to public facilities and providers as to private ones. It is not so much, however, that the various medical records statutes create some sort of cause of action themselves but that they create a condition in which an existing cause of action might be used against public agencies.

There is also a small chance of liability for monetary penalties imposed for violation of the federal Health Insurance Portability and Accountability Act of 1996 (HIPAA), which creates a federal right of privacy in "individually identifiable health information." The statute authorizes the federal secretary of health and human services to impose civil penalties for violations of the privacy regulations promulgated under HIPAA,[22] although the regulations make it clear that the federal government will first attempt to work with a health care provider to achieve compliance with the HIPAA regulations.[23]

Other Statutes

None of the other statutes that prohibit release of records specifically state that a subject of a record may bring a civil action for improper release. Can such a right of action, however, be implied from these statutes? There is one North Carolina case that deals with the issue and answers no, but its treatment of the issue is quite cursory. In *Houpe v. City of Statesville*,[24] the plaintiff police officer had been dismissed by the city following an internal affairs investigation. In response he brought suit, alleging a variety of constitutional and statutory violations. One of his allegations was that two police officials had improperly publicized information from the investigation, and he sought damages for that alleged violation of the personnel privacy statute. The court of appeals addressed this issue in a single paragraph in its opinion and held that, because the statute included only criminal remedies and made no mention of a civil cause of action, no action for damages could be brought under the statute.

Most of the Category 2 exceptions, of course, do not carry criminal penalties, and so the rationale of *Houpe* is not directly applicable. There are a good number of cases nationally, however, that examine generally whether, and under what circumstances, a private right of action for damages may be implied from a statute prohibiting certain conduct or establishing standards of conduct. Since the mid-1970s those decisions have generally followed the lead of the United States Supreme Court in *Cort v. Ash.*[25]

---

21. Watts v. Cumberland County Hosp. Sys., Inc., 75 N.C. App. 1, 330 S.E.2d 242 (1985), *reversed in part on other grounds*, 317 N.C. 321, 345 S.E.2d 201 (1986).

22. 42 U.S.C. § 1320d-5 (2000).

23. 45 C.F.R. §§ 160.400–.426 (2007).

24. 128 N.C. App. 334, 497 S.E.2d 82 (1998).

25. 422 U.S. 66 (1975). There is some uncertainty about the continued validity, in the federal system, of the four-part *Cort* test. A footnote in a recent Kentucky case analyzing a federal statute summarized the issue in this way: "There is some confusion regarding the weight that is to be given to each of the *Cort* factors. Specifically, the United States Supreme Court has reaffirmed its adherence to these factors in dicta,

In *Cort* corporate directors had allegedly authorized use of corporate funds to finance political advertisements, in violation of a federal criminal statute. A shareholder brought an action for damages against the directors, and the question before the court was whether a private cause of action for damages was to be implied from the federal statute. In deciding there was no implicit cause of action under the statute, the Court set out four factors to be considered in deciding such a question:

1. "[I]s the plaintiff one of the class for whose especial benefit the statute was enacted . . .?"[26]
2. "[I]s there any indication of legislative intent, explicit or implicit, either to create such a remedy or to deny one?"[27]
3. Is such a remedy "consistent with the underlying purposes of the legislative scheme"?[28]
4. "[I]s the cause of action one traditionally relegated to state law, in an area [that is] basically the concern of the States . . . ?"[29]

The fourth factor is obviously of little concern to a state court addressing a state statute, but the other three factors have been cited repeatedly by state courts as the factors that do govern their consideration of whether a private cause of action should be implied from a statute.[30] It seems probable, therefore, that the North Carolina appellate courts might also look to the *Cort* factors if presented with a case that is not controlled by *Houpe.*

---

despite two post-*Cort* decisions which elevate the second factor, labeling it 'determinative,' while utilizing the other three factors simply as an aid for deciding the second factor. This inconsistency is pointed out in the concurring opinion" in *Thompson v. Thompson*, 484 U.S. 174, 188–91 (1988) (Scalia, J., concurring). T&M Jewelry, Inc. v. Hicks *ex rel.* Hicks, 189 S.W.3d 526, 529 n.4 (Ky. 2006). A good explanation of developments since *Cort* can also be found in *Wisniewski v. Rodale, Inc.*, 510 F.3d 294 (3d Cir. 2007).

Some recent state cases have applied the *Cort* factors without referencing the subsequent U.S. Supreme Court cases casting doubt on the four-factor test. *See, e.g.*, Schappell v. Motorists Mut. Ins. Co., 934 A.2d 1184 (Pa. 2007) (applying the *Cort* factors and not mentioning post-*Cort* U.S. Supreme Court cases); Machan v. UNUM Life Ins. Co. of Am., 116 P.3d 342 (Utah 2005) (listing *Cort* factors as providing guidance but noting that it is not required to apply *Cort* factors like a federal court would; not mentioning post-*Cort* U.S. Supreme Court cases). Some others apply the *Cort* factors but recognize that they are not equally weighted. *See, e.g.*, Provencher v. Town of Enfield, 936 A.2d 625 (Conn. 2007) (applying the *Cort* factors but citing a subsequent Supreme Court decision (*Touche Ross & Co. v. Redington*, 442 U.S. 560, 576 (1979)) in its explanation that all three factors may not be weighted equally and that the ultimate question is whether the evidence shows that the legislature intended to authorize the private cause of action; also explaining that all factors must be satisfied and the strength of evidence on one factor may influence the outcome as to other factors); Whitey's Boat Cruises, Inc. v. Napali-Kauai Boat Charters, Inc., 132 P.3d 1213, 1224 n.20 (Haw. 2006) (explaining that it would "apply *Cort's* first three factors in determining whether a statute provides a private right of action though understanding that legislative intent appears to be the determining factor").

26. *Cort* at 78 (internal quotation marks omitted).

27. *Id.*

28. *Id.*

29. *Id.*

30. *E.g.*, Cloverleaf Kennel Club, Inc. v. Colo. Racing Comm'n, 620 P.2d 1051 (Colo. 1980); Sawyer Realty Group, Inc. v. Jarvis Corp., 432 N.E.2d 849 (Ill. 1982); Seeman v. Liberty Mut. Ins. Co., 322 N.W.2d 35 (Iowa 1982).

Just as it is striking how consistently the state courts cite and apply the *Cort* factors, so too is it striking how seldom they conclude that a private right of action should be implied from a statute. While the courts frequently acknowledge that a prospective plaintiff is one of the class protected by a statute,[31] they very often determine that allowing a private right of action is not consistent with the legislative scheme set out in the statute. The remedies in the statute itself might be found to be exclusive,[32] or the legislation might obviously be part of a delicate balance of competing interests that would be thrown out of balance by implying a private remedy for damages,[33] or existing common law remedies might be thought sufficient.[34]

The leading case that applies the *Cort* factors to an attempt to bring suit under a public records statute is *Marcus v. Young*,[35] which involved a physician who had been hired to be an expert witness in a lawsuit in a North Carolina federal court. The attorney for the opposing party subpoenaed the medical school the physician had attended, the University of Iowa, for his student records, and the medical school complied with the subpoena. The records apparently were not favorable to the physician, and he was terminated as an expert witness, getting no fee. He thereupon brought an action against the medical school, claiming that the release of the records violated the state public records statute and that a private cause of action should be implied from the statute to remedy such violation. The Iowa Supreme Court ruled that no cause of action would be implied. It is noteworthy that the court argued that such an action would be inconsistent with the general purpose of public records statutes, which is to open government records to the public. If a custodian faced the possibility of damages for wrongly releasing records, he or she would have an incentive to close rather than open records. As the court noted, "[I]t would be counterproductive to allow a private cause of action based on mistaken or negligent dissemination of confidential information. To do so would not encourage disclosure but would hinder it and counteract the primary purpose for which the [public records] statute was passed."[36]

Given the general reluctance of courts to imply a cause of action from a statute that does not itself create one, and the force of the Iowa court's reasoning in *Marcus v. Young*,

---

31. But not always. For example, in *Rayford v. City of Detroit*, 347 N.W.2d 210 (Mich. Ct. App. 1984), police officers who were the victims of a municipal downsizing brought an action for reinstatement, claiming that the applicable local government budget statute had been violated and that the statute gave them a cause of action for reinstatement. The court held that the purpose of the statute was to promote uniform budgeting and avoid deficits and that public employees were not a special class protected by the statute.

32. *E.g.*, Seeman v. Liberty Mut. Ins. Co., 322 N.W.2d 35 (Iowa 1982) (state insurance commissioner sole enforcer of statute proscribing unfair trade practices by insurance company).

33. *E.g.*, Burns Jackson Miller Summit & Spitzer v. Lindner, 451 N.E.2d 459 (N.Y. 1983) (no private cause of action for damages resulting to inconvenienced citizens from strike by public transit workers under statute prohibiting strikes by public employees).

34. *E.g.*, Rhodes v. Mill Race Inn, Inc., 467 N.E.2d 915 (Ill. App. Ct. 1984) (general law of negligence adequate for plaintiff injured by putting her arm through a glass door to a restaurant, when the glass had been installed allegedly in violation of a statute governing use of safety glazing materials).

35. 538 N.W.2d 285 (Iowa 1995).

36. *Id.* at 290. Two other cases that reach the same conclusion as *Marcus* are *Pane v. City of Danbury*, 841 A.2d 684 (Conn. 2004), and *Ferraro v. City of Long Branch*, 714 A.2d 945 (N.J. Super. Ct. App. Div. 1998).

it seems likely that the North Carolina courts would extend the holding in *Houpe* to those Category 2 statutes that do not include criminal penalties, as well as to those that do.

Actions under Section 1983

The 2002 case of *Toomer v. Garrett*[37] illustrates another approach that was successful for one plaintiff. He alleged that officials of the North Carolina Department of Transportation had improperly released information in his personnel file, including his Social Security number, medical diagnoses, and personal financial information, as well as data about his family members. Accepting these allegations as true, the court held that if proven, they would constitute a violation of the plaintiff's substantive due process rights, thereby permitting an action under 42 U.S.C. § 1983. The court also held that the allegations would support an action for common law tortious invasion of privacy. The specific allegations of this case are unusual and narrow, and so the court's holding is not likely to extend to most other prohibited releases of information from Category 2 records—even other releases of personnel file information. In *Pennyfeather v. Tessler*[38] the plaintiff brought an action complaining about the release from his personnel file of his name, address, work schedule, and Social Security number. The court held that the case was not an appropriate one for a Section 1983 suit based on an unconstitutional invasion of privacy, because the information released was not highly personal, was related to the plaintiff's employment, and was released at a personnel hearing.

Access to Excepted Records—Some General Points

Waiver of Confidentiality by Partial Release

Occasionally litigants argue that an agency has revealed in some fashion a record that is by statute not open to public access and that by doing so the agency has waived the statutory protection against public access. A number of courts have recognized the validity of such an argument but relatively few have found such a waiver to have occurred. For example, if the agency has shared a record with some other agency or otherwise used the record in a fashion that is appropriate for the record, the courts have refused to find a waiver of confidentiality.[39] Similarly, if release of the record was involuntary—for example, if it was pursuant to a contested court order—the courts have refused to find a waiver.[40] There have been, though, two sorts of situations in which waiver has been found. First, if the agency

37. 155 N.C. App. 462, 574 S.E.2d 76 (2002).

38. 431 F.3d 54 (2d Cir. 2005).

39. *E.g.*, Rackauckas v. Superior Court, 128 Cal. Rptr. 2d 234 (Ct. App. 2002) (copy of record provided to relevant agency with admonitions of confidentiality; decision based on statute providing for no waiver in disclosures to other agencies who agree to keep information confidential); State *ex rel.* Cincinnati Enquirer v. Sharp, 785 N.E.2d 822 (Ohio Ct. App. 2003) (port authority had received proprietary business information from industrial prospect and shared it with county officials but made clear efforts to maintain confidentiality). *See also* Simmons v. U.S. Dep't of Justice, 796 F.2d 709 (4th Cir. 1986) (unauthorized release by employee not a waiver).

40. *E.g.*, Florida House of Representatives v. U.S. Dep't of Commerce, 961 F.2d 941 (11th Cir. 1992) (contested court order not a waiver, nor is responding to subpoena from Congressional committee).

released the record to some member or members of the public, courts have found a waiver vis-à-vis other members of the public.[41] Second, if the agency allowed the record to be submitted into evidence at a trial or discovered in litigation, and if it did so without any effort at protecting the confidentiality of the record, courts have found a waiver.[42]

Access by Governing Board Members

If a category of record is not open to the public, what right of access to that sort of record does a member of a local government's governing board, or the governing board collectively, have? There can be no single answer to that question; rather, the answer depends on which category of records one is considering. For some sorts of records that are not open to the public, it is the governing board itself that decides who may have access to the record. For others, the records custodian might be able to share the record with the governing board or its individual members to a greater extent than he or she might be able to share it with the public generally. And for still others, members of a local government's governing board have no greater right of access than do members of the public. Here are examples of each of these possibilities.

The Governing Board Controls Access

The strongest examples of records that are controlled by the governing board are the minutes and general accounts of closed sessions.[43] These records uniquely belong to the governing board, and it is the board's responsibility to decide whether and when to make them available to the public or to establish a mechanism for doing so. Another good example is communications to the board from its attorney about litigation;[44] as the principal representative of the client, the board is the appropriate entity to decide on release of the records. And there are still other sorts of records for which it is most sensible for the governing board to make any rules about releasing them to the public—for example, records that include customer billing information,[45] public security plans,[46] and plans of public buildings and infrastructure.[47]

The Governing Board Has Special Rights of Access

Personnel file information is a good example of this category of records.[48] In a mayor–council city or town, the governing board is the statutory supervisor of all employees and as

---

41. *E.g.*, North Dakota *ex rel.* Olson v. Andrus, 581 F.2d 177 (8th Cir. 1978) (voluntary release to organization precluded government from claiming exemption from disclosure in response to request from state); State *ex rel.* Gannett Satellite Info. Network, Inc. v. Petro, 685 N.E.2d 1223 (Ohio 1997) (state auditor made report public until ordered to stop doing so by court; when court order terminated, initial release precluded auditor from claiming exemption from access).

42. *E.g.*, State *ex rel.* Zuern v. Leis, 564 N.E.2d 81 (Ohio 1990) (when investigative report was voluntarily disclosed in discovery during civil trial with no effort to protect confidentiality, sheriff's department was held to have waived any exemption the report might have had against public access).

43. See *infra* chapter 18 for a general discussion of these records.

44. See *infra* chapter 9 for a general discussion of these records.

45. These records are discussed *infra* in chapter 16.

46. These records are discussed *infra* in chapter 20.

47. These records are discussed *infra* in chapter 20.

48. See *infra* chapter 7 for a general discussion of these records.

such is entitled to full access to all personnel files; similarly, school board members enjoy a statutory entitlement to examine all school personnel files. Furthermore, even in manager-system cities and counties, the statutes permit the custodian to allow examination of the personnel files by other government officials in certain situations. A further example of this type of record is trade secret information.[49] If the information was given to the local government as part of a procurement process, for instance, the governing board might need to examine the information in order to make the final procurement decision.

The Governing Board Has No More Rights Than Other Citizens

There are many types of records whose general release is prohibited, with very specific limitations on who may be allowed to inspect the records. Unless the governing board or its individual members fit within the specific limitations, neither the board nor the members have a greater right than any other citizen to access to such records. For example, the statutes dealing with those local tax records that contain income or gross receipts information narrowly limit who may see the records, and governing boards don't fit within the limitations.[50] Similarly, it is difficult to see how it could be appropriate for a county board of commissioners to review patient information from health department records[51] or for any governing board to see Social Security numbers or other personal identifying information that might be in county or city records.[52]

Access by Former Employees or Officials

Just because a person was involved in the creation or maintenance of a record while a public officer or employee does not entitle that person to access to the record once he or she leaves public office or employment. For example, a person may have been on a city council and participated in one or more closed sessions or even prepared the minutes or general account of such a session. Once he or she leaves the council, though, the former member has no greater right of access to the sealed minutes or account than any other member of the public.

Access by Court Order

A number of North Carolina public records statutes that create exceptions to the right of access permit different treatment of a particular record "by order of a court of competent jurisdiction" or comparable language. Here are some prominent examples:

1. Most of the personnel privacy statutes [for example, G.S. 160A-168(c)(4)] permit access to the closed portion of an employee's personnel file "by order of a court of competent jurisdiction."
2. The criminal investigation statute [G.S. 132-1.4(e)] permits a law enforcement agency official who believes that release of a record will jeopardize the

---

49. See *infra* chapter 11 for a general discussion of these records.
50. These records are discussed *infra* in chapter 13.
51. These records are discussed *infra* in chapter 14.
52. These records are discussed *infra* in chapter 15.

prosecution or defense of a criminal trial or investigation to seek "from a court of competent jurisdiction" an order preventing its disclosure.

3. The criminal investigation statute [G.S. 132-1.4(k)] also permits withholding from public access arrest and search warrants, indictments, criminal summonses, and nontestimonial identification orders "when sealed by court order."
4. The statutes denying public access to certain local tax records [for example, G.S. 160A-208.1(a)(1)] permit disclosure "to comply with a court order."

What Is a "Court Order"?

Normally it is not difficult to determine whether a court has issued an order directing that a particular record be made available, either to a specific party or, less likely, to the public at large. One recurring issue, however, is whether a subpoena is a court order within the meaning of these statutes. The better answer is that, in most instances, it is not.

The probable policies underlying allowing release of an otherwise confidential record by court order are (1) to allow a judge to balance the pros and cons of such a release and (2) to permit imposition, through the order, of limitations on the use and further release of the record by the person to whom the record is released. Neither of these policies is realized if a subpoena is treated as a court order. A subpoena may be issued by an attorney for a party to a lawsuit without any need for judicial review or approval of the subpoena.[53] To be sure, when a party to a lawsuit, rather than his or her attorney, issues a subpoena, Rule 45 of the North Carolina Rules of Civil Procedure directs that it be signed by the clerk of court, but even then it is issued in blank form, with no review of the propriety of the subpoena by the clerk.[54] And if a party or his or her attorney receives documents in response to a subpoena, there are no inherent limitations on what that person may do with the documents so received. For these reasons it is unlikely that a court would consider a standard subpoena to qualify as a court order under these statutes. This conclusion is supported by the provisions of two of the personnel privacy statutes—those dealing with public school employees, and those dealing with community college employees.[55] Each of the statutes permits access to an employee's personnel file "by authority of a subpoena or proper court order."[56] If a subpoena were a court order, its listing in the statutes would have been unnecessary.

With the exception of subpoenas issued by federal grand juries, which are dealt with below, there is surprisingly little case law anywhere on this specific issue, but what little there is reinforces the argument made above. The reported appellate case that is most directly relevant is *Stiles v. Atlanta Gas Light Co.*,[57] decided by a federal district court in Georgia. The defendant had issued a subpoena for documents held by the federal Department of Labor, which moved to quash the subpoena on the ground that the federal Privacy Act required a court order before it could release the documents in question. When the

---

53. G.S. 1A-1, N.C.R. Civ. P. 45(a)(4).

54. *Id.*

55. The public school statute is found at G.S. 115C-319 through -321, and the community college statute is found at G.S. 115D-27 through -30.

56. G.S. 115C-321(a)(4) and 115D-29(a)(4).

57. 453 F. Supp. 798 (N.D. Ga. 1978).

defendant argued that a subpoena was a court order, the court disagreed, writing that the Privacy Act's requirement of a court order

> provides for those cases in which, for compelling reasons, the court *specifically* directs that a record be disclosed. Mere issuance in discovery proceedings of a subpoena—which is always subject to the power of the court to quash or limit—does not meet this standard. To so hold would permit precisely the type of privacy invasions the [Privacy] Act sought to prevent.[58]

Also relevant is *Fremont Energy Corp. v. Seattle Post Intelligencer*,[59] decided by the Ninth Circuit Court of Appeals. The plaintiff in the underlying action had subpoenaed a former congressman for documents generated while he was in Congress. When the congressman refused to produce the documents, the federal district court held him in contempt, and he appealed. In beginning its analysis, the court of appeals noted that "because Moss was in violation of no court order, if he is in contempt, it is for failure to comply with the demands of the subpoena duces tecum."[60] That is, the court believed it was clear that a subpoena was not a court order.[61]

The rule might be different for subpoenas issued by federal grand juries. As noted above, there have been a number of cases involving whether such subpoenas were sufficient to require production of state or local government records that were confidential and could be released only pursuant to court order. The cases go both ways, but the majority hold that such a subpoena is sufficient. Some of the cases in the majority base their decision on the Supremacy Clause of the U.S. Constitution,[62] while others hold that a grand jury subpoena is in fact a court order.[63] With either rationale the reasoning appears limited to subpoenas issued by federal grand juries and would not extend to those issued by parties in federal litigation, unless the subpoena was expressly approved by a federal judge or magistrate.

When a local government receives a subpoena for records that are not open to the public absent a court order, it must respond in some fashion; the subpoena cannot simply be ignored. Some local government attorneys telephone the attorney who issued the subpoena and point out the statutory need for a court order, hoping that the attorney will withdraw the subpoena. If he or she is unwilling to do so, however, the local government has two choices. First, it might serve written objections to the subpoena on the party or attorney issuing it. Once such objections have been made, the appropriate Rule of Civil Procedure requires a court order to override them.[64] Second, the local government might apply to the trial court for an order to quash the subpoena. If that route is chosen, a common practice

---

58. *Id.* at 800 (citation omitted, emphasis in original).

59. 688 F.2d 1285 (9th Cir. 1982).

60. *Id.* at 1286.

61. *See also* Baker v. Quick Stop Oil Change & Tune-Up, 580 N.E.2d 528 (Ohio Ct. Com. Pl. 1990) (subpoena issued by notary public, which is permitted by Ohio law, is not court order sufficient to allow release of privileged medical records). *But cf.* Moore v. U. S. Postal Serv., 609 F. Supp. 681 (E.D.N.Y. 1985) (subpoena approved by state-court judge that included words "so ordered" is a court order).

62. *E.g., In re* Grand Jury Subpoena, 198 F. Supp. 2d 1113 (D. Alaska 2002).

63. *E.g., In re* TRW, Inc., 460 F. Supp. 1007 (E.D. Mich. 1978). *Contra In re* Grand Jury Subpoena, 118 F.R.D. 558 (D. Vt. 1987).

64. G.S. 1A-1, N.C.R. Civ. P. 45(c)(3), (4).

is to make copies of the subpoenaed records and take them to court at the time the motion to quash is argued. That will permit the judge to examine the records *in camera* and permit immediate release of the records should the court enter an order to that effect.

Obtaining a Court Order

What procedure should someone follow in order to obtain a court order to examine nonpublic records when the statute provides for one? If the records are sought for ongoing litigation, it would be appropriate to make a motion in the cause for an order calling for production of the relevant records. What, though, if there is no ongoing litigation? The case of *In re Investigation into Injury of Brooks* suggests a method.[65]

In *Brooks,* two Hillsborough police officers were accused of injuring a citizen named Brooks, leading to a town investigation into the charges. The results of the investigation were placed in the officers' personnel files. The local district attorney was also investigating the matter and wished to look at the reports. To do so, he filed an *ex parte* petition with the local superior court seeking release of the personnel files. The petitions contained limited factual allegations about the alleged assault and a statement by the district attorney that the files were "necessary to a full and complete investigation into the injury of Swantee Brooks, and would be in the best interest of the administration of justice." Although the district attorney signed the petitions, they were not supported by any affidavits and did not reference any legal authority permitting the district attorney to seek release of the files. Although the procedural history of the case was a bit fitful, ultimately the trial court issued an order releasing the files to the State Bureau of Investigation, subject to certain limitations to maintain the maximum amount of confidentiality possible. The trial court did not, at this stage, assign a case number to the proceeding.

On appeal from the two officers, the Court of Appeals first held that the superior court had jurisdiction to enter the orders directing release of the personnel files. The court noted that the statute (G.S. 160A-168) permitted release of material in a personnel file by order of a court of competent jurisdiction. The court held that the statutory language, in and of itself, was sufficient to confer jurisdiction on the court to issue such orders. Although the statute does not include any procedures for such a proceeding, the court thought that such procedural provisions were unnecessary. It held, rather, that the matter is a special proceeding as recognized in G.S. 1-1 and 1-3 and is therefore governed by the rules pertinent to such proceedings, as set out in G.S. Chapter 1, Article 33.

Nevertheless, the court disapproved of the procedures followed in the case before it. Relying on the Supreme Court's decision in *In re Superior Court Order,*[66] the court held that "at a minimum," an *ex parte* petition of the sort presented by the district attorney must include or be accompanied by

- "affidavit(s) or similar evidence, including specific factual allegations detailing reasons justifying disclosure;" and
- reference to the "statutory grounds which allow disclosure."

---

65. 143 N.C. App. 601, 548 S.E.2d 748 (2001).
66. 315 N.C. 378, 338 S.E.2d 307 (1986).

Once the petition has been presented, the court should

- docket the petition and orders according to its rules for docketing special proceedings;
- make an independent determination that, in this particular sort of case, "the interests of justice require disclosure of the confidential" material; and
- qualify its order so that the disclosure is the smallest possible to serve the goals of justice.[67]

The *Brooks* decision should provide guidance to public agencies and officers and to trial courts when court orders are sought pursuant to provisions of other public records statutes, such as those noted at the beginning of this section.

Intervention or Suit by the Subject or Owner of a Record

This section discusses whether the subject of a record, who alleges that the record is closed to public access, or a party that has a proprietary interest in such a record has the right to bring an independent lawsuit seeking to enjoin release of the record or has the right to intervene in a lawsuit that has been brought against a record custodian by a party seeking access to the record. While a number of the statutory exceptions to public access under the public records law principally protect the custodial government's own interests,[68] most of the statutory exceptions appear to protect not the government but rather those persons or entities who are the subject of the records or whose business information the records reveal. For example, personnel records contain private information about public employees; law enforcement records include information about one-time subjects of investigations; tax records contain information about individual and business income; hospital records include medical information about patients; and a variety of records include business trade secrets. In many instances of this second category of exceptions to public access, the statute creating the exception does not merely deny public access but goes on to prohibit the custodial government or agency from releasing the protected record, as can be seen from the list of such statutes earlier in this chapter.

With respect to records about individuals or business entities, questions can arise as to whether a particular record falls within a statutory exception, and the government holding the record may not care a great deal about the issue or may be disposed to allow access to the record. Even if no question arises about whether a record falls within an exception, the statute may not expressly prohibit public access to the record, and a custodian may intend to allow access. In such a case, may the subject of the record or the owner of the private

---

67. *Brooks*, 143 N.C. App. at 611, 548 S.E.2d at 755.

68. Examples of such exceptions include those for memoranda from the government's attorney to its governing board, G.S. 132-1.1; minutes of closed sessions, G.S. 143-318.10(e); and records concerning an agency's activities that compete with other service providers, G.S. 131E-97.3 (competitive health care information) and G.S. 159B-38 (joint power agency contract discussions). With these records, it is entirely discretionary with the local government or agency as to whether to assert its right to maintain the confidentiality of the records. No one else is interested in the issue.

business information in the record go to court to protect his or her interests in maintaining the confidentiality of the record? Does such a person have standing to bring an action to enjoin disclosure or a right to intervene in a lawsuit against the custodian of the record to which access is sought?

In *North Carolina Electric Membership Corp. v. North Carolina Department of Economic & Community Development*,[69] the defendant state agency held documents submitted to it by the plaintiff, and a competitor of the plaintiff had requested those documents pursuant to the public records law. The department was prepared to release the documents, and therefore the plaintiff brought an action to enjoin the release, claiming that the documents were trade secrets and protected from release by G.S. 132-1.2. The competitor intervened in the action and, on appeal, argued that there was no jurisdictional provision allowing such a lawsuit. The court of appeals disagreed, holding that the statutory exception to public access necessarily had to create an implied right, in the owner of the documents, to protect their confidentiality. The court wrote:

> We cannot agree with [the intervenor] that the courts have no jurisdiction to issue injunctions to prevent the disclosure of documents. While we recognize the strong policy in favor of disclosure, we must also be cognizant of the protection given certain documents that would otherwise be considered Public Records. The fact that the statute provides an exemption for certain documents leads this Court to the logical conclusion that those claiming that their documents are exempt must have some recourse in our court system. To conclude otherwise, we believe, would offer no protection from agency error or from an agency's abuse of its discretion.[70]

If there is standing to bring such an action directly, then surely a person or entity in the plaintiff's position should be an intervenor of right in any action brought against the agency for access to such a record.[71]

The court of appeals decision accords with the predominant outcome in case law from other jurisdictions, although that case law is not unanimous. Two cases illustrate the predominant position. In *Times Publishing Co. v. A.J.*,[72] records of child abuse were exempted from public access by statute. Nevertheless the sheriff's department, which held a number of such records, was about to release them in response to a public records request. The Florida Supreme Court held that the subjects of the records were entitled to bring an action asserting the statutory exemption from disclosure, based on the policy underlying the

---

69. 108 N.C. App. 711, 425 S.E.2d 440 (1993).

70. *Id.* at 716, 425 S.E.2d at 443. The court also held that it was proper to allow an interlocutory appeal of the trial court's denial of a preliminary injunction. Otherwise, "there would be no reason to proceed with a trial on the merits." *Id.*

71. In *Klein v. Wisconsin Resource Center*, 582 N.W.2d 44 (Wis. Ct. App. 1998), the court held that the subject of a personnel record had standing to bring an action to challenge the legality of a proposed release of that record. In doing so, the court relied on the Wisconsin Supreme Court's decision in *Armade Broadcasting, Inc. v. Stirn*, 516 N.W.2d 357 (Wisc. 1994), which held that such a person was entitled to intervene as of right in a case seeking release of his or her personnel record.

72. 626 So. 2d 1314 (Fla. 1993).

exempting statute. Similarly, in *Beckham v. Board of Education*[73] the Kentucky Supreme Court held that a statutory exemption of personnel files from public access entitled the public employees who were the subject of the files to bring an action against their employer (and the newspaper that was seeking the files) to enjoin public access. The court rejected the newspaper's argument that the decision on whether to allow access to the records was entirely within the discretion of the custodial agency.[74] Therefore, it is likely that the court of appeals decision in *North Carolina Electric Membership Corp.* will be persuasive with other panels of the court of appeals and with the North Carolina Supreme Court.

Even so, it is possible that the decision in *North Carolina Electric Membership Corp.* might be distinguished and held not to apply to all categories of records that are exempt from public access and that contain information about individuals or business entities. The few cases that deny a right of action to enjoin disclosure or a right to intervene are instructive in this regard. The leading case in this category is unquestionably *Chrysler Corp. v. Brown*,[75] decided by the United States Supreme Court under the federal Freedom of Information Act (FOIA). As a federal contractor, Chrysler had submitted a number of reports to the Department of Defense concerning the company's affirmative action goals and performance. The department received an FOIA request for those reports and notified Chrysler of that fact. The company objected to release of the reports, but the department determined to release them anyway. Chrysler then brought an action against the department, seeking to enjoin release of the reports. The Supreme Court held that the FOIA was concerned only with disclosure by government agencies of certain information, leaving to those agencies the discretion as to whether to take advantage of the exceptions to access set out in the statute. The statute contained no prohibitions against release of information within the various exceptions. Consequently, the Court held, the statute created no rights in private parties to require that records within an FOIA exception be kept confidential. (The court did acknowledge that the owner or subject of a document held by a federal agency might bring an action pursuant to the federal Administrative Procedure Act and argue that release of the document would not be in accordance with law because it would violate the Trade Secrets Act.)

Although the North Carolina courts might follow the court of appeals decision in *North Carolina Electric Membership Corp.*, this case suggests that a North Carolina court could also distinguish between statutes that *prohibit* giving public access to records and those that simply provide that certain records are not subject to the public records law or to its right of public access. If a record falls within the former category, courts are likely to

---

73. 873 S.W.2d 575 (Ky. 1994).

74. Other cases allowing an independent action to enjoin access or allowing intervention as of right include *International Brotherhood of Electrical Workers Local 68 v. Denver Metropolitan Major League Baseball Stadium District*, 880 P.2d 10 (Colo. App. 1994) (subcontractor may intervene in action against district seeking documents filed by the subcontractor), and *Bowers v. Shelton*, 453 S.E.2d 741 (Ga. 1995) (subject of records may bring action against custodian to enjoin disclosure to public). See also *Twin-Cities Broadcasting Corp., WJBC-WBNQ Radio v. Reynard*, 661 N.E.2d 401 (Ill. App. Ct. 1996), in which the court held that when one public agency holds records belonging to a second agency, and the first agency has been sued to establish a right of access to the records, the second agency—to whom the records belong—may intervene as of right in the lawsuit to protect its interest in the records.

75. 441 U.S. 281 (1979).

accord the subject or owner of the record a right to seek to enjoin release of the record or to intervene in an action brought to achieve access to the record. If it falls within the latter category, however, then a court might not allow the subject or owner to bring an action to enjoin or to intervene as of right. It is possible to read the *North Carolina Electric Membership Corp.* decision as consistent with this distinction. As chapter 11, "Trade Secrets," points out, a local government or state agency that releases a record containing a trade secret protected by G.S. 132-1.2 may well be liable under the Trade Secrets Protection Act for misappropriation of the trade secret. Therefore, it is reasonable to read G.S. 132-1.2 as prohibiting release of records that fit within its terms. If that is so, then the court's decision in *North Carolina Electric Membership Corp.* addresses a record that falls within the category of records subject to statutes that *prohibit* public access. A North Carolina court could still reach a different conclusion as to a record that is simply *excepted* from the right of public access, without any statutory prohibition on allowing public access.

Litigation—Discovery of Records Not Open to Public Inspection

If a particular record held by a local government is subject to a statute that denies public access to the record or prohibits the local government from releasing the record, what is the status of the record vis-à-vis discovery in litigation?[76] To what extent, if at all, does the record's status under the public records law affect the local government's rights and obligations under the various discovery rules of the North Carolina Rules of Civil Procedure (RCP)?[77]

The General Rule

No North Carolina case fully answers this question, although one state supreme court decision, discussed below, strongly suggests that North Carolina would follow the general rule as articulated in other states.[78] That general rule, based on the decisions of many courts, may be stated as follows:

> When a litigant seeks a copy of a record that is not open to public access or that is excepted from the public records law altogether, the public records exception does not automatically create a privilege against discovery. In appropriate circumstances a government may be able to obtain a protective order respecting a particular record or some information in the record, but as a general rule the

---

76. Two other issues dealing with discovery and public records are dealt with in other statutes. The use of the public records law to obtain documents during litigation, in lieu of discovery, is discussed *infra* in chapter 9, "Confidential Legal Materials." The fact that materials discovered by a local government in litigation then become public records is noted *supra* in chapter 1, at note 32.

77. "Discovery" refers to the rights that a litigant has to seek information, related to the litigation, from the opposing party and others. It includes the right to take depositions, to propose and receive answers to written questions, and to demand that specified documents be produced and copies handed over.

78. The case is *News & Observer Publishing Co. v. State ex rel. Starling*, 312 N.C. 276, 322 S.E.2d 133 (1984). It is discussed in the text, *infra*, at notes 83 through 85.

government should expect that it will have to produce the record, or the information, once a discovery request is made.

Two cases, from many, illustrate this general rule.

In *Gipson v. Bean*[79] the county sheriff had directed two towing companies to seize, tow, and store a large group of farm equipment that was subject to a judgment lien. The judgment was paid, however, without need of selling the equipment, and the equipment was returned to its owners. But without a sale there were no sales proceeds from which to pay the towing companies, and therefore the companies submitted detailed bills to the sheriff and to a deputy county attorney. Ultimately the county declined to pay the bills, and the towing companies brought suit to collect. In order to proceed in their suits, the companies had to demonstrate that they had made a claim to the county and that the county's governing board had rejected the claim. It appeared that the claim was made and rejected, if at all, at a closed session of the governing board, and therefore the towing companies served a subpoena on the county's clerk, seeking the minutes and other records of the closed session. An Arizona statute denied public access to minutes of closed sessions, and the county argued that the statute created a privilege against discovery; therefore the county refused to comply with the subpoena, and the county's refusal was upheld by the trial court. The Arizona Court of Appeals held that the trial court had abused its discretion in upholding the county's refusal to comply with the subpoena and directed that the records be produced. The appellate court noted that the information sought—whether a claim had been presented to the board and whether the board had rejected it—was not within the attorney–client privilege and that the information was in fact essential to the plaintiff's case. The record had to be produced.[80]

In *Henneman v. City of Toledo*,[81] the alleged victim of a police assault, who had sued the city and the officer, sought production of the city's police internal investigation files. The trial court upheld the city's refusal to produce the files, but the Ohio Supreme Court reversed. The court held that the exclusion of these records from public access under the Ohio public records law was irrelevant to whether they were discoverable in civil litigation; the public records provision did not create an automatic privilege against discovery. The court did recognize that there were legitimate concerns for maintaining confidentiality of some of the information in the files, such as names of informants, and therefore directed the trial court to review the files *in camera* before releasing them to the plaintiff. But the court left no doubt that the bulk of the material sought must be made available; it was relevant to the plaintiff's case.[82]

---

79. 753 P.2d 168 (Ariz. Ct. App. 1987).

80. *Accord*, on discovery of minutes of closed sessions, State *ex rel.* Upper Republican Natural Res. Dist. v. Dist. Judges of the Dist. Ct., 728 N.W.2d 275 (Neb. 2007); Sands v. Whitnall Sch. Dist., 754 N.W.2d 439 (Wis. 2008).

81. 520 N.E.2d 207 (Ohio 1988).

82. Other cases following the general rule, as stated in the text, include: *Fears v. Burris Manufacturing Co.*, 436 F.2d 1357 (5th Cir. 1971) (employment security commission files relating to a specific company); *Department of Professional Regulation v. Spiva*, 478 So. 2d 382 (Fla. Dist. Ct. App. 1985) (test scores of successful applicants for state pilot's license); *Dillon v. City of Davenport*, 366 N.W.2d 918 (Iowa 1985) (transcript of closed session of city council); *Lefebvre v. Somersworth Shoe Co.*, 41 A.2d 924 (N.H. 1945) (state health department analysis of industrial fluid); *Huntsville Utility District v. General Trust Co.*, 839

As noted above, a decision of the North Carolina Supreme Court suggests our courts will follow the general rule and allow discovery of records not open to public inspection. In *News & Observer Publishing Co. v. State ex rel. Starling*,[83] the State Bureau of Investigation had investigated various actions of the Wake county school superintendent; after receiving the report, the district attorney had decided there were no grounds to prosecute. The *News and Observer* sued for access to the report under G.S. 114-15, which provides that SBI reports are not public records and "may be made available to the public only upon an order of a court of competent jurisdiction."[84] The supreme court denied the newspaper's right of access to the report. The court held that the quoted language did not create a right of action to seek access to SBI reports. Rather, the language merely referenced the right to seek a court order by someone "otherwise entitled by statute to access,"[85] which the court held to mean someone entitled to the record under the law of discovery. If the newspaper had been in some form of litigation other than a direct suit to obtain the records, and if the records were relevant to that litigation, discovery would have been available. It is not clear from the court's opinion whether the reference in G.S. 114-15 to a court order was crucial to discovery's being available, and for that reason the case cannot fully support a general declaration that North Carolina will follow the general rule, but the case certainly lends significant support to such a declaration. As noted in the text above, between notes 53 and 56, a number of the North Carolina statutes that prohibit release of specific categories of records provide that access is available pursuant to court order. Given the holding in *Starling*, it seems clear that these kinds of records would also be subject to discovery, but the above discussion on court orders indicates that a simple subpoena would not be enough; rather, there would need to be some sort of order issued and signed by a judge.

The general rule, as stated above, ought not to be surprising. In the private sector all records of an individual or entity are closed to public access yet almost all are available through discovery. Allowing discovery of governmental records that are not open to public access merely, in most instances, places a government in the same position as other litigants.

Records Not Subject to Discovery

If local governments are placed on the same playing field as private litigants, the North Carolina Rules of Civil Procedure themselves protect a few categories of government records against discovery. Rule 26(b)(1) provides that discovery is not automatically available for privileged matters; thus, to the extent that local government records fall within accepted privileges, they are protected against discovery. A variety of medical records held by local governments clearly fall within the physician–patient privilege,[86] and the communications from attorney to public client protected against public access under G.S. 132-1.1(a) fall

---

S.W.2d 397 (Tenn. Ct. App. 1992) (bond registration records); and *Madsen v. United Television, Inc.*, 801 P.2d 912 (Utah 1990) (personnel files and police internal investigation files).

83. 312 N.C. 276, 322 S.E.2d 133 (1984).

84. The provision permitting access to criminal investigation records by court order is now found in G.S. 132-1.4.

85. 312 N.C. at 283, 322 S.E.2d at 138 (emphasis omitted).

86. See the statutes discussed *infra* in chapter 14, "Medical and Patient Records."

within the attorney–client privilege.[87] In addition, G.S. 115C-332 states that criminal history information about prospective employees received by a local school administrative unit from the state Department of Justice is "privileged information" and not open to public inspection, and there is comparable language in G.S. 114-19.12 concerning criminal records checks done for fire departments and emergency medical services agencies.[88] It seems likely that these statutory references to "privilege" are intended to create an evidentiary privilege under Rule 26. (It should also be noted that Rule 26(b)(3) protects trial preparation material from discovery and that this provision of the RCP is mirrored in G.S. 132-1.9, which creates an exception from public access for such materials. The Rule and the statute are discussed at length in chapter 9, "Confidential Legal Materials.")

Rule 26(c) permits a trial judge to issue a protective order to prohibit or limit discovery of trade secrets. G.S. 132-1.2(1) provides that the public records law does not authorize or require a government to reveal trade secrets held by it that belong to a private party. Therefore, the government (or the owner of the trade secret, as discussed in the preceding section) might seek a protective order for records subject to that statute.[89] In addition, some of the other, more specific, statutes that deny public access to local government records appear to do so because those records are in the nature of trade secrets of the government itself. These statutes include G.S. 131E-97.3, which protects competitive health care information held by a public hospital, and G.S. 159B-38, which protects contract information held by a joint power agency. The denial of public access to these records lends support to any effort to seek a protective order against their discovery.

A few of the statutes that deny public access to records also specify that the records are not subject to discovery at all, and obviously such a statutory statement overrides the general provisions of Rule 26. Most notably, such a provision is a part of each of the statutes that exempts the records of medical review committees from public access.[90]

Protective Orders

Courts have occasionally denied discovery of records to which public access was statutorily denied, on the ground that the policies of the public records exception would be seriously harmed by allowing any discovery at all. Thus, for example, a New York appellate court

---

87. In *News & Observer Publishing Co. v. Poole*, 330 N.C. 465, 412 S.E.2d 7 (1992), the supreme court stated that G.S. 132-1.1 "defines the scope of the [attorney–client] privilege" under the public records law. *Id.* at 483, 412 S.E.2d at 17.

88. Oddly, this language is absent from the statutes providing for criminal records checks for city and county employees generally, G.S. 114-19.14, 153A-94.2, and 160A-164.2. Although each of these statutes makes clear the information received is "confidential," there is no additional statement that it is "privileged."

89. Other, more specific, statutes also protect from public access proprietary information of a private company held by a government. G.S. 66-169 denies public access to sales records of precious metals dealers filed with a local law enforcement agency. G.S. 95-194 denies public access to information filed with a local fire chief about hazardous chemicals used or manufactured by local businesses. These records also might be possible subjects of protective orders, as trade secrets.

90. G.S. 131E-95 (public hospitals); G.S. 122C-30 (mental health hospitals); and G.S. 122C-191 (area authority facilities). The first of these statutes was interpreted by the supreme court in *Shelton v. Morehead Memorial Hospital*, 318 N.C. 76, 347 S.E.2d 824 (1986).

denied discovery of certain medical information held by the state department of health, on the ground that medical professionals would not provide the information to the government in the future if they knew it was open even to the limited access of discovery.[91] More often, however, courts have rejected these sorts of arguments, holding that the need of the litigant for the information outweighed any speculative consequence of this sort. For example, in *Madsen v. United Television, Inc.*,[92] a city had sought to bar discovery of police internal affairs reports on the ground that allowing access would chill the future willingness of police officers to cooperate with such investigations. The court would have none of it, noting that the machinery of such an investigation itself was more likely to cause noncooperation by police officers than was the chance that the records of the investigation might ultimately be subject to discovery.

While courts have generally been unwilling to deny discovery altogether, they have been amenable to entering protective orders that limit access to and use of records not otherwise open to the public. If there is information in a record that is particularly confidential, such as the name of a law enforcement informant, and that specific information is not itself the subject of the discovery request, courts normally will review the record *in camera*, without attorneys present, and determine whether certain parts of the record might be withheld from discovery.[93] Courts have also been willing to enjoin the parties from any broader disclosure of the information in the record.[94]

Categories of Records Excepted from the Right of Public Access

This last section is a listing of statutes that except various categories of local government records from the right of public access. The first listing sets out those statutes that are discussed separately in the succeeding chapters of this book. The second listing attempts a comprehensive listing of other statutes, not separately discussed, that also create exceptions to the right of access with respect to local government records.[95]

Statutes Discussed in Detail in Other Chapters

Personnel Records [Chapter 7]

G.S. 115C-319 to 115C-321 (Public school employees)
G.S. 115D-27 to 115D-30 (Community college employees)
G.S. 122C-158 (Area authority employees)

---

91. *In re* Love Canal Actions, 460 N.Y.S.2d 850 (App. Div. 1983).
92. 801 P.2d 912 (Utah 1990).
93. *E.g.*, Dillon v. City of Davenport, 366 N.W.2d 918 (Iowa 1985); W. v. U., 354 N.Y.S.2d 721 (App. Div. 1974); Henneman v. City of Toledo, 520 N.E.2d 207 (Ohio 1988).
94. *E.g.*, Dillon v. City of Davenport, 366 N.W.2d 918 (Iowa 1985).
95. There are a larger number of statutes that deny public access to a variety of records held by *state* departments, agencies, and institutions. They are not included in this listing.

G.S. 130A-42 (Health department employees)
G.S. 130A-45.9 (Public health authority employees)
G.S. 131E-257.2 (Public hospital employees)
G.S. 153A-98 (County government employees)
G.S. 160A-168 (City government employees)
G.S. 162A-6.1 (Water and sewer authority employees)
G.S. 115C-209.1 (Public school volunteers)
G.S. 114-19.2 (Criminal records checks for school employees)
G.S. 114-19.3 (Criminal records checks for hospital employees)
G.S. 114-19.12 (Criminal records checks for fire department and EMS employees)
G.S. 114-19.14 (Criminal records checks for county and city employees)

Criminal Investigation and Intelligence Records and Local Jail Records [Chapter 8]
G.S. 132-1.4 (Criminal investigation and criminal intelligence records)
G.S. 7B-3001 (Law enforcement records involving juveniles)

Confidential Legal Materials [Chapter 9]
G.S. 132-1.1(a) (Communications from attorney to client regarding litigation)
G.S. 132-1.9 (Trial preparation materials)

Settlements [Chapter 10]
G.S. 132-1.3 (Settlements of suits brought against governments)
G.S. 143-318.11(a)(3) (Settlements discussed in closed sessions)

Trade Secrets [Chapter 11]
G.S. 132-1.2(1) (Trade secrets received by governments)

Economic Development Records [Chapter 12]
G.S. 132-6(d) (Economic development records)
G.S. 132-1.11 (Incentives disclosures)

Local Tax Records [Chapter 13]
G.S. 153A-148.1 (County tax records)
G.S. 160A-208.1 (City tax records)
G.S. 132-1.1(b) (State, county, and city tax records)

Medical and Patient Records [Chapter 14]
G.S. 8-53 (Privileged physician–patient records)
G.S. 122C-52(a) (Area authority client records)
G.S. 130A-12 (Health department patient medical and financial records)
G.S. 130A-45.8 (Public health authority patient medical and financial records)
G.S. 131E-97 (Health care facility patient medical and financial records)
G.S. 143-518 (EMS client records)

Social Security Numbers and Other Identifying Information [Chapter 15]

G.S. 132-1.10 (Social Security numbers and identifying information)
G.S. 132-1.2(2) (Electronic payment information)

Public Enterprise Billing Information [Chapter 16]

G.S. 132-1.1(c) (Enterprise customer billing records)

Personal Information from Motor Vehicle Records [Chapter 17]

G.S. 20-43.1 (DMV records)
G.S. 20-43.4 (DMV records provided to jury commissions)

Minutes and General Accounts of Closed Sessions [Chapter 18]

G.S. 143-318.10(e) (Minutes and general accounts of closed sessions)

Construction and Procurement Records [Chapter 19]

G.S. 133-33 (Cost estimates and bidders' lists)
G.S. 143-131 (Informal bids)
G.S. 143-129.8 (Information technology bids and proposals)
G.S. 143-129(h) (Public transportation bids and proposals)

Public Security Records [Chapter 20]

G.S. 132-1.6 (Emergency response plans)
G.S. 132-1.7 (Sensitive public security information)
G.S. 132-6.1 (Electronic data-processing records)

Geographic Information System Records [Chapter 21]

G.S. 132-10 (GIS records)

Miscellaneous Records [Chapter 22]

G.S. 125-19 (Library records)
G.S. 132-1.12 (Information about minors participating in public recreation programs)

Statutes Not Discussed in Other Chapters

Law Enforcement Records

Chapter 8 discusses criminal investigation and criminal intelligence records. There are also a few other law enforcement–related statutes that require keeping certain, limited information confidential.

G.S. 14-208.6A and 14-208.10 (Sex offender registration programs) specify that the identity of any victim of a registered offender is not open to the public.

Records Containing Private Business Information

Chapter 11 discusses the exemption from the public records law of business trade secrets. Several more-specific statutes also exempt business information from public access.

G.S. 66-165 (Precious metals dealers' criminal records checks) permits the state Department of Justice to provide criminal record information to a local law enforcement agency about applicants for precious metals dealers' licenses. The statute directs the law enforcement agency to keep the information confidential and declares that it is not a public record.

G.S. 66-169 (Precious metals transactions) requires licensed dealers in precious metals to record each purchase they make of such metals and file a copy with the local law enforcement agency. The section directs that the records filed with the law enforcement agency are not open to public access.

G.S. 95-194 and 95-197 (Hazardous chemical information) require an employer who manufactures or uses hazardous chemicals to provide information about the chemicals to the local fire chief in order to allow the fire department to be prepared to contain fires involving the chemicals. The sections exempt the information received by the fire chief from public access.

G.S. 160A-304 (Taxicab permittees' and licensees' criminal records checks) permits the state Department of Justice to provide criminal record information to a city about applicants for taxicab licenses and permits. The statute directs the city to keep the information confidential and declares that it is not a public record.

Taxpayer Information

G.S. 105-289(e) (Taxpayer information from the state Department of Revenue) permits the Department of Revenue to furnish to local tax officials information that may assist them in property tax administration. The subsection prohibits the local tax officials from allowing public access to the information.

G.S. 105-296(h) (Information about business property) permits the county assessor to require inventories, statements of assets and liabilities, and similar information from business taxpayers. The subsection states that if the information thereby received by the assessor is not required by statute to be on the abstract, the information is not open to public inspection.

G.S. 105A-15 (Taxpayer information) permits the Department of Revenue and state and local agencies making claims under the debt setoff program to share information that is otherwise confidential and requires the agencies with which the information is shared to keep it confidential.

G.S. 105-164.14(f) (Sales tax refunds) directs the Department of Revenue to share information on sales tax refunds with county and city officials and prohibits the recipient officials from disclosing the information to others.

Medical Information

Chapter 14 discusses several statutes that protect from public inspection medical and other information about patients in government-operated health care facilities. A number of other statutes also deal with more specific forms of patient medical information.

G.S. 122C-15 (Consumer Advocate in mental health system) entitles the State Consumer Advocate and any Local Consumer Advocate to have access to patient records to the extent permitted by federal law.

G.S. 130A-143 (Information on communicable diseases) creates a general confidentiality for information and records that identify people with the AIDS virus infection or other communicable diseases who are therefore subject to disease reporting requirements.

G.S. 130A-212 (Information about cancer patients) states that records of and reports about individual patients with cancer are not public records.

G.S. 130A-389 (Certain autopsies), subsections (b) and (c), permits medical examiners to perform autopsies even though the Chief Medical Examiner and the investigating medical examiner do not deem them advisable. Subsection (d) states that the report of such an autopsy is part of the decedent's medical record and not open to public inspection.

G.S. 130A-389.1 and 132-1.8 (Photographs and recordings made pursuant to autopsy) limit the making of copies of photographs and video or audio recordings of autopsies; the statutes maintain the right to inspect such records as long as no copy is made.

G.S. 130A-476 (Access to health information related to terrorist incidents) directs local health directors receiving confidential health information pursuant to this section to maintain the confidentiality of the information.

G.S. 166A-7(d)(5) (Local emergency management) provides that registries identifying functionally and medically fragile persons for local emergency management agencies are not public records.

Vital Records

G.S. 130A-93 (Birth certificates) provides that certain information in birth certificates is not public record.

G.S. 130A-102 (Birth certificates) provides that medical information in a birth certificate is not open to the public.

Peer Review and Other Information about Medical Professionals

G.S. 122C-30 (Mental health hospital medical review committees) states that proceedings of, records produced by, and materials reviewed by medical review committees of hospitals licensed under G.S. Chapter 122C are not public records.

G.S. 122C-191 (Area authority quality assurance committees) states that proceedings of, records produced by, and materials reviewed by quality assurance committees of area authority facilities are not public records.

G.S. 130A-45.7 (Public health authority medical review committees) states that proceedings of, records produced by, and materials reviewed by medical review committees of public health authorities are not public records.

G.S. 130A-45.9(c) (Independent contractors with public health authorities) states that information about the qualifications, competence, performance, character, or fitness of an independent contractor who provides health care services under a contract with a public health authority is not a public record. In addition, the subsection states that documents concerning complaints, charges, and grievances about such contractors are not public records.

G.S. 130A-45.10 (Information about persons with practice privileges at public health authorities) states that records of information obtained by public health authorities as part of the credentialing and peer review of persons having or seeking privileges to practice in a public health facility are not public records.

G.S. 131E-95 (Hospital medical review committees) states that proceedings of, records produced by, and materials reviewed by medical review committees of public hospitals are not public records.

G.S. 131E-97.2 (Information about persons with practice privileges at public hospitals) states that records of information obtained by a public hospital as part of the credentialing and peer review of persons having or seeking privileges to practice in the hospital are not public records.

G.S. 131E-97.1(c) (Health care independent contractors) states that information about the qualifications, competence, performance, character, or fitness of an independent contractor who provides health care services under a contract with a public hospital is not a public record. In addition, the subsection states that documents concerning complaints, charges, and grievances about such contractors are not public records.

Government Operations in Competition with Others

G.S. 130A-45.11 (Competitive health care information) excludes from the public records law information relating to competitive health care activities by or on behalf of a public health authority. All contracts entered into by such an authority, however, are public records unless otherwise exempted from the public records law.

G.S. 131E-97.3 (Competitive health care information) excludes from the public records law information relating to competitive health care activities by or on behalf of a public hospital.

G.S. 131E-99 (Health care contracts) excludes from the public records law the financial terms and other competitive health care information in a contract between a hospital and a managed care organization, insurance company, employer, or other payer.

G.S. 159B-38 (Joint agency contract discussions) excludes from the public records law records of discussions of contracts of joint power agencies relating to construction, ownership, or operation of facilities; use of electric power or energy; or purchase, sale, exchange, interchange, wheeling, pooling, transmission, or use of electric power or energy.

Student Records

G.S. 115C-402 (Public school student records) states that the official record of each public school student is not a public record.

G.S. 115C-174.13 (Student test scores) excludes from the public records law written materials containing identifiable scores of individual students on tests administered under the statewide testing program.

G.S. 115C-366(g) (Addresses of students in the Address Confidentiality Program) permits a school unit to use the actual address of a student in the Address Confidentiality Program in making pupil assignments, as long as the address is kept confidential pursuant to G.S. Chapter 15C.

G.S. 130A-441 (Health assessment reports for children entering kindergarten) requires that such reports be kept confidential.

G.S. 115C-404 (Use of juvenile court information) exempts from the public records law information a juvenile court counselor sends to a school principal about court actions taken respecting a student at the principal's school.

G.S. 132-1.1(f) (Community college applicant information) makes confidential any personally identifiable information from or about an applicant for admission to a community college.

Records about Children

G.S. 7B-2102 (Juvenile photographs and fingerprints) declares that photographs or fingerprints made of juveniles by law enforcement officers are not public records and may not be opened to public inspection.

G.S. 7B-3100 (Sharing information about juveniles) authorizes a variety of local agencies to share confidential information about juveniles but directs that the agency receiving the information maintain its confidentiality.

G.S. 7B-302 (Investigation of child abuse, neglect, or dependency) makes confidential any information received by the county department of social services concerning an investigation of alleged abuse, neglect, or dependency of a child.

G.S. 7B-2901(b) (Records of child abuse, neglect, or dependency) directs the county director of social services to maintain a record of cases of juveniles under the department's protective custody or under placement by the court. The statutes require anyone wishing to examine the records—except the juvenile in question or the guardian ad litem—to obtain a court order.

G.S. 7B-2902 (Records related to child fatality or near fatality cases) provides that, in the case of a child fatality or near fatality that results in criminal charges, a summary of actions taken by a government agency in response to a report that the child may have needed protection is to be disclosed to the public on request, unless disclosure would endanger or harm a child, would jeopardize a criminal investigation or proceeding, or is prohibited by federal law. Confidential records held by the agency, mental health records of the child or the child's family unless directly related to the cause of the harm, the identity of information sources, criminal investigation reports, and criminal intelligence information are not subject to disclosure under this section.

G.S. 7B-1413 (Child abuse and neglect records) allows community child protection teams and child-fatality prevention teams access to various records, including medical records, law enforcement records, and social services records. Subsection (c) makes this information confidential if it is otherwise confidential.

G.S. 14-208.29 (Registered sex offenders who are juveniles) exempts from the public records law information about a juvenile who is required to register as a sex offender.

Social Services Records

G.S. 108A-80 and 108A-73 (Basic social services records) prohibit any person from obtaining, disclosing, or using a list of names or other information about persons applying for or receiving public assistance or other social services when the information comes from records of the department of social services.

G.S. 108A-11 (Access to records by members of board of social services) permits members of county boards of social services to inspect records about applicants for or recipients of public assistance or other social services and prohibits board members from making such information public.

G.S. 48-3-309 (Criminal records checks of adoptive parents) directs the Department of Justice to provide to the Department of Health and Human Services the criminal histories of all persons seeking to become adoptive parents of a child in the custody of or to be placed by a county department of social services. The Department of Health and Human Services and the local department of social services are directed to maintain the confidentiality of the criminal histories received.

G.S. 131D-2 (Information about adult care homes), subsection (b)(5), provides that confidential or privileged information held by a county department of social services concerning inspections of adult care homes, as well as names of residents or complainants, is exempt from public access.

Election Records

G.S. 163-82.10(a) and 132-1.2(4) (Voter registration records) make the following information in a voter registration record confidential and not a public record: electronically captured images of voters' signatures, dates of birth, full or partial Social Security numbers, and driver's license numbers.

G.S. 163-82.10(d) (Voter registration records) requires a board of elections to keep confidential the home address of a voter who is under a protective order or comparable judicial order or is a participant in the Address Confidentiality Program created in G.S. Chapter 15C.

G.S. 163-82.10B (Date of birth in voter records) directs each board of elections to keep confidential the date of birth of each voter-registration applicant and registered voter, subject to certain stated exceptions.

G.S. 163-82.4 (Certain voter registration information) requires that the form used for voter registration state that the following information will remain confidential: (1) the fact that a person submitted an application and then declined to register, and (2) the office at which an applicant submitted a voter registration application.

G.S. 163-228 (Register of absentee voting requests) limits the times in which these records may be inspected.

Miscellaneous Private Information

G.S. 62A-51 and 132-1.5 (Telephone numbers held by 911 systems) require telephone companies to provide subscriber telephone numbers, names, and service addresses to 911 systems. The sections prohibit local governments that operate 911 systems from releasing these telephone numbers except to respond to an emergency.

G.S. 15C-8 and 132-1.1(d) (State and local agency use of addresses of participants in Address Confidentiality Program) set out when a local agency may use a participant's actual rather than his or her substitute address, provide that in general the actual address is not a public record, and set out when the actual address is a public record.

G.S. 47-113.2 (Military discharge documents) restricts public access to military discharge documents filed with the register of deeds.

G.S 159E-11 (Municipal bond registration records) exempts municipal bond registration records from the public records law.

G.S. 130A-189 (Rabies vaccination certificates) prohibits using for commercial purposes the information in the certificate copy submitted to the county animal control agency.

G.S. 132-1.2(5) (Design professionals' seals) prohibits copies being made of the seal of a design professional when the seal is affixed to a document submitted to qualify for a building permit.

Chapter 7—Personnel Records

Statutory Summary

Section 153A-98 of the North Carolina General Statutes [hereinafter G.S.], the county personnel privacy statute; G.S. 160A-168, the city personnel privacy statute; and the parallel statutes that cover other categories of public employees establish special rules of access to the personnel files of public employees.[1] (The other statutes are cited below, and the major differences between statutes are noted as well. This summary, however, covers the county and city statutes and those that are identical to them.)[2] Reflecting a sense that employee records should, for the most part, be private, the statutes deny public access to most items in a public employee's personnel file. A few items are open to public access, as follows:

- the employee's name;
- the employee's age;
- the date the employee was originally employed or appointed by the employing agency;
- the terms of the employee's employment contract, if the employee works pursuant to a contract;
- the employee's current position title;
- the employee's current salary, which is defined to include all compensation;
- the date and amount of the most recent increase or decrease in the employee's salary;
- the date (and probably, nature) of the most recent promotion, demotion, transfer, suspension, separation, or other change in the employee's position classification; and
- the office to which the employee is currently assigned.

---

1. The statutes are set out in appendix 7B at the end of this chapter.
2. Appendix 7A compares the provisions of the several personnel privacy statutes.

The statutes open other materials in the personnel file only to selected persons or pursuant to specific standards. (Under some of the statutes, the employee may waive some or all of the privacy of the file, for specific persons or in general, by having a written waiver placed in the file.) The special rights or opportunities for access are as follows:

- The employee (or an agent of the employee) may inspect his or her entire file, except for letters of reference solicited before employment and medical information a prudent physician would not divulge to his or her patient; the employee may designate a physician to inspect any such medical information.
- Any employee with supervisory responsibility over the subject employee may examine the entire file.
- The custodian may allow an official of any government to inspect the file, except to assist in criminal or tax investigations.
- The governing authorities of the employing agency may release certain information in the file, if they determine that doing so is "essential to maintaining public confidence in the administration of [public] services or to maintaining the level and quality of [public] services."

In addition, access is allowed pursuant to an order from a court of competent jurisdiction.

Subsection (c1) of the statutes excludes certain information from any form of public or employee access, whether part of a personnel file or not. Most importantly, this subsection denies any public or employee access to testing or examination materials used in making appointments or promotions.

The statutes conclude with two criminal penalties. First, if a public official or employee "knowingly, willfully, and with malice" allows access to information in a personnel file by an unauthorized person, the official or employee is guilty of a Class 3 misdemeanor and may be fined up to $500. Second, if an unauthorized person "knowingly and willfully" examines a personnel file in its official filing place or removes or copies any portion of a confidential personnel file, that person is also guilty of a Class 3 misdemeanor and may be fined up to $500.

Parallel Statutes

As was noted above, a series of statutes—ten in total—addresses access to the personnel files of public employees. They are as follows:

- County employees—G.S. 153A-98
- City employees—G.S. 160A-168
- Public school employees—G.S. 115C-319 through 115C-321
- Community college employees—G.S. 115D-27 through 115D-30
- District health department employees—G.S. 130A-42
- Public health authority employees—G.S. 130A-45.9
- Area authority employees—G.S. 122C-158

- Public hospital employees—G.S. 131E-257.2
- Water and sewer authority employees—G.S. 162A-6.1
- State government employees—G.S. 126-22 through 126-30

Four of these statutes are functionally identical—those for county employees, city employees, area authority employees, and water and sewer authority employees. In addition, the district health department statute simply references the county statute, which adds a fifth sort of agency to this list. Throughout this chapter, these essentially identical statutes will be characterized as the *standard statute*. The other five statutes differ more or less from the standard statute. The statutes for public school employees and for community college employees (together, the *education statutes)* permit access to a personnel file by a different list of persons than does the standard statute, notably including governing board members and the school unit's or college's attorney. These statutes also permit access pursuant to a subpoena, as well as by court order. Similarly, the state government statute has a different list of persons entitled to access to a personnel file and other minor differences. The public hospital statute and the public health authority statute exhibit the greatest variation from the standard statute. The hospital statute includes different rules on access to employee compensation information and does not include any authority to release information in order to maintain public confidence in the administration of services or the level and quality of services. The public health authority statute differs most from the standard statute, inasmuch as it includes no authority for any special access to a personnel file, even by the employee. In addition, it includes provisions applicable to licensed medical providers who are employed by or have privileges to practice in an authority facility and provisions concerning access to files about independent contractors with an authority. Each of these variations will be noted and discussed later in the chapter, but the existence of the variations means that officials should examine with care the statute that applies to their particular agency to note any provisions unique to that statute. Appendix 7A at the end of this chapter demonstrates the similarities and differences among the various statutes.

Discussion

Personnel Files in Agencies Not Subject to Any Personnel Privacy Statute

The various personnel privacy statutes do not explicitly cover all North Carolina public employees, and that fact gives rise to two questions. First, just which public employees are clearly covered by the statutes, and particularly, how extensive is the term "county employee"? Second, for those agencies that are not within the terms of the statutes, what is the status of their personnel records?

Who Are County Employees?

G.S. 153A-98 applies to the personnel records of county employees. Clearly that term applies to those employees who are supervised either by the county manager or the board of county commissioners. But what of employees of agencies that are normally considered part of county government but who are supervised by independent officers or independent boards? Are they county employees under the statute as well? It is almost certain that they are.

Let's begin with health department employees. There are two special personnel privacy statutes applicable to public health employees in special agencies. First, G.S. 130A-42 applies to employees of district health departments. Clearly these employees cannot be considered employees of a specific county because their agency operates on a multicounty basis. Therefore, they need their own statute. Second, G.S. 130A-45.9 applies to employees of public health authorities. A public health authority is not part of a county government but rather is a separate corporate entity; furthermore, such an authority can operate on a multicounty basis. For these reasons, employees of such an authority are not necessarily county employees, and therefore G.S. 130A-45.9 was enacted. There is no special statute, however, for employees of a standard county health department. The obvious reason is that there is no need for such a statute—county health department employees are county employees for purposes of G.S. 153A-98.

If that is the case with health department employees, it must also be the case with employees of the other county agencies subject to independent boards and commissions—employees of county social services departments, county boards of elections, and some county library boards.[3]

But what of employees of the sheriff and the register of deeds, both of whom are independently elected officials? The North Carolina courts have held that deputy sheriffs are not county employees in some contexts and are county employees in others. In *Peele v. Provident Mutual Life Insurance Co.*,[4] a dispatcher for the sheriff's department who had been fired by the sheriff brought a wrongful discharge action against the sheriff and the county and county commissioners. The court of appeals affirmed the dismissal of the action against the county and the commissioners on the ground that "plaintiff was an employee of the sheriff and not Watauga County and its Board of Commissioners."[5] Similarly, in *Clark v. Burke County*, a negligence case growing out of a deputy's high speed chase, the court of appeals affirmed summary judgment for the county on the ground that "[a] deputy is an employee of the sheriff, not the county," citing *Peele* in support.[6] On the other side is *Bolick v. County of Caldwell*, another wrongful discharge case brought by a sheriff's department employee.[7] The defendant argued that the county's personnel ordinance did not apply to the plaintiff deputy sheriff because he was not a county employee. The court rejected the argument, holding that a deputy was within the ordinance's meaning of "any Caldwell

---

3. It might be argued that employees in local health, social services, and mental health agencies are subject to the state employee personnel privacy act. That act is found in N.C. Gen. Stat. [hereinafter G.S.] Ch. 126, which establishes the state personnel administration system, and G.S. 126-5(a)(2) provides that the "provisions of *this Chapter*" are to apply to those local employees. Nevertheless, it is clear that the state personnel privacy act does not apply to these local agency employees. G.S. 126-22 declares that the state personnel privacy act applies only to current and former state employees and to applicants for state employment, and G.S. 126-5(a) clearly distinguishes between state employees and the various local agency employees. Indeed, if the state personnel privacy act applied to the local agency employees, there would have been no need to enact the privacy acts for area authority employees and district health department employees.

4. 90 N.C. App. 447, 368 S.E.2d 892 (1988).

5. *Id.* at 449, 368 S.E.2d at 894.

6. 117 N.C. App. 85, 89, 450 S.E.2d 747, 749 (1994).

7. 182 N.C. App. 95, 641 S.E.2d 386 (2007).

County employee."[8] Finally, in *Durham Herald Co. v. County of Durham*,[9] the board of commissioners was in the midst of filling a vacancy in the office of sheriff, and the issue in the case was whether the applications the board had received were subject to the county personnel privacy statute, G.S. 153A-98. The newspaper argued that the statute did not apply to the applications because the sheriff was not an employee of the county. The court rejected the argument but did not explicitly hold that the sheriff was a county employee. Rather, it held that the statute was intended to protect "those who apply to county boards or their agents for positions which those boards and their agents are authorized to fill,"[10] and therefore those applying were "applicants for employment" within the statutory meaning. Although the court chose not to make this point, it seems reasonable to believe that when an "applicant for employment" is actually appointed, he or she is then an "employee," at least for purposes of this statute. After all, if deputy sheriffs or employees within a sheriff's department (or the office of the register of deeds) are not county employees, then they are not covered by any specific personnel privacy statute, and it seems more likely that the General Assembly intended these employees to be covered by the county statute than to be covered by no statute at all.

Agencies Not Explicitly Subject to Any Statute

There are a variety of small, special-purpose agencies that are not explicitly subject to any personnel privacy statute. They include the following:

- Councils of government and regional planning and economic development commissions
- Sanitary districts
- Metropolitan sewerage districts
- Metropolitan water districts
- Regional transportation authorities and regional public transportation authorities
- Regional solid waste management authorities
- Regional libraries
- Public housing authorities
- Alcoholic beverage control (ABC) systems
- Soil and water conservation districts[11]
- Airport authorities and other entities created by local act of the General Assembly

What is the status of personnel records in these various agencies without specific statutes?

---

8. *Id.* at 101, 641 S.E.2d at 390–91.

9. 334 N.C. 677, 435 S.E.2d 317 (1993).

10. *Id.* at 679, 435 S.E.2d at 319.

11. In some soil and water conservation districts, the district's staff are county employees assigned to the district; in others, they are clearly district employees.

One possible answer is that personnel files in these agencies are subject to the general public records statute, and therefore, absent any constitutional claims of personal privacy, all parts of the files are open to public access. The frequently cited Latin phrase *expressio unius est exclusio alterius* stands for the well-accepted proposition that the clear inclusion of certain persons or agencies in a law implies the exclusion of others, not named, from that law.[12] Thus, because the General Assembly has dealt with personnel files on an agency-by-agency basis and has enacted somewhat different statutes for different agencies, the argument would be that the General Assembly did not intend to make special provision for personnel files in agencies not mentioned in any such statute.

Although that is one obvious answer, it is not the only possible answer, and an alternative reading has considerable attraction. Indeed, I find it far preferable. The alternative extends the basic, common elements of all the statutes to these other agencies. It is based upon a number of points.

First, although some of the statutes do differ from the standard statute, they all agree on the fundamental point: subject to certain almost uniform exceptions, personnel files are not open to general public access. There does, therefore, appear to be a state policy regarding access to information in public employee personnel files. Second, some parts of personnel files—for example, medical information or personal financial information—are probably protected from public access by constitutionally based considerations of privacy.[13] Even if no statute addressed personnel files, some parts of the files would be closed to public access because of the constitutional right to privacy. It is more efficient to follow the uniform state policy than to seek to determine, perhaps through litigation, the exact shape of the constitutional bar to access. Third, the General Assembly normally acts by responding to requests. The absence of legislation regulating personnel files of councils of government, sanitary districts, housing authorities, ABC boards, and the other listed agencies is more reasonably explained by assuming that no one has sought such legislation than by assuming an express decision by the General Assembly to treat these categories of public employees differently than the great majority of public employees in the state.

Such an interpretation can be supported textually by a very broad understanding of "county" or "city" employee. One thread common to all the listed entities is that they were either originally created by one or more counties, or cities, or both, or their governing boards are appointed by one more city or county governing boards. That being the case, it is not completely abusive of the statutory language to consider their employees to be, albeit at one remove, employees of the counties or cities that created the entities or that appoint the boards that govern the entities. Under this interpretation, these various entities would follow the county or city personnel privacy statutes which, as noted, are functionally identical.

---

12. Two examples of cases in which the North Carolina Supreme Court relied upon this proposition are *Morrison v. Sears, Roebuck & Co.*, 319 N.C. 298, 354 S.E.2d 495 (1987), and *Campbell v. First Baptist Church of City of Durham*, 298 N.C. 476, 259 S.E.2d 558 (1979).

13. See the discussion of the constitutional right of privacy and personnel records *supra* in chapter 4 at note 27.

Whose Files Are Regulated by These Statutes?

Current and Former Employees

The various personnel privacy statutes make clear, in slightly different ways, that they apply to the personnel files of both current employees and former employees. G.S. 160A-168 and the other standard statutes begin by asserting that the "personnel files of *employees, former employees*, or applicants for employment maintained by a city are subject to inspection and may be disclosed only as provided by this section."[14] There is comparable (though not identical) language in G.S. 115C-319, for public school employees; G.S. 115D-27, for community college employees; and G.S. 130A-45.9, for public health authority employees. Both the public hospital and the state personnel privacy statutes reach the same end by defining "employee" to include both current and former employees.[15] Each of the statutes makes clear that inspection of these personnel files—for both current and former employees—is regulated by the appropriate personnel privacy statute rather than by G.S. 132-6.[16]

There is a unique provision about the files of former employees in the state personnel privacy statute. G.S. 126-22(c) allows full public inspection of the personnel files of former employees separated from state employment for ten years or more, except for material relating to demotions, material relating to disciplinary actions that resulted in the employee's dismissal, and personnel files maintained by any of the state retirement systems. The absence of such a provision in any of the other personnel privacy statutes indicates that, for the agencies subject to those statutes, the files of former employees are to be treated in exactly the same way as files of current employees.

Applicants for Employment

Each of the statutes also applies to the personnel files of applicants for employment, but there are important differences between the standard statutes and the others in their treatment of access to an applicant's file.

Public Access

As is discussed below, each of the personnel privacy statutes except the public health authority statute permits full public access to certain information in the personnel files of current and former employees.[17] Except for the state statute, however, none of them permit access to the files of applicants, although they get to that point somewhat differently.

The standard statutes specify that certain information "with respect to each city [county, water and sewer authority, etc.] employee" is open to the public. Each of these statutes also specifically defines employee to include former employees. They do not include applicants,

---

14. The area authority statute, G.S. 122C-158, does not include former employees in the cited passage, but it defines employee to include former employees.

15. See G.S. 131E-257.2(a) for hospital employees and G.S. 126-22(b)(1) for state employees.

16. The various statutes apply to the files of employees of public employers and not to employees generally. A public agency might sometimes have information about employees of entities that contract with the agency that is comparable to the information in a public employee's personnel file. The personnel privacy statutes do not apply to that sort of information if the subject is not a *public* employee; rather, in the absence of any statute specific to the information, it would be open to public access.

17. The public health authority statute does not seem to permit access of any kind to the files of former employees.

however, within the meaning of employee. Therefore, as the North Carolina Supreme Court has confirmed, the standard statute allows no public access whatsoever to the personnel files of applicants for employment.[18] In the *Elkin Tribune* case, a newspaper sought to inspect all applications submitted for the position of county manager; the court held that it was error for the trial court to order release of the applications to the newspaper. The statutes for public hospitals and public health authorities follow the same pattern.

The two education statutes require that the school board or community college "maintain a record of each of its employees," with certain specified information, and then direct that the specified information be open to public access.[19] These statutes carefully distinguish between employees and applicants, and therefore these sections allowing public access to employee files do not apply to the files of applicants.

G.S. 126-23 requires that each state department and agency maintain a record for each employee with certain information that is open to the public. G.S. 126-22(b)(1) defines employee to include applicants for employment, and therefore the directive of G.S. 126-23 applies to applicant files. Much of the public information is inapplicable to an unsuccessful applicant, but it appears that the names and ages of applicants for state employment are public information.[20]

Access to the Applicant

There is a split among the statutes as to access to the personnel file of an applicant by the applicant himself or herself. The two education statutes and the state statute each specifically grant to an applicant the same right of access to his or her file that is given to a current or former employee.[21] The standard statute, however, does not entitle an applicant to any access at all. The standard statute, as well as the public hospital statute, permits access to the file by the employee, and, as mentioned above, employee is defined specifically to include former employees but not applicants. Therefore, while a current or former employee has a broad right of access to his or her file under the standard statute and the public hospital statute, an unsuccessful applicant has none.[22] As was noted earlier, the public health authority statute does not permit access by the employee himself or herself, nor does it permit access by an applicant.

Limited Rights of Access

Each of the personnel privacy statutes sets out several limited rights of access to a personnel file. Again, with respect to the file of an applicant, the standard statute (and the public

---

18. Elkin Tribune, Inc. v. Yadkin County Bd. of Comm'rs, 331 N.C. 735, 417 S.E.2d 465 (1992).

19. See G.S. 115C-320 for public schools and G.S. 115D-28 for community colleges.

20. The sort of information that is public bears little relevance to applicants, so it is possible that a court might interpret G.S. 126-23 to apply only to current and former state employees.

21. See G.S. 115C-321(a)(1) for school employees, G.S. 115D-29 for community college employees, and G.S. 126-24(1) for state employees.

22. When a current or former employee applies for a different job within his or her government or agency, the employer should open a new file for the employee as an applicant. In that way, the restrictions on access to applicant files will apply to that new file. If the application materials were integrated with the existing personnel file of such an inside applicant, the normal rules of access to an employee's personnel file might otherwise apply.

hospital statute) is somewhat differently structured than the other statutes. The limited rights of access are set out in subsection (c) of the standard and public hospital statutes, and the introductory paragraph of that subsection states that it applies to "employee's personnel file[s]." Because of the statutes' definition of "employee," these rights of access apply to the files of current and former employees but not to the files of applicants. Essentially there is no right of access to the file of an applicant except for those persons involved in the appointment or employment process.

The two education statutes and the state statute, however, allow limited access to "personnel file[s]," a term that includes files of both current and former employees and applicants. Therefore, each of the limited rights of access allowed under those statutes applies just as much to the files of applicants as to the files of current or former employees.

The Subject's Waiver of Confidentiality

Sometimes a government or agency that is filling a high profile position, such as city or county manager, wishes to make public the short list of persons being considered for the position. Given the statutory provisions described above, a government or agency that wishes to release names or other information about persons applying for a public job should secure the permission of those persons before doing so.

Elected Officials

It seems certain that the county personnel privacy act applies to the personnel files of the sheriff, the register of deeds, and any other elected full-time official (such as an elected tax collector). As was noted above in the discussion on applicants, the North Carolina Supreme Court has held that persons applying for appointment as sheriff were "applicants for employment" within the meaning of the county statute,[23] and it is highly unlikely that a court would not extend the holding to reach the personnel file of a sheriff, once he or she was appointed or elected. That being the case, the county statute would also apply to the personnel file of the register of deeds and to any other elected full-time county official.

The status of personnel files for elected board members—such as county commissioners, city council members, or school board members—is much less clear. The local personnel privacy statutes extend by their own terms to "employees." Because sheriffs and registers of deeds are full time, normally making their living from their elected positions, it does not stretch the language to consider them employees. But it is otherwise with governing board members. Theirs is normally a part-time position and is not the predominant source of their income. We would not consider them county or city employees in the usual sense of the word, and the law clearly treats them as nonemployees in certain contexts. For example, they are not employees for purposes of the Local Governmental Employees' Retirement System and therefore cannot be enrolled in the system.[24] On the other hand, they are treated as employees in other contexts. The Internal Revenue Service, for example, considers them to be employees for income tax purposes, and therefore local governments

---

23. Durham Herald Co. v. County of Durham, 334 N.C. 677, 435 S.E.2d 317 (1993).

24. G.S. 128-21(10) defines employee for purposes of the retirement system and excludes "such employees who hold office by popular election as are not required to devote a major portion of their time to the duties of their office."

withhold taxes from any compensation they receive and issue them W-2 forms rather than 1099s.[25] Some local governments also include their governing board members in some employee benefit programs, especially group health or life insurance. Although elected officials probably shed some expectation of privacy when they stand for public office,[26] it is not clear that this loss extends to the kind of information normally found on an application for health or life insurance. Perhaps the personnel privacy statutes permit maintaining confidentiality of those documents that record transactions in which board members are treated as if they were employees. If such a distinction were permitted, insurance applications and W-4 forms might be protected by the statutes, but not applications filled out for a vacant seat on the board of county commissioners nor the home addresses and cell phone numbers of board members.[27]

Volunteers

Local governments make extensive use of volunteers in carrying out their work. Citizens serve, with at most nominal compensation, on a variety of boards and commissions. Police departments are often assisted by volunteer auxiliary officers, and volunteers are widespread in fire departments and rescue squads. Recreation departments and public hospitals, among other departments, also rely heavily on volunteers. A local government is likely to have a variety of documents relating to individual volunteers: application forms, performance evaluations, payroll records, and perhaps letters of reference. Many of these documents contain information comparable to that found in the personnel files of public employees. Therefore, the same concerns for privacy that led to protections for employee files probably extend to files about volunteers.

But volunteers are not usually considered employees. Although the Internal Revenue Service requires that they be treated as employees for withholding purposes,[28] and although it is possible to locate court decisions that treat volunteers as if they were employees,[29]

---

25. Internal Revenue Serv., Public Employer Tax Guide 6 (Feb. 2008), *available at* www.docstoc.com/docs/696720/Public-Employer-s-Tax-Guide.

26. In *In re Kading*, 235 N.W.2d 409, 417 (Wis. 1975) (footnotes omitted), the Wisconsin Supreme Court said, with reference to a rule requiring judicial officials to disclose financial information:

> It is the fact that Judge Kading is not solely a private citizen. Judge Kading is by voluntary choice a public official. While public officials, of course, do not waive their constitutional rights, they are nevertheless set apart from other members of society in terms of certain rights, as the law on libel makes clear. One who willingly puts himself forward into the public arena, and accepts publicly conferred benefits after election to public office, is legitimately much more subject to reasonable scrutiny and exposure than a purely private individual.

See *Klaus v. Minnesota State Ethics Commission*, 244 N.W.2d 672 (Minn. 1976), which collects numerous cases upholding against privacy attacks the constitutionality of disclosure requirements for elected officials.

27. In *Federated Publications, Inc. v. Boise City*, 915 P.2d 21 (Idaho 1996), the court held that the names and resumes of applicants for appointment to a vacancy on the city council were not personnel records of city employees and therefore were not exempt from public records access.

28. *See* Internal Revenue Serv., Public Employer Tax Guide 6 (Feb. 2008), *available at* www.docstoc.com/docs/696720/Public-Employer-s-Tax-Guide ("Volunteer firefighters are considered employees and their remuneration is generally subject to all withholding taxes.").

29. *E,g.*, Ryles v. Durham County Hosp. Corp., 107 N.C. App. 455, 420 S.E.2d 487 (1992) (uncompensated training apprentice held to be hospital employee for workers' compensation purposes); Whittington v. Sowela Technical Inst., 438 So. 2d 236 (La. Ct. App. 1983) (student nurse who drove van on class field trip

most decisions distinguish volunteers from employees.[30] Given that fact, and the general approach of the courts to read exceptions to public access narrowly, it is probable that the personnel privacy statutes do not extend to personnel-like records that concern volunteers of various kinds. This conclusion is reinforced by two statutes. First, G.S. 115C-209.1, enacted in 2003, exempts from public inspection the files kept by school administrative units for school volunteers. If volunteers were employees, such a statute would be unnecessary. Second, G.S. 126-5(c1)(4) makes it clear that members of *state* boards and commissions are in general not state employees and therefore not subject to state personnel laws, but the statute makes an exception for the state's personnel privacy statute and subjects records concerning such persons to that statute. There is no comparable provision for members of local government boards and commissions, an absence that reinforces the likelihood that the local government personnel privacy statutes do not extend to such people or to other volunteers.

If volunteers are not employees for purposes of the personnel privacy statutes, no other exception to the public records law applies generally to records about volunteers, and therefore, absent some intrusion into a volunteer's constitutional right of privacy, it is likely that such records—with the possible exception of tax-related records—are entirely open to public access.

Independent Contractors

A final group of individuals for whom governments might occasionally have records that are comparable in nature to personnel records are certain independent contractors. A county, for example, might accept applications from local attorneys for the position of county attorney. If the attorney is to be full time, he or she would be an employee, and the applications received would be exempt from public access under the county personnel privacy statute. But if the attorney is to remain in private practice, with the county as only one of many retained clients, he or she would not be a county employee but rather would be an independent contractor. In that case, the applications and any other records concerning the attorney (or any comparable contractor) would not be exempt from inspection as personnel records; they would be public records and open to public inspection and copying. The court of appeals assumed that independent contractors were not employees in *News Reporter Co. v. Columbus County*, decided in 2007.[31] The county's emergency services director had written the county commissioners a letter concerning the performance of a local physician who had been serving as the county's medical director, and the newspaper was seeking a copy of the letter. The court noted in passing that the physician was an independent contractor and therefore "defendants appropriately do not argue that the letter is entitled to protection under § 153A-98 as a personnel record."[32]

---

that was integral part of educational program held to be employee for purposes of imposing liability on educational institution for automobile accident that happened on trip).

30. *E.g.*, City of Fort Calhoun v. Collins, 500 N.W.2d 822 (Neb. 1993) (volunteer firemen not employees of fire department, nor of city served by department, for purposes of state Fair Employment Practices Act).

31. 184 N.C. App. 512, 646 S.E.2d 390 (2007).

32. *Id.* at 515, 646 S.E.2d at 393.

This conclusion is reinforced by the state's statutory treatment of records concerning physicians and other medical providers holding staff privileges at public hospitals and public health authorities or others acting as independent contractors with such entities. Both G.S. 130A-45.9 (for public health authorities) and G.S. 131E-97.1 (for public hospitals) exempt from public access information about the qualifications, competence, performance, and the like of "an independent contractor who provides health care services under a contract" with a public health authority or public hospital. These provisions would be unnecessary if the records qualified as personnel records.[33]

The Kinds of Documents within a Personnel File

The various personnel privacy statutes regulate access to the "personnel files" of public employees. What kinds of documents are included within such a file? This section discusses that question. Note that the discussion focuses on the substantive types of materials that can be part of a personnel file. The form of a particular record is unimportant. An e-mail that evaluates a subordinate is as much a part of the subordinate's personnel file as would be a written memorandum with the same content.

The Statutory Examples

The personnel privacy statutes themselves set out an illustrative list of documents that are part of a personnel file, and some of the other provisions of the statutes suggest the inclusion of other documents not on the illustrative list. The provision in the standard statute setting out the illustrative list, which is substantially the same in most of the other statutes, states that a personnel file consists, "by way of illustration but not limitation,"[34] of information relating to the employee's

> application, selection or nonselection, performance, promotions, demotions, transfers, suspension and other disciplinary actions, evaluation forms, leave, salary, and termination of employment.

This language clearly indicates that a very important category of information in a personnel file comprises items that record or form the basis for various personnel actions—hiring, promoting, compensating, disciplining, and discharging. These items include application forms, letters of reference, evaluations and performance ratings, training records, and so

---

33. In *Southwest Anesthesia Service, P.A. v. Southwest Medical Center*, 937 P.2d 1257 (Kan. Ct. App. 1997), the court held that a statutory exemption from access for records relating to employees did not extend to records concerning physicians holding staff privileges at a public hospital; it found that the physicians were not employees.

34. Three of the statutes—the state statute and the two education statutes—do not include the language in quotes. The state statute uses the verb "includes" but omits the phrase quoted in the text, and so the difference may be unimportant. The education statutes, however, use the verb "consists of," which suggests that the statutory listing may be exclusive. This raises the possibility that there might be information in a personnel file of an agency subject to the standard statute that would not be part of the personnel file of a public school or community college employee, but it is very difficult to speculate as to just what the information might be.

on. Letters of resignation probably also fall into this category.[35] The statutory listing also mentions information concerning leave, and therefore records concerning annual leave, sick leave, petty leave, and other forms of leave are part of an employee's personnel file.

Other provisions in the statute indicate that additional kinds of documents are part of a personnel file as well. The list of items that are specifically public includes the employee's current title and the office to which the employee is currently assigned. These listings suggest that other status information, such as shift assignments, is also part of the personnel file. One category of items that the statute closes to the employee himself or herself is medical information "that a prudent physician would not divulge to his patient." Obviously, then, medical information about an employee, whether from a required physical, as part of a wellness program, or otherwise, is also part of the personnel file.

In summary, the statute itself indicates at least four kinds of documents that are part of an employee's personnel file: (1) items that record or form the basis of personnel actions; (2) information about leave; (3) information about the employee's position, office, and so forth; and (4) medical information about the employee. Here is a list of some sorts of items that would be part of a personnel file:

- Applications and applicant resumes
- Comments about applicants
- Complaints against employees
- Conflict-of-interest forms
- Employee work plans or performance goals for the upcoming year[36]
- Employee work schedules
- ID photographs[37]
- Insurance beneficiaries
- Insurance claims history[38]
- Interview notes or recordings
- Letters about working with other employees[39]

---

35. In *Oregonian Publishing Co. v. Portland School District No. 1J*, 925 P.2d 591 (1996), the court held that a school principal's resignation letter was not part of the principal's personnel file. The court based its conclusion, however, on the facts that the letter had been sent to all faculty and staff at the school and printed in the school newspaper.

36. Versaci v. Superior Court, 26 Cal. Rptr. 3d 92 (Ct. App. 2005) (superintendent's performance goals for the year part of her personnel file).

37. Henderson v. City of Chattanooga, 133 S.W.3d 192 (Tenn. Ct. App. 2003) (employee photographs part of their personnel files). *State ex rel. Plain Dealer Publishing Co. v. City of Cleveland*, 831 N.E.2d 987 (Ohio 2005) held that ID photographs of police officers were not open to public access but did so under an exemption other than for personnel records. The court did not reach the question of whether such photographs were part of the officers' personnel files.

38. Michelson v. Wyatt, 880 A.2d 458 (N.J. Super. Ct. App. Div. 2005) (employee health insurance claims history part of personnel file).

39. In *News Reporter Co. v. Columbus County*, 184 N.C. App. 512, 646 S.E.2d 390 (2007), the county's emergency services director had written a letter to the county commissioners, who were considering reappointment of the county medical director, discussing his experience in working with the medical director. The court held that those portions of the letter that discussed the author's ability to work with the medical director were appropriately part of the *author's* personnel file.

- Qualification and promotion examination scores[40]
- W-4 forms

Employment Contracts

School superintendents operate, by statute, under contracts with their employing school boards;[41] and city and county managers, other chief executives, and full-time attorneys often enter into such contracts as well. There has been some question in the past as to whether such contracts were part of the employee's personnel file. The initial answer was given by the court of appeals in a case involving executives of a public hospital.[42] The court held that, under the public hospital personnel privacy statute, the executives' contracts with the hospital were part of their personnel files.[43] The result was that most of the provisions in the contract were not available for public access. Because the relevant provisions of the public hospital statute were essentially identical to the other personnel privacy statutes, the consequence was that all these employment contracts were part of the employee's personnel file. The General Assembly responded to the case in 2007, enacting amendments to each of the personnel privacy statutes.[44] As amended, each of the statutes makes clear that an employment contract is in fact part of the employee's personnel file, but they also, with one exception, make clear that the entire contract is within that part of a personnel file that is open to the public.[45]

The Meaning of "Gathered"

The various personnel privacy statutes define a personnel file as comprising information gathered by the employing entity.[46] Some plaintiffs have argued that the word "gathered" imposes limitations on the content of a personnel file. In *Elkin Tribune, Inc. v. Yadkin County Board of County Commissioners*, the newspaper argued that employment applications that were *sent to* the county were not gathered by the county;[47] and in *Knight Publishing Co. v. Charlotte-Mecklenburg Hospital Authority*, the newspaper argued that contract and payroll documents were also not gathered by the authority.[48] The courts have rejected these arguments, preferring a more expansive understanding of the meaning of gathered. In *Knight Publishing*, the court concluded that a personnel file is "comprised of information

---

40. *See* DeLaMater v. Marion Civil Serv. Comm'n, 554 N.W.2d 875 (Iowa 1996) (court accepts that a person's score on civil service examination part of his or her personnel file).

41. G.S. 115C-271.

42. Knight Publ'g Co. v. Charlotte-Mecklenburg Hosp. Auth., 172 N.C. App. 486, 616 S.E.2d 602 (2005).

43. The holding was contrary to the outcome of comparable cases decided in other states, all of which held that the terms of such employment contracts were open to public access. Denver Publ'g Co. v. Univ. of Colo., 812 P.2d 682 (Colo. App. 1990) (contracts between university and chancellors); Reppert v. S. Ill. Univ., 874 N.E.2d 905 (Ill. App. Ct. 2007) (university employment contracts); University Sys. of Md. v. Baltimore Sun Co., 847 A.2d 427 (Md. 2004) (university coaches' contracts); Librach v. Cooper, 778 S.W.2d 351 (Mo. Ct. App. 1989) (school superintendent's contract).

44. S.L. 2008-508.

45. The exception is G.S. 131E-257.2, which does not list an employment contract as one of the public items in a personnel file.

46. The public health authority statute, G.S. 130A-459, does not define "personnel file."

47. 331 N.C. 735, 417 S.E.2d 465 (1992).

48. 172 N.C. App. 486, 616 S.E.2d 602 (2005).

and documents, including employee contracts and payroll documents, which are amassed, accumulated, and collected into one place by the employer."[49]

Another issue involves the gathering entity. The state personnel privacy act, in G.S. 126-22, previously defined a personnel file as comprising information "gathered by the *department, division, bureau, commission, council, or other agency* . . . which employs" the person who is the subject of the file.[50] In *News & Observer Publishing Co. v. Poole*,[51] the supreme court emphasized the italicized words and held that information about a state employee originally gathered by some state agency other than that employee's employing agency is not part of the employee's personnel file. In *Poole*, information about employees of North Carolina State University (NCSU) was gathered by the State Bureau of Investigation (SBI); therefore, it was not part of the personnel files of those employees. Their employing agency was NCSU, not the SBI. In this regard the various local government personnel privacy statutes differ somewhat from the state statute. If the statutes were parallel, the local government statutes would define the personnel file as comprising information gathered by the employee's department, agency, and so forth. Instead, however, the local government statutes speak of information gathered by the "city" or by the "county" or by the "local board of education," and so forth. That usage appears to cover any information in an employee's personnel file: if the information is in the local government's possession, it has perforce been gathered by the local government.

Internal Investigations and Use of Force Reports

When local governments conduct internal investigations into the actions of specific employees, the question arises as to whether the information gathered through such an investigation is part of the employee's personnel file. It almost certainly is. The information, or any report based on it, clearly might form the basis of personnel action taken regarding the employee. Even if the investigation reveals no misconduct or error by the employee, and therefore no personnel action is taken, the outcome of the investigation does not change its essential nature as a personnel matter. This issue has arisen in a number of states that restrict access to personnel records, and a significant majority of the cases held that the records of such an investigation are part of the personnel file of the affected employee or employees.[52]

---

49. *Id.* at 492, 616 S.E.2d at 607.

50. G.S. 126-22 was amended in 2007 and now states that a "personnel file" is information "gathered by an employer," and "employer" is defined as "any State department, university, division, bureau, commission, council, or other agency." The change does not seem to be substantive.

51. 330 N.C. 465, 412 S.E.2d 7 (1992).

52. *E.g.*, BRV, Inc. v. Superior Court, 49 Cal. Rptr. 3d 519 (Ct. App. 2006) (investigation into allegations of misconduct by school superintendent); Des Moines Indep. Cmty. Sch. Dist. Pub. Records v. Des Moines Register & Tribune Co., 487 N.W.2d 666 (Iowa 1992) (investigation of job performance of teachers); Kent County Deputy Sheriff's Ass'n v. Kent County Sheriff, 616 N.W.2d 677 (Mich. 2000); Demers v. City of Minneapolis, 486 N.W.2d 828 (Minn. Ct. App. 1992) (police department internal investigation); Wilson v. McNeal, 575 S.W.2d 802 (Mo. Ct. App. 1978) (police department internal investigation); Hounsell v. N. Conway Water Precinct, 903 A.2d 987 (N.H. 2006) (investigation into allegations that one employee harassed another); Union Leader Corp. v. Fenniman, 620 A.2d 1039 (N.H. 1993) (police department internal investigation); Pawtucket Teachers Alliance Local No. 920 v. Brady, 556 A.2d 556 (R.I. 1989) (investigation

In a 1995 advisory opinion, the attorney general agreed that internal investigation records are part of the employee's personnel file and then dealt with an additional issue under the statute.[53] The opinion concerned a city's practice in dealing with citizen complaints about a police officer and consequent internal investigations of the officer's actions. Once an investigation was complete, the city wrote the complainant and summarized the results of the investigation; that is, whether the charges were sustained or not sustained, whether the officer was exonerated, and whether the charges were unfounded. The city's letter to the complainant did not specify whether disciplinary action was taken against the officer. The attorney general concluded that the records of the investigation were part of the officer's personnel file and were thus closed to public access under G.S. 160A-168. That being the case, the attorney general went on to advise, the city's letters to complainants reporting the results of investigations released information that also was part of personnel files. Before sending such a letter, therefore, the city needed to comply with one of the exceptions to confidentiality set out in G.S. 160A-168(c). Those include requesting that the employee in question sign a release or asking the manager and council to invoke the provisions of G.S. 160A-168(c)(7) that specify what data may be released from a personnel file.[54]

It should be noted that if internal investigation records are part of an employee's personnel file, the employee is entitled to access to the complete investigation.

Use of force reports. A related issue is whether law enforcement use of force reports are part of an officer's personnel file. Typically, a law enforcement officer fills out such a report any time force is used in making an arrest. A Texas case demonstrates that the status of these reports under the public records law may depend on the use made of the record by the law enforcement agency. The police department in *City of San Antonio v. San Antonio Express-News*[55] used the reports to track trends in the use of force by the city's police department but not to evaluate individual officers. The court therefore held that the reports were not part of the officers' personnel files. On the other hand, if a department used such reports in evaluating and disciplining officers, it is likely the court would hold them to be part of the officers' personnel files.

Settlements with Employees

If an employee is disciplined or discharged by a local government, or simply feels that he or she has been mistreated, the employee might file a grievance, initiate some sort of administrative proceeding, or bring a lawsuit. If the matter is settled, a question then arises about the status of the settlement documents. The employee will frequently want them to be sealed, and the local government may want that result as well.

---

into principal's administration of school). *Contra* Worcester Telegram & Gazette Corp. v. Chief of Police, 787 N.E.2d 602 (Mass. App. Ct. 2003) (police internal affairs investigation).

53. Letter to Keith D. Burns, 22 May 1995, Advisory Opinion No. 182, *available at* www.ncdoj.gov/About-DOJ/Legal-Services/Legal-Opinions.aspx.

54. It is worth noting that several cities have obtained local acts from the General Assembly that permit each city to release the disposition of disciplinary charges against a police officer to the person alleged to have been aggrieved by the officer's actions. S.L. 1997-305 (Charlotte); S.L. 1998-142 (Durham); S.L. 2001-20 (Greensboro); and S.L. 2003-238 (Wilmington).

55. 47 S.W.3d 556 (Tex. App. 2000).

Settlement documents fit within the definition of items within the employee's personnel file. They typically contain information concerning the employee's "selection or nonselection, performance, promotions, . . . suspension and other disciplinary actions, . . . and termination of employment." But recognizing that settlement documents are appropriately part of the employee's personnel file does not determine whether the documents are subject to public inspection. G.S. 132-1.3 provides that settlement documents in any suit or administrative proceeding against the state or a local government are public records and are open to public inspection. The possible conflict between the settlement statute and other statutes, such as the personnel privacy acts, that provide for confidentiality of specific records is considered in the chapter on settlements, chapter 10, and the reader is referred to that discussion.

Attorney Communications

In an advisory opinion issued in 2001, the attorney general's office wrote that communications about specific employees from a local government attorney to the local government's officials were part of the employees' personnel files and therefore not subject to public inspection.[56] (Because they are part of a personnel file, though, they would consequently be open to inspection by the concerned employee.)

Minutes and General Accounts of Closed Sessions

One of the purposes for which a public body may hold a closed session, under the open meetings law, is to "consider the qualifications, competence, performance, character, fitness, conditions of appointment, or conditions of initial employment of an individual public officer or employee or prospective public officer or employee."[57] As is discussed more fully *infra* in chapter 18, "Minutes and General Accounts of Closed Sessions," the open meetings law requires a public body to prepare minutes and a general account of any closed session. The law also permits sealing such minutes or general account, but only "so long as public inspection would frustrate the purpose of a closed session."[58] Local governments often seal permanently the minutes of closed sessions held to consider personnel matters, on the ground that it would always frustrate the purpose of the closed session to allow public inspection of the minutes. The question then arises, are such sealed minutes part of the discussed employee's personnel file, or are the minutes some other sort of record that a public body can seal permanently because its content is so comparable to the content of a personnel file? The consequence of the answer lies in whether the employee who was discussed has access to the sealed minutes. If they are part of his or her personnel file, he or she is entitled to access; if not, there is no special right of access for the employee.

No court has addressed this issue, but my own conclusion is that the minutes and general account of a closed session held to discuss an employee are part of that employee's personnel file. If it is detailed enough, the general account of such a closed session may contain an evaluation of the employee in question that is comparable to evaluations of other employees

---

56. Letter to Grady Joseph Wheeler, Jr., 30 May 2001, Advisory Opinion No. 497, *available at* www.ncdoj.gov/About-DOJ/Legal-Services/Legal-Opinions.aspx.

57. G.S. 143-318.11(a)(6).

58. G.S. 143-318.10(e).

made by their supervisors. Sometimes the minutes and general account will reflect some sort of action taken with respect to an employee, such as placing the employee on probation or agreeing on performance goals for the upcoming year. These are the same sorts of material that would be in the personnel file of an employee were the actions taken by the manager rather than by the governing board. Given the comparability of the material to that routinely placed in personnel files, the minutes and general account should be considered part of the personnel file, and therefore the employee is entitled to full access to those minutes and general accounts.

Documents Possibly Excluded from Personnel Files

Not all information that a local government maintains on specific employees is part of the employee's personnel file. This section suggests some categories of material that might not be part of a personnel file.

Financial Records

Local governments typically maintain a variety of payroll records that contain information about specific employees. These records include time sheets and cards and other information indicating the number of hours worked by each employee and perhaps information on leave taken; accounting records showing the amounts paid to each employee; and documents that indicate various deductions and withholdings from each employee's paycheck. At least some of this information is probably not part of an employee's personnel file.

Basic Accounting System Records

A local government's accounting records are generally open to public inspection. Even though the detailed records show the amount paid each employee each month, these are more appropriately considered accounting records—showing the use of public resources—than personnel records.

Garnishment Records

Occasionally public employees will be subject to garnishment orders, and money will be deducted from their paychecks as a result. The documentation of such an action is almost certainly not part of an employee's personnel file. The garnishment has nothing to do with his or her actions as an employee. Rather, it results from the employee's actions as a private citizen, and the financial apparatus of the government is being used to help resolve the private matter. Even if the garnishment somehow results in some sort of disciplinary action against the employee, that ought not to affect the original nature of the record. An employee might be discharged because he or she is charged with a crime, but that personnel action does not convert the original incident report into a personnel file document.

Time Sheets

Time sheets present a more difficult issue, and the answer might differ from one government to another. A simple time card, of the sort used to punch in at an old fashioned time machine, simply records when a person arrives and leaves work and is created solely for payroll purposes. If that is what is meant by a time sheet, it is much more a financial record than a personnel record and probably is not part of the employee's personnel file.[59] Often, however, time sheets are more elaborate and record not only the specific hours of work but also the amount of annual, petty, or sick leave that the employee takes and the amount of overtime earned or compensatory time taken. Such a more elaborate time sheet is probably part of the employee's personnel file, given the definition of personnel file in the various statutes. The various statutory definitions specifically include within a personnel file information about both leave and salary.

Payroll Deductions and Withholdings

These also present a difficult issue. Clearly the source documents upon which payroll deductions and withholdings are made are part of the personnel file. The usual practice, in units large enough to separate the financial and human resources (HR) functions, is for the HR department to record and maintain the information upon which the deductions and withholdings are made and then give the finance department just enough information for it to be able to prepare the payroll. It is the HR department that has custody of tax withholding forms, insurance applications, deferred compensation applications, and the like, and those basic documents are clearly part of the employee's personnel file.[60] Even if a unit does not have a separate HR department, and the basic documents are in the finance department's custody, the documents retain their character as personnel documents. The payroll stubs or comparable records themselves, however, are clearly finance department documents and record only the *amounts* withheld or deducted. Nevertheless, revealing even the amount of tax withheld or the insurance premium deducted may give a window into the employee's private life that the various personnel privacy statutes are intended to keep covered. For that reason, the most that can be said for these financial records is that the law remains unclear.

Travel Records

Records that support an employee's request for reimbursement for work-related travel expenses or for advance for such travel are open to public access; they are financial in nature and are not part of the employee's personnel file.[61]

---

59. In *State ex rel. Kim v. Wachenschwanz*, 757 N.E.2d 367 (Ohio 2001), the court held that records created by each police officer indicating his or her time on duty and mileage on duty were public record. The defendant agency, however, made no attempt to argue that these records were part of the employees' personnel files. In *Alaska Wildlife Alliance v. Rue*, 948 P.2d 976 (Alaska 1997), the court held that time sheets were not part of an employee's personnel file. The Alaska statute does not include a definition of personnel file comparable to the North Carolina statutes'.

60. In *Blankenship v. City of Hoover*, 590 So. 2d 245 (Ala. 1991), the court held that W-2 forms were not subject to public access under that state's public records law.

61. In *News & Observer Publishing Co. v. Wake County Hospital System, Inc.*, 55 N.C. App. 1, 284 S.E.2d 542 (1981), the court held that expense account records for the system's president and trustees were open to public access, but it is not clear that the defendants sought to characterize these records as part of anyone's personnel file.

The attorney general's office reached the same conclusion in 1993. Letter to John M. Bahner, Jr., 5 April 1993, Advisory Opinion No. 11, *available at* www.ncdoj.gov/About-DOJ/Legal-Services/

Employee Telephone Numbers and E-mail Addresses

An employee's office telephone number and e-mail address have nothing to do with the sorts of information included in the statutory definition of a personnel file and for that reason are almost certainly not part of the employee's personnel file. This would include both desk telephones and employer-issued cell phones. Therefore, these numbers and addresses are open to public access.

Reports about Departmental Processes and the Like

After the school district in *Oregonian Publishing Co. v. Portland School District No. 1J*[62] received a report alleging the misuse and theft of school property, it asked the school district's police department to investigate the matter. As a result of the police report describing problems with property control at the school, three employees either resigned or were terminated. The Oregon Supreme Court noted that the report focused on property control procedures at the school and made recommendations for improvements in those procedures; it did not address the performance of specific employees or make recommendations about specific employees. Therefore, the court held, the report was not part of any employee's personnel file. The opinion makes sense, and it is likely that a North Carolina court would reach a similar conclusion.

Release of Criminal Records Checks

Several statutes permit the state Department of Justice to provide criminal records information about applicants for employment to many local agencies, as follows:

- To a city or county, about any applicant for city or county employment—G.S. 114-19.14.
- To a local Homeland Security director, local fire chief, county fire marshal, or emergency services director or, if there is no such person, to a local law enforcement agency, about any applicant to become a paid or volunteer firefighter or emergency medical service worker for a local government—G.S. 114-19.12.
- To a school administrative unit, about any applicant for school employment—G.S. 114-19.2.
- To a public hospital, about employees or prospective employees— G.S. 114-19.3.
- To a G.S. Chapter 122C provider, about employees or prospective employees—G.S. 114-19.10.

Each of these statutes directs that the information provided to the local unit or agency be kept confidential, but there is one subtle difference in their confidentiality provisions. The public school statute directs that the information be kept confidential as provided in the public school personnel privacy statute. That would seem to mean that the criminal records information held by a school administrative unit is part of the personnel file of the

---

Legal-Opinions.aspx . The opinion advised that "[t]ravel records relate to the expenditure of public funds; any relationship to the [employee's] employment is secondary or incidental. Thus, in our opinion, G.S. 115C-319 [the public school employee personnel privacy statute] does not apply in this instance."

62. 987 P.2d 480 (Or. 1999).

subject of the information and that the information is accessible in the same way as other information in the file. The other statutes, by contrast, state simply that the recipient agency is to keep the record confidential; they do not refer to the applicable personnel privacy statute. This difference suggests that a local government or agency subject to one of these other statutes should not make the criminal records information part of the subject's personnel file but should keep it separate and not allow access to the information as they would if it were part of the personnel file.[63]

The Statutory List of Public Information

The statutory list of items within a personnel file that are open to public access is generally straightforward. A number of comments are in order, however.

Employees and Former Employees—Usually Not Applicants

As was noted in the discussion under "Applicants for Employment," except for the state statute, none of the statutes permits any public access whatsoever to the files of applicants for employment.[64] Therefore, the public access rules discussed below apply only to the files of current and former employees, except for public health authorities, for which the discussion applies only to current employees.[65] (In the remainder of this section, the use of the word "employee" includes former employees.)

The Employee's Name

Coupling the Name with Other Information

The statutes make an employee's name a public portion of the personnel file, along with certain other information about the employee. Occasionally local governments, in responding to public access requests, have attempted to separate the names from the other information. A government might, for example, provide a list of all employees and a list of all salaries but not show which salary belongs to which employee. Or a government might admit that an employee was placed on suspension but not name the employee. Such an attempt at decoupling the information is almost certainly not permitted by the various statutes. The list of public information is intended to provide a snapshot of information about each public employee, and that statutory intention cannot be served if each item of public information is not tied to a specific employee.

---

63. If a local government obtains criminal history information about an employee or applicant for employment through some method other than a criminal history records check through the Department of Justice, that information would presumably become part of the employee's or applicant's regular personnel file.

64. The state statute, as noted, arguably permits access to the names and ages of applicants for state employment.

65. The public health authority statute, G.S. 130A-45.9, specifically applies generally to personnel files of former employees. Subsection (b), however, which specifies what part of a file is open to public inspection, specifically applies only to "employees," and that term is not—as it is in the other statutes—defined to include former employees.

The Idaho case of *Magic Valley Newspapers, Inc. v. Magic Valley Regional Medical Center*[66] is illuminating on this matter. The newspaper had sought a list of the names and salaries of all hospital employees making more than $50,000 annually; the hospital provided the information but blackened out the names. The hospital noted that the statute made public employees' current salaries and salary histories public but that it did not make public the names of employees. Therefore, the hospital argued, unless the requester provided a name in its request, the public agency could not provide a name in response to the request. The court was unimpressed. Noting that the information to be disclosed would be meaningless if not coupled to a name, it directed the hospital to show the names along with the salaries. In North Carolina the statutes specifically make employee names a public item in personnel files, and so the argument for coupling information is even stronger.

Undercover Officer Names

The city and county statutes, in subsection (c1)(3), permit denying public access to "[i]nformation that might identify an undercover law enforcement officer or a law enforcement informer." Clearly this gives authority for a local government to refuse to provide the name of an undercover officer, particularly if the name is coupled to the officer's position.

Salary Information

The Meaning of "Salary"

In their original form, the various statues made public an employee's "current salary" but did not make clear whether, with respect to hourly employees, salary meant the amount paid over a particular time period or the employee's rate of pay. The term also seemed to exclude any bonuses, benefits, or the like paid to an employee.[67] In 2007, however, the General Assembly rewrote the various statutes and defined—and probably enlarged—the term. The standard statute, the educational statutes, and the state statute now define salary to include "pay, benefits,[68] incentives, bonuses, and deferred and all other forms of compensation paid by the employing entity."[69] For an hourly employee, the public information is clearly the total amount paid, not the rate of pay, and as the quoted language states, it also includes bonuses or incentives, benefits, and all deferred compensation. It probably also includes compensatory time owed to an employee.[70]

---

66. 59 P.3d 314 (Idaho 2002).

67. The attorney general's office did conclude, in 1997, that the term salary included the amount of disability income being received by a current or former employee. Letter to Janice Faulkner, 18 March 1997, Advisory Opinion No. 298, *available at* www.ncdoj.gov/About-DOJ/Legal-Services/Legal-Opinions.aspx. Under the statutory amendments discussed below, there is no question but that such income is included within the meaning of "salary."

68. The attorney general's office has construed the word "benefits" to include the balances due to an employee of various sorts of leave—vacation leave, sick leave, bonus leave, and compensatory time. Letter to Laura B. Luger, 15 June 2009, *available at* www.ncdoj.gov/About-DOJ/Legal-Services/Legal-Opinions.aspx.

69. There is no basis in the definition of salary to conclude that it includes the amounts withheld from an employee's paycheck for taxes, insurance, and the like. Those amounts are not *paid to* the employee by the government.

70. In *Mississippi Department of Wildlife, Fisheries & Parks v. Mississippi Wildlife Enforcement Officers Ass'n*, 740 So. 2d 925 (Miss. 1999), the court characterized compensatory time as an element of an employee's compensation.

The 2007 legislation made slightly different provision, however, for public health authorities and public hospitals. First, with respect to public health authorities, G.S. 130A-45.9(b) makes public for an employee the "total compensation of current and former positions." The language is ambiguous. It might be taken to mean, for the current year, total compensation, in which case it would be appropriate to apply to public health authorities the same definition of salary as is found in the standard statute. But the addition of "former positions" to the phrase suggests a different meaning. Total compensation in former positions might be a cumulative number, the total amount paid over time in all former positions held by an employee within an authority. If that is the meaning for former positions, it might then also be the meaning for the current position—that is, not the total compensation for the current year, but the total amount paid to the employee through the duration of his or her current position, which obviously might be over several years. Under that meaning, only the cumulative totals, and not the employee's current salary and other compensation, would be public records. The statute might also be read to require more detail—that is, total compensation in all positions might mean a listing of the annual compensation paid to an employee for each year he or she worked for an authority. That would certainly be more useful to the public than a simple cumulative number. It would be helpful for the legislature to clarify the statute.

In regard to public hospital employees, the statute, G.S. 131E-257.2, is clear, but the policy is strikingly different from that applicable to other public employees. The salary information of almost all hospital employees is closed to public access. Only the salary information of the hospital's chief executive officer and other "Covered Officers" and "key employees" is open to public access. A hospital may have up to five covered officers: the chief executive officer and the next four most highly compensated executive officers, who are persons appointed by the hospital's governing board to serve as officers. In addition, the statute makes public the salary information of the five most highly compensated key employees, who are defined as persons having "responsibilities, power, or influence similar to those of an officer"; these employees apparently might be appointed by someone other than the governing board. For the covered officers and key employees, the statute makes public (1) the person's base salary, (2) the person's bonus compensation, (3) the person's plan-based incentive compensation, and (4) the dollar value of all of the person's other compensation, including any perquisites or other personal benefits.

Retirement Benefits

The 2007 amendments relating to compensation state that salary includes various forms of compensation "paid by the employing entity." Shortly after the adjournment of the 2007 General Assembly, the question arose as to whether the amount paid to former employees in retirement benefits was included within the meaning of salary, and two members of the state Senate sought an advisory opinion from the attorney general's office, which was issued in February 2008.[71] While the letter and response dealt only with former state employees, the reasoning would apply as well to retired local government employees in various state-

71. Letter to Tony Rand & David W. Hoyle, 5 February 2008, Advisory Opinion No. 584, *available at* www.ncdoj.gov/About-DOJ/Legal-Services/Legal-Opinions.aspx .

administered retirement systems. The letter pointed out that retirement benefits for state employees are not paid by the "employing entity" but by the Department of State Treasurer, and therefore on first blush they did not seem to come within the statutory terms. But the letter went on to point out that for retired employees of that department, the employing entity and the entity paying retirement benefits were one and the same, so that uniquely among retired state employees, those who had worked for the Department of State Treasurer would have their retirement benefits open to public access. The letter pointed out that this seemed an absurd result that could not have been intended by the General Assembly and therefore concluded that the legislature "did not intend to exclude retirement benefit information from the records required to be maintained for public inspection." If it is absurd to distinguish between employees retired from the Department of State Treasurer and those retired from other state departments and agencies, it seems equally absurd to distinguish between state employees and local government employees when the statutory language is identical. Therefore, the standard statute and educational statutes should be read to include state-administered retirement benefits as part of the salary of local government employees as well as state government employees.[72]

If a local government is administering a local retirement system or is making supplemental retirement payments to retired law enforcement officers, the payment is clearly coming from the employing entity, and the amounts paid are public record.

Salary History

In addition to an employee's current compensation, most of the statutes also make public the date and amount of an employee's "most recent increase or decrease in salary." (The exceptions are the public health authority statute and the public hospital statute, which are discussed separately below.) First, given the expanded definition of salary, the quoted phrase probably also means the date and amount of the most recent increase or decrease in the other components of compensation beyond salary. For example, if an employee's deferred compensation has increased, that amount and the date of the increase are probably public. Second, and more important, note that it is only the most recent increase or decrease that is public. It is the amount of the employee's last raise that is public, and the dates and amounts of earlier raises—each public at one time, when it was the most recent—are no longer part of the public information in a personnel file. That is, only the most recent change in compensation is public, rather than an employee's complete salary history.

As was noted above, the public health authority statute makes public an employee's total compensation of current and former positions. This might either require that an authority provide the cumulative amount paid to an employee in all the years he or she has worked for the authority, or it might require a listing of the total compensation paid to the employee for each year he or she has worked. If the latter, a public health authority would be under quite a different regime with respect to salary history than any other public employer.

---

72. Some local government employees are part of privately-administered retirement systems, such as the IMCA system. The logic of the attorney general's opinion would not extend to such systems, and their records would therefore not be part of an employee's or former employee's personnel file; they would not be public records at all.

In the case of public hospitals, it is only current compensation that is public. There is no provision in the statute for making public the amount or date of any increase or decrease in compensation.

Position Title and Office to Which Assigned and Work Assignments

The various statutes make public an employee's current position title and the office to which the person is currently assigned.[73] Given the nature of this information, it seems likely a personnel file would also include an employee's current work assignment or work schedule, and that these items would not be open to public access.

Date [and Substance] of Last Personnel Action

Date or Date and Substance?

Each of the statutes includes within the public information in a personnel file the "*date* of the most recent promotion, demotion, transfer, suspension, separation, or other change in position classification." Literally, the language makes public the date upon which the personnel action was taken but not the nature of that personnel action. Many local officials and employees, and many members of the public, assume that despite the language, the statutes intend that the nature of the action be public as well. There is, however, internal evidence within several of the statutes that supports a reading that only the date is meant. Under that reading, all that can be disclosed is that some unspecified personnel action was taken on a certain date with respect to an identified employee. As is discussed below, most of the statutes permit a release of otherwise protected information in order to maintain public confidence in the administration of public services (or words to that effect). The provision in G.S. 160A-168(c)(7) is representative:

> The city manager, with concurrence of the council, or, in cities not having a manager, the council may inform any person *of the employment or nonemployment, promotion, demotion, suspension or other disciplinary action, reinstatement, transfer, or termination of a city employee* and the reasons for that personnel action.

If the automatically public information in a personnel file included the substance of the most recent personnel action as well as its date, the italicized language just quoted would normally be unnecessary; the action in question would already be public. Indeed, the attorney general's office took the position over thirty years ago that when the statutes said "date," they meant date. When asked whether the news media could be informed that a state employee had been suspended pending an investigation, the office responded by saying "No. The news media may be told only the date of an employee's most recent suspension."[74] In addition, most of the statutes also make public the "date and amount" of the employee's most recent change in compensation. This demonstrates that the General Assembly knew how to phrase the statute to include more than the date when it wished to.

---

73. The public health authority statute, G.S. 130A-45.9, does not include the office to which a person is assigned among the public information in a personnel file.

74. Letter to J. Phil Carlton, 47 Op. N.C. Att'y Gen. 141 (1977).

Despite this evidence from within the statutes and the published opinion of the attorney general, it is a widespread practice among local governments to make public both the date and the nature of the most recent personnel action. Indeed, at least one local government has been ordered by a superior court judge to release the nature of the action as well as the date.[75] Until the General Assembly or an appellate court clarifies the matter, whether the nature of the latest personnel action is public will remain uncertain.

Administrative Leave

Whether it is the date, or both the date and the nature of the action, the requirement that the information be made public applies to the most recent "promotion, demotion, transfer, suspension, separation, or other change in position classification." The question arises, is an administrative leave with pay an "other change in position classification"? (If an employee is placed on administrative leave *without* pay, it is hard to see how that differs from a suspension and it therefore would be such a change.) Local governments most frequently place an employee on administrative leave with pay when there is some sort of allegation against the employee or some other event (such as a law enforcement officer's discharge of a firearm) that compels the government to investigate the employee's conduct. If the allegation proves unfounded or the other event does not warrant discipline, the employee comes off administrative leave and there is usually no permanent record of the matter included in the personnel file. If the allegation proves true or investigation reveals the need for some sort of personnel action, whatever action is taken becomes the most recent action specified in the statute.

The items listed in the statute are not quite a set of parallel actions. They include four actions that clearly constitute a "change in position classification": promotion, demotion, transfer, or separation. And they include suspension, which is not strictly speaking a change in classification; once the suspension is served, the employee returns to the same position. One possible reading of the statutory list is that it includes any change in position classification and any suspension, but nothing that is neither a change in classification nor a suspension. If that reading is correct, is administrative leave with pay a suspension? It resembles a suspension in that the employee is temporarily barred from performing the duties of his or her employment. It differs from a suspension, however, in that first, the employee continues to be paid, and second and more importantly, a suspension is a disciplinary action, while administrative leave is a status imposed while the government determines whether disciplinary action is warranted. My conclusion is that administrative leave with pay in the circumstances described above is not the sort of action that triggers the statutory duty of disclosure.[76]

---

75. Lakeland Ledger Publ'g Corp. v. City of Wilmington, No. 03 CVS 2482 (N.C. Super. Ct., New Hanover County, Dec. 3, 2003). In response to a request, the city had disclosed that on a certain date unspecified employment actions had been taken with respect to two identified employees. The court ordered the city to disclose the type of employment action that was taken. Specifically, if the action was a suspension, the city was required to state that the action was a suspension as well as providing the beginning and ending dates of the suspension and indicating whether a decrease in salary accompanied the suspension.

76. This was the conclusion reached by the trial judge in an action brought against the City of Durham in 2007—that administrative leave is neither a suspension nor a change in position classification. Capitol Broad. Co. v. City of Durham, No. 07 CVS 001218 (N.C. Super. Ct., Durham County, Dec. 21, 2007).

Home Addresses and Telephone Numbers

Finally, an employee's home address and home telephone number are not on the list of items open to public access. This suggests that this information should not be included within an employee directory—which is usually disseminated at least to all employees—without giving the employee an opportunity to object.

Release to the Tax Collector

All of the personnel privacy statutes—save the public health authority statute, which does not permit any limited release of information in a file, and the public school employees statute—permit the custodian of a personnel file to allow other government officials to inspect the confidential portions of the file "when such inspection is deemed by [the custodian] to be necessary and essential to the pursuance of a proper function of the inspecting agency." The custodian may not permit such an inspection, however, to assist "in an investigation of [the employee's] tax liability" (the language of the standard statute and the public hospital statute) or "in a tax investigation" (the language of the community college statute and the state statute).

The restrictions might be thought to conflict with the Machinery Act provision, G.S. 105-368(i)(1), that entitles any local tax collector to require any employer to provide to the collector a list of the names and home addresses of each of the employer's employees. Indeed, the Machinery Act makes it a misdemeanor to refuse to supply such a list. In 1983, however, in an attorney general's opinion that addressed the provision in the state personnel privacy statute, the two statutes were reconciled.[77] The opinion distinguished between the duties of the county tax *assessor* and those of a local tax *collector*. That is, whereas the assessor's responsibility is to determine a person's tax liability, the collector's responsibility is simply to collect tax liabilities that already exist. Therefore, the prohibition in the personnel privacy statutes applies to requests from an assessor but not a collector. A records custodian may, without violating the statutes, supply a tax collector with the home addresses of public employees.[78] Indeed, the opinion concludes that, because of the mandate in the Machinery Act, the custodian has no discretion; the list must be supplied.[79]

---

77. Letter to Sarah T. Morrow, 52 Op. N.C. Att'y Gen. 85 (1983).

78. The opinion concluded that "[c]onsequently it is our opinion that a request for the home address of a State employee by an ad valorem tax collector pursuant to G.S. 105-368(i)(1) does not constitute a request for information for purposes of 'assisting in a tax investigation.'" *Id.* at 86.

79. "[T]here would appear to repose no discretion in the agency head with which to deny the request from the tax collector." *Id.* at 87.

Because the public school statute and the public health authority statute do not include an authorization to share personnel file information with officials of other governments, and therefore do not include the prohibition on sharing information to assist in a tax liability investigation, there is no question but that the tax collector is entitled to the names and addresses of public school and public health authority employees. Those employers should be treated no differently than private employers, who must also release that information.

Provisions for Access to Personnel Files

Each of the personnel privacy statutes—except the statute for public health authorities—permits access to a personnel file by specific persons or under specific circumstances, although there are some differences among the statutes. This section discusses those provisions.[80]

The standard statute and the public hospital statute, but not any of the others, include a provision that lists four kinds of information and specifies that even if these sorts of information are considered part of a person's personnel file they "need not be disclosed to an employee nor to any other person."[81] Note that the statutes say the information "need not" be disclosed. This is an authorization not to disclose, not a requirement. Here are the four sorts of information listed:

1. Testing or examination material used to help with appointment, employment, or promotion, if releasing the material would compromise the objectivity or the fairness of the testing or examination process. Thus, a local government need not release the questions and answers of a promotion examination.
2. Investigative materials about possible criminal actions of an employee, until either the investigation is completed and no criminal action brought or a criminal action is brought and has been completed.[82]
3. Information that might identify an undercover law enforcement officer or a law enforcement informer.
4. Notes, preliminary drafts, and internal communications concerning an employee. If these materials, however, are used as a basis for any official personnel decision, the employee or his or her agent is entitled to inspect the materials. Presumably "any official personnel decision" includes a decision on the amount of an employee's merit increase, as well as suspensions, leaves, and changes in position classification.

The absence of this listing from the state statute, the education statutes, and the public health authority statute implies that the listed information is either part of an employee's personnel file and therefore subject to the normal rules of access to such a file, or it is not part of an employee's personnel file and therefore open to public access as a normal public record.

---

80. 29 C.F.R. § 1630.14, a federal regulation adopted pursuant to the Americans with Disabilities Act, sharply limits access to the results of medical examinations performed on current and potential employees. The listing in this federal regulation supersedes the broader authorization for access to employee personnel files under the various personnel privacy statutes as to this one sort of medical information.

81. This provision is set out in subsection (c1) of the city and county statutes and in subsection (d) of the other three statutes.

82. This provision is somewhat inconsistent with G.S. 132-1.4, which covers criminal investigation records generally. That statute does not open such records, to a suspect or anyone else, after the investigation is closed, while this one seems at least to open the records to the employee if he or she was the person being investigated. A reconciliation of the two statutes is set out *infra* in chapter 8 at notes 26 and 27.

Inspection Only, or Copying as Well?

Each of the statutes that provide for access to personnel files permits the files to be "examined" or "inspected." None of the statutes specifically include any right to *copy* material in such a file. Is copying included in the rights of access that are set out? My own conclusion is that copying is included within the special rights of access that are given, for the reasons set out in the next paragraph.

Some of the special rights of access that are set out in the statutes cannot be satisfactorily exercised if the person making the examination or inspection cannot copy the material as well. For example, the standard statute permits a physician of the employee's choice to "examine" the employee's medical record, and the state statute permits the employee's medical record to be "disclosed" to a physician of the employee's choosing. If the physician is to do a professional job of advising the patient, however, he or she can do so much more effectively if the record can be copied as well as examined; otherwise the physician would have to rely on memory. Each of the statutes also permits examination of a personnel file pursuant to a court order, and it is clear that litigants armed with court-approved subpoenas are seeking copies of the records, not simply the right to read them. It is worth noting that one provision of the standard statute permits access to personnel files by academic researchers in certain circumstances without expressly permitting copying information from the files, but again, it is unlikely that such a researcher could make effective use of the information without being able to copy it.[83] Therefore, the discussion that follows assumes that the special statutory rights to examine or inspect the files also include the right to make copies of material within the files.

The Employee or the Employee's Agent

Each of the statutes that allow access to a personnel file permits an employee or a former employee to have almost complete access to his or her personnel file. (In addition, the state statute and the two education statutes give the same right to an applicant for employment; the standard statute and the public hospital statute do not permit access by an applicant.)

Material Not Open to the Employee

The various statutes list a few items that the employee or former employee may not see in the personnel file.

First, each of the statutes provides that an employee or former employee may not inspect letters of reference that were solicited before employment as part of the selection process. Some local governments do not seek letters of reference; rather, they call references, discuss the employee, and prepare notes of the conversation that are then placed in an applicant's file. Such notes are the functional equivalent of a letter of reference, and it seems reasonable to treat them the same way.[84] It should be noted that this exception to the employee's right

---

83. This provision can be found in subsection (c2) of the city and county statutes and subsection (e) of the area authority and water and sewer authority statutes.

84. Such an approach did not seem reasonable to a majority of a three-member panel of the Colorado Court of Appeals. That court held that a statute that limited access to "letters of reference" was not activated by notes about such a telephone conversation; notes simply were not a "letter." The Colorado Supreme Court disagreed, however, and reversed the decision of the court of appeals, concluding that the

of access to the file does not include evaluations of the employee, as an applicant, made by persons involved in the selection process. If the file includes such evaluations, the employee has access to them.

Second, the standard statute and the state statute provide that an employee or former employee does not have a right of access to "information concerning a medical disability, mental or physical, that a prudent physician would not divulge to his patient." It should be noted that such information is likely to be exceedingly rare. While at one time physician paternalism supported withholding information from patients in order to avoid harm to the patient's well-being, current medical ethics specify that "[w]ithholding medical information from patients without their knowledge or consent is ethically unacceptable."[85] If a personnel file contains such information, however, the statutes permit a physician designated by the employee to look at that medical information.[86] It seems appropriate for a local government official who thinks it best to deny an employee access to such medical information to do so only upon advice from a physician or other health care professional. How else could the government know whether a prudent physician would not divulge the information to the patient? In addition, the government should inform the employee that medical information is being withheld from the employee. Unless the employee knows that there is undisclosed medical information in the file, he or she will be unable to exercise the statutory right to have a physician examine the information on his or her behalf.

Third, some local governments routinely seek periodic updates of driver history information from the SBI's Division of Criminal Information about those employees whose work assignments include operation of government-owned vehicles. This sort of information is clearly part of the employee's personnel file, but unlike other information in the file, the driver history information is not open to the employee who is the subject of the information. The Department of Justice's regulations governing access to driver history information prohibit allowing the person whose driver history is recorded to have access to the information through his or her employer; rather, the person must follow the mechanisms established for all drivers through the Division of Motor Vehicles.[87]

The Employee's Agent

Each of the statutes that allow access to the personnel file by the employee also allows access by the employee's "duly authorized" or "properly authorized" agent. In general this is clear. Occasionally, though, a question arises about access if the employee or former

---

forms on which notes from conversations with references were recorded qualified as "letters of reference" that were protected from disclosure. City of Westminster v. Dogan Constr. Co., 914 P.2d 455 (Colo. App. 1995), *rev'd*, 930 P.2d 585 (Colo. 1997).

85. Council on Ethical and Judicial Affairs, American Medical Association, Opinion E-8.082 Withholding Information from Patients (Nov. 2006), *available at* www.ama-assn.org/ad-com/polfind/Hlth-Ethics.pdf.

86. The public hospital statute includes an authorization for allowing a physician designated by the employee to examine the employee's medical record, G.S. 131E-257.2(c)(2), even though the statute does not include a provision denying the employee access to the same information.

87. N.C. Admin. Code tit. 12, ch. 4F, § .0701(e) (Nov. 2008) [hereinafter N.C.A.C.]. The driver history information should not be made available to officials of other governments or to the public either; the regulations limit access to it to officials of the employing agency. 12 N.C.A.C. 4F .0701(d).

employee has died: does the employee's right of access succeed to his or her heirs or personal representative? Although the statutes provide no clear answer to the question, I think the better answer is that an heir or personal representative does succeed to the employee's right of access, as his or her agent.

It is possible that the deceased employee might have had some sort of claim against the government that employed him or her. If the employee had survived, he or she would have had an absolute right of access to the file in order to support that claim; the employee would not have needed to resort to a subpoena or court order. It seems reasonable, then, to allow the person who has succeeded to the employee's right to pursue the claim to have the same right of access to the personnel file as the employee. Therefore, at least in the circumstance of pursuing a claim of the employee, I believe the heir or personal representative should be considered the authorized agent of the employee.

Release by the Employee

The standard statute and the public hospital statute (but none of the others) expressly permit an employee to sign a written release allowing the employing government or agency to provide specified information to anyone named in the release. (With the other statutes it may be that the employee would have to obtain the information himself or herself and then share it rather than have the employer share the information directly with the third party.) If the employee does sign such a release, it appears that the employer is then bound to provide the information specified in the release; the employer does not have the discretion to refuse to do so. After all, the employee is entitled to obtain the information directly, so it would serve no point for the government to have any right to refuse to cooperate with a release.[88]

The Employee's Supervisors

Each of the local government statutes that permit any sort of limited access to a personnel file permits such access by anyone with "supervisory authority" over the employee.[89] In general the quoted language includes any person with authority to make employment

88. As has been noted several times, under the standard statute and the public hospital statute an applicant has no right of access to his or her application file, and these statutes are structured so that the right to direct a release of information in the file does not apply to applicants either. Nevertheless it is a frequent practice of governments seeking to appoint a chief administrator or other high-level employee to ask a final group of applicants for permission to release to the public their names and other details about them. Although technically the statutes might be read to not allow even this sort of release of applicant information, if the applicant and government both agree to the release, it is hard to see how anyone else might object.

89. The state statute, in G.S. 126-24(2), permits access by the "supervisor of the employee," which may carry a narrower meaning than anyone with "supervisory authority" over the employee. The two education statutes permit access by the superintendent (or president) and "other supervisory personnel," which may include persons who do not directly supervise the employee.

It should also be noted that G.S. 122C-192(a) permits the state's Secretary of Health and Human Services to review the personnel records of all employees of area authorities.

decisions that concern the employee—about, for example, work hours, responsibilities, or discipline.[90] Here are some comments about city and county government in particular.

Cities and Towns Operating under the Council-Manager Form of Government

A city or town manager usually has direct supervisory responsibility over very few employees but nonetheless has statutory power to discharge almost all city or town employees.[91] That statutory power could not be responsibly exercised if the manager did not have access to the personnel file of each such employee. Therefore, the manager is clearly a person with supervisory authority over each employee for whom he or she has the power of discharge. In addition, in some cities and towns the manager is directed by the governing board to supervise the work of the clerk, even though that official may be appointed by the board itself. When there has been that sort of delegation, the manager has sufficient supervisory authority to have access to the clerk's personnel file.

Cities and Towns Operating under the Mayor-Council Form of Government

Under the mayor-council form of government, the governing board has statutory power to hire and fire employees.[92] It may delegate that power to an administrator,[93] even as a manager may delegate his or her supervisory powers to department heads or others, but the statutory authority remains in place. For that reason, even when the governing board has appointed an administrator, it continues to have supervisory authority over town employees and for that reason has access to employee personnel files.[94]

Counties

There are a variety of county employees over whom neither the manager nor the governing board has any supervisory authority. These include employees in the offices of the sheriff and register of deeds and employees in departments headed by persons appointed by independent boards, such as public health, mental health, social services, and elections. Because they do not have supervisory authority, neither the manager nor the board of commissioners has any right of access to the personnel files of these employees under this provision of the county personnel privacy statute.

---

90. Persons with supervisory authority do not include management-level employees who have no role in the supervision of a particular employee. For example, the term does not include a local government's attorney (except for employees in his or her office) and does not include assistant or deputy managers who have supervisory responsibility for some departments and agencies but not others. These management employees would have to fit under some other authorization in order to be permitted access to a personnel file. The two education statutes specifically permit release of personnel information to the attorney representing the school board or college board of trustees. For other governments and agencies, the most appropriate such authorization is probably that for officials of the same or other governments.

91. G.S. 160A-148(1).

92. G.S. 160A-155.

93. *Id.*

94. G.S. 160A-168(c)(3) does speak of any "city employee" with supervisory authority over the employee whose file is sought, and as noted earlier, governing board members are not city employees. But if that fact were to disallow access by the board, then literally no one might be able to examine personnel files in some smaller towns. If the board is exercising supervisory authority over an employee, it needs to be able to examine that employee's personnel file.

There are a few county employees who are appointed by the board of commissioners rather than by the manager—the clerk and the tax administrator (or the tax assessor and the tax collector if the county has not combined these positions). If the board has delegated supervisory power over these employees to the county manager, the manager then has the requisite supervisory authority to be entitled to access to these employees' personnel files under this provision of the statute; because of its legal authority, the board also is entitled to access under this provision.

Release to Government Officials

Each of the statutes, except the public school statute and the public health authority statute, permits the custodian of a personnel file to allow a governmental official—federal, state, or local—to inspect any part of a personnel file when the custodian deems the inspection to be "necessary and essential to the pursuance of a proper function of the inspecting agency."[95] It should be noted that this provision allows sharing information from a personnel file within the employing government or agency as well as with other governments or agencies, although some such sharing within an employing entity may well be permissible without such a provision. For example, the provision clearly allows a custodian to allow persons who are part of the government's employee grievance procedures, such as citizen members of a grievance panel, to inspect a personnel file. Each of the statutes with a provision of this sort prohibits the release of information for the purposes of assisting in a criminal prosecution of the employee or assisting in an investigation of the employee's tax liability.[96] The statutes do permit, however, releasing an employee's name, address, and telephone number in order to assist in a criminal investigation.[97]

Criminal Investigations and the Public School Statute

The public school statute, in G.S. 115C-321(a1) through (a3), includes a unique set of provisions allowing release of information in personnel files to assist in criminal investigations of certain specified crimes. The subsections require notice to the employee, who then has an opportunity to seek judicial protection of the information, and they provide that any statements or admissions by the employee found in the personnel file are inadmissible in any subsequent criminal proceeding against the employee.

Release to Board Members

Sometimes an individual member of a governing board, or the board as a whole, wishes to examine some or all of an employee's personnel file. Whether that is allowable depends on three factors:

1. which personnel privacy statute governs,
2. the form of government of the unit in question, and
3. whether the entire board concurs in the wish to examine.

---

95. G.S. 122C-15(d) entitles a State/Local Consumer Advocate within the state's mental health system to have complete access to the personnel files of employees of area authorities.

96. See the discussion of turning over employee addresses to the tax collector *supra* at notes 77 through 79.

97. The state statute, G.S. 126-24(5), and the community college statute, G.S. 115D-29(a)(5), do not include provisions allowing the release of the employee's name, address, and telephone number.

The two education statutes expressly permit access to an employee's personnel file by members of the agency's governing board.[98] Each of these statutes entitles "members" of the governing boards to inspect the file, rather than referring to the boards collectively, and therefore the statutes appear to entitle individual board members to inspect personnel files without need for authorization from the full board.

None of the other statutes, however, includes an express authorization for access by board members, and therefore the matter is more complicated for other governments and agencies. Board member access, if it is to be allowed, must be fitted into one of the other categories of special access to personnel files. Moreover, with these other statutes, access should be provided to the full board or, if to a single member, by authority of the entire board.

One category of special access is for an "employee having supervisory authority" over the employee whose file is sought. As was noted earlier, in cities and towns without managers the governing board is by law the appointing authority of all employees and therefore the supervisor of all employees, and for that reason the board collectively may examine any employee's personnel file.[99] If a city or county has a manager, however, or if there is a full-time director of the agency (as with health departments, area authorities, or water and sewer authorities, for example), the manager or director has final supervisory authority over almost all employees.[100] The board supervises only the manager or director and perhaps a few other employees. Therefore, while the special access to personnel files allowed to supervisors permits access by the manager or director, it does not permit access by the board or any board member. If the board or any member of the board is to have access to an employee's personnel file in these governments or agencies, it must be under some other provision of the statutes.

One possibility is under the provision, described above, that permits a custodian to allow access to a personnel file by any official of a local government when doing so is "necessary and essential to the pursuance of a proper function" of the inspecting agency. If a board collectively wished to examine the personnel file of an employee, or if a single member of the board, acting under authority of the board, sought to examine a file, and if the custodian was satisfied that such an examination met the statutory standard, this provision authorizes the access. If, however, a single member of a board sought access and did so without prior authorization from the entire board, it is difficult to see how the "necessary and essential" test could be met. Single board members in units with managers or other executive directors do not normally have responsibilities that justify examination of employees' personnel files.

There is one final possibility, and that is under the provision, discussed below, that allows the manager or board to inform any person of certain information in an employee's personnel file in order to maintain confidence in public services or in the level of public services. This provision is probably more suitable, however, if information is to be made available to the public generally rather than just to the board or a member thereof.

---

98. *See* G.S. 115C-321(a)(3) (public school employees); G.S. 115D-29(a)(3) (community college employees).

99. See the discussion *supra* accompanying notes 92 through 94.

100. *See* G.S. 160A-148(1) (city manager); G.S. 153A-82(1) (county manager); G.S. 130A-45.5(c)(12) (public health authority director); G.S. 122C-121(c)(1) (area authority director).

Release by the Manager or Other Chief Administrator or Governing Board

One consequence of the privacy of most information in a personnel file is that it has sometimes allowed an employee who has been disciplined or discharged to make public his or her version of events while the public employer has been unable to respond with its version. The employee is under no prohibition on releasing information that is part of a personnel file and therefore can speak openly about the circumstances of any personnel action. That the employee does so, however, does not waive his or her right to have the file kept confidential, and so the employer is not able to respond with its own version of what happened. When just this set of events occurred not long after enactment of the first personnel privacy statutes, those statutes were amended to allow a limited release of otherwise-confidential information from a personnel file.[101]

The release is made by the chief administrator—manager, superintendent, president, director—of the government or agency, with the concurrence of the governing board in the case of cities and counties. If there is no such administrator, then the release is made by the board itself. (The two education statutes permit the board to initiate such a release and to direct the superintendent or president to do so.) Before releasing the information, the administrator or board, as specified in the relevant statute, must make a written determination that the release is

> "essential to maintaining public confidence in the administration of [public] services or to maintaining the level and quality of [public] services" [the standard statute], or
> "essential to maintaining the integrity of the board or to maintaining the level or quality of services provided by the board" [the education statutes].

This determination is itself to become part of the personnel file of the affected employee and is to be a part of the file open to public inspection.[102]

The statute gives no role in the process to the employee, and there is no requirement that the government or agency give the employee any notice of its intent to release information from the file. It may be that an employee would have a right to seek an injunction against release if the employee could somehow show that the government or agency abused its discretion in making the determination required as a condition of release, but that is probably a very difficult showing to make.

It should be noted that the power to release information under this provision does not extend to all information in an employee's personnel file. Rather, it only applies to the fact of an employee's "employment or nonemployment, promotion, demotion, suspension or other disciplinary action, reinstatement, transfer, or termination . . . and the reasons for that personnel action." The list includes "termination," and that term includes both voluntary and involuntary termination. Therefore, a government or agency could use this provision to make public the reasons for a resignation, just as it may make public the reasons for a discharge. But there are many items that may be part of a personnel file that do not

101. Neither the public hospital statute nor the public health authority statute includes a provision of the sort discussed in this section.

102. The two education statutes do not specify that the determination is to be part of the employee's personnel file, although they do direct that it be retained and open to public inspection.

fit within the quoted list of actions, and this provision gives no authority to make those items public.

Finally, it should be noted that there is no prohibition under this provision on release of the listed items in order to assist in a criminal investigation. Should one of the listed actions, or more probably the reasons for the action, reveal possible criminal conduct by the employee, the statute still permits release, even if the release is limited to law enforcement agencies.

Release Pursuant to a Subpoena or Court Order

The two education statutes specifically permit release of information in a personnel file "by authority of a subpoena or proper court order," and each of the other statutes, except the public health authority statute, permits release "[b]y order of a court of competent jurisdiction."[103] Chapter 6 discusses the meaning of "court order" and the procedure for seeking such an order, and the reader is referred to that discussion.[104] I would just add the obvious point that these provisions offer an opportunity for the employing government or agency to seek permission to release information in a personnel file beyond the circumstances set out in each of the statutes. For example, if a local government became aware that information in a personnel file pointed to the employee as the person who committed a crime, the government might seek a court order to permit release of that information to the appropriate law enforcement agency.

Release by the Retirement Systems Division

In 2008 the General Assembly amended some of the personnel privacy statutes, but not all, to permit the Retirement Systems Division of the Department of State Treasurer to release the names and mailing addresses of former employees to certain nonprofit organizations that represent retired state, local, or public school employees. (There were no amendments to the water and sewer authority statute, area authority statute, public health authority statute, or public hospital statute, and therefore these authorizations do not apply to employees subject to those statutes.) In order to receive the names and addresses of retired state or public school employees, the organization must represent at least 10,000 retired employees; in order to receive the names and addresses of retired county, city, or community college employees, the organization must represent at least 2,000 retired employees.

Release to Prospective Employers

Prospective employers are not among those with special access to personnel files, but there are several routes by which information in an employee's or former employee's personnel file may be shared with a prospective employer. First, the employee might waive his or her rights of confidentiality in the file and allow information to be shared with the prospective employer. Second, if the prospective employer is another government agency, the custodian can share the information under the provision allowing access to officials of the federal government, any state government, or any local government, when access is necessary

---

103. The state statute, in G.S. 126-24, uses the phrase "by authority of a proper court order."
104. *See supra* chapter 6 notes 53 through 67 and accompanying text.

and essential to the proper functioning of the inspecting government or agency. Seeking information about a prospective employee certainly fits within that standard. Third, if the prospective employer is a private agency, so that the second route is not available, some categories of information can be shared under the provision allowing release by the manager or other chief administrator or the governing board if doing so meets the standards of the appropriate statute.

G.S. 1-539.12 establishes immunity from civil liability for an employer who discloses information about a current or former employee's job history or performance to a prospective employer, as long as the information given is not false or, if it is false, the employer did not know that it was. This statute does not modify the personnel privacy statutes, however, and therefore does not grant public employers any greater right to release information from a personnel file to a prospective employer than that given by the various personnel privacy statutes.

Release to Professionals

Outside Legal Counsel

When a local government or its insurance carrier retains outside counsel to represent the government in a dispute with or involving an employee, may the outside attorney examine the employee's personnel file? If the issue involves any of the matters that may be released pursuant to a determination by the manager or other chief administrator or by the board that doing so is necessary to maintaining the integrity of or confidence in public services, that provision is adequate to allow release to the outside attorney. But if the issue arises in a workers' compensation dispute, the attorney may need access to medical information in the file, and that kind of information is not subject to release under the above provisions. Workers' compensation disputes are heard before the Industrial Commission, however, and the regulations of the commission establish a general right of access to medical information that appears to be broad enough to allow access by outside counsel to medical information about a government or agency employee.[105]

In other circumstances, a local government may simply have to assert that it cannot be properly represented unless the outside attorney has access to confidential information in the file. In the Illinois case of *Aufox v. Board of Education,* the court accepted that approach. In *Aufox*, the parents of a special education student complained about the school district allowing its attorneys to have access to the student file of their child, pointing out that the applicable statute did not specifically allow such access. The court held that such a right of access was inherent in the statutory authority to employ counsel. "It would seem impossible for an attorney to represent a school district at a hearing concerning a student's special education placement without access to information from school records concerning that placement."[106]

---

105. 4 N.C.A.C. § 10A .0607.

106. 588 N.E.2d 316, 319 (Ill. App. Ct. 1992). The case was followed in *Ibata v. Board of Education*, 851 N.E.2d 658 (Ill. App. Ct. 2006).

Annual Auditor

When a certified public accountant undertakes the statutorily required annual audit of a local government agency, a standard part of the auditing process is to obtain employee addresses in order to compare those addresses with vendor addresses and to obtain employee W-2s in order to check payroll records. Both items—addresses and W-2s—are part of the employee's personnel file, and no statute expressly permits release of the information to the auditor. Nevertheless, the employing government should make the information available. G.S. 159-34 requires local governments and public authorities to be audited each year, and it further requires that the audit be conducted pursuant to generally accepted auditing standards. Because the tests set out above are necessary in order to conduct a professionally acceptable audit, the provision in G.S. 159-34 must be understood as an additional exception to the confidentiality requirements of the various personnel privacy statutes.

Remedies for Improper Release or Examination

Eight of the statutes—the five standard statutes, the state statute, the public school statute, and the public hospital statute—include almost identical provisions establishing penalties for allowing or undertaking unauthorized access of a personnel file. (The other two statutes—for community colleges and for public health authorities—have no remedial provisions.) The statutes establish penalties for these two sets of actions:

1. "Knowingly, willfully, and with malice" permitting any person to have unauthorized access to information in a personnel file.[107]
2. "Knowingly and willfully" examining a personnel file in its official filing place, or removing or copying any portion of a file, without authority pursuant to the appropriate personnel privacy statute.[108]

In each case the statutes provide that violation is a Class 3 misdemeanor, punishable by a maximum fine of $500.[109]

These statutes do not per se prohibit open discussion of a public employee's performance. For example, if a city council decided to hold an open discussion of the manager's performance over the past year, the council members would most likely be contributing their own observations and experiences during that time period rather than drawing on material they had found in the manager's personnel file. Therefore, there would be no unauthorized release of information in the file. Indeed, even if the council members were to refer to material in the personnel file during the course of such an open discussion, there would have to be proof of malice before there could be a conviction for violating the first of the two remedial provisions. Similarly, the statutes do not prohibit governing board members

107. The state statute, G.S. 126-27, does not include the requirement of malice, and the area authorities statute, G.S. 122C-158, does not include any of the phrase in quotes but simply prohibits unauthorized release.

108. The area authorities statute, G.S. 122C-158, does not use the "knowingly and willfully" phrase, but it does require that the violator know that he or she was not authorized to do the prohibited act.

109. The water and sewer authority statute, G.S. 162A-6.1, makes a violation a Class 2 misdemeanor.

from public criticism of public employees. Typically, such criticism is an expression of the personal opinion of the board member and not a release of information in a personnel file. These points demonstrate that these are fairly narrow provisions; especially the first, because of its requirement of malice.

I know of no prosecutions under any of the statutes for violation of these provisions, and so there is not yet any certain sense of the meaning of the terms knowingly, willfully, or with malice within the context of these statutes.

Appendix 7A—Personnel Privacy Statutes Compared

Provision	Standard Statute	Public Schools	Community Colleges	Public Hospitals	Public Health Authorities	State Statute
Applies to files of current and former employees	Yes	Yes	Yes	Yes	Yes	Yes
Applies to files of applicants	Yes	Yes	Yes	Yes	Yes	Yes
Applies to files of volunteers	No	Yes (separate statute)	No	No	No	Members of boards and commissions
Applies to files of independent contractors	No	No	No	Health care providers (separate statute)	Health care providers	No
Permits public access to files of former employees	No	No	No	No	No	Ten years after separation
Permits public access to files of applicants	No	No	No	No	No	Perhaps
Permits public access to employee compensation	Yes, all forms of compensation	Yes, all forms of compensation	Yes, all forms of compensation	A few select employees only	Total compensation in current and former positions	Yes, all forms of compensation
Permits public access to salary history	Most recent change only	Most recent change only	Most recent change only	No	Total compensation in current and former positions	Most recent change only
Includes provisions for special access	Yes	Yes	Yes	Yes	No	Yes
Permits access by employee or agent	Yes	Yes	Yes	Yes	No	Yes
Restricts access by employee to some medical information	Yes	No	No	No	No	Yes
Permits access by applicant	No	Yes	Yes	No	No	Yes

(continued)

(*continued*)

Provision	Standard Statute	Public Schools	Community Colleges	Public Hospitals	Public Health Authorities	State Statute
Permits employee to allow access to file	Yes	No	No	Yes	No	No
Permits access by one or more supervisors	Yes, anyone with supervisory authority over employee	Yes, superintendent and other supervisory personnel	Yes, president and other supervisory personnel	Yes, anyone with supervisory authority over employee	No	Yes, supervisor
Permits release to officials of federal, state, or local government	Yes	No	Yes	Yes	No	Yes
Permits release to law enforcement agencies, re employee	No	Yes	No	No	No	No
Permits release to governing board members	Silent	Yes	Yes	Silent	No	No
Permits release to unit's attorney	Silent	Yes	Yes	Silent	No	Silent
Permits limited release of information to public	Yes	Yes	Yes	No	No	Yes
Permits release pursuant to court order or subpoena	Court order	Court order or subpoena	Court order or subpoena	Court order	No	Court order
Permits release of limited information by Retirement System	County and city employees but not WASA or mental health employees	Yes	Yes	No	No	Yes
Provides need not release testing material	Yes	No	No	Yes	No	No
Provides need not release information about criminal investigation of employee	Yes	No	No	Yes	No	No
Provides need not release identity of undercover officers	Yes	No	No	Yes	No	No
Provides need not release certain notes or drafts	Yes	No	No	Yes	No	No
Includes remedial provisions	Yes	Yes	No	Yes	No	Yes

Appendix 7B—Statutes

The "Standard Statute" (G.S. 153A-98)

§ 153A-98. Privacy of employee personnel records.

(a) Notwithstanding the provisions of G.S. 132-6 or any other general law or local act concerning access to public records, personnel files of employees, former employees, or applicants for employment maintained by a county are subject to inspection and may be disclosed only as provided by this section. For purposes of this section, an employee's personnel file consists of any information in any form gathered by the county with respect to that employee and, by way of illustration but not limitation, relating to his application, selection or nonselection, performance, promotions, demotions, transfers, suspension and other disciplinary actions, evaluation forms, leave, salary, and termination of employment. As used in this section, "employee" includes former employees of the county.

(b) The following information with respect to each county employee is a matter of public record: name; age; date of original employment or appointment to the county service; the terms of any contract by which the employee is employed whether written or oral, past and current, to the extent that the county has the written contract or a record of the oral contract in its possession; current position title; current salary; date and amount of the most recent increase or decrease in salary; date of the most recent promotion, demotion, transfer, suspension, separation or other change in position classification; and the office to which the employee is currently assigned. For the purposes of this subsection, the term "salary" includes pay, benefits, incentives, bonuses, and deferred and all other forms of compensation paid by the employing entity. The board of county commissioners shall determine in what form and by whom this information will be maintained. Any person may have access to this information for the purpose of inspection, examination, and copying, during regular business hours, subject only to such rules and regulations for the safekeeping of public records as the board of commissioners may have adopted. Any person denied access to this information may apply to the appropriate division of the General Court of Justice for an order compelling disclosure, and the court shall have jurisdiction to issue such orders.

(c) All information contained in a county employee's personnel file, other than the information made public by subsection (b) of this section, is confidential and shall be open to inspection only in the following instances:

(1) The employee or his duly authorized agent may examine all portions of his personnel file except (i) letters of reference solicited prior to employment, and (ii) information concerning a medical disability, mental or physical, that a prudent physician would not divulge to his patient.

(2) A licensed physician designated in writing by the employee may examine the employee's medical record.

(3) A county employee having supervisory authority over the employee may examine all material in the employee's personnel file.

(4) By order of a court of competent jurisdiction, any person may examine such portion of an employee's personnel file as may be ordered by the court.

(5) An official of an agency of the State or federal government, or any political subdivision of the State, may inspect any portion of a personnel file when such inspection is deemed by the official having custody of such records to be inspected to be necessary and essential to the pursuance of a proper function of the inspecting agency, but no information shall be divulged for the purpose of assisting in a criminal prosecution of the employee, or for the purpose of assisting in an investigation of the employee's tax liability. However, the official having custody of such records may release the name, address, and telephone number from a personnel file for the purpose of assisting in a criminal investigation.

(6) An employee may sign a written release, to be placed with his personnel file, that permits the person with custody of the file to provide, either in person, by telephone, or by mail, information specified in the release to prospective employers, educational institutions, or other persons specified in the release.

(7) The county manager, with concurrence of the board of county commissioners, or, in counties not having a manager, the board of county commissioners may inform any person of the employment or nonemployment, promotion, demotion, suspension or other disciplinary action, reinstatement, transfer, or termination of a county employee and the reasons for that personnel action. Before releasing the information, the manager or board shall determine in writing that the release is essential to maintaining public confidence in the administration of county services or to maintaining the level and quality of county services. This written determination shall be retained in the office of the manager or the county clerk, is a record available for public inspection and shall become part of the employee's personnel file.

(c1) Even if considered part of an employee's personnel file, the following information need not be disclosed to an employee nor to any other person:

(1) Testing or examination material used solely to determine individual qualifications for appointment, employment, or promotion in the county's service, when disclosure would compromise the objectivity or the fairness of the testing or examination process.

(2) Investigative reports or memoranda and other information concerning the investigation of possible criminal actions of an employee, until the investigation is completed and no criminal action taken, or until the criminal action is concluded.

(3) Information that might identify an undercover law enforcement officer or a law enforcement informer.

(4) Notes, preliminary drafts and internal communications concerning an employee. In the event such materials are used for any official personnel decision, then the employee or his duly authorized agent shall have a right to inspect such materials.

(c2) The board of county commissioners may permit access, subject to limitations they may impose, to selected personnel files by a professional representative of a training, research, or academic institution if that person certifies that he will not release information identifying the employees whose files are opened and that the information will be used solely for statistical, research, or teaching purposes. This certification shall be retained by the county as long as each personnel file so examined is retained.

(c3) Notwithstanding any provision of this section to the contrary, the Retirement Systems Division of the Department of State Treasurer may disclose the name and mailing address of former local governmental employees to domiciled, nonprofit organizations representing 2,000 or more active or retired State government, local government, or public school employees.

(d) The board of commissioners of a county that maintains personnel files containing information other than the information mentioned in subsection (b) of this section shall establish procedures whereby an employee who objects to material in his file on grounds that it is inaccurate or misleading may seek to have the material removed from the file or may place in the file a statement relating to the material.

(e) A public official or employee who knowingly, willfully, and with malice permits any person to have access to information contained in a personnel file, except as is permitted by this section, is guilty of a Class 3 misdemeanor and upon conviction shall only be fined an amount not more than five hundred dollars ($500.00).

(f) Any person, not specifically authorized by this section to have access to a personnel file designated as confidential, who shall knowingly and willfully examine in its official filing place, remove or copy any portion of a confidential personnel file shall be guilty of a Class 3 misdemeanor and upon conviction shall only be fined in the discretion of the court but not in excess of five hundred dollars ($500.00).

Public School Personnel Privacy Statute (G.S. 115C-319 through 115C-321)

§ 115C-319. Personnel files not subject to inspection.

Personnel files of employees of local boards of education, former employees of local boards of education, or applicants for employment with local boards of education shall not be subject to inspection and examination as authorized by G.S. 132-6. For purposes of this Article, a personnel file consists of any information gathered by the local board of education which employs an individual, previously employed an individual, or considered an individual's application for employment, and which information relates to the individual's application, selection or nonselection, promotion, demotion, transfer, leave, salary, suspension, performance evaluation, disciplinary action, or termination of employment wherever located or in whatever form.

Nothing in this section shall be construed to prevent local boards of education from disclosing the certification status and other information about employees as required by Section 1111(h)(6) of P.L. 107-110.

§ 115C-320. Certain records open to inspection.

Each local board of education shall maintain a record of each of its employees, showing the following information with respect to each employee: name, age, date of original employment or appointment, the terms of any contract by which the employee is employed whether written or oral, past and current, to the extent that the board has the written contract or a record of the oral contract in its possession, current position, title, current salary, date and amount of most recent increase or decrease in salary, date of most recent promotion, demotion, transfer, suspension, separation, or other change in position classification, and the office or station to which the employee is currently assigned. For the purposes of this section, the term "salary" includes pay, benefits, incentives, bonuses, and deferred and all other forms of compensation paid by the employing entity. Subject only to rules and regulations for the safekeeping of records adopted by the local board of education, every person having custody of the records shall permit them to be inspected and examined and copies made by any person during regular business hours. The name of a participant in the Address Confidentiality Program established pursuant to Chapter 15C of the General Statutes shall not be open to inspection and shall be redacted from any record released pursuant to this section. Any person who is denied access to any record for the purpose of inspecting, examining or copying the record shall have a right to compel compliance with the provisions of this section by application to a court of competent jurisdiction for a writ of mandamus or other appropriate relief.

§ 115C-321. Confidential information in personnel files; access to information.

(a) All information contained in a personnel file, except as otherwise provided in this Chapter, is confidential and shall not be open for inspection and examination except to any of the following persons:

(1) The employee, applicant for employment, former employee, or his properly authorized agent, who may examine his own personnel file at all reasonable times in its entirety except for letters of reference solicited prior to employment.

(2) The superintendent and other supervisory personnel.

(3) Members of the local board of education and the board's attorney.

(4) A party by authority of a subpoena or proper court order may inspect and examine a particular confidential portion of an employee's personnel file.

(a1) Notwithstanding any other provision of this Chapter, information contained in a personnel file that is relevant to possible criminal misconduct may be made available to law enforcement and the district attorney to assist in the investigation of:

(1) A report made to law enforcement pursuant to G.S. 115C-288(g), or

(2) Any report to law enforcement regarding an arson, attempted arson, destruction of, theft from, theft of, embezzlement from, embezzlement of any personal or real property owned by the local board of education.

(a2) The employee shall be given five working days prior written notice of any disclosure under subsection (a1) of this section to permit the employee to apply to the district court for an in camera review prior to the date of disclosure to determine if the information is relevant to the possible criminal misconduct. Failure of the employee to apply for a review shall constitute a waiver by the employee of any relief under this subsection.

(a3) Statements or admissions made by the employee and produced under subsection (a1) of this section shall not be admissible in any subsequent criminal proceeding against the employee.

(b) Notwithstanding any other provision of this Chapter, any superintendent may, in his discretion, or shall at the direction of the Board of Education, inform any person or corporation of any promotion, demotion, suspension, reinstatement, transfer, separation, dismissal, employment or nonemployment of any applicant, employee or former employee employed by or assigned to the local board of education or whose personnel file is maintained by the board and the reasons therefor and may allow the personnel file of the person or any portion to be inspected and examined by any person or corporation provided that the board has determined that the release of the information or the inspection and examination of the file or any portion is essential to maintaining the integrity of the board or to maintaining the level or quality of services provided by the board; provided, that prior to releasing the information or making the file or any portion available as provided herein, the superintendent shall prepare a memorandum setting forth the circumstances which he and the board deem to require the disclosure and the information to be disclosed. The memorandum shall be retained in the files of the superintendent and shall be a public record.

(b1) Notwithstanding any provision of this section to the contrary, the Retirement Systems Division of the Department of State Treasurer may disclose the name and mailing address of former public school employees to domiciled, nonprofit organizations representing 10,000 or more retired State government, local government, or public school employees.

(c) A public official or employee who knowingly, willfully, and with malice permits any person to have access to information contained in a personnel file, except as permitted by this section, is guilty of a Class 3 misdemeanor and upon conviction shall only be fined an amount not in excess of five hundred dollars ($500.00).

(d) Any person, not specifically authorized by this section to have access to a personnel file, who shall knowingly and willfully examine in its official filing place, remove, or copy any portion of a personnel file shall be guilty of a Class 3 misdemeanor and upon conviction shall only be fined not in excess of five hundred dollars ($500.00).

Community College Personnel Privacy Statute (G.S. 115D-27 through 115D-30)

§ 115D-27. Personnel files not subject to inspection.

Personnel files of employees of boards of trustees, former employees of boards of trustees, or applicants for employment with boards of trustees shall not be subject to inspection and examination as authorized by G.S. 132-6. For purposes of this Article, a personnel file consists of any information gathered by the board of trustees which employs an individual, previously employed an individual, or considered an individual's application for employment, and which information relates to the individual's application, selection or nonselection, promotion, demotion, transfer, leave, salary, suspension, performance evaluation, disciplinary action, or termination of employment wherever located or in whatever form.

§ 115D-28. Certain records open to inspection.

Each board of trustees shall maintain a record of each of its employees, showing the following information with respect to each employee: name, age, date of original employment or appointment, the terms of any contract by which the employee is employed whether written or oral, past and current, to the extent that the board has the written contract or a record of the oral contract in its possession, current position, title, current salary, date and amount of most recent increase or decrease in salary, date of most recent promotion, demotion, transfer, suspension, separation, or other change in position classification, and the office or station to which the employee is currently assigned. For the purposes of this section, the term "salary" includes pay, benefits, incentives, bonuses, and deferred and all other forms of compensation paid by the employing entity. Subject only to rules and regulations for the safekeeping of records adopted by the board of trustees, every person having custody of the records shall permit them to be inspected and examined and copies made by any person during regular business hours. Any person who is denied access to any record for the purpose of inspecting, examining or copying the record shall have a right to compel compliance with the provisions of this section by application to a court of competent jurisdiction for a writ of mandamus or other appropriate relief.

§ 115D-29. Confidential information in personnel files; access to information.

(a) All information contained in a personnel file, except as otherwise provided in this Article, is confidential and shall not be open for inspection and examination except to the following persons:

(1) The employee, applicant for employment, former employee, or his properly authorized agent, who may examine his own personnel file at all reasonable times in its entirety except for letters of reference solicited prior to employment;

(2) The president and other supervisory personnel;

(3) Members of the board of trustees and the board's attorney;

(4) A party by authority of a subpoena or proper court order may inspect and examine a particular confidential portion of an employee's personnel file; and

(5) An official of an agency of the federal government, State government or any political subdivision thereof. Such an official may inspect any personnel records when such [an] inspection is deemed by the college of the employee, applicant, or former employee whose record is to be inspected as necessary and essential to the pursuance of a proper function of said agency; provided, however, that such information shall not be divulged for purposes of assisting in a criminal prosecution, nor for purposes of assisting in a tax investigation.

(b) Notwithstanding any other provision of this Article, any president may, in his discretion, or shall at the direction of the board of trustees, inform any person or corporation of any promotion, demotion, suspension, reinstatement, transfer, separation, dismissal, employment or nonemployment of any applicant, employee or former employee employed by or assigned to the board of trustees or whose personnel file is maintained by the board and the reasons therefor and may allow the personnel file of the person or any portion to be inspected and examined by any person or corporation provided that the board has determined that the release of the information or the inspection and examination of the file or any portion is essential to maintaining the integrity of the board or to maintaining the level or quality of services provided by the board; provided, that prior to releasing the information or making the file or any portion available as provided herein, the president shall prepare a memorandum setting forth the circumstances which he and the board deem to require the disclosure and the information to be disclosed. The memorandum shall be retained in the files of the president and shall be a public record.

(c) Notwithstanding any provision of this section to the contrary, the Retirement Systems Division of the Department of State Treasurer may disclose the name and mailing address of former community college employees to domiciled, nonprofit organizations representing 2,000 or more active or retired State government, local government, or public school employees.

§ 115D-30. Remedy of employee objecting to material in file.

An employee, former employee or applicant for employment who objects to material in his file may place in his file a statement relating to the materials he considers to be inaccurate or misleading. An employee, former employee or applicant for employment who objects to material in his file because he considers it inaccurate or misleading, and the material has not been placed there in connection with a grievance procedure established by the board of trustees, may seek the removal of such material from the file through grievance procedures to be established by each board of trustees.

Public Health Authority Personnel Privacy Statute (G.S. 130A-45.9)

§ 130A-45.9. Confidentiality of personnel information.

(a) Except as provided in subsection (b) of this section, the personnel files of employees or former employees and the files of applicants for employment maintained by a public health authority are not public records as defined by Chapter 132 of the General Statutes.

(b) The following information with respect to each employee of a public health authority is a matter of public record: name; age; date of original employment or appointment; beginning and ending dates, position title, position descriptions, and total compensation of current and former positions; the terms of any contract by which the employee is employed whether written or oral, past and current, to the extent that the authority has the written contract or a record of the oral contract in its possession, and date of the most recent promotion, demotion, transfer, suspension, separation, or other change in position classification. In addition, the following information with respect to each licensed medical provider employed by or having privileges to practice in a public health facility shall be a matter of public record: educational history and qualifications, date and jurisdiction or original and current licensure; and information relating to medical board certifications or other qualifications of medical specialists. For the purposes of this subsection, the term "total compensation" includes pay, benefits, incentives, bonuses, and deferred and all other forms of compensation paid by the employing entity.

(c) Information regarding the qualifications, competence, performance, character, fitness, or conditions of appointment of an independent contractor who provides health care services under a contract with a public health authority is not a public record as defined by Chapter 132 of the General Statutes. Information regarding a hearing or investigation of a complaint, charge, or grievance by or against an independent contractor who provides health care services under a contract with a public health authority is not a public record as defined by Chapter 132 of the General Statutes. Final action making an appointment or discharge or removal by a public health authority having final authority for the appointment or discharge or removal shall be taken in an open meeting, unless otherwise exempted by law. The following information with respect to each independent contractor of health care services of a public health authority is a matter of public record: name; age; date of original contract; beginning and ending dates; position title; position descriptions; and total compensation of current and former positions; and the date of the most recent promotion, demotion, transfer, suspension, separation, or other change in position classification.

Public Hospital Personnel Privacy Statute (G.S. 131E-257.2)

§ 131E-257.2. Privacy of employee personnel records.

(a) Notwithstanding the provisions of G.S. 132-6 or any other general law or local act concerning access to public records, personnel files of employees and applicants for employment maintained by a public hospital are subject to inspection and may be disclosed only as provided by this section. For purposes of this section, an employee's personnel file consists of any information in any form gathered by the public hospital with respect to an employee and, by way of illustration but not limitation, relating to the employee's application, selection or nonselection, performance, promotions, demotions, transfers, suspensions and other disciplinary actions, evaluation forms, employment contracts, leave, salary, and termination of employment. As used in this section, "employee" includes both current and former employees of a public hospital.

(b) The following information with respect to each public hospital employee is a matter of public record:

(1) Name.
(2) Age.
(3) Date of original employment.
(4) Current position title.
(5) Date of the most recent promotion, demotion, transfer, suspension, separation or other change in position classification.
(6) The office to which the employee is currently assigned.

In addition, the following information with respect to each licensed medical provider employed by or having privileges to practice in a public hospital shall be a matter of public record: educational history and qualifications, date and jurisdiction or original and current licensure; and information relating to medical board certifications or other qualifications of medical specialists.

(b1) In addition, the following information for the last completed fiscal year, beginning with the fiscal year ending in 2008, of a public hospital with respect to each Covered Officer and the five key employees (who are not Covered Officers) with the highest annual compensation of a public hospital is a matter of public record:

(1) Base salary.
(2) Bonus compensation.
(3) Plan-based incentive compensation.
(4) Dollar value of all other compensation, which includes any perquisites and other personal benefits.

(b2) As used in this section:

(1) "Covered Officer" means each of the following:

a. All individuals serving as the public hospital's chief executive officer or acting in a similar capacity at any time during the last completed fiscal year, regardless of compensation level.

b. The public hospital's four most highly compensated executive officers, determined by the aggregate amount reportable under subdivisions (1) through (4) of subsection (b1) of this section, other than the chief executive officer, who were serving as executive officers at the end of the last completed fiscal year.
c. Any individual for whom disclosure would have been provided pursuant to sub-subdivision b. of this subsection but for the fact that the individual's service as an executive officer of the public hospital terminated during the last completed fiscal year.

(2) "Executive officer" means each employee of the public hospital specifically appointed by the governing board of the public hospital to serve as an officer.
(3) "Key employee" means any person having responsibilities, powers, or influence similar to those of an officer. The term includes the chief management and administrative officials of a public hospital.

(b3) The governing board of a public hospital shall determine in what form and by whom this information will be maintained. Any person may have access to this information for the purpose of inspection, examination, and copying, during regular business hours, subject only to such rules and regulations for the safekeeping of public records as the governing board of the public hospital may have adopted. Any person denied access to this information may apply to the appropriate division of the General Court of Justice for an order compelling disclosure, and the court shall have jurisdiction to issue such orders.

(c) All information contained in a public hospital employee's personnel file, other than the information made public by subsection (b) of this section, is confidential and shall be open to inspection only in the following instances:

(1) The employee or the employee's duly authorized agent may examine all portions of the employee's personnel file, except letters of reference solicited prior to employment.
(2) A licensed physician designated in writing by the employee may examine the employee's medical record.
(3) A public hospital employee having supervisory authority over the employee may examine all material in the employee's personnel file.
(4) By order of a court of competent jurisdiction, any person may examine such portion of an employee's personnel file as may be ordered by the court.
(5) An official of an agency of the State or federal government, or any political subdivision of the State, may inspect any portion of a personnel file when the inspection is deemed by the person having custody of the file to be inspected to be necessary and essential to the pursuance of a proper function of the inspecting agency, but no information shall be divulged for the purpose of assisting in criminal prosecution of the employee, or for the purpose of assisting in an investigation of the employee's tax liability. However, the official having custody of the records may release the name, address, and telephone number from a personnel file for the purpose of assisting in a criminal investigation.
(6) An employee may sign a written release, to be placed with the employee's personnel file, that permits the person with custody of the file to provide, either in

person, by telephone, or by mail, information specified in the release to prospective employers, educational institutions, or other persons specified in the release.

(d) Even if considered part of an employee's personnel file, the following information need not be disclosed to an employee nor to any other person:

(1) Testing or examination material used solely to determine individual qualifications for appointment, employment, or promotion in the public hospital's service, when disclosure would compromise the objectivity or the fairness of the testing or examination process.

(2) Investigative reports or memoranda and other information concerning the investigation of possible criminal actions of an employee, until the investigation is completed and no criminal action taken, or until the criminal action is concluded.

(3) Information that might identify an undercover law enforcement officer or a law enforcement informer.

(4) Notes, preliminary drafts, and internal communications concerning an employee. In the event such materials are used for any official personnel decision, then the employee or his duly authorized agent shall have a right to inspect such materials.

(e) The governing board of a public hospital may permit access, subject to limitations they may impose, to selected personnel files by a professional representative of a training, research, or academic institution if that representative certifies that he or she will not release information identifying the employees whose files are opened and that the information will be used solely for statistical, research, or teaching purposes. This certification shall be retained by the public hospital as long as each personnel file so examined is retained.

(f) The governing board of a public hospital that maintains personnel files containing information other than the information mentioned in subsection (b) of this section shall establish procedures whereby an employee who objects to material in his or her file on grounds that it is inaccurate or misleading may seek to have the material removed from the file or may place in the file a statement relating to the material.

(g) A public hospital director, trustee, officer, or employee who knowingly, willfully, and with malice permits any person to have access to information contained in a personnel file, except as is permitted by this section, is guilty of a Class 3 misdemeanor; however, conviction under this subsection shall be punishable only by a fine not to exceed five hundred dollars ($500.00).

(h) Any person not specifically authorized by this section to have access to a personnel file designated as confidential, who shall knowingly and willfully examine in its official filing place, or remove, or copy any portion of a confidential personnel file shall be guilty of a Class 3 misdemeanor; however, conviction under this subsection shall be punishable, in the discretion of the court, by a fine not to exceed five hundred dollars ($500.00).

State Government Personnel Privacy Statute (G.S. 126-22 through 126-30)

§ 126-22. Personnel files not subject to inspection under § 132-6.

(a) Except as provided in G.S. 126-23 and G.S. 126-24, personnel files of State employees shall not be subject to inspection and examination as authorized by G.S. 132-6.

(b) For purposes of this Article the following definitions apply:

(1) "Employee" means any current State employee, former State employee, or applicant for State employment.

(2) "Employer" means any State department, university, division, bureau, commission, council, or other agency subject to Article 7 of this Chapter.

(3) "Personnel file" means any employment-related or personal information gathered by an employer, the Retirement Systems Division of the Department of State Treasurer, or by the Office of State Personnel. Employment-related information contained in a personnel file includes information related to an individual's application, selection, promotion, demotion, transfer, leave, salary, contract for employment, benefits, suspension, performance evaluation, disciplinary actions, and termination. Personal information contained in a personnel file includes an individual's home address, social security number, medical history, personal financial data, marital status, dependents, and beneficiaries.

(4) "Record" means the personnel information that each employer is required to maintain in accordance with G.S. 126-23.

(c) Personnel files of former State employees who have been separated from State employment for 10 or more years may be open to inspection and examination except for papers and documents relating to demotions and to disciplinary actions resulting in the dismissal of the employee and personnel files maintained by the Retirement Systems Division of the Department of State Treasurer.

(d) Notwithstanding any provision of this section to the contrary, the Retirement Systems Division of the Department of State Treasurer may disclose the name and mailing address of former State employees to domiciled, nonprofit organizations representing 10,000 or more retired State government, local government, or public school employees.

§ 126-23. Certain records to be kept by State agencies open to inspection.

Each department, agency, institution, commission and bureau of the State shall maintain a record of each of its employees, showing the following information with respect to each such employee: name, age, date of original employment or appointment to the State service, the terms of any contract by which the employee is employed whether written or oral, past and current, to the extent that the agency has the written contract or a record of the oral contract in its possession, current position, title, current salary, date and amount of most recent increase or decrease in salary, date of most recent promotion, demotion, transfer, suspension, separation, or other change in position classification, and the office or station to which the employee is currently assigned. For the purposes of this section, the term "salary" includes pay, benefits, incentives, bonuses, and deferred and all other forms of compensation paid by the employing entity. Subject only to rules and regulations for the safekeeping of the records, adopted by the State Personnel Commission, every person having custody of such records shall permit them to be inspected and examined and copies thereof made by any person during regular business hours. Any person who is denied access to any such record for the purpose of inspecting, examining or copying the same shall have a right to compel compliance with the provisions of this section by application to a court of competent jurisdiction for a writ of mandamus or other appropriate relief.

§ 126-24. Confidential information in personnel files; access to such information.

All other information contained in a personnel file is confidential and shall not be open for inspection and examination except to the following persons:

(1) The employee, applicant for employment, former employee, or his properly authorized agent, who may examine his own personnel file in its entirety except for (i) letters of reference solicited prior to employment, or (ii) information concerning a medical disability, mental or physical, that a prudent physician would not divulge to a patient. An employee's medical record may be disclosed to a licensed physician designated in writing by the employee;

(2) The supervisor of the employee;

(3) Members of the General Assembly who may inspect and examine personnel records under the authority of G.S. 120-19;

(4) A party by authority of a proper court order may inspect and examine a particular confidential portion of a State employee's personnel file; and

(5) An official of an agency of the federal government, State government or any political subdivision thereof. Such an official may inspect any personnel records when such inspection is deemed by the department head of the employee whose record is to be inspected or, in the case of an applicant for employment or a former employee, by the department head of the agency in which the record is maintained as necessary and essential to the pursuance of a proper function of said agency; provided, however, that such information shall not be divulged for purposes of assisting in a criminal prosecution, nor for purposes of assisting in a tax investigation.

Notwithstanding any other provision of this Chapter, any department head may, in his discretion, inform any person or corporation of any promotion, demotion, suspension, reinstatement, transfer, separation, dismissal, employment or nonemployment of any applicant, employee or former employee employed by or assigned to his department or whose personnel file is maintained in his department and the reasons therefor and may allow the personnel file of such person or any portion thereof to be inspected and examined by any person or corporation when such department head shall determine that the release of such information or the inspection and examination of such file or portion thereof is essential to maintaining the integrity of such department or to maintaining the level or quality of services provided by such department; provided that prior to releasing such information or making such file or portion thereof available as provided herein, such department head shall prepare a memorandum setting forth the circumstances which the department head deems to require such disclosure and the information to be disclosed. The memorandum shall be retained in the files of said department head and shall be a public record.

§ 126-25. Remedies of employee objecting to material in file.

An employee, former employee or applicant for employment who objects to material in his file may place in his file a statement relating to the material he considers to be inaccurate or misleading. An employee, former employee or applicant for employment who objects to material in his file because he considers it inaccurate or misleading may seek the removal of such material from his file in accordance with the grievance procedure of that department, including appeal to the State Personnel Commission. When a department, division, bureau, commission, or other agency agrees or is ordered by the State Personnel Commission or by the General Court of Justice of this State to remove inaccurate or misleading material from an employee's file, which information was placed in the file by the supervisor or other agent of management, it shall destroy the original and all copies of the material removed and may not retain any inaccurate or misleading information derived from the material removed.

§ 126-26. Rules and regulations.
The State Personnel Commission shall prescribe such rules and regulations as it deems necessary to implement the provisions of this Article.

§ 126-27. Penalty for permitting access to confidential file by unauthorized person.
Any public official or employee who shall knowingly and willfully permit any person to have access to or custody or possession of any portion of a personnel file designated as confidential by this Article, unless such person is one specifically authorized by G.S. 126-24 to have access thereto for inspection and examination, shall be guilty of a Class 3 misdemeanor and upon conviction shall only be fined in the discretion of the court but not in excess of five hundred dollars ($500.00).

§ 126-28. Penalty for examining, copying, etc., confidential file without authority.
Any person, not specifically authorized by G.S. 126-24 to have access to a personnel file designated as confidential by this Article, who shall knowingly and willfully examine in its official filing place, remove or copy any portion of a confidential personnel file shall be guilty of a Class 3 misdemeanor and upon conviction shall only be fined in the discretion of the court but not in excess of five hundred dollars ($500.00).

§ 126-29. Access to material in file for agency hearing.
A party to a quasi-judicial hearing of a State agency subject to Article 7 of this Chapter, or a State agency subject to Article 7 of this Chapter which is conducting a quasi-judicial hearing, may have access to relevant material in personnel files and may introduce copies of such material or information based on such material as evidence in the hearing either upon consent of the employee, former employee, or applicant for employment or upon subpoena properly issued by the agency either upon request of a party or on its own motion. Nothing in this Article shall impose liability on any agent or officer of the State for compliance with this provision, notwithstanding any other provision of this Article.

§ 126-30. Fraudulent disclosure and willful nondisclosure on application for State employment; penalties.
(a) Any employee who knowingly and willfully discloses false or misleading information, or conceals dishonorable military service; or conceals prior employment history or other requested information, either of which are significantly related to job responsibilities on an application for State employment may be subjected to disciplinary action up to and including immediate dismissal from employment. Dismissal shall be mandatory where the

applicant discloses false or misleading information in order to meet position qualifications. Application forms for State employment shall include a statement informing applicants of the consequences of such fraudulent disclosure or lack of disclosure.

(b) The employing authority within each department, university, board, or commission, shall verify the status of credentials and the accuracy of statements contained in the application of each new employee within 90 days from the date of the employees employment. Failure to verify the application shall not bar action under subsection (a) above.

(c) The State Personnel Commission shall issue rules and procedures to implement this section for all departments, agencies and institutions which are not exempted from the State Personnel Act under G.S. 126-5(c1). Each agency, department and institution which is exempted under G.S. 126-5(c1) shall issue regulations to implement this section pursuant to the rulemaking procedures applicable to it.

Chapter 8—Criminal Investigation and Intelligence Records and Local Jail Records

PART 1—Criminal Investigation and Intelligence Records

Statutory Summary

Section 132-1.4 of the North Carolina General Statutes [hereinafter G.S.] establishes special rules of access to records generated while a law enforcement agency is investigating alleged or known violations of the criminal law, broadly defined.[1] The section also applies to records generated while a law enforcement agency is seeking to "anticipate, prevent, or monitor" violations of the criminal law, referred to in the statute as "criminal intelligence information." In general, the statute excludes such records from the public records

1. The statute is set out in appendix 8A at the end of this chapter.

law, thereby denying public access to them.[2] (The statute simply denies any right of public access; it does not prohibit release of the records by a law enforcement agency.) This kind of statute is common among the fifty states, and North Carolina's probably reflects a set of purposes comparable to those listed by the North Carolina Supreme Court in discussing the statute making State Bureau of Investigation (SBI) records confidential:

> Reports based on criminal investigations are often exempt from disclosure because they are based on hearsay and consist largely of the opinions and conclusions of the investigators. The need for protection of confidentiality of government informants and the protection of investigative techniques used by law enforcement agencies also have been generally accepted as justifying prohibitions on disclosure of police and investigative records. . . . An equally important reason for prohibiting access to police and investigative reports arises from recognition of the rights of privacy of individuals mentioned or accused of wrongdoing in unverified or unverifiable hearsay statements of others included in such reports.[3]

The statute excepts a few law enforcement records from the exclusion; that is, it declares these records to be public records and open to public access. These open records consist of details of criminal incidents, information about persons arrested or charged, the circumstances of arrests, contents of 911 telephone calls, radio communications between law enforcement personnel, and information about victims of crime and persons who file complaints or report violations. If necessary to protect the health or safety of a victim or witness, however, a law enforcement agency may withhold that person's name and address from public access.

---

2. Other statutes may require that a law enforcement agency share some criminal investigation records with other public agencies. For example, N.C. GEN. STAT. [hereinafter G.S.] § 7B-302 requires law enforcement agencies to share information with the local director of social services when the latter official is investigating a complaint about child abuse.

3. News & Observer Publ'g Co. v. State *ex rel.* Starling, 312 N.C. 276, 282–83, 322 S.E.2d 133, 138 (1984) (citation omitted). A comparable statement of purposes is found in *Bougas v. Chief of Police of Lexington*, 354 N.E.2d 872, 876 (Mass. 1976):

> Included among the purposes in providing this exemption [for criminal justice investigatory materials] would be the avoidance of premature disclosure of the [State's] case prior to trial, the prevention of the disclosure of confidential investigative techniques, procedures, or sources of information, the encouragement of individual citizens to come forward and speak freely with police concerning matters under investigation, and the creation of initiative that police officers might be completely candid in recording their observations, hypotheses and interim conclusions.

The federal Freedom of Information Act (FOIA) suggests an alternative list of policies served by such a statute. It excludes law enforcement records from public access but only when access would (1) interfere with enforcement, (2) deprive the defendant of a fair trial, (3) invade personal privacy, (4) disclose the identity of a confidential source, (5) disclose investigative techniques or guidelines, or (6) endanger someone's life or safety. 5 U.S.C. § 552(b)(7) (2006).

Discussion

Agencies to Which the Statute Applies

Although the statute's clear focus is on the records of city police departments and county sheriffs' departments (as well as state law enforcement agencies), it in fact reaches many additional agencies, including some not normally considered law enforcement agencies. The statute applies to information relating to investigations of or gathering of intelligence about "violations of the law" by any "public law enforcement agency," and the two quoted phrases are defined in the statute.

Violations of the law are defined as "crimes and offenses that are prosecutable in the criminal courts in this State or the United States and infractions." Thus, if an act exposes the actor to prosecution for committing a felony, a misdemeanor, or an infraction, the investigation of that act can generate records covered by the statute. Because G.S. 14-4 makes violation of almost all city or county ordinances either a misdemeanor or an infraction, the investigation of ordinance violations of almost any sort falls within the statute. (A county or city has the option of decriminalizing an ordinance entirely, making it enforceable only through civil penalties.[4] If an ordinance has been decriminalized, the statute does not cover records generated in an investigation of a violation of that ordinance.)

Counties and cities often enforce local ordinances that carry criminal or infraction penalties in ways other than through those penalties. If a utility department's operating rules have been violated, for example, the department is more likely to cut off service than to bring criminal charges; and planning departments enforce zoning ordinances more often by injunction or civil penalties than by criminal enforcement. But the statute does not condition its definitions on the usual enforcement methods or on the enforcement method likely to be used against a particular violation. Rather, if violation of a statute, ordinance, or rule or regulation can cause the violator to be answerable in a criminal proceeding or in an infraction proceeding, it is a violation of the law as defined in G.S. 132-1.4.

Public law enforcement agency is defined to include "any State or local agency, force, department, or unit responsible for investigating, preventing, or solving violations of the law." Thus, any organizational unit within a county or city that is responsible for enforcement of a statute, ordinance, or rule or regulation that carries misdemeanor or infraction penalties is capable of generating records that are covered by the statute.[5] Some of the possible examples of such units, in addition to police and sheriffs' departments, include those

---

4. See G.S. 153A-123 for counties and G.S. 160A-175 for cities.

5. In a letter to the chief deputy secretary of state, the attorney general's office distinguished between an agency with responsibility for *reporting* violations of a law and one with responsibility for *investigating* those violations once reported. Only the latter is a public law enforcement agency. Letter to Rodney S. Maddox, 3 April 2006, Advisory Opinion No. 580, *available at* www.ncdoj.gov/About-DOJ/Legal-Services/Legal-Opinions.aspx.

involved with code enforcement;[6] animal control;[7] arson investigations;[8] utilities, if operating rules have been adopted by ordinance; zoning administration; environmental health;[9] sedimentation control;[10] housing or employment discrimination, if regulations have been adopted by ordinance; business license tax collection;[11] and welfare fraud investigations.[12]

In *McCormick v. Hanson Aggregates Southeast, Inc.*,[13] the North Carolina Court of Appeals held that the Raleigh City Attorney's Office was a public law enforcement agency. The court cited a provision in the city's charter that directed the city attorney "to prosecute and defend all suits-at-law or in equity in which the City of Raleigh may become the plaintiff or defendant" and a city ordinance that granted to the city attorney criminal enforcement powers over misdemeanors and infractions. It is not clear that this holding extends to attorneys for other cities or for counties, although it should. As noted, the court relied on a specific charter provision and a city ordinance in support of its holding that the attorney's office was a public law enforcement agency. The charter provision, however, is quite unusual, and many cities or counties do not have the sort of ordinance cited by the court. Most cities and counties rely upon the general law, or a charter or local act provision similar to the general law, which simply directs the governing board to appoint a city or county attorney who is to be the board's legal adviser.[14] There is no specific direction in the general law comparable to that found in Raleigh's charter. Therefore, if a court were to focus on statutory or comparable powers in determining whether an office or department was a public law enforcement agency, most county or city attorneys would not qualify.[15] A court should not focus solely on formal powers, however. Most county or city attorneys do as a matter of practice engage in the same ordinance enforcement activities as Raleigh's, and a court should focus as much on the actual activities of an agency as on its formal statutory or comparable powers. If an office or department is in fact investigating violations of the law or gathering criminal intelligence information because that is its responsibility under

---

6. G.S. 153A-357 and 160A-417 make it a misdemeanor to proceed with construction without the permits required by the State Building Code, and other sections of G.S. Chapter 153, Article 18, Part 4, and G.S. Chapter 160A, Article 19, Part 5, make it a misdemeanor to violate specific orders of county or city building inspectors.

7. Violation of a local animal control ordinance would be a misdemeanor under G.S. 14-4. In addition, local animal control agencies enforce state laws, such as those regulating dangerous dogs, the violation of which is a misdemeanor. G.S. 67-4.2 and 67-4.3.

8. G.S. 58-79-1 directs municipal fire chiefs to investigate suspicious fires, and the resulting report, sent to the attorney general, is a public record. Other arson investigation files held by the Department of Insurance are exempt from public inspection, however, under G.S. 58-2-100.

9. G.S. 130A-25 makes it a misdemeanor to violate any rule of a local board of health, any rule of the Commission for Public Health, and any provision of G.S. Chapter 130A.

10. Knowing violation of a local sedimentation ordinance or of state sedimentation rules is a misdemeanor under G.S. 113A-64(b).

11. Failure to pay privilege taxes is a misdemeanor under G.S. 105-109.

12. Welfare fraud is a crime under G.S. 108A-39.

13. 164 N.C. App. 459, 596 S.E.2d 431 (2004).

14. G.S. 160A-173 directs the "council [to] appoint a city attorney to serve at its pleasure and to be its legal adviser," and G.S. 153A-114 has almost identical language with respect to boards of county commissioners and county attorneys.

15. A county social services attorney clearly would qualify, however. The duties of the position are set out in G.S. 108A-18, and they clearly include enforcement of various criminal statutes.

the organizational structure of the agency or the government of which it is a part, it should be considered a public law enforcement agency.

Obviously, the statute does not cover all records of each organizational unit that qualifies as a public law enforcement agency, just as it does not cover all records generated by police or sheriffs' departments. Nevertheless, if a department or agency generates records while investigating a possible violation of a law or ordinance that carries criminal or infraction penalties, those records are within the statutory coverage. As a practical matter, most of these agencies other than police and sheriffs' departments rarely insist upon the statutory protections available for these records. The most common use of the statute by these non-police agencies may be to protect the identity of complaining witnesses in disputes between neighbors—for example, disputes involving nuisances caused by pets.

Criminal Investigation and Criminal Intelligence Records

Specific Kinds of Records

What kinds of specific records held by public law enforcement agencies are excluded from public access by the statute? The statute itself provides some detail. It defines "records of criminal investigations" as including "information derived from witnesses, laboratory tests, surveillance, investigators, confidential informants, photographs, and measurements." In addition, the listing of investigative material that is public also offers assistance in determining the kinds of records that are excluded from public access by the statute: while basic information about persons arrested or charged is public, statements from such persons are not; while radioed communications among law enforcement officers are public, written communications about an investigation are not; and while the identity of the victim and any complaining witness is public, the identities of other witnesses located and interviewed by the law enforcement agency are not. Finally, court decisions under comparable statutes in other states offer examples of records that appear to fall within the statute's coverage: witness statements;[16] booking photographs (that is, mug shots, although many departments release these anyway);[17] results of breathalyzer, polygraph, and other tests;[18] autopsy photographs and other autopsy records;[19] letters alleging criminal activities;[20] physical evidence such as weapons, clothing, and the like; and evidence logs.[21]

---

16. *E.g.*, State *ex rel.* Hamblin v. City of Brooklyn, 616 N.E.2d 883 (Ohio 1993).

17. *E.g.*, Patterson v. Allegan County Sheriff, 502 N.W.2d 368 (Mich. Ct. App. 1993).

18. *E.g.*, State *ex rel.* Outlet Commc'ns, Inc. v. Lancaster Police Dep't, 528 N.E.2d 175 (Ohio 1988).

19. *E.g.*, Shuttleworth v. City of Camden, 610 A.2d 903 (N.J. Super. Ct. App. Div. 1992); Journal/Sentinel, Inc. v. Aagerup, 429 N.W.2d 772 (Wis. Ct. App. 1988). Under G.S. 130A-389, autopsy reports in North Carolina are public record. (Under G.S. 130A-389.1, autopsy photographs and videos are open to public inspection but not copying.) The statute does not address the notes upon which the report is based, however, and if a crime is suspected those notes fit the definition of records of criminal investigations. (If no crime is suspected, the notes are probably part of the deceased's medical records and not public record for that reason. *Cf.* G.S. 130A-389(d).)

20. Ortiz v. U.S. Dep't of Health & Human Servs., 70 F.3d 729 (2d Cir. 1995).

21. G.S. 147-90 provides that if a private citizen is killed as a result of firearm use by a law enforcement officer, the surviving spouse or next of kin may request the district attorney to have the State Bureau of Investigation investigate the incident. The statute provides that statements prepared by or on behalf of

Criminal intelligence information is a little hazier and probably more idiosyncratic. The statute defines such information as records compiled "to anticipate, prevent, or monitor possible violations of the law." Here are some random examples of records that seem to fit this definition:

- Pawn tickets collected by a law enforcement agency as a routine matter in order to locate fenced goods
- Recordings of telephone calls made by jail inmates
- Registrations of home alarm systems, including such information as the homeowner's name and address, contact information, and work schedule
- Film from a surveillance camera placed in a public place by a law enforcement agency[22]

The information must have been collected to anticipate, prevent, or monitor violations of the law, however. If a law enforcement agency maintains a database of persons residing in nursing homes, for example, to help in identification if an elderly person is found wandering and disoriented, there is no connection to violations of the law and the database would not be covered by this statute.

Information about a Person or Group of Persons

Both the definition of "records of criminal investigations" and the definition of "records of criminal intelligence information" speak of information that "pertains to a person or group of persons." Many investigations, of course, begin without any focus on a particular person, and some never are able to focus on any particular person. If there is no focus on a particular person or group of persons, are the files of that investigation excluded from the statute and therefore open to public access?

The answer is that they almost certainly are not. Given the probable purposes of the statute, it makes no sense to make investigative records public simply because no suspect has yet been identified. The better understanding of the statutory language is that it covers records that document law enforcement agency efforts to identify specific suspects, as opposed to records with a more general focus, such as those that set out an agency's investigatory procedures.

Closed or Inactive Investigations

A number of criminal investigation records statutes enacted by other states limit their applicability to records that are part of active investigations.[23] Once an investigation has closed because there has been a prosecution or a decision not to prosecute, criminal investigation records in those other states become public. The North Carolina statute, however, does not distinguish between active and inactive or closed investigations, a point recog-

---

the district attorney pursuant to this statute may be released only as provided by G.S. 132-1.4 or other applicable law.

22. G.S. 66-11(c)(1) provides that reports and receipts forwarded to a law enforcement agency by a secondary metals recycler are records of criminal investigation or intelligence under G.S. 132-1.4.

23. The Florida statute is one example. *See* Tribune Co. v. Pub. Records, P.C.S.O. # 79-35504 Miller/Jent, 493 So. 2d 480 (Fla. Dist. Ct. App. 1986).

nized by the state court of appeals. In *Gannett Pacific Corp. v. North Carolina State Bureau of Investigation*,[24] the SBI had conducted an investigation of a fire that took place in the Mitchell County Jail in 2002. Once the investigation was complete and no prosecution had been brought, the plaintiff newspaper sought copies of the SBI's investigative files. When the agency refused, the newspaper sued and urged the court to adopt a balancing approach, under which the reviewing court would weigh the purposes for secrecy against the public's need for disclosure. The court of appeals rejected the argument, noting that the statute makes no distinction between ongoing and completed investigations. It pointed out that the purposes of statutes such as G.S. 132-1.4

> include, but are not limited to the following: (1) protection of confidentiality of government informants; (2) protection of investigative techniques used by law enforcement agencies; (3) criminal investigation reports contain the opinions and conclusions of the investigators and may be based on hearsay. These justifications do not dissipate upon conclusion of an investigation or where no actual prosecution takes place.[25]

Several of the personnel privacy statutes include the following provision:

> Even if considered part of an employee's personnel file, the following information need not be disclosed to an employee nor to any other person:
>
> . . .
>
> (2) Investigative reports or memoranda and other information concerning the investigation of possible criminal actions of an employee, *until the investigation is completed and no criminal action taken, or until the criminal action is concluded.*[26]

The italicized portion of this provision suggests that, at least, an employee who is the subject of a criminal investigation is entitled to inspect the investigative file once the investigation or any criminal proceeding is complete. That is, of course, inconsistent with the general rule applicable to criminal investigation records.

The personnel privacy act provisions regarding investigative reports were first enacted in 1981, in the city and county personnel privacy statutes,[27] and then included automatically in several separate personnel privacy statutes that were enacted later and modeled on the city and county statutes. The criminal investigation statute was not enacted until 1993 and as

---

24. 164 N.C. App. 154, 595 S.E.2d 162 (2004).

25. *Id.* at 160, 595 S.E.2d at 166 (citation omitted). The Ohio Supreme Court made a similar point. It noted that one purpose of the Ohio statute "is to avoid the situation in which the release of confidential law enforcement investigatory records would subject a person to adverse publicity where he may otherwise never have been identified with the matter under investigation." Unless such a person was charged, "there is no reason why the suspect should be subjected to potential adverse publicity where he or she may otherwise have never been implicated in the investigation." State *ex rel.* Thompson Newspapers, Inc. v. Martin, 546 N.E.2d 939, 942 (Ohio 1989).

26. This language is found in the county personnel privacy statute, G.S. 153A-98(c1)(2); the city personnel privacy statute, G.S. 160A-168(c1)(2); the water and sewer authority personnel privacy statute, G.S. 162A-6.1(d)(2); the area authority personnel privacy statute, G.S. 122C-158(d)(2); and the public hospital personnel privacy statute, G.S. 131E-257.2(d)(2). The italics have been added for emphasis.

27. 1981 N.C. Sess. Laws ch. 926, §§ 3 and 7.

the later statute perhaps might be thought to be controlling for that reason alone. There is a way to reconcile the statutes, however, without having to leave the personnel privacy provisions without any force. The introductory language of the personnel privacy provisions states that "even if" these records are part of a personnel file, they are to be treated in this special way. As a matter of fact, though, such a criminal investigation would not normally be considered part of a personnel file, and therefore the personnel privacy acts would not apply at all. Only if the results of a criminal investigation were used to take some sort of personnel action against the employee would the material be part of the personnel file. If that were to happen, then the personnel privacy provisions would apply, and the employee would have the same access to the material as he or she has to any other material in the file that might support a personnel action against the employee.

Investigations That Demonstrate No Crime Was Committed

Law enforcement agencies investigate numerous incidents that turn out not to involve criminal behavior. A death turns out to be suicide. A motor vehicle accident turns out to be just that—an accident, with no criminal offense or infraction involved.[28] Allegations of one kind or another turn out to be unfounded. If the result of an investigation demonstrates that there was no criminal activity involved, does the statute cover the records of the investigation so as to deny public access to them?

Quite probably it does. Although these investigations have led to a conclusion that no crime was committed, the law enforcement agency was not sure of that fact until the investigation was completed.[29] The investigation was a bona fide criminal investigation while it was being conducted, and several of the policies that underlie the statute are furthered by maintaining confidentiality of this kind of file: protecting the reputation of those investigated; protecting the confidentiality of investigative techniques and, possibly, the identity of informants; and encouraging witnesses to come forward. Indeed, this sort of investigation is merely one form of inactive investigation[30] and should therefore be subject to the same sort of rules as other inactive or closed investigations: the file is still confidential under the criminal investigation records statute.[31]

---

28. G.S. 20-166.1(e) requires local police departments to complete and send to the state Division of Motor Vehicles a report on each motor vehicle collision the department is required to investigate. G.S. 20-166.1(i) makes the reports public records in the custody of the division. That being the case, the reports are probably public records in the custody of the local police department as well. That the reporting forms are public records, however, does not mean necessarily that any notes and other supporting materials held by the police department are also public records. Their status is governed by the discussion in the text accompanying this note.

29. If it is clear from the beginning that no crime was committed, perhaps there can be no criminal investigation for purposes of the statute. *See* State *ex rel.* Ware v. City of Cleveland, 562 N.E.2d 946 (Ohio Ct. App. 1989) (because city police treated death of jail inmate as suicide from the outset, police cannot claim records of investigation are criminal investigative records).

30. The Ohio case quoted from and cited *supra* in note 25 actually was an example of an investigation that concluded no crime was committed. There had been allegations against a local official but no criminal charges were brought.

31. A case that supports the conclusion in the text is *Barfield v. City of Fort Lauderdale Police Department*, 639 So. 2d 1012 (Fla. Dist. Ct. App. 1994). In that case two police officers had shot a citizen, and a police dog had bitten another man. The police department routinely treated such events as possibly

Records Otherwise Public Made Part of the Investigation

G.S. 132-1.4(f) prohibits a law enforcement agency from denying public access to public records in the custody of some other public agency simply because the law enforcement agency has used the public record in the course of its investigation. Thus, a police department could not close off access to accounting records in the city's finance department simply because the police had consulted or copied the records in investigating an alleged embezzlement of city moneys. The statutory provision is most naturally read as prohibiting the law enforcement agency from attempting to seal the public record regardless of the record's location. Even if the law enforcement agency seized and retained physical possession of the original record, the statutory provision seems to require the agency to allow access to the original as a public record. "The use of a public record in connection with a criminal investigation . . . shall not affect its status as a public record."[32] If a law enforcement agency makes a copy of the original record, however, the copy is part of the investigative file and need not be disclosed to the public.

This analysis might seem somewhat inconsistent with the 1996 case of *Times-News Publishing Co. v. State*[33] from the North Carolina Court of Appeals. The court was faced with the issue of public access to criminal investigation records that had been introduced into evidence in a murder trial and then returned to the district attorney when the supreme court ordered a new trial. The records at issue included the murder weapon, blood scrapings, crime scene photographs, fingerprints, and the victims' clothing. After the records had been returned to the district attorney, a newspaper company demanded access to them under the public records law. Acknowledging that the records were originally protected

---

criminal and investigated them and turned the results over to the district attorney. The plaintiff sought access to the investigative records, arguing that they were not really criminal investigative records. The court ruled for the police department, arguing that the statute was not limited to those cases in which arrest or prosecution was a certainty or even likely; the purpose of the investigation was to determine if arrest or prosecution was warranted, and it required confidentiality to proceed. *Accord* Viotti v. U.S. Air Force, 902 F. Supp. 1331 (D. Colo. 1995) (exception to federal Privacy Act for "investigatory material compiled for law enforcement purposes" applies even when no criminal charges are brought); Haynie v. Superior Court, 31 P.3d 760 (Cal. 2001) (when deputies stopped a van in response to a telephoned report they did not know no criminal conduct was involved and therefore records are criminal investigation records); An Unincorporated Operating Div. of Ind. Newspapers, Inc. v. Trs. of Ind. Univ., 787 N.E.2d 893 (Ind. Ct. App. 2003) (exception to public access for "information compiled in the course of the investigation of a crime" does not depend on prosecution resulting from the investigation); Seck v. City of Overland Park, 27 P.3d 919 (Kan. Ct. App. 2000) (although death turned out to be a suicide, the court emphasized that at the beginning of the investigation it was a potential homicide and therefore the associated records were criminal investigation records); Jensen v. Schiffman, 544 P.2d 1048 (Or. Ct. App. 1976) (criminal investigations were "not limited to literal investigations of crimes, but [include] investigations to determine whether a crime has been committed," *Jensen* at 1050). (In *Griffin v. City of Knoxville*, 821 S.W.2d 921 (Tenn. 1991), the court granted public access to records associated with a suicide, but at that time Tennessee's public records law had no exception for criminal investigation records.)

32. G.S. 132-1.4(f). This statutory rule differs from the United States Supreme Court's interpretation of the federal Freedom of Information Act. In *John Doe Agency v. John Doe Corp.*, 493 U.S. 146 (1989), the Court held that records originally compiled for some purpose other than criminal investigation, and as such normally available under FOIA, became criminal investigation records when they were later used in an investigation.

33. 124 N.C. App. 175, 476 S.E.2d 450 (1996).

from public access under G.S. 132-1.4, the newspaper argued that statutory confidentiality was lost once the records were introduced into evidence at the first trial. The court of appeals disagreed. Although the newspaper might have been correct during the period after the records were placed into evidence and before they were returned to the district attorney, upon being returned the records once again became subject to G.S. 132-1.4 and were closed to public access. Although this outcome might seem inconsistent with G.S. 132-1.4(f), it should be noted that these records began as criminal investigation records and not as some other sort of public records. The outcome might well have been different had the records been open to the public before they became part of the investigation.

Law Enforcement Materials That Are Not Criminal Investigation or Criminal Intelligence Records

Not all materials held by law enforcement agencies qualify as criminal investigation records or criminal intelligence records. While police or sheriffs' departments may have good reasons for wanting to withhold some of these other materials from public access, G.S. 132-1.4 provides no basis for their doing so. This section discusses some of the kinds of materials that are not protected from public access by the statute.

Operations Manuals, Procedures Books, and the Like

Many police and sheriffs' departments have developed manuals or compiled notebooks that set out general departmental policies and procedures on a variety of topics. For much of the information in these manuals, no one would claim any need for confidentiality. But some of the information might well be compromised by public access. A manual might, for example, set out the department's policies on dealing with a person holding hostages, its procedures for determining roadblock locations or for protecting presidential candidates, or its plans for drug interdiction. Publicizing any of these might make the publicized policy or procedure worthless. Nevertheless, these materials do not fit into the definition of either criminal investigation or criminal intelligence materials.

Some of the procedures or plans might, however, fit into a different exception to public access. G.S. 132-1.7, entitled "Sensitive public security information," excepts from the definition of "public record" both the "specific details of public security plans and arrangements" and "plans to prevent or respond to terrorist activity." (This section is discussed at length *infra* in chapter 20.) Certainly at least some of the sorts of plans or procedures set out in departmental operations manuals and similar publications fit under the quoted exceptions to public access. Material in a manual that does not fit under G.S. 132-1.7, however, appears to be standard public record, fully open to public access.

Routine Follow-Ups on Use of Force, Chases, and the Like

Many law enforcement agencies routinely conduct internal investigations each time an officer uses a weapon, each time an officer pursues an automobile, each time a police dog touches a person, and for other comparable incidents. Some of these incidents may be treated as potentially criminal, and therefore the investigative files would qualify as records of criminal investigations. Firearm discharge investigations might be examples of this category.[34] Not all such investigations involve potentially criminal behavior, however—many automobile pursuits do not, and police dog incidents usually do not. These investigations are undertaken as part of departmental management to determine if officers are following established procedures and if those procedures need modification. Investigations undertaken for this latter set of purposes do not appear to qualify as criminal investigations, and therefore the records of the investigation are not subject to G.S. 132-1.4.[35] In many cases the records will qualify, though, as personnel records and be made part of the personnel files of the officers involved. (Investigations of dog-related incidents would not be part of a personnel file unless the investigation involved the performance of the dog's handler.)

Information about Officers

Law enforcement officers are often concerned about their personal safety and seek to shield their home addresses and telephone numbers from public access. As was noted in chapter 7, "Personnel Records," that information is not a public part of the personnel file of any public employee. There is no basis in any of the exceptions to the public records statutes, however, for excepting other records that might contain that sort of information. For example, there is no basis for denying public access to deed or tax records simply because they might reveal a police officer's home address.

Law enforcement officers also sometimes seek to deny public access to their work telephone numbers or the numbers of agency-issued cell phones, usually in order to restrict unwanted usage of those phones. There is no basis for doing so, however, in the criminal investigation statute, in any of the personnel privacy statutes, or in any other statute establishing an exception to the right of public access. The numbers are open to public access.

Permit Applications

Law enforcement agencies, particularly sheriffs' departments, are charged by statute with approving applications for a variety of permits. Examples include handgun[36] and concealed handgun permits,[37] pawnbrokers' licenses,[38] and permits for dealers in precious metals.[39] Many city ordinances also charge police departments with issuing various sorts of permits, such as for taxicab operators. Although the statutes have a purpose in requiring that these permits and licenses be approved by a police agency, that purpose is probably to facilitate investigation of the applicants and to give the police agency a list of persons in the community involved in the business or activity regulated. It cannot be reasonably argued that the police agency holds the permitting or licensing responsibility in order to engage in

---

34. *But see* Reinstein v. Police Comm'r, 391 N.E.2d 881 (Mass. 1979) (firearms discharge reports are prepared for internal monitoring and not criminal prosecution and therefore are not law enforcement records).

35. *Accord* Cowles Publ'g Co. v. City of Spokane, 849 P.2d 1271 (Wash. Ct. App. 1993) (dog incident report prepared as routine administrative matter and not for criminal investigation).

36. G.S. 14-402.

37. G.S. 14-415.11.

38. G.S. 91A-6. The statute provides for issuance of the license by the appropriate city or county agency. Many local governments have designated their law enforcement agencies as the appropriate agency.

39. G.S. 66-165.

criminal intelligence or criminal investigation activities. Unless the statute establishing the permit or license requirement exempts the records associated with the permit or license from public access, they are public records.[40] Thus, the applications for these permits and licenses, any list made or maintained of permit or license holders, and any reports required from permit or license holders are public record.[41]

Public Material in Law Enforcement Files

Summary

As stated in the statutory summary at the beginning of this chapter, and as set out in subsection (c) of the statute itself, certain criminal investigation or criminal intelligence records are open to public inspection and copying. These records contain (1) basic information about violations or apparent violations of law; (2) basic information about persons who have been arrested; (3) basic information about the circumstances and manner of arrests; (4) the contents of 911 and other emergency telephone calls; (5) the contents of radioed communications between or among law enforcement employees; and, subject to possible delay, (6) the name, age, sex, and address of a complaining witness.

Incident and Arrest Reports in General

Of the above categories of information that is public, the first three and the sixth correspond generally to state-provided forms that are widely used by local police and sheriffs' departments. As part of its statutory mandate to gather criminal justice statistics, the Division of Criminal Information in the State Bureau of Investigation has promulgated forms for incident/investigation reports and arrest reports that it asks local law enforcement agencies to use in transmitting information to the division. When G.S. 132-1.4 was enacted, law enforcement agencies generally filled out paper versions of these forms and mailed them to the division in Raleigh. The first page (of two) of the incident/investigation report asks for information that generally corresponds to the first and sixth categories of public information listed in the previous paragraph,[42] and the one-page arrest report asks for information that corresponds to the second and third categories of information so listed. As long as the paper forms were used, local law enforcement agencies recognized these correlations and routinely made available to the public the front page of the incident/investigation report and the entire arrest report.

Despite this widespread practice, the first page of the incident/investigation report in fact includes more information than the statute requires be made public. Most importantly,

---

40. Compare *Superintendent of Police v. Freedom of Information Commission*, 609 A.2d 998 (Conn. 1992), in which the court held that the information on pistol permits was a public record and not protected from public access by any doctrine of privacy.

41. G.S. 66-169 creates one exception to this statement. The statute requires dealers in precious metals to maintain a record of precious metals purchases and deposit a copy of the record with the law enforcement agency that granted the dealer a permit. It then provides that the transaction record is not open to public access under G.S. 132-6.

42. When a law enforcement agency investigates a motor vehicle accident, the officer prepares a collision report that is sent to the state's Division of Motor Vehicles. This report probably constitutes the incident/ investigation report for that event, and in general the first page of the report includes the information about an incident that is required to be made public under the criminal investigation statute.

the statute makes public the "name, sex, age, and address" of the complaining witness or victim, while the report also includes fields for the victim's race, home or business telephone number, employer, and other information. Indeed, as is noted below, the statute may require that information about the victim be made public only when the victim is the complaining witness, but the incident/investigation report includes victim information whether the victim or some other person reported the crime. Today, rather than creating and sending off paper versions of the report, most law enforcement agencies fill out the form electronically and electronically send it to the division. That process has made it possible to create an incident report for distribution to the public that more closely follows the content specified in the statute, and many agencies in fact create a special version of the incident report for that purpose.[43]

Incidents Involving Juvenile Offenders

G.S. 7B-3001(b) provides that "[u]nless jurisdiction of the juvenile has been transferred to superior court,[44] all law enforcement records and files concerning a juvenile shall be kept separate from the records and files of adults and shall be withheld from public inspection." How does this provision interact with the requirements in G.S. 132-1.4(c) that incident reports and arrest records be open to public access, when the incident in question involves a juvenile offender? Interestingly, G.S. 132-1.4(l) provides that investigation records "of alleged child abuse shall be governed by Article 29 of Chapter 7B of the General Statutes," whose predecessor was the same section that—at the time G.S. 132-1.4 was enacted—also made confidential law enforcement records generated when a crime was committed by a juvenile.[45] Because there is no comparable provision in G.S. 132-1.4 with respect to what is now G.S. 7B-3001(b), it seems that G.S. 7B-3001(b) does not automatically control; rather, it must be reconciled, as best it can be, with the requirements of G.S. 132-1.4(c).

A West Virginia case suggests a possible reconciliation with respect to the incident/investigation report. In West Virginia, as in North Carolina, incident reports are open to public inspection but law enforcement records "concerning a child" are not. The West

---

43. Such an approach was upheld in *State ex rel. Goodman v. St. Louis Board of Police Commissioners*, 181 S.W.3d 156 (Mo. Ct. App. 2005). The Missouri statute made public "the date, time, specific location, name of the victim and immediate facts and circumstances surrounding the initial report of a crime or incident." The court held that this listing was exclusive and therefore that the law enforcement agency could delete the following from its incident reports for motor vehicle accidents: driver's license numbers, license plate numbers, victims' addresses and phone numbers, and victims' day and month (but not year) of birth.

G.S. 20-166.1 requires law enforcement agencies to prepare motor vehicle accident forms and submit them to the state Division of Motor Vehicles (DMV). Subsection (i) of the statute provides that the copy sent to DMV is a public record, but that does not apply to the copy retained by the local law enforcement agency. The report is the equivalent of an incident report, and only those items made public by G.S. 132-1.4 need be made public by a local law enforcement agency.

44. G.S. 7B-2200 provides:

> After notice, hearing, and a finding of probable cause the [district] court may, upon motion of the prosecutor or the juvenile's attorney or upon its own motion, transfer jurisdiction over a juvenile to superior court if the juvenile was 13 years of age or older at the time the juvenile allegedly committed an offense that would be a felony if committed by an adult. If the alleged felony constitutes a Class A felony and the court finds probable cause, the court shall transfer the case to the superior court for trial as in the case of adults.

45. Records of child abuse are now governed by G.S. 7B-2901.

Virginia Supreme Court interpreted the juvenile records statute as concerned with protecting the identity of the juvenile. Therefore, it reconciled the two statutes by directing that incident reports involving offenses committed by juveniles be made public but also directing that the name of the juvenile and any other information that might identify the juvenile be removed from the report.[46] The North Carolina statute also seems concerned with protecting the identity of the juvenile and thus could be served by a similar reconciliation. Many local law enforcement agencies already follow such a practice.

With respect to arrest reports, the answer probably lies in the technical point that juvenile offenders are not "arrested"; they are "taken into temporary custody."[47] Given the general policy of G.S. 7B-3001(b) that juvenile records are not public, it is sensible to read the wording of G.S. 132-1.4(c) literally and exclude from it custodial situations that do not involve arrests. Such an interpretation accords with the widespread practice of local law enforcement agencies. The reports they prepare on taking juveniles into temporary custody are not routinely made available for public inspection and copying.

The Name, Address, and Identity of a Victim or Complaining Witness

G.S. 132-1.4(c)(6) makes generally public the "name, sex, age, and address of a complaining witness." G.S. 132-1.4(b)(5) defines a "complaining witness" as "an alleged victim or other person who reports a violation or apparent violation of the law to a public law enforcement agency."

Identity of victims—generally. The statutory definition of complaining witness is ambiguous. The term is defined as the "victim or other person who reports a violation," and the quoted language can be read in either of two ways. First, it might be read to refer to a victim who reports a violation and to any other person who reports a violation. So read, the definition of a complaining witness includes a victim only when that person was the one reporting the crime. Any other victim would not be included, and information about such a victim would not be required to be made public. Alternatively, the quoted language might be read to refer to (1) victims and (2) persons who report violations; that is, the words "who reports a violation" would modify only "other person" and not "victim." Under this reading, information about a victim would always be public, and so would information about any complaining witness who was not the victim.

Although no court has been called upon to resolve this ambiguity, the widespread practice of law enforcement agencies is to assume that the second reading is correct and to make available information about victims whether they reported the crime or not.

Victims of child abuse. A number of statutes are concerned with protecting the identity of and other information about children who are the victims of child abuse. G.S. 7B-2901(a) directs that court records about "juvenile cases . . . alleging abuse, neglect, or dependency . . . be withheld from public inspection." Subsection (b) of the same statute directs each county department of social services to maintain records of juveniles under the department's protective custody or under placement by a court and generally permits access to these records only by court order. G.S. 7B-3100 directs the state Department of Juvenile

46. Ogden Newspapers, Inc. v. City of Williamstown, 453 S.E.2d 631 (W. Va. 1994).
47. *See* G.S. 7B-1900.

Justice and Delinquency Prevention to adopt rules governing the sharing of information among public agencies about particular cases of child abuse, neglect, or dependency, and law enforcement agencies are among those listed as being subject to these rules. Any shared information is to remain confidential. Finally, G.S. 132-1.4(l) provides that records of investigations of alleged child abuse are to be governed not by G.S. 132-1.4 but by Article 29 of Chapter 7B of the General Statutes. Nevertheless, the sections in G.S. Chapter 7B do not in fact specifically address how law enforcement agencies should treat incident and arrest reports in cases that involve child abuse. There are three possibilities.

First, the records could be treated in the same way as incident reports and arrest records for other crimes, on the ground that the Juvenile Code statutes do not specifically require otherwise. Second, the records could be entirely excluded from public access, given the Juvenile Code's clear policy of confidentiality and the cross-reference in G.S. 132-1.4(l). Third, as a middle ground, the incident report and any arrest record could be made public, but with any information that might disclose the identity of the child redacted. This alternative gives recognition to both G.S. 132-1.4 and the Juvenile Code provisions and is comparable to the suggested treatment of a juvenile's identity when he or she commits a crime rather than being the victim of one. It is also the alternative most often chosen by law enforcement agencies.

Temporarily withholding information about a complaining witness. Although G.S. 132-1.4(c)(6) provides that the name, sex, age, and address of a complaining witness are open to public access, subsection (d) of the statute establishes a possible exception to this rule. It provides that if release of a complaining witness's name or address is "reasonably likely to pose a threat to the mental health, physical health, or personal safety" of the witness or is likely to compromise the investigation, the law enforcement agency *shall* temporarily[48] withhold the name and address from public inspection. By and large, local law enforcement agencies have implemented this set of provisions without controversy. Many agencies by policy do not release the name or address of victims of rape or other sexual assaults, assuming that such a release would always be reasonably likely to threaten the victim's health or safety,[49] and some agencies have similar policies for other classes of incidents, such as threatening or obscene telephone calls, possible suicides, or certain incidents in which the victim is a juvenile. For other offenses, agencies will consider sealing the victim's (or other witness's) name and address if asked to do so by that person.

The principal legal issue that this set of provisions gives rise to is the consequence if a victim or other complaining witness requests that his or her name and address not be released, the law enforcement agency refuses to honor the request, and some harm thereafter comes to the victim or witness, arguably as a result of his or her name and address being known. Does the statute's statement that an agency *shall* withhold the name and address

---

48. The statute does not indicate when the temporary period of confidentiality should end. If there is an arrest, the victim's name will appear on the arrest warrant, and at that point there is no further point to confidentiality. But if no suspect is identified and therefore no arrest is made, the policies behind the provision suggest that confidentiality should continue. The temporary period could in effect become permanent.

49. In *Cape Publications v. City of Louisville*, 147 S.W.3d 731 (Ky. Ct. App. 2003), the court held that a city policy of routinely redacting from incident reports the names of victims of rapes and sexual assaults was reasonable, interpreting a public records statute somewhat different from North Carolina's.

from public access if there is danger to the complaining witness's health or safety create a duty to do so that is owed directly to the witness? For example, might a law enforcement agency be liable if it released the name and address of a rape victim who was thereafter either harassed by the alleged rapist or suffered mental health problems that clearly were attributable to his or her public identification as a rape victim?

One condition that must be met before a person or entity may be held liable to another in tort is that the defendant must have owed some sort of duty of care to the plaintiff (that is, the person complaining of injury). In normal circumstances, law enforcement agencies do not owe any such duty to specific individuals; rather, an agency's responsibilities are to the public at large. As a result, a law enforcement agency normally cannot be held liable for failure to provide protection to an individual who has been the victim of crime.[50] This rule, known as the public duty doctrine, is subject to two exceptions: first, when there is a special relationship between the injured party and the law enforcement agency, such as in the case of a confidential informant; and second, when the law enforcement agency imposes a special duty upon itself by promising special protection to an individual and then fails to provide the protection.[51] The North Carolina Supreme Court has characterized the second exception as narrow, to be applied only when the agency's promise and the individual's reliance on it and resulting injury are unmistakable.[52]

Neither of these exceptions appears to apply to a situation in which a law enforcement agency releases the name or address of a complaining witness and the witness thereafter suffers some sort of injury. There is clearly no special relationship between the witness and the agency; the witness is simply one of many victims of or witnesses to a crime. Nor has the agency made any promise of protection to the witness. Therefore, if the public duty doctrine applied to such a situation, it apparently would protect the law enforcement agency from liability to the complaining witness. It is not clear, however, that the public duty doctrine would apply.

By stating that a law enforcement agency *shall* withhold access to a complaining witness's name and address when release would endanger the witness's health or safety, the statute might itself create a special duty owed to the witness, taking a failure to withhold access out of the *public* duty doctrine. Even if the statute does create an exception to the public duty doctrine, though, that fact would not automatically impose liability on an agency that released a victim's name and address with unfortunate consequences. It would still be necessary to prove that the release was negligent. If the underlying crime was rape or other sexual assault, the widespread practice of not releasing information about victims of such crimes might be important in determining the standard of reasonableness. For other crimes for which there is no comparable pattern of departmental policies, the facts would probably have to be egregious in order for a unit to be held negligent; a department's judgment that there was little likelihood of harm to a victim or other witness from release

---

50. Braswell v. Braswell, 330 N.C. 363, 410 S.E.2d 897 (1991). See also *Coleman v. Cooper*, 89 N.C. App. 188, 366 S.E.2d 2 (1988), *disapproved in part on other grounds by* Hunt *ex rel.* Hasty v. N.C. Dep't of Labor, 348 N.C. 192, 499 S.E.2d 747 (1998), in which the court of appeals held that law enforcement agencies have no individual duty to provide protection to witnesses.

51. *Braswell*, 330 N.C. at 370–71, 410 S.E.2d at 901–2.

52. *Id.* at 372, 410 S.E.2d at 902.

of the person's name and address would probably be upheld unless that judgment was clearly unreasonable. Nevertheless, given the uncertainty about the effect of the statutory language, law enforcement agencies might properly decide that it is prudent to honor any request from a victim or other complaining witness that his or her name and address not be released.[53]

Incident report includes victim's address. A possible conflict exists between the statute's requirement that the "location" of a violation is information that must be made public and the statute's direction that the address of a complaining witness be withheld from public access if release would endanger the health or safety of the witness. Say, for example, that a police department's normal policy was to not release the name or address of the victim of a sexual assault. If a woman were sexually assaulted in her home, however, the incident report normally would include her address as the location of the crime. There is no specific authorization in G.S. 132-1.4 to deny public access to the location of any incident, but releasing the location would also indicate the address of the victim.

Just this set of facts occurred in Indiana, which has essentially the same statutory rules for criminal investigation records as does North Carolina: the location of any crime is a public record, but the name of a rape victim is not. The Indiana Supreme Court held that in such a situation the police need not release the exact location of the incident; the general location would do. The court argued that one purpose of protecting the identity of victims of sexual assaults was to encourage them to come forward, and to require that the exact location of the incident be made public would completely frustrate that purpose inasmuch as it would amount to naming the victim.[54]

911 and Radio Records

Law enforcement agencies and other operators of 911 and dispatch centers routinely tape all telephone and radio communications coming into and leaving these centers. (In a backhanded fashion, G.S. 132-1.4(i) appears to require that such tapes be retained for at least thirty days,[55] but the common practice is to keep them for at least sixty days and often longer.) The effect of the statute's provisions governing 911 and radio communications is to open these tapes to public inspection and to entitle citizens to a copy of a particular 911 or radio communication upon request. This section discusses a number of points about these statutory provisions.

Applicability to data or video transmissions. The statute makes public the "contents of communications . . . that are broadcast over the public airways."[56] When the statute was written, this clearly referred to voice communications among law enforcement personnel, but technology advances have raised questions about other forms of communication. Voice communications travel over radio frequencies assigned to law enforcement agencies by

---

53. See *Hyde v. City of Columbia*, 637 S.W.2d 251 (Mo. Ct. App. 1982), in which the court held (in an appeal from dismissal of the complaint) that a police department could be liable in negligence for releasing, contrary to departmental policy, the name and address of a victim of attempted rape. There is no discussion in the case, however, of the public duty doctrine.

54. Post-Tribune v. Police Dep't, 643 N.E.2d 307 (Ind. 1994).

55. The subsection provides that "[l]aw enforcement agencies shall not be required to maintain any tape recordings of '911' or other communications for more than 30 days from the time of the call."

56. G.S. 132-1.4(c)(5).

the Federal Communications Commission (FCC). Some law enforcement agencies also transmit video recordings or data from patrol cars to headquarters through one or another form of wireless technology. Given that these other transmissions also take place over radio frequencies assigned by the FCC, are they therefore communications "that are broadcast over the public airways"?

In a technical sense they are; the public airways are in fact radio frequencies assigned to various users by the FCC. But it is likely that the statutory language was not intended to be that technical. That is because station-to-station communications, such as between a dispatch center and a patrol car or between two patrol cars, are technically not broadcast at all. A broadcast signal is one that goes to listeners in general rather than to a specific recipient; the radio signals emitted by a commercial radio station are broadcast, while the signals from one amateur radio operator to another are not.[57] Therefore, the statutory usage of "broadcast" was not intended to be technical, and probably the phrase "public airways" was not either. When the statute was enacted, it was common for citizens to be able to listen to law enforcement voice communications through the use of a radio scanner, and it seems more likely that such a capability is what the statute intended by the term public airways.

In addition, the statute speaks of communications "between or among *employees*" of law enforcement agencies. Voice communications are clearly between two or more human beings. Video or data transmissions, however, are usually directed to a computer rather than to an individual and thus are not between or among employees. For these reasons, it is most likely that the statute requires the release of any tapes of voice communications between or among law enforcement personnel but not of video or data transmissions, even if done through radio frequencies.

Identifying a complaining witness. The provision of G.S. 132-1.4 that requires 911 tapes to be made public contains a provision that seems inconsistent with the separate provision that normally makes public the name, sex, age, and address of a complaining witness. The 911 provision states that it does not apply to tape "contents that reveal the name, address, telephone number, or other information that may identify the caller, victim, or witness." How are these competing provisions to be reconciled?

The honest answer is that there is no clear way to do so. Here, though, are a couple of possibilities. First, it may be that if the only source of the information about the witness is the 911 tape, then the provision that focuses on the 911 tapes takes precedence. Because the tape cannot be the source of information about any complaining witness, information about the witness can be made public only if it is recorded in some other law enforcement document. Alternatively, it may be that the exception in the 911 provision is intended only as a reinforcement to the authorization to withhold access to information about a complaining witness when that person is under some threat to his or her health or safety. If so, the purpose of the provision would be to avoid an unintentional release of information about the witness; if no such threat were present, the information would be open, pursuant to the provision making specific information about complaining witnesses public. The first

57. The FCC's regulations define "Broadcasting Service" as "[a] radiocommunications service in which the transmissions are intended for direct reception by the general public." 47 C.F.R. § 2.1 (2007).

possibility seems more compatible with the statutory language, but neither explanation is fully satisfying.

Who decides on access to 911 or radio communication tapes? Many 911 dispatch centers operate independently of law enforcement or other emergency services. These centers are the responsibility of separate departments and their personnel are not law enforcement employees. In such an arrangement, it is most appropriate that decisions about access to 911 or radio tapes be made by the agency that responded to the 911 call rather than by the department operating the center. G.S. 132-1.4(c)(4) provides that certain contents of 911 communications are not open to public access, and G.S. 132-1.4(e) allows a law enforcement agency to seek judicial protection of other information in a 911 call or radio communication if release would affect the State's case or undermine an investigation. If a request to listen to or have a copy of a conversation is made, placing decision making with the law enforcement agency rather than with the nominal custodian of the record permits the agency to protect the record against access when it believes doing so is appropriate.[58]

No right to scan. As was noted earlier, when the statute was enacted it was common for the news media and citizens to listen to radio communications between 911 centers and police officers or emergency personnel on scanners that were commercially available. In the intervening years, however, many law enforcement agencies have purchased radio technology that makes it impossible to follow radio communications on scanners. G.S. 132-1.4 does not prohibit use of such new technology. The public records law in general does not entitle anyone to observe a record being established; a person is only entitled to examine the record once it is completed. So, too, G.S. 132-1.4 does not entitle anyone to listen while the communication record is being established; a person is only entitled to listen to and have a copy of the communication once it has occurred.[59]

911 tapes of non–law enforcement calls. Dispatch and 911 centers are not limited to law enforcement matters; they also receive and dispatch fire calls and emergency medical service (EMS) calls. G.S. 132-1.4, however, deals only with criminal investigation records; it has no application to records involving either fire calls or EMS calls. Therefore, the statute's provisions allowing some denial of access to law enforcement communications do not automatically apply to these other calls. (Some fires may involve arson, and any 911 calls about such a fire might be relevant to the arson investigation.) In the absence of any suspected crime, calls and dispatches related to fires are subject to the same rules of access and copying as other public records, described in the first several chapters of this book. The status of EMS records as medical records, which are not open to public access, is discussed *infra* in chapter 14, "Medical and Patient Records."

---

58. G.S. 132-6(a) recognizes that the nominal holder of a record might not be the legal custodian. It provides that "'custodian' does not mean an agency that holds the public records of other agencies solely for purposes of storage or safekeeping . . . ."

59. The attorney general's office agrees with this conclusion. Letter to J. Mark Payne, 22 January 2002, Advisory Opinion No. 524, *available at* www.ncdoj.gov/About-DOJ/Legal-Services/Legal-Opinions.aspx.

Miscellaneous Matters

Releases Not Required by Statute

As was noted in the first paragraph of this chapter, G.S. 132-1.4 is a statute that simply denies public access to a group of government records; it does not prohibit the government from releasing these records. Law enforcement agencies recognize this point and frequently release criminal investigation information that they are not required to release under the statute.[60] A common reason for release is that doing so will help in solving the crime. If a law enforcement agency is seeking to identify a suspect, for example, and the person appears on an ATM-machine video that has been collected by the agency, the agency might release the video and ask for help from the public in making the identification. Some law enforcement agencies also release certain sorts of information as a general policy. For example, some agencies will release to the employing agency any information they might have about a domestic violence event involving a law enforcement officer employed by some other agency, as a matter of interagency courtesy.

In the usual case, release of such information neither undermines the agency's ability to maintain the confidentiality of other information associated with the same investigation nor opens the agency to any liability for the release. Occasionally a targeted release might give rise to a claim that the agency has waived its right to deny release of the same material to others, but as long as there is a reasonable justification for the limited nature of the release such a claim should be unavailing. The circumstances under which such a waiver claim might succeed are set out in chapter 6, in the discussion accompanying notes 39 through 42. Even more rarely a reckless release of information might give rise to an action for damages for invasion of privacy; this possibility is also discussed in chapter 6, in the text accompanying notes 11 through 13.

Court Orders Sealing Information

G.S. 132-1.4(e) permits a law enforcement agency to seek a court order preventing disclosure of information that would otherwise be available to the public under the statute. It may seek such an order because of a concern that release of the information will

- jeopardize the right of the State to prosecute a defendant, or
- jeopardize the right of the defendant to receive a fair trial, or
- undermine an ongoing or future investigation.

The statute speaks only to law enforcement agencies seeking such a court order, but the grounds set out suggest that at least two other parties ought to have a comparable right—the district attorney's office, which should be in the best position to judge whether release would jeopardize a prosecution; and the defendant (or his or her attorney), who should be in the best position to judge whether release would jeopardize his or her right to a fair trial. Perhaps a court's inherent right to seal records in order to assure the fair administration of

60. One such release is required by statute. G.S. 15A-903(a)(1) requires release to a defendant, on the defendant's motion, of "the complete files of all law enforcement and prosecutorial agencies involved in the investigation of the crimes committed or the prosecution of the defendant." G.S. 15A-903(c) requires a similar release to the State.

justice would provide a basis for extending the express authorization of the statute to the prosecution and defense.[61]

The statute does not set out a procedure for securing the court order authorized in G.S. 132-1.4(e). Some local governments have been successful in simply filing a motion before superior court, possibly with notice to anyone who has sought a copy of the records in question, but this procedure has not been tested on appeal. It may be that an appellate court would require any party seeking an order under subsection (e) to follow the somewhat more elaborate procedure set out in *In re Investigation into Injury of Brooks*, a case discussed at length in chapter 6 at notes 65 and 67.

Unserved Warrants

G.S. 132-1.4(k) provides that certain court records are public records and are open to the public unless sealed by court order. The listing includes "arrest and search warrants *that have been returned by law enforcement agencies.*" G.S. 15A-257 requires an officer who has executed a search warrant to return the warrant to the clerk of court, together with an inventory of items seized in the search. G.S. 15A-301(d) directs the officer who executes an arrest warrant to return it to the clerk of court; the subsection also directs that an unexecuted arrest warrant be returned within 180 days after issuance. Until the return is made, though, the peculiar phraseology of the statute seems to intend that the warrant is not yet open to public access. There are good reasons for keeping these warrants confidential until they are served, and the statutory provision seems to recognize them.[62]

PART 2—Jail Records

Statutory Summary

There is no statute that expressly excepts local jail records from public access, although, as noted below, a combination of statutes appear to make inmate medical records not available to the public.

Discussion

Jail Logs

G.S. 162-57 directs the person having charge of prisoners in a county jail to "keep a record showing, the name, age, date of sentence, length of sentence, crime for which convicted, home address, next of kin, and the conduct of each prisoner received." Sheriffs and other

---

61. *See* Virmani v. Presbyterian Health Servs. Corp., 350 N.C. 449, 515 S.E.2d 675 (1999).

62. In *In re Search Warrants*, COA08-1280, filed 6 October 2009, the court of appeals discussed the standards and procedures for a court order sealing a search warrant that had been served.

local jailers also normally keep comparable records on persons who have been arrested and are in the jail awaiting trial. Neither the records about inmates who have been convicted of a crime nor those about persons arrested are concerned with the criminal investigation that led to the person's arrest; rather, they are kept to assist in managing the jail. Therefore, these jail records are not criminal investigation records as defined in G.S. 132-1.4.

G.S. 148-74 and 148-76 establish a record-keeping system in the Department of Correction (DOC) for persons who have been committed to the department's custody, and the North Carolina Court of Appeals has held that these statutes make these inmate records confidential.[63] Prisoners in county jails, however, have been committed to the custody of the local sheriff, not the Department of Correction,[64] and for that reason the DOC statutes apparently do not apply. The DOC statutes also have no applicability to persons who are in jail awaiting trial. Therefore, these basic jail records are open to public inspection.

Inmate Medical Records

The rules appear to be different with respect to medical records about jail inmates. Both the statutes and state regulations appear to assume that these records are confidential, although no statute expressly says so. G.S. 153A-222, which deals with state inspections of local jails, expressly permits inspectors to have access to inmate medical records "[n]otwithstanding the provisions of G.S. 8-53 or any other provision of law relating to the confidentiality of communications between physician and patient." That is, the statute seems to assume that the records are not open to public access. And the regulations promulgated by the state Department of Health and Human Services respecting local jails require the jail's medical plan to include procedures that address the "[m]aintenance and confidentiality of [inmate] medical records."[65] Many inmate medical records are generated through the interaction of the inmate with a physician or other person acting under a physician's control, and therefore the general provision in G.S. 8-53 that privileged medical communications are not open to public access covers these records. But not all inmate medical records are generated in this way. In some jails, for example, the health screening form administered to all incoming inmates is done by a jailer rather than a medical professional. Nevertheless, it seems appropriate for local jails to maintain confidentiality for all inmate medical records, regardless of the circumstances under which they were generated, because there is probably some element of constitutional privacy protection for the records, given the nature of the information in them, and because a variety of state statutes demonstrate a strong state policy in favor of such confidentiality.[66]

---

63. Goble v. Bounds, 13 N.C. App. 579, 186 S.E.2d 638, *aff'd*, 281 N.C. 307, 188 S.E.2d 347 (1972).

64. G.S. 15A-1352.

65. 10A N.C.A.C. 14J .1001(b)(6) (2008).

66. For the constitutional protection, see *supra* chapter 4; for the North Carolina statutes, see *infra* chapter 14.

Appendix 8A—Statute

G.S. 132-1.4

§ 132-1.4. Criminal investigations; intelligence information records; Innocence Inquiry Commission records.

(a) Records of criminal investigations conducted by public law enforcement agencies, records of criminal intelligence information compiled by public law enforcement agencies, and records of investigations conducted by the North Carolina Innocence Inquiry Commission, are not public records as defined by G.S. 132-1. Records of criminal investigations conducted by public law enforcement agencies or records of criminal intelligence information may be released by order of a court of competent jurisdiction.

(b) As used in this section:

(1) "Records of criminal investigations" means all records or any information that pertains to a person or group of persons that is compiled by public law enforcement agencies for the purpose of attempting to prevent or solve violations of the law, including information derived from witnesses, laboratory tests, surveillance, investigators, confidential informants, photographs, and measurements.

(2) "Records of criminal intelligence information" means records or information that pertain to a person or group of persons that is compiled by a public law enforcement agency in an effort to anticipate, prevent, or monitor possible violations of the law.

(3) "Public law enforcement agency" means a municipal police department, a county police department, a sheriff's department, a company police agency commissioned by the Attorney General pursuant to G.S. 74E-1, et seq., and any State or local agency, force, department, or unit responsible for investigating, preventing, or solving violations of the law.

(4) "Violations of the law" means crimes and offenses that are prosecutable in the criminal courts in this State or the United States and infractions as defined in G.S. 14-3.1.

(5) "Complaining witness" means an alleged victim or other person who reports a violation or apparent violation of the law to a public law enforcement agency.

(c) Notwithstanding the provisions of this section, and unless otherwise prohibited by law, the following information shall be public records within the meaning of G.S. 132-1.

(1) The time, date, location, and nature of a violation or apparent violation of the law reported to a public law enforcement agency.

(2) The name, sex, age, address, employment, and alleged violation of law of a person arrested, charged, or indicted.

(3) The circumstances surrounding an arrest, including the time and place of the arrest, whether the arrest involved resistance, possession or use of weapons, or pursuit, and a description of any items seized in connection with the arrest.

(4) The contents of "911" and other emergency telephone calls received by or on behalf of public law enforcement agencies, except for such contents that reveal the name, address, telephone number, or other information that may identify the caller, victim, or witness.

(5) The contents of communications between or among employees of public law enforcement agencies that are broadcast over the public airways.

(6) The name, sex, age, and address of a complaining witness.

(d) A public law enforcement agency shall temporarily withhold the name or address of a complaining witness if release of the information is reasonably likely to pose a threat to the mental health, physical health, or personal safety of the complaining witness or materially compromise a continuing or future criminal investigation or criminal intelligence operation. Information temporarily withheld under this subsection shall be made available for release to the public in accordance with G.S. 132-6 as soon as the circumstances that justify withholding it cease to exist. Any person denied access to information withheld under this subsection may apply to a court of competent jurisdiction for an order compelling disclosure of the information. In such action, the court shall balance the interests of the public in disclosure against the interests of the law enforcement agency and the alleged victim in withholding the information. Actions brought pursuant to this subsection shall be set down for immediate hearing, and subsequent proceedings in such actions shall be accorded priority by the trial and appellate courts.

(e) If a public law enforcement agency believes that release of information that is a public record under subdivisions (c)(1) through (c)(5) of this section will jeopardize the right of the State to prosecute a defendant or the right of a defendant to receive a fair trial or will undermine an ongoing or future investigation, it may seek an order from a court of competent jurisdiction to prevent disclosure of the information. In such action the law enforcement agency shall have the burden of showing by a preponderance of the evidence that disclosure of the information in question will jeopardize the right of the State to prosecute a defendant or the right of a defendant to receive a fair trial or will undermine an ongoing or future investigation. Actions brought pursuant to this subsection shall be set down for immediate hearing, and subsequent proceedings in such actions shall be accorded priority by the trial and appellate courts.

(f) Nothing in this section shall be construed as authorizing any public law enforcement agency to prohibit or prevent another public agency having custody of a public record from permitting the inspection, examination, or copying of such public record in compliance with G.S. 132-6. The use of a public record in connection with a criminal investigation or the gathering of criminal intelligence shall not affect its status as a public record.

(g) Disclosure of records of criminal investigations and criminal intelligence information that have been transmitted to a district attorney or other attorney authorized to prosecute a violation of law shall be governed by this section and Chapter 15A of the General Statutes.

(h) Nothing in this section shall be construed as requiring law enforcement agencies to disclose the following:

(1) Information that would not be required to be disclosed under Chapter 15A of the General Statutes; or

(2) Information that is reasonably likely to identify a confidential informant.

(i) Law enforcement agencies shall not be required to maintain any tape recordings of "911" or other communications for more than 30 days from the time of the call, unless a court of competent jurisdiction orders a portion sealed.

(j) When information that is not a public record under the provisions of this section is deleted from a document, tape recording, or other record, the law enforcement agency shall make clear that a deletion has been made. Nothing in this subsection shall authorize the destruction of the original record.

(k) The following court records are public records and may be withheld only when sealed by court order: arrest and search warrants that have been returned by law enforcement agencies, indictments, criminal summons, and nontestimonial identification orders.

(l) Records of investigations of alleged child abuse shall be governed by Article 29 of Chapter 7B of the General Statutes.

Chapter 9—Confidential Legal Materials

PART 1—G.S. 132-1.1(a): Communications from Lawyer to Client

Statutory Summary

Section 132-1.1(a) of the North Carolina General Statutes[1] [hereinafter G.S.] embodies a limited legislative acceptance of confidentiality for governmental legal materials that are within the attorney–client privilege: it temporarily closes to public access a limited set of materials generated within the attorney–client relationship when the client is a local government or state agency. The statute exempts from public examination and copying *only*

1. The statute is set out in appendix 9A at the end of this chapter.

those communications from an attorney to a public body in state or local government when those communications involve (1) a claim by or against the public body or the government for which it acts or (2) a judicial action or administrative proceeding to which the public body is a party or by which it is affected. The exemption is temporary, however. A communication covered by the statute becomes fully open to public access three years after the date the public body received it (or sooner if released by the public body).

Discussion

The Limited Scope of the Statute

In *News & Observer Publishing Co. v. Poole*,[2] the North Carolina Supreme Court held that G.S. 132-1.1 is the only statutory expression of the attorney–client privilege that affects the public records law: "In the context of what [government] agencies must disclose pursuant to the Public Records Act, [G.S. 132-1.1(a)] itself defines the scope of the privilege."[3] If a communication between attorney and client does not meet the terms of G.S. 132-1.1(a), it is not exempt from inspection under the public records law. Or, to state the matter another way, simply because a record has been produced within the attorney–client relationship and is therefore privileged under the laws of evidence does not mean that record is closed to public access under the public records law. Rather, it is open unless it fits within the terms of G.S. 132-1.1(a).[4] That being the case, it is important to recognize how limited the privilege is under this statute.

First, the statute covers only communications from the attorney to the client. It does not cover communications from the client to the attorney, and thus those communications are not exempt from public access.

Second, the statute covers only communications that involve claims, litigation, or administrative proceedings. If a government's attorney writes a letter to a governmental body giving legal advice on a question not involved in litigation or potential litigation, the statute does not cover the letter. Consequently, such a letter is open to public access. It should be noted, however, that the statute is not limited to matters under active litigation. It separately mentions "claim[s] against or on behalf of" the government and "judicial action." Therefore, a communication from attorney to client about a claim that has not yet ripened to litigation is still covered by the statutory exception.

Third, the statute covers only communications to a "public board, council, commission or other governmental body." It does not cover communications to an individual officer or employee, such as a letter from a city attorney to the city manager or from a county

2. 330 N.C. 465, 412 S.E.2d 7 (1992).

3. *Id.* at 482–83, 412 S.E.2d at 17.

4. Even if a record that is within the attorney–client privilege is open to the public under the *Poole* decision, it still might remain privileged under the laws of evidence. In *Newsday, Inc. v. State Department of Transportation*, 833 N.E.2d 210 (N.Y. 2005), the state DOT argued that because certain records were not subject to discovery under the federal rules of civil procedure, therefore they should not be open to public access under the state's public records statute. The New York court rejected the argument, noting that if the records were obtained under the statute, they would still not be admissible in any federal litigation.

attorney to the sheriff, even if those communications concern a claim or litigation. In most cases, however, such a communication could be sent first to a governmental body, such as the city council or board of county commissioners, with a copy to the interested officer or employee. A suit or claim against such an individual in that person's official capacity is a suit against the governmental unit itself, and therefore any communication about the suit could appropriately be made to the governing body of the unit. Because G.S. 132-1.1(a) exempts from inspection the principal copy of such a communication—that is, the copy going to the board—it probably also exempts any copy sent to an individual officer or employee. The governmental entity is the client of a governmental attorney,[5] and so writing both to the board and to an individual officer or employee does not destroy the confidentiality of any communication.[6]

Fourth, note that the statute permits the communications to be exempted three years from the date they are received by the governing body and no longer, even if the subject litigation is still ongoing. On the other hand, the three-year provision also applies even if the litigation ended a few months after the communication was made: the government need not release the communication until the three years have run.

Attorney Billing Statements

Some attorneys representing local governments provide detailed billing statements to their governmental clients. These statements set out the nature of each event or action being charged to the client in a form something like this:

> Review of materials regarding __[name of employee]__ and legal research regarding proper administrative prerequisites to issuing warning letter.
>
> Conference with __[department head]__ concerning proposed memorandum to be sent to departmental employees.
>
> Preparation of legal analysis in section B(2) of brief including facts and case law on nature of boundary description in annexation ordinance.
>
> Conference with __[faculty member at School of Government]__ concerning proper method for filling vacancy in mayor's office.

Occasionally, pursuant to the public records law, a local government receives a request to inspect and copy such statements. These requests raise the question of whether the statements are privileged or otherwise exempt from access.[7]

---

5. North Carolina State Bar, Rules of Professional Conduct, Rule 1.13(a) (2008).

6. In *MCI Construction, LLC v. Hazen and Sawyer, P.C.*, 213 F.R.D. 268 (M.D.N.C. 2003), the plaintiff was prosecuting a motion to compel production of certain documents from the city co-defendant. The documents were communications, both oral and written, from the city's outside litigation counsel to the city manager about the litigation within which the motion was made. Because the communications were more than three years' old, the court ordered production. None of the parties nor the court took any note that the communications were with the city's manager rather than the council; all assumed that N.C. Gen. Stat. [hereinafter G.S.] § 132-1.1 was still relevant.

7. In *Womack Newspapers, Inc. v. Town of Kitty Hawk*, 181 N.C. App. 1, 639 S.E.2d 96, *petition for review withdrawn*, 361 N.C. 370, 644 S.E.2d 564 (2007), the trial court ordered the town to provide to plaintiffs copies of the town's attorney's billing statements, except for those dealing specifically with claims or

Although there is no North Carolina case law on point, a number of courts in other states and in the federal system have considered whether attorney billing statements of this nature are protected by the attorney–client privilege. The result is mixed, although it appears that a majority of courts have held that they are not privileged. For example, the Missouri Court of Appeals noted that the

> billing statements [in the case] merely *identify* attorney Wohler's preparation of pleadings, phone calls, meetings, and discussions with other attorneys or individuals. The subject billing statements do not include *detailed* entries which advise, analyze or discuss privileged communications. The mere fact that City Attorney Wohler prepared the billing statements does not render those statements confidential. The billing statements are extraneous to Wohler's legal advice or work product.[8]

Even if these billing statements were privileged under the rules of evidence, that would not by itself exempt them from public access under the public records law. As was pointed out earlier in this chapter, the North Carolina Supreme Court in *Poole* held that unless an attorney–client communication fits within the terms of G.S. 132-1.1(a), it is open to public access, even if it is otherwise privileged.

If an attorney's billing statement, however, is concerned with work done by the attorney on "any claim against or on behalf of the governmental body or the governmental entity for which such body acts, or concerning the prosecution, defense, settlement or litigation of any judicial action, or any administrative or other type of proceeding," then it appears to fit within the terms of G.S. 132-1.1(a), regardless of whether it is or is not privileged. That is, the statute allows a local government to deny public access, for three years, to any written communication from an attorney representing the local government if the communication concerns the matters listed in the above quotation. The statute does not require that the communication be privileged but just that it be made "within the scope of the attorney–client relationship." A billing statement for legal services is certainly made within that relationship. To the extent that a billing statement reports activities not within the quoted language, however, G.S. 132-1.1(a) does not exempt it from public access.[9]

Attorney–Client Communications under the Open Meetings Law

The open meetings law offers an opportunity for maintaining the confidentiality of some attorney–client communications that are not within the scope of G.S. 132-1.1(a). G.S. 143-318.11(a)(3) permits a public body to hold a closed session "[t]o consult with an attorney

---

litigation. Before the court of appeals addressed the issue, however, the town voluntarily released the statements, and as a result the appellate court declined to reach the issue.

8. Tipton v. Barton, 747 S.W.2d 325, 332 (Mo. Ct. App. 1988). Other cases reaching the same conclusion include *Beavers v. Hobbs*, 176 F.R.D. 562 (S.D. Iowa 1997); *City of New Haven v. Freedom of Information Commission*, 493 A.2d 283 (Conn. App. Ct. 1985); and *Cypress Media, Inc. v. City of Overland Park*, 997 P.2d 681 (Kan. 2000). In *City Pages v. State*, 655 N.W.2d 839 (Minn. Ct. App. 2003), the court held that any parts of the billing records that actually provided or indicated legal advice were covered by the privilege.

9. It is possible that specific entries in such a billing statement might be covered by other statutory exceptions to access. The first entry in the hypothetical bill set out in the text might, for example, be part of the personnel file of the employee involved. *See* discussion *supra* chapter 7, note 56 and accompanying text.

employed or retained by the public body in order to preserve the attorney–client privilege between the attorney and the public body." Thus, a closed session may appropriately be the occasion for communications from the client public body to the attorney, on any subject within the privilege, and the occasion for similar communications from the attorney to the client, including communications on matters not involving claims or litigation. The minutes and general account of such a closed session might detail the client's communications to the attorney or might incorporate a written memorial of the attorney's advice to the client. G.S. 143-318.10(e) permits a public body to withhold the minutes or general account of a closed session from public access "so long as public inspection would frustrate the purpose of [the] closed session." Thus, the open meetings law establishes the possibility of exempting additional attorney–client communications from public inspection if those communications are made in closed session and incorporated into the minutes or general account of the session.

Letters to or from Opposing Counsel

If a local government receives a letter from an attorney representing someone with a claim against the government, G.S. 132-1.1(a) offers no basis for denying public access to the letter, nor does any other statutory exception to the right of public access. The letter would be available for public inspection. Similarly, if the local government's attorney responded to the letter on the local government's behalf, that letter too would be open to public inspection, inasmuch as it would not fit within the confines of G.S. 132-1.1(a).

Materials in Possession of an Attorney Representing a Local Government

Most attorneys who represent local governments are in private practice. As part of their representation, they conduct and memorialize research, write and receive letters and e-mails, prepare memoranda and other documents, and so on. Under a decision of the North Carolina Court of Appeals, most of this material is subject to the public records law, even in the physical possession of the attorney. (If the attorney is in the employ of the local government, records in his or her office are obviously subject to the public records law.) In *Womack Newspapers, Inc. v. Town of Kitty Hawk*,[10] the newspaper sought a variety of records associated with oceanfront condemnations undertaken by the town; these included records related to engineering, surveying, and other professional services rendered in connection with the condemnation litigation. The town argued that because these records were in the possession of the town's attorney, a law firm engaged in private practice, they therefore were not subject to the public records law. The court rejected the argument, setting out three alternative rationales for its decision.

First, the court reiterated earlier holdings that a city attorney is a public officer, because the position is created by statute. (G.S. 160A-173 provides that the city council "shall appoint a city attorney to serve at its pleasure and to be its legal adviser.") Because the public records law extends to records in the possession of any public officer, these records were therefore public records. This specific rationale would reach records held in the private law offices

---

10. 181 N.C. App. 1, 639 S.E.2d 96, *petition for review withdrawn*, 361 N.C. 370, 644 S.E.2d 564 (2007).

of persons or firms designated as city or county attorneys,[11] but attorneys who represent school boards and other local government entities are not mentioned by statute and therefore do not appear to be public officers. Therefore, this first rationale would not reach these other attorneys.

Second, the court looked to the rules of professional conduct applicable to an attorney's files, which the court summarized by saying that "[i]n North Carolina, anything in a client's file, which is in the hands of the client's attorney, belongs to the client, with the exception only of the attorney's notes or work product."[12] Therefore, the court went on, the client town, not the law firm town attorney, owned the contested documents. Obviously, this rationale reaches beyond city and county attorneys to reach any attorney who represents a local government entity in a specific transaction or specific litigation.[13]

Third, the court pointed out the policy implications of a contrary result:

> Allowing defendants to prevail on their argument that these documents were the private property of the Town Attorney, and not property of the Town itself, would be permitting the Town to place documents such as these in the hands of a so-called independent contractor in order to escape the public records disclosure requirements. If an argument such as this were to prevail there would be nothing to prevent municipalities and other governmental agencies from skirting the public records disclosure requirements simply by hiring independent contractors to perform governmental tasks and to have them retain all documents in conjunction with the performance of those tasks that municipalities and agencies chose to shield from public scrutiny.[14]

It should be noted that the combination of the first and second rationales opens the possibility of different treatment of records held by city and county attorneys, on the one hand, and records held by attorneys representing other kinds of local governments, on the other.

---

11. G.S. 153A-114 provides that the "board of commissioners shall appoint a county attorney to serve at its pleasure and to be its legal adviser."

12. 181 N.C. App. at 13, 639 S.E.2d at 104. The court mentions that the attorney's notes and work product do not belong to the client and therefore are not public records. The same would presumably apply to an attorney's trust account records, which also do not belong to the client.

13. A number of cases in other states have dealt with records held by an attorney retained by an insurance company to handle matters pursuant to an insurance policy issued to a local government. By and large the cases held that the attorney is, as a practical matter, representing the insured (the local government) and not the insurer (the insurance company), even though he or she was actually retained by the company. Therefore, the records have been held to belong to the government insured and to be public records. *E.g.*, Knightstown Banner, LLC v. Town of Knightstown, 838 N.E.2d 1127 (Ind. Ct. App. 2005); Tribune-Review Publ'g Co. v. Westmoreland County Hous. Auth., 833 A.2d 112 (Pa. 2003). In the latter case the insurance company retained complete control of the defense of an action and did not communicate with the insured, and the settlement documents were retained by the insurance company; nevertheless, the court held that the settlement documents were public record.

14. 181 N.C. App. at 14, 639 S.E.2d at 105. The Connecticut case of *Town of Windham v. Freedom of Information Commission*, 711 A.2d 738 (Conn. App. Ct. 1998), takes a different position. As part of his representation of the town in defending a proceeding brought by an individual, the town's attorney (a retained lawyer) took affidavits from town employees and a selectman; they were never introduced in the proceeding, however. When the other party to the proceeding demanded copies as public record, the Connecticut court held that because the attorney was not a town employee and retained the documents, the affidavits were not subject to the public records law.

The second rationale relies on the rules of professional conduct, which provide that the client does not have a right to the "attorney's notes or work product." Therefore, materials relevant to the representation but comprising the lawyer's notes or work product would not be public record. The first rationale, however, looks to the status of the city (or county) attorney as a public officer. If status is the key, then any documents held by the officer are public records. This would seemingly include the attorney's notes or work product, unless they were excluded from public access by other principles of the public records law (such as the trial preparation exception discussed in the next part of this chapter). Thus, there might be greater public access to records held by a city or county attorney than to records held by attorneys representing other sorts of local government agencies.

PART 2—G.S. 132-1.9: Trial Preparation Materials

Statutory Summary

G.S. 132-1.9[15] establishes an exclusive framework for providing public access to public records that also qualify as "trial preparation materials," which are essentially materials prepared in anticipation of litigation or for use in a trial or other sort of civil legal proceeding. (The statute does not apply to records prepared for a criminal proceeding; rather, G.S. 132-1.4 is the appropriate statute for those records.) The statute's enactment was occasioned by the North Carolina Court of Appeals' decision in *McCormick v. Hanson Aggregates Southeast, Inc.*[16] In that case, the court held that the work product privilege, which protects trial preparation materials from discovery, *did not* create an exception to the public records law and that therefore materials of that nature held by the Raleigh City Attorney were open to public inspection.[17] This statute in effect reverses the rule of the case.

The rules established by the statute are fairly straightforward. Before the litigation or other proceeding for which the materials have been prepared has begun, or during the litigation or other proceeding, a party to the litigation or other proceeding may have access to the materials only through the rules of discovery. A person who is not a party to the litigation or other proceeding has no right to the materials at all. Once the litigation or other proceeding is completely over, the materials become subject to the normal rules of access to public records.

---

15. The statute is set out in appendix 9A.

16. 164 N.C. App. 459, 596 S.E.2d 431 (2004).

17. The North Carolina Court of Appeals was not alone in reaching such a conclusion about the status of trial preparation materials under public records laws. Other courts that reached a similar conclusion include *Scott v. Smith*, 728 S.W.2d 515 (Ark. 1987); *Hillsborough County Aviation Authority v. Azzarelli Construction Co.*, 436 So. 2d 153 (Fla. Dist. Ct. App. 1983); and *General Electric Co. v. Department of Environmental Protection*, 711 N.E.2d 589 (Mass. 1999).

Discussion

What Sorts of Proceedings Are Covered?

The statute applies to materials that are generated in anticipation of or for legal proceedings that are subject to either the federal or state rules of civil procedure—essentially trials in the state or federal courts. The statute also applies to materials generated in anticipation of or for legal proceedings not subject to the state or federal rules—proceedings such as those in front of state or federal administrative or quasi-judicial agencies or, indeed, in front of local quasi-judicial bodies such as a board of adjustment or a board of equalization and review.

What Are Trial Preparation Materials?

G.S. 132-1.9(h)(2) provides that the term "trial preparation material"—often also referred to as attorney work product—is to be defined pursuant to Rule 26 of the North Carolina Rules of Civil Procedure, whether the proceeding in question is subject to those rules or not. That is, if a local government prepares materials for an administrative hearing that would be trial preparation materials if prepared for a case in superior court, those materials are trial preparation materials for purposes of the public records statute. The policy behind the protection of work product in litigation, and therefore behind its temporary exemption from public access under the public records law, was stated by the North Carolina Court of Appeals in 2006:

> It is essential that a lawyer work with a certain degree of privacy, free from unnecessary intrusion by opposing parties and their counsel. Proper preparation of a client's case demands that he assemble information, sift what he considers to be the relevant from the irrelevant facts, prepare his legal theories and plan his strategy without undue and needless interference. That is the historical and the necessary way in which lawyers act within the framework of our system of jurisprudence to promote justice and to protect their clients' interest.[18]

Rule 26(b)(3) distinguishes between two types of trial preparation materials. One type, often labeled *opinion work product*, consists of "the mental impressions, conclusions, opinions, or legal theories of an attorney or other representative of a party concerning the litigation in which the material is sought or work product of the attorney or attorneys of record in the particular action." These materials are absolutely immune from discovery and include, for example, notes and internal memoranda prepared by attorneys evaluating an agency's chance of success in actual or threatened litigation, or notes of an attorney setting out his or her theory of the case and strategy for the litigation. This type of work product, though, is not limited to opinions and the like of attorneys; it explicitly also includes comparable material produced by "other representatives" of the governmental entity.

The second type of trial preparation material, *ordinary* or *fact work product*, consists of other materials "prepared in anticipation of litigation or for trial," such as reports made to an attorney by an investigator or other professionals such as engineers or public accountants, reports made by staff of the public agency, or records of interviews of

18. Wachovia Bank, Nat'l Ass'n v. Clean River Corp., 178 N.C. App. 528, 533, 631 S.E.2d 879, 883 (2006). The court was quoting from *Hickman v. Taylor*, 329 U.S. 495, 510-11 (1947).

potential witnesses conducted by or at the direction of the attorney.[19] Unlike an attorney's mental impressions and conclusions, these materials are subject to discovery upon a litigant's showing of substantial need for the materials and undue hardship in obtaining them through alternative means.

Trial preparation materials do not include materials prepared in the ordinary course of business or for purposes unrelated to litigation, no matter how useful the materials might be in litigation. Rule 26(b)(3) protects only materials prepared for or in anticipation of litigation,[20] and therefore that is equally true of G.S. 132-1.9.

Access to Trial Preparation Materials

The statute sets out separate rules for access to trial preparation materials, depending on the status of the litigation or other proceeding.

Before the Litigation or Other Proceeding Has Begun

If someone is denied a record on the ground that it is trial preparation material but the litigation or other proceeding has not yet begun, that person may petition a court pursuant to G.S. 132-9 for a determination of whether the material was in fact prepared in anticipation of a legal proceeding. G.S. 132-1.9(b) calls on the custodian to provide, upon request, a written justification for the assertion that the materials have been prepared in anticipation of a legal proceeding, and the court proceeding would allow a judge to review that justification. If the judge agreed with the government entity, the materials would not be open to public inspection; if the judge disagreed, the materials would be open to inspection unless they fit within some other exception to access.

During Litigation—Opposing Parties

Once a legal proceeding has begun, a party to the proceeding may have access to trial preparation materials only in accordance with the rules for discovery set out in Rule 26. A party to a lawsuit may not seek the materials as a public record under the usual rules applicable to public records. A party to some other sort of legal proceeding not covered by the Rules of Civil Procedure may apply to court under G.S. 132-9 for access to the records, but in deciding whether to allow access the court is to apply the principles of Rule 26.

During Litigation—Nonparties

If a person is not a party to the legal proceeding for which the trial preparation materials were prepared, he or she has no right of access to the materials. This appears to be true whether the materials in question are opinion work product or ordinary work product. It also appears to be true even if a party to the litigation has been successful in obtaining a copy of ordinary work product through the discovery process; that fact does not give any new right to a person not party to the litigation. A nonparty's only recourse is to petition a

---

19. An extensive collection of cases involving these kinds of materials is found in 8 Charles Alan Wright, Arthur R. Miller & Richard L. Marcus, Federal Practice and Procedure § 2024 (2d ed. 1994 & Supp. 2008).

20. James L. Underwood, A Guide to Federal Discovery Rules 27–29 (2d ed. 1985) discusses the factors that courts have developed in deciding whether material was prepared in anticipation of litigation.

court under G.S. 132-9 and assert that the materials do not in fact qualify as trial preparation materials.

Following the Litigation or Other Proceeding

Once the litigation is entirely complete, including all appeals and postjudgment proceedings, the materials become subject to the regular rules of public records. If no litigation or other proceeding was ever brought, the materials become subject to the public records laws once all applicable statutes of limitation and periods of repose have expired. Of course, if the materials qualify for any other exceptions to access, the custodian can claim the protection of those other exceptions.

PART 3—The Use of the Public Records Law in Lieu of Discovery

There are a variety of reasons why a party to litigation may be cut off from discovery of certain records or information held by the other party to the litigation. The time for discovery may be past; the record or information may not be sufficiently relevant to the litigation to support discovery; or the record or information may be privileged or otherwise not discoverable on substantive grounds. As was noted at the beginning of part 2 of this chapter, in *McCormick v. Hanson Aggregates Southeast, Inc.*[21] the court of appeals held that the Rules of Civil Procedure, which protect trial preparation materials from discovery, *did not* create an exception to the public records law and that therefore materials of that nature held by the Raleigh City Attorney were open to public inspection. Although the entity seeking the materials was not then in litigation against the city, it did have an appeal pending before the city's board of adjustment, and it is reasonable to believe that litigation was ultimately likely. Therefore, it is also reasonable to read the case to permit a person or entity in litigation with a local government or state agency to obtain trial preparation materials through a public records request, even though those materials would not be available through discovery. The specific holding of *McCormick*, of course, has been reversed by statute, as elaborated in part 2 of the chapter, but it is likely that the more general principle of the case remains good law. That is, a litigant who is foreclosed by the rules of discovery from obtaining a document may seek to obtain the same document through a public records request. G.S. 132-1.9 prohibits this tactic when the documents in question are trial preparation materials, but the statute does not apply in other situations in which discovery is not available.

Such an outcome is supported by decisions in the courts of at least nine other states.[22] These courts argue that simply because a person becomes a party to litigation with a gov-

---

21. 164 N.C. App. 459, 596 S.E.2d 431 (2004).

22. Scott v. Smith, 728 S.W.2d 515 (Ark. 1987) (plaintiff sought litigation files held by agency's attorney and court held that protection of work product in the Arkansas Rules of Civil Procedure was a procedural matter limited to that context; access was allowed); City of Fayetteville v. Edmark, 801 S.W.2d 275 (Ark.

ernment, that person does not surrender his or her rights under the public records laws. In addition, if the record is open to public access, anyone may demand to inspect and copy it; if a litigant is denied access simply because the record is not available through discovery, that litigant could simply ask a friend who is not involved in the litigation to get the record and thereby obtain the record indirectly. So, why require the subterfuge?

There is one court of appeals case that is an exception to this general principle, but it is not at all clear that the case should be relied upon. In *Shella v. Moon*,[23] the court was presented with a litigant who sought documents from a state agency under the public records law when those documents were not available under discovery.[24] Denying the litigant's request, the court argued that allowing her to prevail "would make a mockery of our discovery rules."[25] Despite this language, the decision may not state the law in North Carolina. First, the discussion about the records is dicta. The court had already held that, inasmuch

1990) (newspaper given access to memoranda written by attorney for city assessing strength of city's position in potential litigation); Chief of Police v. Freedom of Info. Comm'n, 746 A.2d 1264 (Conn. 2000) (even though particular record was requested but not produced through discovery, it was still available under public records law); Wait v. Fla. Power & Light Co., 372 So. 2d 420 (Fla. 1979) (party in litigation with city before U.S. Nuclear Regulatory Commission allowed access under public records law to materials that might be privileged or confidential; opinion does not detail nature of materials); Hillsborough County Aviation Auth. v. Azzarelli Constr. Co., 436 So. 2d 153 (Fla. Dist. Ct. App. 1983) (party in contract litigation with aviation authority permitted access to "work product" under public records law, even though those materials were not available through discovery); Orange County v. Fla. Land Co., 450 So. 2d 341 (Fla. Dist. Ct. App. 1984) (party in litigation with county permitted access to memoranda developed by county's attorney relating to case); Kentucky Lottery Corp. v. Stewart, 41 S.W.3d 860 (Ky. Ct. App. 2001) (court permitted public records access to documents not available through discovery, noting the absurdity of allowing nonparty to obtain public records but not allowing party to do so); Bauer v. Maestri, 676 So. 2d 1096 (La. Ct. App. 1996) (litigant against parish who has been unsuccessful in discovery requests permitted to obtain same material under public records law; opinion does not detail why the materials were not discoverable); Central Mich. Univ. Supervisory-Technical Ass'n, MEA/NEA v. Bd. of Trs. of Cent. Mich. Univ., 567 N.W.2d 696 (Mich. Ct. App. 1997) (parties to lawsuits may proceed in their discretion either through discovery or through the public records law); M. Farbman & Sons, Inc. v. N.Y. City Health & Hosp. Corp., 464 N.E.2d 437 (N.Y. 1984) (plaintiff in contract litigation against defendant permitted to gain access to materials probably not subject to discovery; discovery barred because request was insufficiently specific); Burke v. Yudelson, 378 N.Y.S.2d 165 (App. Div. 1976) (party in contract litigation with city permitted to gain access to materials that might not have been subject to discovery; opinion does not indicate why the materials may have been protected from discovery); Gilbert v. Summit County, 821 N.E.2d 564 (Ohio 2004) (party to lawsuit against public entity may use the public records law to obtain copies of documents for the lawsuit, even though the time for discovery has passed); State *ex rel.* Lank v. Rzentkowski, 416 N.W.2d 635 (Wis. Ct. App. 1987) (party in litigation with town permitted to gain access to materials needed for lawsuit, even though discovery barred because request made after period for discovery had lapsed). *See also* State *ex rel.* Parker v. Lucas Co. Dept. of Job and Family Servs., 893 N.E.2d 558 (Ohio Ct. App. 2008) (materials subject to protective order during litigation are open to the public under the public records law once the litigation has ended). Using the public records law rather than discovery is recommended in Robert D. Peltz, *Use of the Florida Public Records Act as a Discovery Tool in Tort and Administrative Litigation Against the State*, 39 U. MIAMI L. REV. 291 (1985).

23. 125 N.C. App. 607, 481 S.E.2d 363 (1997).

24. The defendant in a Department of Transportation condemnation action was seeking a copy of the department's appraisal of her property, which the department argued was part of its attorney's work product.

25. *Shella*, 125 N.C. App. at 611, 481 S.E.2d at 365.

as the state had offered to provide the plaintiff with the records, the action was moot.[26] Second, the case was poorly briefed by the plaintiff, who appeared on her own behalf and offered, essentially, only factual arguments in her brief. The court was therefore not presented with case law from other jurisdictions that reaches a different conclusion. Finally, the sentiment expressed in the quoted language from *Shella* is inconsistent with the outcome in *McCormick*, where the documents in dispute were work product prepared because of a dispute with the other party that the city expected to ripen to litigation and which the court nevertheless allowed the other party to obtain under the public records law. For these reasons, it appears more likely that the general principle that underlies *McCormick* is the rule in North Carolina.

---

26. In *MCI Construction, LLC v. Hazen & Sawyer, P.C.*, 213 F.R.D. 268, 271 (M.D.N.C. 2003), the federal district court stated that there was no North Carolina case in which "a court has refused to require the release of privileged documents classified as public records under the [Public Records] Act because litigation is pending." The court noted and cited *Shella* but only for the proposition that the state had already turned over the records; that is, the mootness cancelled out the remainder of the court of appeals' opinion in the view of the federal magistrate judge.

Appendix 9A—Statutes

G.S. 132-1.1(a)

§ 132-1.1. Confidential communications by legal counsel to public board or agency; State tax information; public enterprise billing information; Address Confidentiality Program information.

(a) Confidential Communications.—Public records, as defined in G.S. 132-1, shall not include written communications (and copies thereof) to any public board, council, commission or other governmental body of the State or of any county, municipality or other political subdivision or unit of government, made within the scope of the attorney–client relationship by any attorney-at-law serving any such governmental body, concerning any claim against or on behalf of the governmental body or the governmental entity for which such body acts, or concerning the prosecution, defense, settlement or litigation of any judicial action, or any administrative or other type of proceeding to which the governmental body is a party or by which it is or may be directly affected. Such written communication and copies thereof shall not be open to public inspection, examination or copying unless specifically made public by the governmental body receiving such written communications; provided, however, that such written communications and copies thereof shall become public records as defined in G.S. 132-1 three years from the date such communication was received by such public board, council, commission or other governmental body.

G.S. 132-1.9

§ 132-1.9. Trial preparation materials.

(a) Scope.—A request to inspect, examine, or copy a public record that is also trial preparation material is governed by this section, and, to the extent this section conflicts with any other provision of law, this section applies.

(b) Right to Deny Access.—Except as otherwise provided in this section, a custodian may deny access to a public record that is also trial preparation material. If the denial is based on an assertion that the public record is trial preparation material that was prepared in anticipation of a legal proceeding that has not commenced, the custodian shall, upon request, provide a written justification for the assertion that the public record was prepared in anticipation of a legal proceeding.

(c) Trial Preparation Material Prepared in Anticipation of a Legal Proceeding.—Any person who is denied access to a public record that is also claimed to be trial preparation material that was prepared in anticipation of a legal proceeding that has not yet been commenced may petition the court pursuant to G.S. 132-9 for determination as to whether the public record is trial preparation material that was prepared in anticipation of a legal proceeding.

(d) During a Legal Proceeding.—

(1) When a legal proceeding is subject to G.S. 1A-1, Rule 26(b)(3), or subject to Rule 26(b)(3) of the Federal Rules of Civil Procedure, a party to the pending legal proceeding, including any appeals and postjudgment proceedings, who is denied

access to a public record that is also claimed to be trial preparation material that pertains to the pending proceeding may seek access to such record only by motion made in the pending legal proceeding and pursuant to the procedural and substantive standards that apply to that proceeding. A party to the pending legal proceeding may not directly or indirectly commence a separate proceeding for release of such record pursuant to G.S. 132-9 in any other court or tribunal.

(2) When a legal proceeding is not subject to G.S. 1A-1, Rule 26(b)(3), and not subject to Rule 26(b)(3) of the Federal Rules of Civil Procedure, a party to the pending legal proceeding, including any appeals and postjudgment proceedings, who is denied access to a public record that is also claimed to be trial preparation material that pertains to the pending legal proceeding may petition the court pursuant to G.S. 132-9 for access to such record. In determining whether to require the custodian to provide access to all or any portion of the record, the court or other tribunal shall apply the provisions of G.S. 1A-1, Rule 26(b)(3).

(3) Any person who is denied access to a public record that is also claimed to be trial preparation material and who is not a party to the pending legal proceeding to which such record pertains, and who is not acting in concert with or as an agent for any party to the pending legal proceeding, may petition the court pursuant to G.S. 132-9 for a determination as to whether the public record is trial preparation material.

(e) Following a Legal Proceeding.—Upon the conclusion of a legal proceeding, including the completion of all appeals and postjudgment proceedings, or, in the case where no legal proceeding has been commenced, upon the expiration of all applicable statutes of limitations and periods of repose, the custodian of a public record that is also claimed to be trial preparation material shall permit the inspection, examination, or copying of such record if any law that is applicable so provides.

(f) Effect of Disclosure.—Disclosure pursuant to this section of all or any portion of a public record that is also trial preparation material, whether voluntary or pursuant to an order issued by a court, or issued by an officer in an administrative or quasi-judicial legal proceeding, shall not constitute a waiver of the right to claim that any other document or record constitutes trial preparation material.

(g) Trial Preparation Materials That Are Not Public Records.—This section does not require disclosure, or authorize a court to require disclosure, of trial preparation material that is not also a public record or that is under other provisions of this Chapter exempted or protected from disclosure by law or by an order issued by a court, or by an officer in an administrative or quasi-judicial legal proceeding.

(h) Definitions.—As used in this section, the following definitions apply:

(1) Legal proceeding.—Civil proceedings in any federal or State court. Legal proceeding also includes any federal, State, or local government administrative or quasi-judicial proceeding that is not expressly subject to the provisions of Chapter 1A of the General Statutes or the Federal Rules of Civil Procedure.

(2) Trial preparation material.—Any record, wherever located and in whatever form, that is trial preparation material within the meaning of G.S. 1A-1, Rule 26(b)(3), any

comparable material prepared for any other legal proceeding, and any comparable material exchanged pursuant to a joint defense, joint prosecution, or joint interest agreement in connection with any pending or anticipated legal proceeding.

Chapter 10—Settlements

Statutory Summary

Section 132-1.3 of the North Carolina General Statutes[1] [hereinafter G.S.] defines "public record" to include "all settlement documents in any suit, administrative proceeding or arbitration" brought against the state, any local government, or any state or local government agency.[2] With two exceptions, it prohibits these governments and agencies, and their attorneys, from entering into any settlement in such a proceeding that provides that the settlement terms are to be confidential. The first exception exempts from the entire statute medical malpractice actions brought against public hospitals. Thus, these documents are not public record. The second exception permits a court or administrative tribunal to seal a settlement (and thereby close it to public inspection) if two conditions are met: (1) there is an interest served by sealing that overrides the normal presumption of openness, and (2) that interest can be protected only by sealing the settlement.

G.S. 143-318.11(a)(3)[3] is part of the open meetings law. It permits closed sessions of a public body in order to discuss and give instructions to an attorney about the handling

1. The statute is set out in appendix 10A at the end of this chapter.

2. For purposes of this statute, there is no distinction between a *settlement* and a *consent judgment*. The statute itself defines "settlement documents" to include "consent orders," and the North Carolina Supreme Court has defined a "consent judgment" as a form of settlement, standing "as the agreement of the parties, made a matter of record at their request." Cason v. Shute, 211 N.C. 195, 196, 189 S.E. 494, 495 (1937).

3. The statute is set out in appendix 10A at the end of this chapter.

or settlement of a judicial or administrative proceeding or an arbitration. If the terms of a settlement are discussed in closed session, the provision requires that, once the settlement is concluded, the terms of the settlement are to be reported to the public body and then entered into its minutes.

Discussion

G.S. 132-1.3 and Prior Case Law

The effect of G.S. 132-1.3 is not to open settlements to public access but rather to close some that probably would otherwise have been open. In addition, the statute leaves the law concerning public access to settlements somewhat confused.

This statute was not enacted until 1989; before its enactment, access to the terms of a settlement was governed by the general provisions of the public records law. The case law in North Carolina was, and elsewhere overwhelmingly still is, that the terms of settlement of any litigation or administrative proceeding involving a local government or state agency are public record and that any attempt by the litigants to seal such a settlement is unavailing. In *News & Observer Publishing Co. v. Wake County Hospital System, Inc.*,[4] the North Carolina Court of Appeals held that the terms of settlement of three lawsuits brought against the hospital system by medical professional associations were public record and open to public access; this decision is clearly consistent with the North Carolina Supreme Court's later holding in *News & Observer Publishing Co. v. Poole*[5] that all materials held by a public agency are public record, and open to public inspection, unless some statute provides otherwise. In addition, as noted above, courts in other states have consistently held that the terms of settlements in judicial or administrative actions involving governmental agencies are public; in several of those decisions, the courts expressly rejected the litigants' agreement to seal the terms of the settlement.[6] Therefore, before enactment of the statute, it is likely that the law in North Carolina was that all settlement documents were open to public access and that a court had no discretion to order that a settlement's terms be held

4. 55 N.C. App. 1, 284 S.E.2d 542 (1981).

5. 330 N.C. 465, 412 S.E.2d 7 (1992).

6. Anchorage Sch. Dist. v. Anchorage Daily News, 779 P.2d 1191 (Alaska 1989) (settlement is public record, even though the parties had agreed that the terms would be confidential); Register Div. of Freedom Newspapers, Inc. v. County of Orange, 205 Cal. Rptr. 92 (Ct. App. 1984) (settlement is public record, even though other party had been assured that the terms would be confidential); Miami Herald Publ'g Co. v. Collazo, 329 So. 2d 333 (Fla. Dist. Ct. App. 1976) (abuse of discretion for trial court to seal monetary terms of settlement to which city was a party); Lexington-Fayette Urban County Gov't v. Lexington Herald-Leader Co., 941 S.W.2d 469 (Ky. 1997) (settlement documents are public records, even though they include confidentiality agreements); Dutton v. Guste, 395 So. 2d 683 (La. 1981) (settlement documents are public records); Board of Comm'rs v. Las Cruces Sun-News, 76 P.3d 36 (N.M. Ct. App. 2003) (settlement documents are public records); State *ex rel.* Sun Newspapers v. Westlake Bd. of Educ., 601 N.E.2d 173 (Ohio Ct. App. 1991) (settlement is public record, even though the parties had agreed that the terms would be confidential); Tribune-Review Publ'g Co. v. Westmoreland County Hous. Auth., 833 A.2d 112 (Pa. 2003) (settlement documents are public records); Morning Call, Inc. v. Lower Saucon Twp., 627 A.2d 297 (Pa. Commw. Ct. 1993) (settlement is public record, even though the parties had agreed that the terms would be confidential).

confidential. Because the statute exempts medical malpractice settlements pertaining to public hospitals from public access and expressly authorizes a court to seal other settlements' terms, it reduces public access to settlements.

The statute also creates confusion about some settlements. It applies only to settlements of cases that are brought *against* a public agency; it says nothing about settlements in suits in which the agency is the plaintiff. If there is a settlement in a case in which an agency is the plaintiff, does the court have any power to order the terms of settlement sealed (as it clearly does under G.S. 132-1.3 when an agency is the defendant)? There is no way of knowing the answer to the question. The inclusion of such a power in the statute may suggest to a court that such a power is consistent with the state's public records policies, or it may suggest that there must be express statutory authority before a court exercises such a power.

Suits against Individual Officers and Employees

G.S. 132-1.3 applies to settlements of suits against "any agency of North Carolina government or its subdivisions, as defined in G.S. 132-1." G.S. 132-1 in turn defines the listed term to include "every public office, public officer or official." Therefore, suits against individuals who are public officers or officials are expressly included in the statute. But what of suits against those public employees who cannot be characterized as officers or officials? How, if at all, does the statute apply?

If an action is brought against an employee in that person's official capacity, the law is clear that the suit is actually against the unit or agency for which he or she works,[7] and therefore G.S. 132-1.3 applies. If the action is brought against the employee in his or her individual capacity, however, the liability is the individual's. Even so, the defendant's unit or agency might have purchased insurance that covers such individual liabilities or, even if there is no insurance, the unit or agency might provide an attorney for and pay any judgment against an individual defendant.[8] When either of these situations applies—(1) a unit or agency has purchased such insurance and the insurance carrier is defending the individual employee, or (2) the unit or agency itself has retained counsel for the employee and pays any judgment against the defendant—is any settlement reached considered a public record, either under this statute or under the rule of the *Wake County Hospital* case?[9]

If the employee's unit directly pays for the defendant's counsel and then pays any judgment against the individual defendant, the action probably should be treated, for public records purposes, as an action against the unit itself. At the least the rule of *Wake County Hospital* would apply to such a settlement; it would be public record.

If the employee's defense is provided under an insurance contract, however, the matter is less clear. Although the unit's insurance premiums might be affected by any settlement or

---

7. *E.g.*, Prudential Ins. Co. of Am. v. Powell, 217 N.C. 495, 8 S.E.2d 619 (1940) (members of state commission); Gregory v. City of Kings Mountain, 117 N.C. App. 99, 450 S.E.2d 349 (1994) (city gas superintendent); Whitaker v. Clark, 109 N.C. App. 379, 427 S.E.2d 142 (1993) (county social services employees).

8. N.C. Gen. Stat. [hereinafter G.S.] § 160A-167 authorizes cities, counties, and other local agencies to purchase such insurance or provide an attorney.

9. If an employee is sued in his or her individual capacity and bears the full cost of the defense, with no contribution from or involvement by his or her unit, the defendant is no different than any other private litigant, and G.S. 132-1.3 has no application to any settlement that might be reached in the suit.

judgment in such a case, the unit is much less likely to be involved in settlement discussions. Rather, the insurance carrier might discuss the matter with the employee or might simply act on its own discretion. Some insurance policies that cover local government entities leave the question of settlement entirely to the insurance carrier. In such a situation, courts might consider the terms of any settlement to be the private records of the individual defendant rather than records that belong to the employing unit.[10]

Drafts of Settlements

If the parties to litigation circulate among themselves drafts of proposed settlements, are those drafts public record? The answer depends on which party proposed the draft.

If the public agency proposed the draft, the draft would appear to be trial preparation material and thus protected against public access by G.S. 132-1.9, discussed in the immediately preceding chapter. As that chapter notes, the protection against public access continues for as long as the litigation continues, even if the materials in question have been shared with the opposing party.

If the other party, not a governmental unit or agency, proposed the draft, it would not be the government's trial preparation material and thus would not be covered by G.S. 132-1.9. Under the decision of *News & Observer Publishing Co. v. Poole*,[11] drafts of public record are themselves public record;[12] and because the settlement itself will be public record once reached, the logic of *Poole* would be that the draft is public record once received by the governmental unit or agency.[13]

The Interplay of G.S. 132-1.3 with Other Statutes

Settlements That Might Be Subject to Other Public Records Statutes

Settlement documents in lawsuits and other proceedings brought against public agencies sometimes include information that might properly be withheld from public inspection under other statutes. Most commonly, perhaps, settlement documents in a suit between an agency and a current or former employee, brought to contest the employee's discharge or other disciplinary action taken against the employee, might include information about the employee's performance that is properly part of the employee's personnel file.[14] A school pupil might claim that the school administrative unit is not providing him or her the special education required by law, and the settlement documents in the pupil's lawsuit might detail the special education that the unit will provide; that information is normally part of the pupil's records and is confidential by law.[15] A patient of a county health department might bring a malpractice action against the department, and the settlement documents

---

10. If the unit was given a copy of any settlement of a suit against an individual employee, the unit's copy would appear to be a public record unless protected by the appropriate personnel privacy act.

11. 330 N.C. 465, 412 S.E.2d 7 (1992).

12. See the discussion in chapter 1, in the text accompanying notes 36 through 44.

13. This was the outcome in *State ex rel. Cincinnati Enquirer v. Dupuis*, 781 N.E.2d 163 (Ohio 2002).

14. Most of the personnel files of most public employees are exempt from public access. See the discussion in chapter 7 of this book.

15. G.S. 115C-402.

might include medical information about the patient that is normally exempt from public inspection.[16]

When some or all of the information included within settlement documents might properly be withheld from public inspection under some other statutory exception to the public records laws, which provision governs? Does the settlement statute create an exception to the confidentiality provisions of the statute permitting or requiring confidentiality, or does the other statute create an exception to the rules on settlements? There are cogent arguments for either answer.

The argument for maintaining confidentiality of settlements when the information falls within other statutes permitting or requiring confidentiality begins with the recognition, as is discussed at the beginning of this chapter, that G.S. 132-1.3 in a sense simply affirms what is already the law absent the statute. Courts have held that settlements entered into by local governments are public records, even if the parties to the settlements purport to agree to keep them confidential. So, too, personnel records, student records, and medical records are public records and, in the absence of the various statutes making these records confidential, would be open to public inspection. If settlements are part of personnel files, or student records, or medical records, which by statute are not open to the public, that exception to the right of access applies as much to the settlement as to any other part of the file or record.

The opposing argument, for allowing access to settlements involving information otherwise protected by confidentiality statutes, focuses on the language of the settlement statute and on the timing of the enactments of the settlement statute and of the various other statutes. The settlement statute itself speaks broadly, extending to *all* settlement documents in *any* suit or proceeding against a local government. The absence of any express exception for suits or proceedings in which the terms of settlement might include otherwise confidential information may be significant inasmuch as the statute makes one express exception, for medical malpractice actions against public hospitals. (This provision is particularly telling with respect to medical malpractice actions brought against local health departments, as opposed to public hospitals.) In addition, the settlement statute was enacted in 1989—after each of the cited confidentiality statutes, which date from the mid-1970s and mid-1980s. If the General Assembly had intended the earlier statutes as exceptions to the later statute, it could easily have said so explicitly.

Unfortunately there is no way to state with certainty which of these arguments is correct or would convince an appellate court.[17] Perhaps this suggests searching for some middle

---

16. G.S. 130A-12. Medical records are discussed generally in chapter 14 of this book.

17. The issue has arisen in at least two other states, both of which held the settlement to be open to public inspection, but in each case the statutory context differed significantly from North Carolina's.

In *Des Moines Independent Community School District Public Records v. Des Moines Register & Tribune Co.*, 487 N.W.2d 666 (Iowa 1992), the statute excluded from public access "personal information in confidential personnel records." The court first noted that courts generally held settlements to be public. It then went on to admit that the settlement at issue had some elements that were public in nature and some that were personal, but it held that the settlement was public because "public funds were being paid to settle a private dispute." 487 N.W.2d at 669.

In *Yakima Newspapers, Inc. v. City of Yakima*, 890 P.2d 544 (Wash. Ct. App. 1995), the statute excluded from public access "[p]ersonal information in files maintained for employees . . . to the extent that

ground, one that seeks a partial reconciliation of the settlement statute with the various confidentiality statutes. At least two such middle grounds are possible, each more attractive than the stark choice outlined above. First, different parts of any settlement could be treated differently: those terms of the settlement that have nothing to do with an employee's performance, or a student's record, or a patient's medical record, could be made public, while those that clearly fall within the various confidentiality statutes could be held confidential. Under such a reconciliation, for example, the amount of any money payments agreed to by the public agency would certainly be open to public inspection.[18] Alternatively, the existence of an apparent conflict between the two statutes might be grounds for seeking court approval of sealing some portion of a settlement, a step expressly allowed by G.S. 132-1.3.

G.S. 132-1.3 and the Open Meetings Law Provision

Two differences between the statutes. There are a couple of differences between G.S. 132-1.3 and G.S. 143-318.11(a)(3) that are worth noting. First, G.S. 132-1.3 merely states that settlement documents are public records and thus open to public inspection and copying. The statute does not impose on the public agency any duty other than allowing public access. The open meetings law provision, however, establishes an affirmative duty of publicity. If the terms of a settlement are discussed in a closed session of a public body, the final terms of that settlement must be reported to the public body and entered into the public body's minutes. (By "terms of that settlement" the statute probably intends the actual terms themselves and not a summary.)

Second, the materials subject to G.S. 132-1.3 are more inclusive than those subject to the open meetings law provision. Settlement documents under G.S. 132-1.3 include not only the terms of the settlement but also any correspondence associated with reaching the settlement and any checks written by the government pursuant to the settlement. While these additional materials are public records, they are not subject to the provisions of G.S. 143-318.11(a)(3) and would not need to be entered into the minutes of the public body.

Dealing with sealed settlements under the open meetings law. In certain narrow circumstances G.S. 132-1.3 permits a judge, administrative agency, or arbitrator to seal a settlement, thereby denying public access to its terms. But the public records provision says nothing about the requirements of the open meetings law, and therefore a properly sealed settlement, if it has been discussed by a public body in closed ses-

---

disclosure would violate their right to privacy." The court read the statute to exclude materials from disclosure only if disclosure would be highly offensive to a reasonable person *and* the materials were not of legitimate public concern. The court held that the document at issue was subject to disclosure because those seeking to keep it confidential failed to show that the document was not of legitimate public concern. The North Carolina personnel privacy statutes, by contrast, are not qualified in any way; subject to the statutory exceptions, all information in a personnel file is closed to public access.

18. The attorney general has issued an opinion that seems to agree with this approach. It states that if the terms of a settlement with an employee include material that was originally part of the employee's personnel file, that information need not be made public. Letter to Fred M. Carmichael, 26 November 1997, Advisory Opinion No. 338, *available at* www.ncdoj.gov/About-DOJ/Legal-Services/Legal-Opinions.aspx.

sion, apparently still must be reported to the public body and its terms entered into the public body's minutes.[19] If so, is the order sealing the settlement merely an illusion?

Not necessarily. The open meetings law, in G.S. 143-318.11(a)(1), permits a public body to hold a closed session in order "[t]o prevent the disclosure of information that is privileged or confidential pursuant to the law of this State." Because a properly sealed settlement is confidential pursuant to G.S. 132-1.3, a public body may hold a closed session to receive the report about the settlement, and the terms of the settlement should be set out in the minutes of that closed session. (I would suggest reporting the fact of the settlement to the public body in open session, then going into closed session to report on the specific terms.) G.S. 143-318.10(e) permits a public body to seal the minutes of a closed session as long as "public inspection would frustrate the purpose of [the] closed session," and sealing the minutes that include the terms of a confidential settlement fits within that authorization.

Admittedly, the statutory reconciliation just suggested is not fully satisfying. The difficulty is that the two statutes—public records and open meetings—have conflicting intentions in the circumstances of a settlement properly sealed under G.S. 132-1.3. One shields such a settlement from public disclosure while the other demands public disclosure. Both intentions cannot be secured simultaneously. The suggested reconciliation does, however, respect the language of the open meetings provision, and perhaps this is the best that can be done. A local government that is party to a properly sealed settlement might request the sealing official or entity to include in its order a direction that the terms be presented in closed session, as suggested above. Such a step would provide slightly stronger support to the course of action outlined in this section.

Settlements of Federal Litigation and Federal Administrative Proceedings

When a public agency is involved in a suit in federal court or in a proceeding before a federal administrative agency, if the suit or proceeding is then settled and if the court or the agency orders or approves the sealing of some or all of the terms of settlement, the principles of federal supremacy cause the federal tribunal's act to override the provisions of G.S. 132-1.3 or G.S. 143-318.11(a)(3).[20] Those terms of settlement are not to be public records nor do they need to be entered into the public minutes of any public body that discussed the settlement in closed session. Before a federal court approves sealing a settlement, however, it is highly likely that it would consider the provisions of North Carolina law in deciding whether to do so. In *Pansy v. Borough of Stroudsburg*, for example, the federal Third Circuit Court of Appeals held that

> where it is likely that information is accessible under a relevant freedom of information law, a strong presumption exists against granting or maintaining an order of confidentiality [for a settlement] whose scope would prevent disclosure of that information pursuant to the relevant freedom of information law. In the good cause balancing test [that governs whether to grant such an order], this

---

19. Indeed, the terms of a medical malpractice settlement entered into by a public hospital, which is expressly excepted from G.S. 132-1.3, are also expressly excepted from the open meetings law requirement.

20. *Cf.* Pansy v. Borough of Stroudsburg, 23 F.3d 772 (3d Cir. 1994).

> strong presumption tilts the scales heavily against entering or maintaining an order of confidentiality.[21]

If a federal proceeding is settled and the parties attempt to agree to keep the settlement confidential but do not have court or agency approval to do so, there is no conflict between federal law and state law because there is no federal approval of the confidentiality agreement. Therefore, the North Carolina statutes would still apply.

Agreements Not to Discuss Settlements and Confidentiality Agreements Applicable Only to the Nongovernmental Party

There are two variants on the basic sort of agreement discussed in this chapter. In one the government acknowledges that the terms of settlement are public record but agrees to do no more than the law requires. The government also agrees that its officials and employees will not affirmatively disclose settlement terms. In the second the government does not agree to maintain confidentiality of the settlement, but the other party (assuming it is not also a governmental entity) does. Does the law permit these sorts of provisions?

Agreements to Do No More Than the Law Requires

This sort of agreement is literally not covered by G.S. 132-1.3. In such an agreement, the government has acknowledged that the settlement terms are public record and that it must reveal them pursuant to the statute if called upon to do so. But the government also agrees that it will not disclose the terms unless requested to do so pursuant to the public records law. It therefore appears that it would be within a government's authority to enter into such an agreement.

Confidentiality Imposed on Only the Nongovernmental Party

A settlement agreement under which only the nongovernmental party agrees to hold the terms confidential seems clearly outside the realm of G.S. 132-1.3. The governmental party has made no effort at evading the statutory declaration that settlements are public records. The one question about such a settlement arises from the language in the second sentence of G.S. 132-1.3(a), which directs that no North Carolina governmental entity "shall approve, accept or enter into any settlement . . . if the settlement provides that its terms and conditions shall be confidential." Does that language prohibit a settlement agreement under which one party, but not the other, agrees not to disclose the settlement? Probably it does not. After all, if one party is entirely free to disclose the terms of the settlement, it can hardly be said that the settlement is confidential. Furthermore, as applies to the nongovernmental party, there is nothing unusual about such a provision, and there is no stated state policy against private litigants agreeing to maintain the confidentiality of their settlements.

---

21. *Id.* at 791. *Accord* Ford v. City of Huntsville, 242 F.3d 235 (5th Cir. 2001) (holding that a newspaper had a right under the federal rules of civil procedure to intervene in a lawsuit to contest a confidentiality order that was inconsistent with state public records law). *See also* Daines v. Harrison, 838 F. Supp. 1406 (D. Colo. 1993) (refusing to enforce an earlier order sealing a settlement, in part because settlements were public record under state law).

Appendix 10A—Statutes

G.S. 132-1.3

§ 132-1.3. Settlements made by or on behalf of public agencies, public officials, or public employees; public records.

(a) Public records, as defined in G.S. 132-1, shall include all settlement documents in any suit, administrative proceeding or arbitration instituted against any agency of North Carolina government or its subdivisions, as defined in G.S. 132-1, in connection with or arising out of such agency's official actions, duties or responsibilities, except in an action for medical malpractice against a hospital facility. No agency of North Carolina government or its subdivisions, nor any counsel, insurance company or other representative acting on behalf of such agency, shall approve, accept or enter into any settlement of any such suit, arbitration or proceeding if the settlement provides that its terms and conditions shall be confidential, except in an action for medical malpractice against a hospital facility. No settlement document sealed under subsection (b) of this section shall be open for public inspection.

(b) No judge, administrative judge or administrative hearing officer of this State, nor any board or commission, nor any arbitrator appointed pursuant to the laws of North Carolina, shall order or permit the sealing of any settlement document in any proceeding described herein except on the basis of a written order concluding that (1) the presumption of openness is overcome by an overriding interest and (2) that such overriding interest cannot be protected by any measure short of sealing the settlement. Such order shall articulate the overriding interest and shall include findings of fact that are sufficiently specific to permit a reviewing court to determine whether the order was proper.

(c) Except for confidential communications as provided in G.S. 132-1.1, the term "settlement documents," as used herein, shall include all documents which reflect, or which are made or utilized in connection with, the terms and conditions upon which any proceedings described in this section are compromised, settled, terminated or dismissed, including but not limited to correspondence, settlement agreements, consent orders, checks, and bank drafts.

G.S. 143-318.11(a)(3)

§ 143-318.11. Closed sessions.

(a) Permitted Purposes.—It is the policy of this State that closed sessions shall be held only when required to permit a public body to act in the public interest as permitted in this section. A public body may hold a closed session and exclude the public only when a closed session is required:

. . .

(3) To consult with an attorney employed or retained by the public body in order to preserve the attorney–client privilege between the attorney and the public body, which privilege is hereby acknowledged. General policy matters may not be discussed in a closed session and nothing herein shall be construed to permit a public body to close a meeting that otherwise would be open merely because an attorney

employed or retained by the public body is a participant. The public body may consider and give instructions to an attorney concerning the handling or settlement of a claim, judicial action, mediation, arbitration, or administrative procedure. **If the public body has approved or considered a settlement, other than a malpractice settlement by or on behalf of a hospital, in closed session, the terms of that settlement shall be reported to the public body and entered into its minutes as soon as possible within a reasonable time after the settlement is concluded.** (emphasis added)

Chapter 11—Trade Secrets

Statutory Summary

Section 132-1.2(1) of the North Carolina General Statutes[1] [hereinafter G.S.] exempts from the public records law confidential, privately owned, business information that is held by a public agency. For information to qualify for the exemption, four conditions must be met:

1. The information is a "trade secret" as that term is defined in G.S. 66-152(3), the state's Trade Secrets Protection Act.
2. The information is owned by a "private person" as that term is defined in the Trade Secrets Protection Act.
3. The owner discloses or furnishes the information to the public agency in one of a number of listed contexts: bidding on or performing a contract with a public agency; applying for a publicly granted license, permit, or special benefit; responding to a public agency's request for proposals; undertaking an industrial development project; or demonstrating compliance with some law, ordinance, or regulation.
4. The owner of the information indicates that it is confidential or a trade secret when the information is first disclosed or furnished to the public agency.

---

1. The statute is set out in appendix 11A at the end of this chapter.

Discussion

The Four Conditions

Introduction

First-time readers of G.S. 132-1.2(1) frequently conclude that it establishes *four* exceptions to public access, one under each separate lettered paragraph in the subsection. The conclusion is incorrect. The four paragraphs are cumulative, and for information to be exempt from public access the requirements of all four paragraphs must be met.

The Material Is a Trade Secret

The first condition that must be met, in order for the exemption created by G.S. 132-1.2(1) to apply, is that the information in question be a trade secret as that term is defined in G.S. 66-152(3). The definition reads as follows:

> "Trade secret" means business or technical information, including but not limited to a formula, pattern, program, device, compilation of information, method, technique, or process that:
>
> a. Derives independent actual or potential commercial value from not being generally known or readily ascertainable through independent development or reverse engineering by persons who can obtain economic value from its disclosure or use; and
>
> b. Is the subject of efforts that are reasonable under the circumstances to maintain its secrecy.

This definition is drawn from and quite similar to that found in the Uniform Trade Secrets Act, which in turn is based on the principles set out in the Restatement of Torts.[2] The definition is broad and encompassing. As two commentators stated soon after the Trade Secrets Protection Act was enacted, "[t]he prime requisite of a trade secret . . . is secrecy. The owner derives value from the secret because he knows it, and his competitors do not."[3] The court of appeals, in a 1999 decision, set out the sorts of advantages that maintenance of trade secrets might bring to a company:

> The information sought is collected by the CLPs ["competitive local providers" of telephone service] for their own use and, except for the requirement that it be disclosed to the Commission, is not available to the public. Indeed, to provide

---

2. Joseph E. Root III & Guy M. Blynn, *Abandonment of Common-Law Principles: The North Carolina Trade Secrets Protection Act*, 18 Wake Forest L. Rev. 823, 836–37 (1982). The authors write that North Carolina's "definition of 'trade secret' tracks the Uniform Act's definition with minor variations that should improve the operation of the North Carolina Act. Both Acts provide trade secrets protection to information that: (1) is business or technical information, (2) has actual or potential economic value stemming from its secrecy, and (3) the owner has made the object of reasonable efforts to keep secret." *Id.* at 836 (footnotes omitted).

3. *Id.* at 826. In *Billmayer v. City of Kalispell*, 160 P.3d 869 (Mont. 2007), an engineer who had done a floodplain study for a developer that had then been filed with the city objected to allowing copies to be made of the study documents. Because, however, he was willing to allow the documents to be read, just not copied, the court had no trouble in holding that they did not constitute trade secrets; there was not the requisite attempt to maintain secrecy.

> public access to this information would provide competitors rather extensive insight into the business plans and operations of a particular CLP, information that otherwise would not be available generally. Disclosure of this information would allow competitors to discover how a CLP serves its customers, a CLP's plans for entering the local market and how quickly it acquires new customers, and in which areas of the state the CLP is focusing its marketing efforts and the relative effectiveness of those efforts. Most importantly, disclosure of such information would thwart the creativity and innovation that competition brings to the marketplace, and prohibit the competitive environment our legislature intended to create.[4]

The North Carolina courts have not had a great many occasions to interpret the Trade Secrets Protection Act since its enactment in 1981, but the decisions that have been rendered recognize the breadth of the statutory definition. One extended discussion is found in *Barr-Mullin, Inc. v. Browning*,[5] in which the issue was whether a computer software program, embedded in industrial machinery sold by the plaintiff, was a trade secret. The court held that it was. The program was embedded in a programmable read-only memory chip, sold in object code form. (The court distinguished between computer *object code* and computer *source code*; the latter is the code in which programmers write programs.) Because the software was sold in object code, expert testimony indicated that "it [was] practically impossible to make any meaningful changes to the software,"[6] which the court took as evidence that the company was trying to maintain the secrecy of the program. This fact, plus the company's practice of allowing access to the software only to employees and consultants, demonstrated sufficient efforts to maintain the software's secrecy.

In *Wilmington Star-News, Inc. v. New Hanover Regional Medical Center, Inc.*,[7] the focus was on a contract between a public hospital and a health maintenance organization (HMO), under which the hospital agreed to provide medical services to members of the HMO. The contract included a list of prices the HMO would pay for specific services performed by the hospital. When the newspaper sought a copy of the contract, the trial court granted it summary judgment. The court of appeals held that, based on the evidence available to the trial court, "a reasonable trier of fact could conclude that the price lists constitute trade secrets."[8] In *Drouillard v. Keister Williams Newspaper Services, Inc.*,[9] the court of appeals affirmed a trial court finding that customer lists and bidding formulas were trade secrets.[10]

---

4. State *ex rel.* Utilities Comm'n v. MCI Telecomms. Corp., 132 N.C. App. 625, 634–35, 514 S.E.2d 276, 282–83 (1999).

5. 108 N.C. App. 590, 424 S.E.2d 226 (1993).

6. *Id.* at 596, 424 S.E.2d at 229.

7. 125 N.C. App. 174, 480 S.E.2d 53 (1997).

8. *Id.* at 182, 480 S.E.2d at 57.

9. 108 N.C. App. 169, 423 S.E.2d 324 (1992).

10. In *Harrington Manufacturing Co. v. Powell Manufacturing Co.*, 26 N.C. App. 414, 216 S.E.2d 379 (1975), the court held that customer lists were not trade secrets for purposes of the protection of trade secrets from civil discovery. The discovery statute has since been amended, and this case antedates the statutory definition of trade secrets in the Trade Secrets Protection Act; therefore, it is probably no longer good law on whether customer lists are trade secrets.

And in *Byrd's Lawn & Landscaping, Inc. v. Smith,*[11] the court of appeals extended trade secret status to detailed cost records setting out the materials, labor, and equipment used in the commercial landscaping contracts that were the core of the plaintiff's business.

Although there have not been a great number of North Carolina cases deciding whether particular information is a trade secret, there have been many cases nationally. Courts, as well as commentators, stress that any determination of whether information is a trade secret is heavily dependent on the facts of each situation—on whether there is economic value to maintaining the secrecy of the information and on what steps the owner has taken to maintain that secrecy. The fact-based nature of the inquiry is also suggested by the influential comment to the Restatement of Torts (which has been quoted by the North Carolina appellate courts) that lists the following factors as useful in determining whether information is a trade secret:

> (1) the extent to which the information is known outside of [a person's] business; (2) the extent to which it is known by employees and others involved in his business; (3) the extent of measures taken by him to guard the secrecy of the information; (4) the value of the information to him and to his competitors; (5) the amount of effort or money expended by him in developing the information; (6) the ease or difficulty with which the information could be properly acquired or duplicated by others.[12]

Despite the inquiry's being dependent on the facts surrounding the particular alleged secret, the cases from around the country exhibit a good bit of uniformity in their outcomes. Because the North Carolina definition is based on the Uniform Act definition, and because both are similar to the Restatement's definition, cases from elsewhere give guidance to the meaning of the term in this state.[13] Among the kinds of information that have been widely held to constitute trade secrets are industrial formulas, industrial processes, designs of industrial machinery, computer software incorporated in products, plans and specifications for a wide range of products, retail customer lists, marketing plans, sales

---

11. 142 N.C. App. 371, 542 S.E.2d 689 (2001).

12. RESTATEMENT OF TORTS § 757 cmt. b (1939). A recent example, among several, of use of this listing by the North Carolina courts is found in *Sunbelt Rentals, Inc. v. Head & Engquist Equipment, L.L.C.*, 174 N.C. App. 49, 53, 620 S.E.2d 222, 226 (2005). These factors have been widely used by other courts as well in deciding trade secrets cases. *See, e.g.*, Citizens' Util. Bd. v. Or. Pub. Util. Comm'n, 877 P.2d 116 (Or. Ct. App. 1994).

13. One source that is not a good guide to the meaning of trade secret is the trade secret exemption to the federal Freedom of Information Act (FOIA) and the cases interpreting it. This exemption protects from access "trade secrets and commercial or financial information obtained from a person [that is] privileged or confidential." 5 U.S.C. § 552(b)(4) (2006). In order to give meaning to the second part of the exemption—commercial or financial information—most of the federal courts interpreting this exemption limit trade secrets to plans, formulas, processes, or devices involved in manufacturing, a meaning that is much narrower than that of the Uniform Trade Secrets Act or the Restatement of Torts. The differences between the FOIA meaning of trade secrets and that of the Uniform Act and the Restatement are pointed out in 1 GUIDEBOOK TO THE FREEDOM OF INFORMATION AND PRIVACY ACTS § 4:2 (Justin D. Franklin & Robert F. Bouchard eds., 2d ed. 2006 & Supp. 2007). Because the North Carolina statute is based on the Uniform Act, the FOIA cases are not probative of the meaning of trade secrets.

forecasts, and pricing formulas (and sometimes, as in the *New Hanover Regional Medical Center* case, the prices themselves).[14]

Two kinds of materials have an uncertain status as trade secrets. The first is a privately held company's audited financial statements. Local governments receive such statements in a number of contexts: as part of an application for a loan, as part of a bid or proposal submitted to the government to be used to determine the submitter's financial responsibility, or as part of an application for a business license or permit. Although the case law is mixed,[15] financial statements of a privately held business appear to qualify as trade secrets. The information might be useful to a competitor, and many businesses carefully maintain the confidentiality of their statements.

The second kind of material with questionable trade secret status is building plans submitted to a local inspection office for approval under the state building code. Sometimes other builders or designers wish to make a copy of such plans for their own building, and the author of the filed plans might object. It is difficult to characterize building plans and drawings as trade secrets: not only are they submitted to a public office and made available to various construction contractors and subcontractors, but the exterior of any building is obviously not secret once it is constructed, and the interior plan can be recreated by anyone who visits the building.[16]

The Material Belongs to a Private Party

No protection for government-owned trade secrets. The second condition that must be met to satisfy the exemption requirement is that the material must belong to "a private 'person' as defined in G.S. 66-152(2)." The cited statute defines "person" to include government agencies, so the condition in G.S. 132-1.2(1) excludes public owners of trade secrets from the exemption to the public records law, and therefore a local government or other public agency may not use G.S. 132-1.2(1) to deny public access to trade secrets that belong to the

---

14. The cases are collected and summarized in 1ROGER M. MILGRIM & ERIC E. BENSEN, MILGRIM ON TRADE SECRETS § 1.09 (2008). Another good source is HENRY H. PERRITT, JR., TRADE SECRETS: A PRACTITIONER'S GUIDE (2d ed. 2008); chapter three collects and summarizes many cases.

15. The Kentucky public records law denies public access to "records . . . generally recognized as confidential or proprietary, which if openly disclosed would permit an unfair commercial advantage to competitors of the entity that disclosed the records." KY. REV. STAT. ANN § 61.878(1)(c)(1) (LexisNexis Supp. 2008). The Kentucky Supreme Court held that audited financial statements of a privately held company fit within the quoted provision. Marina Mgmt. Servs., Inc. v. Commonwealth, 906 S.W.2d 318 (Ky. 1995). See also *Hoy v. Kentucky Industrial Revitalization Authority*, 907 S.W.2d 766 (Ky. 1995), in which the Kentucky Supreme Court stated that "[i]t does not take a degree in finance to recognize that such information [as financial statements and other financial information] concerning the inner workings of a corporation is 'generally recognized as confidential or proprietary.'" *Id.* at 768. Two other cases (one a trial court decision), however, hold that financial statements are not trade secrets. William Kaufman Assocs. v. Levy, 345 N.Y.S.2d 836 (Sup. Ct. 1973) (real estate company's financial statements submitted to tax authorities; the court simply states that the data in question were not of such a character that they could be regarded as trade secrets); Apodaca v. Montes, 606 S.W.2d 734 (Tex. Civ. App. 1980) (financial statements of bail bondsman submitted to licensing agency; held not a trade secret, because competitors' statements would also be public record).

16. It may be a violation of federal copyright law to *copy* design plans. They are protected by copyright, 17 U.S.C. § 102 (2006), and if they have not been published it is a violation of federal copyright law even to make a copy of them. Demetriades v. Kaufmann, 680 F. Supp. 658 (S.D.N.Y. 1988). It is not, however, the responsibility of a local inspection office to enforce federal copyright law.

government or agency or some other local government or public agency.[17] This point was recognized in the *New Hanover Regional Medical Center* case, discussed above. After deciding that the price lists at issue in the case might be trade secrets, the court noted that the lists were the result of negotiations between the public hospital and the HMO and were written in a contract between those two entities. Therefore, "it would defy logic to insist that [these] price lists belong solely to [the HMO] and not also to [the public hospital]."[18] Because the lists were not solely the property of a private person, G.S. 132-1.2 did not apply.[19]

Nonprofit entities can own trade secrets. Local governments sometimes receive materials from nonprofit entities that claim trade secret status and wonder whether such an entity can in fact own a trade secret. The answer is yes. The Trade Secrets Protection Act itself does not distinguish between for-profit and nonprofit entities in its definition of "person," and in fact the North Carolina Court of Appeals has extended the protections of G.S. 132-1.2(1) to a nonprofit entity. The plaintiff in *North Carolina Electric Membership Corp. v. North Carolina Department of Economic & Community Development*, which was successful in obtaining injunctive relief to bar release of claimed trade secrets,[20] was organized under G.S. Chapter 117, which makes clear that electric membership corporations (EMCs) are nonprofit organizations. G.S. 117-10 characterizes EMCs as "corporation[s] not organized for pecuniary profit."

The Material Is Submitted to the Government in a Specific Manner

The statute lists a number of contexts in which the government holding the trade secret information might have received it. These circumstances cover those who are

- performing a public contract;[21]
- bidding on a public contract;
- applying for a government permit or license;[22]
- applying to participate in some kind of government program;[23]

---

17. Some state public records laws do deny public access to trade secrets owned by government agencies. *See, e.g.*, Servais v. Port of Bellingham, 904 P.2d 1124 (Wash. 1995) (interpreting a Washington statute that denies public access to "valuable formulae, designs, drawings, and research data obtained by any agency . . . when disclosure would produce private gain and public loss").

18. 125 N.C. App. 174, 182, 480 S.E.2d 53, 57 (1997).

19. In *State ex rel. Utilities Commission v. MCI Telecommunications Corp.*, 132 N.C. App. 625, 514 S.E.2d 276 (1999), the court suggested in dicta that the statute would also not apply to facially private entities that were sufficiently controlled by government to be considered public agencies for public records purposes. In the case the court also held that a regulated public utility was a private person, despite the extent of government regulation over its activities.

20. 108 N.C. App. 711, 425 S.E.2d 440 (1993).

21. For example, in *Freedom Newspapers, Inc. v. Denver & Rio Grande Western Railroad*, 731 P.2d 740 (Colo. App. 1986), the railroad claimed that the prices it charged under a contract to deliver coal to a public utility district were a trade secret, and in *Douglas Asphalt Co. v. E.R. Snell Contractor, Inc.*, 639 S.E.2d 372 (Ga. Ct. App. 2006), the court agreed that asphalt formulas developed by paving contractors and on file with the Georgia Department of Transportation were trade secrets.

22. For example, in *State ex rel. The Plain Dealer v. Ohio Department of Insurance*, 687 N.E.2d 661 (Ohio 1997), the issue involved a large number of documents submitted to the department by an insurance company as part of a proceeding to approve a possible acquisition.

23. *North Carolina Electric Membership Corp. v. North Carolina Department of Economic & Community Development*, 108 N.C. App. 711, 425 S.E.2d 440 (1993), involved alleged trade secrets submitted to the

- responding to a government's request for proposals for a program or contract;[24]
- negotiating with a government about an industrial development project; or
- complying with a federal, state, or local requirement that the information be submitted.[25]

The Owner Indicates That a Record Is Confidential

As the final condition for qualifying information for exemption from access, G.S. 132-1.2(1)(d) requires that the information be "designated or indicated" as confidential or a trade secret at the time the information is first disclosed to the public agency.[26] In *North Carolina Electric Membership Corp. v. North Carolina Department of Economic & Community Development*,[27] the court of appeals interpreted this requirement in a forgiving way. The materials in question had been submitted to the state agency some years before the enactment of G.S. 132-1.2(1), and so there had been no effort by the owner of the materials to expressly designate them as confidential or a trade secret. The court held, nevertheless, that the circumstances under which the materials were submitted to the state might support a finding that the owner had "indicated" that they were confidential. The court appears to be saying that if the owner of the trade secret in any manner conveys its concern for the confidentiality of the materials, it has met this condition. The one bit of evidence the court gave for its conclusion on this point was that the state agency sought a response from the materials' owner before releasing them for public inspection. By making such a request, the court stated, the agency acknowledged that the materials might contain trade secrets and that the owner had made the agency aware of that possibility. (The opinion does not detail just what the owner did to indicate that the materials were confidential.)

---

department by the plaintiff membership corporation in order to apply, through the department, for federal funding.

24. For example, in *Envirotest Partners v. Commonwealth Department of Transportation*, 664 A.2d 208 (Pa. Commw. Ct. 1995), the plaintiff submitted a proposal to inspect vehicle emissions on behalf of the Commonwealth of Pennsylvania and the proposal included descriptions of the technology that the plaintiff would use to do the inspections; the plaintiff asserted that the technology was a trade secret. And in *State ex rel. Fisher v. PRC Public Sector, Inc.*, 650 N.E.2d 945 (Ohio Ct. App. 1994), the winning bidder on a contract for an automated fingerprint identification system included trade secrets about its systems in its bid.

25. For example, in *State Department of Natural Resources v. Arctic Slope Regional Corp.*, 834 P.2d 134 (Alaska 1991), a company submitted oil well drilling data to a state agency pursuant to a statutory requirement to do so. All parties agreed that the data contained trade secrets. In another example, in *American Family Mutual Insurance Co. v. Missouri Department of Insurance*, 169 S.W.3d 905 (Mo. Ct. App. 2005), the insurance company was required to submit periodic reports to the state department, and the court upheld a trial court judgment that some of the information constituted trade secrets. In North Carolina, local governments often require industrial companies seeking sewer pretreatment permits to disclose information that might include trade secrets about the companies' industrial wastes; and *State ex rel. Utilities Commission v. MCI Telecommunications Corp.*, 132 N.C. App. 625, 514 S.E.2d 276 (1999), *see* discussion *supra* note 20, involved information that the company was required to submit to the state Utilities Commission.

26. A number of courts have held that a failure to so designate materials submitted to a government is strong evidence that the materials are not trade secrets, inasmuch as the owner of the materials has not taken adequate steps to maintain their confidentiality. *E.g.*, Cubic Transp. Sys., Inc. v. Miami-Dade County, 899 So. 2d 453 (Fla. Dist. Ct. App. 2005).

27. 108 N.C. App. 711, 425 S.E.2d 440 (1993).

If a local government regularly receives information that might be a trade secret, it may wish to take steps to alert the owners of the information to their responsibilities under this section. For example, a local government that is seeking procurement bids that might include bidders' trade secrets could include in the specifications a notice to bidders to label all trade secret information as such. Or a local government that adopts a sewage pretreatment ordinance that requires reporting from industrial companies might include a requirement that any trade secret information included in such a report be properly labeled as a trade secret.

Release of Trade Secrets

G.S. 132-1.2(1) provides that nothing in the public records law is to be construed "to require or authorize" an agency to release information that qualifies for protection from access under the subsection. Suppose a local government possessing information that meets the four conditions nevertheless releases it, either intentionally or by mistake. Would the local government or its officials thereby incur any liability to the owner of the trade secret?

Although there can be no certain answer to the question, there is a plain risk that a government could be held liable in damages for such a release. G.S. 132-1.2(1) itself contains no penalties, either civil or criminal, for release of trade secret information, but that fact is not dispositive. Courts in other states have occasionally held public records custodians individually liable in tort when the custodians have released records that were not open to public access under the public records statute. The relevant cases are discussed in chapter 6, in the text accompanying notes 11 through 13. More importantly, the North Carolina Trade Secrets Protection Act itself may threaten liability if a local government releases trade secret information against the wishes of the owner of the information. G.S. 66-153 entitles the owner of a trade secret that has been misappropriated to bring a civil action to remedy the wrong, and G.S. 66-154(b) specifies that such an owner may recover damages for its economic loss. G.S. 66-152(1) defines "misappropriation" to include "disclosure . . . of a trade secret of another without express or implied authority or consent." These statutory provisions, together with the statement in G.S. 132-1.2(1) that nothing in the public records law "authorizes" disclosure of trade secrets, suggest that a primary purpose of the public records provision is to make clear that the public records laws are not authority for disclosure of trade secrets. This leaves local governments and other public agencies holding such information under the same constraints and the same liabilities as private parties holding the trade secrets of others.[28]

---

28. In *State ex rel. Fisher v. PRC Public Sector, Inc.*, 650 N.E.2d 945 (Ohio Ct. App. 1994), the state government, which had received trade secrets in response to a request for proposals, assumed that it would be liable under that state's trades secrets statute for wrongful disclosure of a secret.

Governments that release trade secrets may, in some circumstances, face an additional source of liability. Trade secrets are property, and their owners are entitled to the general protections accorded to property against government actions. One court has held that if a government *requires* the owner of a trade secret to disclose that secret to the government and then the government itself discloses the secret to others, a taking has occurred and the government is liable for compensation. Noranda Exploration, Inc. v. Ostrom, 335 N.W.2d 596 (Wis. 1983). The Alaska Supreme Court seemed to accept this analysis in *State Department of Natural Resources v. Arctic Slope Regional Corp.*, 834 P.2d 134 (Alaska 1991). See also *Ruckelshaus v. Monsanto Co.*, 467 U.S. 986 (1984), which held that the release of some private trade secrets

Because liability is possible, local governments that hold materials that might include trade secrets should proceed cautiously if a request is received to inspect or copy the materials under the public records law. The government might ask the business that owns the materials whether it would object to release of the information. If it does, the safest course would be to require that the party requesting the materials bring suit to inspect them under the public records law, then seek to join the owners as defendants and let the owner fight the issue out with the plaintiff.

---

by the federal government would constitute a taking when the government had assured the private owners of confidentiality when the information was disclosed to the government.

Appendix 11A—Statute

G.S. 132-1.2

§ 132-1.2. Confidential information.

Nothing in this Chapter shall be construed to require or authorize a public agency or its subdivision to disclose any information that:

(1) Meets all of the following conditions:

a. Constitutes a "trade secret" as defined in G.S. 66-152(3).

b. Is the property of a private "person" as defined in G.S. 66-152(2).

c. Is disclosed or furnished to the public agency in connection with the owner's performance of a public contract or in connection with a bid, application, proposal, industrial development project, or in compliance with laws, regulations, rules, or ordinances of the United States, the State, or political subdivisions of the State.

d. Is designated or indicated as "confidential" or as a "trade secret" at the time of its initial disclosure to the public agency.

Chapter 12—Economic Development Records

Statutory Summary

Section 132-6(d) of the North Carolina General Statutes[1] [hereinafter G.S.] permits a local government or other public agency to deny public inspection of records related to specific economic development projects. (The exception does not cover records related to general economic development policies and practices, which therefore must be made available for public inspection.) Once there has been a public announcement of a company's commitment to a specific project, or a final decision by the company not to undertake the project, the government must release any records not otherwise made confidential by law. If the business has committed to North Carolina but not to a specific location in the state, the

1. The statutes summarized in these two paragraphs are set out in appendix 12A at the end of this chapter.

state must release its records, but local governments may continue to withhold theirs until the company has selected a specific location.

G.S. 132-1.11 contains two other requirements related to economic development, but each mandates the creation of new documents rather than establishing new exceptions to the right of access. Subsection (a) requires any local government that has used a cost-benefit analysis or similar assessment of incentives offered for a specific project to prepare a detailed description of its assumptions and methodologies. This description may be withheld from public inspection along with other records associated with that project, but it must be released when those other records are released. Subsection (b) requires a local government that engages in economic development to prepare and make available to interested businesses a statement describing when public records may be withheld from public inspection, what sorts of records may be withheld, and what steps are taken to maintain the confidentiality of records.

Discussion

G.S. 132-6(d)—The Authorization to Deny Public Access

Economic development activities involving private companies require secrecy. Companies that are locating or expanding commonly demand confidentiality as a condition of considering a community as a location for a particular facility. Companies often hire consultants to help identify and narrow the list of possible communities in which to invest, and in many instances the consultants' discussions with local economic development officials never reveal the company's name. Even after the identity of the company has become known to local officials, the company will often continue to demand that its identity and plans remain confidential. If either becomes public before the company would prefer, the company may well drop the community from its search.

There is an additional pressure for secrecy—from the local government itself. It is engaged in negotiation with the company. As in any negotiation, the local government strengthens its negotiating ability if it can shield its position from the other party, in this case the company.

The North Carolina General Assembly has recognized these practical needs for confidentiality, not only in the public records law but also in the open meetings statute.[2] As noted above in the summary, the public records laws permit economic development officials to shield some economic development records from public access, thus allowing secrecy to continue until a local government and a company have reached tentative agreement on an incentive package and the company has agreed to undertake the project or until the company has decided to go elsewhere.

The Kinds of Records

The statute permits a local government or other public agency to deny access to "records relating to the proposed expansion or location of specific business or industrial projects

---

2. N.C. Gen. Stat. [hereinafter G.S.] § 143-318.11(a)(4).

. . . so long as their inspection, examination or copying would frustrate the purpose for which such public records were created." The kinds of records that might relate to a specific business or industrial project include correspondence with a company or its agents or associates; information from the company about its business practices and procedures, its business plans, and its financial condition; internal government memoranda about the project; appraisals of land or buildings that might be conveyed to the company; draft contracts with the company; and the minutes or general accounts of closed sessions held concerning the project. They would also include any cost-benefit or other assessment made about potential incentives as well as the description of methodologies and assumptions prepared in accordance with G.S. 132-1.11(a).

It should be noted that it is possible that some of the material provided by the company qualifies as trade secrets. Assuming the company has made the required declaration that the material is a trade secret or confidential, as discussed in chapter 11, this material may not be released along with other documents associated with a project once a final determination has been made on whether or not to build the project.

The Kinds of Projects

The statute applies to records relating to "the proposed expansion or location of specific business or industrial projects." This statutory language applies to the overwhelming majority of projects for which a local government might be considering offering incentives. But there are a few kinds of projects that do not fit the language well, and therefore the statute might not apply to records about such projects.

Retention of a Company

Suppose a manufacturing company approaches the county economic development director and discloses that it is going to close one of its two facilities, one of which is located within the county. The company then asks what incentives the county might offer to keep the local facility open. Are any records related to this request—materials from the company, interoffice memoranda within the agency, draft incentive proposals, and the like—within the exception to public access set out in G.S. 132-6(d)?

The needs for confidentiality that underlie the authorization to deny public access apply to this situation. One reason companies demand confidentiality when they investigate whether to locate a *new* facility within a community is that they may be planning to close an existing facility elsewhere and do not want it known in that community or by the employees of that facility. Whatever we may think of this as a matter of company policy, it is often company practice, and the public records law recognizes the realities of business practice. If a company approaches a local government and reveals that it may be closing a facility within the community, this information may not be publicly known and the company may expect local officials to respect the company's request for continued confidentiality.

The other reason for the public records exception is the local government's own need for confidentiality as it prepares for negotiations with the company. That need is as strong when the government is seeking to retain a facility as when it is seeking to attract one. In sum, the policy justifications for the exception to the right of public access generally still apply when the issue is what measures might be taken to retain a business facility.

Even so, is the statutory language itself broad enough to support denying public access to any records generated because of the possible closing? The statute permits denying public access to records relating to "the proposed expansion or location of specific business or industrial projects." It might be thought hard to characterize a plant closing as an "expansion or location" or as a "project." From the company's standpoint, however, a closing in one location often entails expansion in another location, and so the overall project might fit within the statutory language. Given the policy considerations set out above, a local government is probably justified in denying access to records associated with a facility closing unless a court reaches a contrary conclusion.

Governmental Facilities

Does the statute reach efforts by a local government to attract facilities of another government, such as a state prison? Here the argument in favor of applying the statute to such projects is considerably weaker. The state simply does not enjoy the same expectations of confidentiality about its process for locating a prison that a company does for its process for locating a manufacturing plant. The state facility has been authorized through a very public budget process, and the North Carolina public records law contains no shield denying public access to state documents related to locating a new facility. Therefore, the facility owner will not be demanding confidentiality when a local government is seeking to attract a governmental facility.

Admittedly a local government seeking a governmental facility may need to bargain with the government placing the facility and thus may wish for confidentiality in developing its bargaining position, but that need alone is probably inadequate to support application of the exception to such a project. After all, the statute speaks of location of "business or industrial projects," and a state facility is neither a business nor an industry in common parlance. For these reasons it is unlikely that the statutory language can be stretched to include a facility of some other government.

Eventual Release of the Records

G.S. 132-6(d) does not create a permanent exception to the right of public access. Rather, a local government may deny public access only so long as is necessary to avoid "frustrat[ing] the purpose for which such public records were created." The statute goes on to elaborate on when that point is conclusively presumed to have been reached: either once a commitment by the business to proceed with the project has been announced, or once the business has made a final decision not to proceed and has communicated that decision to the government or agency involved in the project. Once either point is reached, the associated records are to be available for disclosure "as soon as practicable," but in any event within twenty-five days of the announcement or final negative decision.

Sometimes a business will announce a commitment to North Carolina but delay selection of a specific site within the state. This happened with the Dell facility that eventually located in Forsyth County: the company announced that it was coming to the Triad region of North Carolina but left open the possibility of locating within any of several counties within that region. When that happens, the statute requires that any state records that have been created about the project be released but permits the various local governments interested in the project to maintain the confidentiality of their records until the final site selection has occurred. (The statute also permits the state to maintain the confidentiality of its records related to a local government's efforts to attract the project.)

The Dormant Inquiry

Local economic development agencies routinely receive inquiries from companies about economic development opportunities and policies within their jurisdictions, and the companies making the inquiries frequently request confidentiality about the request. Often there is no follow-up to this initial inquiry, and the company is never heard from again. Even when there has been some follow-up, the company may not feel sufficiently engaged with the agency to notify it that it has decided to go elsewhere. When there has been a final decision by a company to locate an expansion elsewhere but no communication of that decision to a local government or other public agency, how is the local government to implement the requirement of releasing the records associated with that inquiry?

Sometimes the government will read or hear of the company making a location announcement in some other community and will recognize that the facility involved was the one that occasioned the company's inquiry. At that point the records should be opened to public access. More often, though, the government will not know enough about the company to ascertain what facility was involved or will not see or hear of the company's final decision. In such a case, the most sensible course for the local government or agency is to develop some kind of policy about how long inquiries will be considered active after the last contact from the company and then more or less automatically open the records of the inquiry once that period has elapsed. Economic development professionals are probably in the best position to judge what an appropriate period of time might be.

Negotiations after the Location Announcement

The statute appears to assume that a company will not make its location announcement until it has reached final agreement with the host local government on any incentive arrangement, and therefore there will be no need for further confidentiality about the project. It is certainly true that there is no longer any need for confidentiality to protect the company—it has, after all, made the location announcement—but that is often not in fact true for the local government. This is because even after the announcement, there are frequently further negotiations between the company and the relevant local government while the various details of any incentives arrangements are being worked out. Nevertheless, the statute does not appear to allow the local government to maintain any confidentiality for records it may generate as part of its side of the negotiation: once the basic locational decision is announced, all records associated with the project must be opened to public access. This suggests that local governments should seek as far as possible to make reality accord with the statutory assumption and not allow announcement of any locational decision until the details of any incentives agreement with a company have been finalized.[3]

---

3. The open meetings law, in G.S. 143-318.11(a)(4), requires that board action approving an incentive package take place in open session. Even if the formal announcement has not yet been made, so that other documents associated with the project might still be confidential, it seems unlikely that the law permits denying public access to the draft of a contract that was voted on and approved in open session.

Closed Session Minutes and General Accounts

The open meetings law permits a public body, such as a board of county commissioners, a city council, or an economic development commission, to hold closed sessions to consider "the location or expansion of industries or other businesses in the area served by the public body."[4] The minutes or general account of such a closed session may be sealed "so long as public inspection would frustrate the purpose of [the] closed session."[5] Once other records associated with an economic development project have been opened to public access, it would be difficult to argue that opening the minutes or general account of any closed sessions associated with the project would frustrate the purpose of the closed session, and therefore they should usually be unsealed at that point as well.

Confidentiality Agreements

Sometimes a company that is interested in locating within a community will ask the local government or governments it is negotiating with, and possibly the individual board members and officials involved, to sign agreements to maintain the confidentiality of all aspects of the project until the final decisions have been made. Although these agreements have generated some controversy,[6] they appear to be permissible within the existing state of the law.

First, with respect to the government or agency itself, it is simply agreeing by contract to maintain the confidentiality of records (and closed sessions under the open meetings law) that is permitted by North Carolina law. The confidentiality itself is clearly consistent with settled state policy and therefore there should be no impediment to a local government agreeing to do that which the law permits. Of course, the local government could not by such an agreement purport to impose greater confidentiality on records than is permitted by the existing statutes.

Second, with respect to individual board members or other officials, they are signing as individuals, and the law does not impose on them as individuals any duty of public disclosure.

G.S. 132-1.11(b)—Disclosure of Public Records Requirements

The statute requires a local government or other public agency that (1) proposes incentives, (2) negotiates incentives, or (3) accepts an application for incentives to disclose—apparently to the company involved—that any information received by the government or agency is

4. G.S. 143-318.11(a)(4).

5. G.S. 143-318.10(e). Minutes and general accounts of closed sessions generally are the subject of chapter 18, *infra*.

6. In 2007 a bill was introduced in the General Assembly that would have stated that the "confidentiality agreements involving specific economic development proposals that restrict the ability of elected officials acting in their official capacity to communicate with the public are contrary to public policy and do not apply to any elected official, or to any person who was an elected official at the time of signing the agreement." H1663, 1st ed., 2007 Sess. (N.C. 2007).

subject to the public records law. More specifically, the statute requires that the disclosure must "fully and accurately describe"

- when confidential information may be withheld from public disclosure,
- what qualifies as confidential information, and
- how the government or agency prevents disclosure of confidential information.

The apparent purpose of this subsection is to give notice, to companies that might share with the government or agency trade secrets or other information that might be exempt from public disclosure, of the boundaries of the relevant exceptions to public access and the procedures that the company must follow in order to take advantage of those exceptions. Most importantly, probably, the government or agency should give notice to the company of the need for the company to identify trade secrets as such when they are shared with the public entity. Otherwise, as noted *supra* in chapter 11, the trade secrets exception to the public records law will not be available.

Appendixes 12B and 12C at the end of this chapter include examples of two disclosure statements developed in response to this statutory requirement: a form letter developed by the State Department of Commerce and a statement developed by Union County, respectively. These statements are presented as examples, not models, to give local governments a sense of the sort of disclosure that is required.

G.S. 132-1.11(a)—Assumptions and Methodologies

Some local governments and other public agencies, when considering whether to offer incentives to an economic development project—and, if so, how much in the way of incentives—will make some sort of assessment of the likely return to the government from its investment in incentives, with the return measured by jobs created within the community and by additional government revenues generated because of the project. Sometimes this is a simple matter of accepting the company's promises about investment and jobs and comparing them to the dollar cost of the incentives. Other times, however, the government will seek to measure the multiplier effect of the company's investment—including likely investment and job creation by suppliers to the original project, likely creation of service jobs because of the wages paid to the holders of the new jobs, and likely increase in property and sales tax revenues because of these secondary consequences. These more elaborate assessments are then the basis for public decision making about incentives and public justification for those incentives.

G.S. 132-1.11 does not require public agencies to make such assessments, but if a government does engage in such a process, the statute requires that it prepare a detailed description of the assumptions it made and the methodologies it used to reach its conclusions. The apparent purpose of this requirement is to permit the public and other governmental officials to better monitor the decisions and decision-making process associated with offering economic development incentives.

Appendix 12A—Statutes

G.S. 132-6(d)

§ 132-6. Inspection and examination of records.

. . .

(d) Notwithstanding the provisions of subsections (a) and (b) of this section, public records relating to the proposed expansion or location of specific business or industrial projects may be withheld so long as their inspection, examination or copying would frustrate the purpose for which such public records were created; provided, however, that nothing herein shall be construed to permit the withholding of public records relating to general economic development policies or activities. Once the State, a local government, or the specific business has announced a commitment by the business to expand or locate a specific project in this State or a final decision not to do so and the business has communicated that commitment or decision to the State or local government agency involved with the project, the provisions of this subsection allowing public records to be withheld by the agency no longer apply. Once the provisions of this subsection no longer apply, the agency shall disclose as soon as practicable, and within 25 business days, public records requested for the announced project that are not otherwise made confidential by law. An announcement that a business or industrial project has committed to expand or locate in the State shall not require disclosure of local government records relating to the project if the business has not selected a specific location within the State for the project. Once a specific location for the project has been determined, local government records must be disclosed, upon request, in accordance with the provisions of this section. For purposes of this section, "local government records" include records maintained by the State that relate to a local government's efforts to attract the project.

G.S. 132-1.11

§ 132-1.11. Economic development incentives.

(a) Assumptions and Methodologies.—Subject to the provisions of this Chapter regarding confidential information and the withholding of public records relating to the proposed expansion or location of specific business or industrial projects when the release of those records would frustrate the purpose for which they were created, whenever a public agency or its subdivision performs a cost-benefit analysis or similar assessment with respect to economic development incentives offered to a specific business or industrial project, the agency or its subdivision must describe in detail the assumptions and methodologies used in completing the analysis or assessment. This description is a public record and is subject to all provisions of this Chapter and other law regarding public records.

(b) Disclosure of Public Records Requirements.—Whenever an agency or its subdivision first proposes, negotiates, or accepts an application for economic development incentives with respect to a specific industrial or business project, the agency or subdivision must disclose that any information obtained by the agency or subdivision is subject to laws regarding disclosure of public records. In addition, the agency or subdivision must fully and accurately describe the instances in which confidential information may be withheld from disclosure, the types of information that qualify as confidential information, and the methods for ensuring that confidential information is not disclosed.

Appendix 12B—State Disclosure Letter

Re: Important Information Describing the State of North Carolina's Public Records Laws and the Exclusive Methods to Be Used by Companies That Seek to Protect Trade Secrets and Qualifying Confidential Information.

Dear __________:

Thank you for your interest in North Carolina. As we begin to work together and share information about your project, I wanted to make you aware of some relevant information regarding public records and the protection of confidential information for economic development projects.

As a state agency, the Department of Commerce (the "Department") is subject to the North Carolina General Statutes relating to public records and confidential information. These statutes provide certain very specific protections for confidential materials. In particular, in the context of economic development projects, the Department is permitted to withhold public records relating to proposed expansion or location of businesses and projects in North Carolina so long as the release of these materials would "frustrate the purpose for which they were created." A copy of G.S. 132-6(d), which establishes this protection, is attached for your information and review, along with other sections of the General Statutes relating to public records, confidential information and economic development projects.

In light of these statutory provisions, the Department's policy is not to release public records relating to specific proposed economic development projects until such time as a final decision concerning the location has been made and the decision is announced (at which time the statutes require disclosure). At that point, if any part of the information that has been provided to the Department qualifies as tax information and/or a trade secret and has been properly identified as such at the time of delivery, that information may be retained as confidential by the Department under other statutory provisions. These are G.S. 132-1.2 (The Public Records Law) and G.S. 66-152 (The Trade Secrets Protection Act), copies of which are attached. Taxpayer information is protected from disclosure, except in limited specified circumstances; by G.S. 105-259 (the general confidentiality provisions governing taxpayer information). *"Trade secrets" are exempt from otherwise required disclosure if certain conditions are met. A "trade secret" is business or technical information that derives commercial value from not being generally known or readily ascertainable, and which is the subject of reasonable efforts to maintain its secrecy.*

In order to protect the confidentiality of trade secrets, tax information and other confidential business information, you and your client must:

- **Make all designations of confidential materials at the time documents are first submitted to the Department** (and on every occasion thereafter when those materials are resubmitted). This applies to written communications, in whatever form, including e-mails.

- **Clearly, prominently, and specifically designate in writing what information is "CONFIDENTIAL—TRADE SECRET".** Indiscriminate designations of information as "confidential," such as form language automatically inserted into e-mails or into the margins of documents will not be regarded as sufficient designations, i.e., the designations must embrace only specific confidential words, numbers, descriptions, etc., and not whole sentences or groups of sentences. A method of accomplishing this may be to provide both a "clean" version, and a version with qualifying confidential material redacted, at the time of submission.

Let me reiterate that all information regarding the project will be treated as confidential while the project is considering its site location. It will be produced in response to a public records request only after the project has publicly announced a final decision with respect to site selection (whether to proceed or not proceed). Thus, the only information the company or its representatives should designate in writing as "CONFIDENTIAL—TRADE SECRET" is (1) true individual taxpayer tax information or (2) information that (a) meets the test of a trade secret and (b) will continue to meet that test following the project's announcement. The procedures described in this letter are the only procedures by which materials that qualify as trade secrets may be withheld from public disclosure.

Our experience with other companies and projects indicates that very little information shared during the site selection and recruitment process is likely to justify confidential treatment following an announcement.

Under the Public Records Law, the Department is required to produce public records as soon as they become available, and no later than 25 business days following the date of request. If a public records request is received, the Department will examine the records that have been submitted to it. If the company or its representatives have specifically designated certain information as "CONFIDENTIAL—TRADE SECRET" we will respect that designation, provided that the Department determines that (1) the claim of confidentiality is credible and (2) it is not overly broad or indiscriminate.

In the unlikely event a challenge is brought by a member of the public contesting the designation of certain information as confidential, the company should be prepared to defend its designation at its own expense, given that the information necessary to establish trade secrecy is uniquely in its possession. In our experience, legal challenges to appropriate confidential designations are very rare.

On a final note, if your company seeks information on any of the state's targeted, performance-based incentive programs, please be aware that *only* state officials in charge of incentive programs can propose incentives under those programs and preliminary representations about state incentives when made by local developers or third parties cannot be relied upon and will not be honored by the State. Also, if your company chooses to seek incentives, please be aware that certain employment and financial information regarding the company will be required to be submitted.

Appendix 12C—Union County Disclosure Form

NOTICE OF COUNTY'S DUTY TO DISCLOSE PUBLIC RECORDS

I. General Duty to Disclose "Public Records"

Pursuant to N.C.G.S. § 132-1, Union County must allow inspection of "public records" and provide copies of the same, if requested, unless otherwise specifically provided by law. The term "public records" is broadly defined to include, among other things, all documents, papers, letters, maps, photographs, and all other documentary material, regardless of physical form or characteristics, made or received in connection with the transaction of public business. Consequently, if requested, Union County must allow public inspection and/or provide copies of all information relating to economic development within the County, including information provided to the County by participating businesses, unless disclosure is otherwise protected by law.

II. Protection of Information About "Proposed" Economic Development Projects

The County may lawfully deny access to public records relating to the proposed expansion or location of specific businesses or industrial projects so long as the inspection, examination, or copying of those records would frustrate the purpose for which they were created, in accordance with N.C.G.S. § 132-6(d). Public records may not be withheld under this subsection once the State, a local government, or the specific business has announced a commitment by the business to expand or locate a specific project in this State or a final decision not to do so, and the business has communicated that commitment or decision to the State or local government agency involved with the project. Once these events take place, the County must disclose, as soon as practicable, but in any event no later than 25 business days, all requested information about the announced project that is not otherwise "confidential."

In addition, N.C.G.S. § 143-318.10(e), authorizes the County to withhold the minutes or account of a closed session from public inspection so long as such inspection would frustrate the purpose of that session. One of the purposes for which the Board of County Commissions may hold a closed session is to discuss matters relating to the location or expansion of industries or other businesses in the area, including agreement on a tentative list of economic development incentives that it may offer in negotiations. See, § 143-318.11(a)(4). The act of approving the execution of an economic development contract or commitment or authorizing payment of economic development expenditures must, however, be made in open session. Following such approval or authorization, when disclosure of the minutes or account would no longer frustrate the purpose of the closed meeting, this protection no longer applies. Thus, the minutes may be released except to the extent that any information contained there remains subject to some other exception from North Carolina's Public Records Law.

III. Continued Protection of Information That Is Confidential or Otherwise Protected by Law

Possible grounds for continuing to deny public access to economic development information, even after the above protections no longer apply, include by way of illustration but not limitation, the following:

Trade Secrets

N.C.G.S. § 132-1.2 authorizes the County to deny public access to information that meets the following four conditions:

1. It constitutes a "trade secret" as defined in N.C.G.S. § 66-152(3) (see below);
2. It is the property of a private "person," defined in N.C.G.S. § 66-152(2) to include, among others, a corporation or any other legal or commercial entity;
3. It is disclosed or furnished to the public agency in connection with the owner's performance of a public contract or in connection with a bid, application, proposal, industrial development project, or in compliance with laws, regulations, rules, or ordinances of the United States, the State, or political subdivisions of the State; and
4. It is designated or indicated as "confidential" or as a "trade secret" at the time of its initial disclosure to the public agency. [Emphasis added.]

"Trade secret," as defined in N.C.G.S. § 66-152(3), means business or technical information, including but not limited to a formula, pattern, program, device, compilation of information, method, technique, or process that:

1. Derives independent actual or potential commercial value from not being generally known or readily ascertainable through independent development or reverse engineering by persons who can obtain economic value from its disclosure or use; and
2. Is the subject of efforts that are reasonable under the circumstances to maintain its secrecy.

Personal Identifying Information

Numbers or other information that can be used to access a person's financial resources, including the following, enjoy continued protection under N.C.G.S. § 132-1.10:

Social security numbers	Drivers license numbers
State identification card numbers	Passport numbers
Checking account numbers	Savings account numbers
Credit card numbers	Debit card numbers
Personal Identification Number (PIN)	Digital signatures
Biometric data	Fingerprints
Passwords	

Tax Information

N.C.G.S. § 132-1.1(b) protects from public disclosure state and local "tax information," defined as information from any source concerning the liability of a taxpayer for a tax including, among other things: information contained on a tax return, a tax report, or an application for a license for which a tax is imposed; information obtained through an audit of a taxpayer or by correspondence with a taxpayer; and information on whether a taxpayer has filed a tax return or a tax report. Similarly, N.C.G.S. § 160A-208.1 protects local tax records that contain information about a taxpayer's income or receipts.

Other Types of Information

State and Federal protections covering other types of information may also apply.

IV. Measures to Prevent Disclosure of Exempt Information

The County has a duty not to disclose legally protected information. Therefore, before responding to any public records request, the County will check to determine if any legal protections apply. With respect to trade secrets or other confidential business information, the County will notify a business of any request for information that the business has identified as "confidential" or as a "trade secret," so that the business may defend any claims or disputes arising from efforts of others to cause such information to be disclosed. Note, however, that the responsibility for identifying information that a business provides to the County as "confidential" or a "trade secret" rests with the business. If the County determines that information marked by a business as "confidential" or as a "trade secret" does not qualify for protection under N.C.G.S. § 132-1.2, or if the County is unable to make such determination, the County will notify the business of the request and of the date that the requested records will be released unless the business obtains a court order enjoining that disclosure. If the business fails to obtain the court order enjoining disclosure, the County will release the requested information on the date specified.

Chapter 13—Local Tax Records

PART 1—G.S. 153A-148.1 and G.S. 160A-208.1: Local Tax Information

Statutory Summary

Sections 153A-148.1 (relating to counties) and 160A-208.1 (relating to cities and towns) of the North Carolina General Statutes[1] [hereinafter G.S.] prohibit the release of information about a taxpayer's income or receipts" that appears in local tax records, the purpose being to protect taxpayer privacy.[2] The two statutes do not simply exclude this information from

1. The statutes are set out in appendix 13A at the end of this chapter.

2. Financial information of this sort is probably not within the constitutionally protected zone of privacy and thus a statute is necessary if there is to be any limit on public access. *Cf.* Booth Newspapers, Inc. v. Kent County Treasurer, 438 N.W.2d 317 (Mich. Ct. App. 1989) (holding that hotels' tax records that contain occupancy information cannot be withheld under the state public records law privacy exemption and specifically determining that there is no common law or constitutional right to privacy concerning that type of information). See also *Portland Adventist Medical Center v. Sheffield*, 735 P.2d 371 (Or. 1987), in which the court held that statutory provisions exempting property and income tax returns from public inspection did not permit the court to create a parallel exemption for information submitted to obtain a property tax exemption.

public access at the discretion of tax officials; rather, the statutes *prohibit* tax officials from releasing the information. If a local official or employee violates the statute and releases protected information, that person has committed a Class 1 misdemeanor; in addition to other punishment, the statute requires that the violator be dismissed from public office or employment and bars the person from holding any other public office or employment for five years after the violation.

Discussion

The Taxes Covered by These Sections

G.S. 153A-148.1 and G.S. 160A-208.1 prohibit the release of local tax records that contain information about a taxpayer's income or receipts. What taxes generate records with that kind of information?

Privilege License Taxes

If a city levies a license tax on the privilege of operating a business inside the city, pursuant to G.S. 160A-211, and measures the tax by gross receipts, license tax applications submitted to the city will either estimate or state the taxpayer's business receipts. G.S. 160A-208.1 prohibits the release of that information. Many cities, however, do not measure privilege license taxes by gross receipts; rather, they levy privilege license taxes at a flat rate, such as $100 per business. Even cities that use a gross receipts measure will tax some categories of businesses at a flat rate. Taxpayer information related to privilege license taxes levied at a flat rate or on some basis other than gross receipts does not include income or receipts information and thus is not covered by the statute.

Property Taxes

Two provisions for property tax relief—the homestead exclusion enacted by G.S. 105-277.1 and the homestead circuit breaker enacted by G.S. 105-277.1B—depend upon the income of the property owner, and for that reason the application for each of these includes income information. In addition, a county assessor may have income or receipts information from some taxpayers because the information is necessary for appraisal of the taxpayer's property. Commercial real estate, for example, is often appraised by capitalizing the income from the property, which obviously requires knowing what the income is. Therefore, G.S. 153A-148.1 covers some property tax records.[3]

Car Rental Taxes and Heavy Equipment Rental Taxes

G.S. 153A-156 and G.S. 160A-215.1 permit counties and cities, respectively, to levy taxes "on the gross receipts from the short-term lease or rental of vehicles at retail to the general

---

3. See also N.C. Gen. Stat. [hereinafter G.S.] § 105-289(e), which allows the state to share information with county assessors but closes the information to public inspection, making it specifically subject to G.S. 153A-148.1 and G.S. 160A-208.1; and G.S. 105-296(h), which closes to public inspection "[i]nventories, statements of assets and liabilities, or other information secured by the assessor . . . but not expressly required . . . to be shown on the abstract" for a particular business enterprise.

public," and G.S. 153A-156.1 and G.S. 160A-215.2 permit counties and cities, respectively, to levy taxes "on the gross receipts from the short-term lease or rental of heavy equipment." Because both these taxes are measured by gross receipts, G.S. 153A-148.1 and G.S. 160A-208.1 cover returns from companies paying the taxes.

Occupancy Taxes and Prepared Food Taxes

Many counties and cities levy occupancy taxes pursuant to local acts from the General Assembly, and a few counties levy prepared meals taxes pursuant to local acts. Occupancy taxes tax the letting of motel and hotel rooms and comparable short-term rentals, while prepared food taxes tax meals served in restaurants and other prepared foods, such as those at grocery delicatessen counters. Both taxes are measured by gross receipts, and therefore G.S. 153A-148.1 and G.S. 160A-208.1 cover returns from taxpayers for both taxes.

Cable Television Franchise Taxes

Until relatively recently, many cities and some counties franchised cable television companies and levied a franchise fee or franchise tax that was measured by gross receipts.[4] North Carolina law now permits such companies to seek a statewide franchise, however, and therefore very few, if any, cities or counties still have active franchises. To the extent that any such franchises are still in effect, the franchise tax returns are covered by G.S. 153A-148.1 and G.S. 160A-208.1.

Noncovered Taxes

Other local taxes are not measured by gross receipts, and a taxpayer would not provide tax officials with receipts or income information in conjunction with those taxes. Therefore, G.S. 153A-148.1 and G.S. 160A-208.1 do not cover records associated with these other taxes, which include motor vehicle taxes,[5] animal taxes,[6] deed transfer taxes,[7] and admission taxes.[8]

Other Gross Receipts Information

These two statutes do not establish a general prohibition on revealing information found in public records that discloses a person's or business's income or receipts; they apply only to such information that is found in local government tax records. Tax records are probably the public records most likely to include such information, but they are not the only ones. At least two other kinds of government-held records might include income or receipts

4. The authority for the tax was G.S. 153A-154 for counties and G.S. 160A-214 for cities.

5. G.S. 20-97. These taxes are levied at a flat rate on all vehicles within the taxing jurisdiction.

6. G.S. 153A-153 (for counties); G.S. 160A-212 (for cities). These taxes are levied at a flat rate (or occasionally at two flat rates, depending on the animal's gender).

7. Seven counties are authorized by local act to levy a tax on the transfer of land. *E.g.*, 1985 N.C. Sess. Laws ch. 525 (Dare County). These taxes are typically levied at a rate of 1 percent of the consideration paid for the property. In addition, G.S. 105-601 authorizes all counties to levy a land transfer tax at a maximum rate of 0.4 percent but requires voter approval before a county may do so; through 2008 no county had been successful at obtaining the necessary voter approval.

8. Greensboro is authorized to levy a flat per-ticket tax on events at the Greensboro Coliseum. 1989 N.C. Sess. Laws ch. 383.

information, and no statute expressly exempts these other kinds of records from public inspection and copying.

First, local governments sometimes require persons or businesses to provide income statements and other financial information as a condition of receiving a benefit from the government or participating in a government program. A housing authority, for example, might require income information from an applicant for public housing to determine whether the person qualifies for such housing. Or a city might operate a community development program that makes loans to local businesses for improving the older buildings in which they operate or to moderate-income homeowners for improving their homes. The loan application package would almost certainly require financial statements from any business or homeowner seeking a loan. Business financial statements might be exempted from public inspection as trade secrets,[9] but no statute exempts these kinds of individual financial statements from public inspection.[10]

Second, local governments sometimes lease space they own by using commercial leases that tie the amount of rent paid to the gross receipts of the lessee. A city operating an airport might, for example, enter into such a lease with airport concessionaires, or a coastal city might enter into such a lease for dock space at a city-owned marina. The lease is clearly public record, and a person familiar with the lease terms could, by using the government's accounting records, determine the gross receipts of the lessee. Here, too, no statute expressly exempts this kind of information from public inspection.[11]

Issues in Tax and Financial Information

The prohibition in G.S. 153A-148.1 and G.S.160A-208.1 raises a number of compliance issues, which are discussed in this section.

Information the Statutes Prohibit Releasing

Do the statutes prohibit release of income or receipts information only or release of the entire tax record? In a city that measures privilege license taxes by gross receipts, a taxpayer typically submits an annual application for the license. This application sets out the taxpayer's gross business receipts for the preceding year and also includes a range of other information. At the least this other information includes the taxpayer's business name and location and the nature of the business. It might also include such information as whether the business is incorporated and, if so, the names of corporate officers; whether the business is part of a chain; and identifying information about the business owner, such as his or her home address and telephone number and his or her Social Security number or driver's license number.

---

9. G.S. 132-1.2(1) exempts from public inspection trade secrets received by governments in certain circumstances. Chapter 11 discusses that statute.

10. In *Forsberg v. Housing Authority*, 455 So. 2d 373 (Fla. 1984), the court held that financial records submitted to a housing authority by applicants for public housing were open to public inspection and copying. In *Doe v. Sears*, 263 S.E.2d 119 (Ga. 1980), the court held that information that revealed the income of public housing tenants whose rental accounts were in arrears was public record.

11. It might be that gross receipts submitted by a lessee are trade secrets, although "in connection with a lease" is not among the transactions listed in G.S. 132-1.2(1) as transactions within which trade secrets received by government are protected from public access. *See supra* chapter 11.

The two statutes begin by providing that local tax records containing information about a taxpayer's income or receipts are not public records. In addition, the two statutes that establish uniform administrative provisions for county and city occupancy taxes each specify that "[a] room occupancy tax return filed with the [county or city] finance officer is not a public record and may not be disclosed except in accordance with G.S. 153A-148.1 or G.S. 160A-208.1."[12] Therefore, there is not automatic right of access to any portion of these records. But the inquiry does not end there. The two statutes—G.S. 153A-148.1 and G.S. 160A-208.1—do not prohibit disclosure of the "tax records." Rather, they prohibit disclosure any "information about the amount of a taxpayer's income or receipts." The result is that while there is no *right* of public access to any portion of the tax record, the prohibition on release applies only to that portion that discloses a taxpayer's income or receipts. The government is free to release the other portions of the tax records if it wishes to do so.

Sharing Information with Other Governments

May a local tax office with records that disclose the income or receipts of a taxpayer share that information with other government agencies, especially with the state Department of Revenue or the tax offices of other local governments? For example, if a city tax office administering an occupancy tax learns the gross receipts of a local motel, may it share that information with the county assessor, who might use the information in appraising the motel? The answer differs between the two statutes, but even under the county statute such sharing is limited. G.S. 153A-148.1 and G.S. 160A-208.1 each contain a number of exceptions to their prohibition on release of income or receipts information, but the lists are different. The city statute's exceptions do not include sharing the information with the Department of Revenue or with other local governments. The county statute's exceptions, however, permit sharing with regional public transportation authorities, regional transportation authorities, and the state Department of Revenue. Furthermore, G.S. 105-259, the state tax confidentiality statute, and G.S. 105-289(e), which sets out the Department of Revenue's responsibilities in the property tax system, specifically permit the Department of Revenue to share some tax information with local tax officials.[13] The differences among the various statutes are telling and lead to these conclusions:[14]

- A county tax office may share income or receipts information with (1) a regional public transportation authority, (2) a regional transportation authority, or (3) the state Department of Revenue but no other governments.
- A city tax office may not share income or receipts information with any other government.

---

12. G.S. 153A-155(d); G.S. 160A-215(d).

13. The authorizations to share information found in G.S. 105-259 are set out and discussed *infra* in part 2 of this chapter. G.S. 105-289(e) permits the department to provide a wide variety of information to local tax officials.

14. In *Fayette County v. Martin*, 130 S.W.2d 838 (Ky. 1939), *overruled in part on other grounds by* City of St. Matthews v. Voice of St. Matthews, Inc., 519 S.W.2d 811 (Ky. 1974), a Kentucky statute permitted the State Tax Commission to share information with cities but did not mention counties. The court held that therefore the commission could not share such information with a county.

It should be noted that these conclusions indicate that a county or city tax office may not share occupancy tax returns from specific businesses with the tourism development authority to which the tax proceeds are remitted; sharing with such an authority is not included in the lists discussed above.

The Amount of Taxes on Posted Licenses

Typically, a local privilege license ordinance requires that the license itself be posted in a public place within the business and that this license set out the amount of the tax.[15] When the tax is measured by gross receipts, however, including the amount of the tax on the license and then requiring that the license be posted at a public location on the business's premises appears to violate the prohibition in G.S. 160A-208.1.[16] The license itself, after all, is normally the receipt for payment of the tax and thus qualifies as a tax record. Armed with the amount of the tax and knowledge of the city's tax rate, any citizen could easily estimate the amount of gross receipts reported by the business. Therefore, it would be prudent for a city that measures privilege license taxes by gross receipts to delete the amount of tax paid from the posted license.[17]

This conclusion—that the statute covers records that indirectly reveal a taxpayer's income or receipts—is bolstered by a 2008 addition to the list of permitted disclosures in each statute. For properties classified under the homestead circuit breaker program established by G.S. 105-277.1B, the 2008 addition specifically allows a tax office to include on a property tax receipt the amount of taxes due and the amount of taxes deferred. Such a receipt does not show the property owner's income, but that income can be roughly calculated by the amount of taxes that are deferred. If the receipt were not listed in the statutes, apparently it would not be a public record.[18]

---

15. These requirements are part of the School of Government's model privilege license tax ordinance, which has been widely adopted by local governments. The posting requirement is in § 27, while the requirement that the license set out the amount of the tax is in § 17. The model ordinance is found in appendix A of William A. Campbell, North Carolina City and County Privilege License Taxes (UNC Institute of Government, 5th ed. 2000).

16. Counties are not authorized to levy privilege license taxes on a gross receipts basis, and so this is an issue solely for cities and towns.

17. The Kentucky case of *Hardin County Schools v. Foster*, 40 S.W.3d 865 (Ky. 2001), reinforces the suggestion that governments should be cautious in releasing otherwise-public records if doing so could lead to the inadvertent release of confidential records or information. In ordering a school to release certain information about student disciplinary cases, the court directed it to "redact . . . information that would reasonably lead to identification of the student" involved. *Id.* at 869.

18. The statutes do not include a comparable exception for tax records that would reveal that an owner participates in the homestead exclusion program established by G.S. 105-277.1. For example, the basic property record might show the appraised value for the property and then the tax assessed, which would be one-half the expected amount because of the exclusion. Therefore, someone reading the record could conclude that the owner's income was less than the current eligibility limit. The reader would not know, however, how much less than the limit the income was. Perhaps, because the record would only show a cap on the owner's income and not the specific income, the statute does not apply and the record would be open to public access. After all, if the record was removed from public access, a person looking for it could also conclude that the owner was participating in the program.

Budget Information

A potential conflict exists between the prohibitions in G.S. 153A-148.1 and G.S. 160A-208.1 and the common annual financial reporting practices undertaken by local governments pursuant to G.S. 159-34. One of the required schedules in a local government's financial statements compares the government's actual revenues and expenditures with the amounts of revenues and expenditures shown in the adopted budget ordinance. Some local governments list actual revenues in sufficient detail that the proceeds of some of the gross receipts taxes listed earlier in this chapter are set out separately. If, for example, a city had only a single car rental agency, setting out the amount the city received from the car rental tax would indirectly disclose the gross receipts of that agency within the city. While it might be argued that the annual financial report is not a tax record, given the serious consequences of violating G.S. 160A-208.1 or G.S. 153A-148.1 it would be prudent for a city or county to group its various gross receipts tax revenues in such a way that the amount of tax paid by a single business is not separately stated.

PART 2—G.S. 105-259: State Tax Information Shared with Local Governments

G.S. 105-259[19] is the state tax privacy statute and generally prohibits "[a]n officer, an employee, or an agent of the State" from disclosing "tax information." The term "tax information" is considerably broader than the income and receipts information covered by the county and city tax privacy statutes discussed *supra* in part 1 of this chapter. It is defined to include the following:

1. Information contained on a tax return, a tax report, or an application for a license for which a tax is imposed
2. Information obtained through an audit of a taxpayer or by correspondence with a taxpayer
3. Information on whether a taxpayer has filed a tax return or a tax report
4. A list or other compilation of the names, addresses, Social Security numbers, or similar information concerning taxpayers[20]

The statute also includes a long list of exceptions—persons or entities to which a state official, employee, or agent may release confidential tax information.[21] Several of these exceptions permit release of specific information to various local government entities

19. The statute is set out in appendix 13A at the end of this chapter.

20. G.S. 105-259(a)(2).

21. Other statutes sometimes permit or direct release of the information as well. G.S. 105A-15 permits the department to share tax information with claimant agencies under the debt set-off program, and then restricts the recipients' use of the information.

- to provide a government agency with a list of taxpayers who have paid specific state privilege license taxes [subsection (b)(4)];
- to give information about a county's sales and use tax to the chair of the board of county commissioners [subsection (b)(5)];
- to furnish a city's finance officials with a list of electric utility taxable gross receipts and piped natural gas tax revenues attributable to that city [subsection (b)(5b)];
- to provide certain information about car rental agencies to regional public transportation authorities or regional transportation authorities [subsection (b)(5c)];
- to provide to a city or county information on retailers who might be subject to the city's or county's occupancy tax or prepared food tax [subsection (b)(5d)];
- to furnish to a designated county or city official a list of claimants who have received a refund of the county's sales and use tax [subsection (b)(6a)].

If a local government receives information from the state Department of Revenue pursuant to one of the paragraphs in G.S. 105-259(b), is that information open to the public or is the local government under some sort of direction to maintain the information's confidentiality?

The local government should almost certainly maintain that confidentiality, although the basis for that advice is somewhat round about. G.S. 105-259 itself does not contain any prohibition on release of tax information by a local government that has received the information from the Department of Revenue. There are almost fifty separate paragraphs permitting the department to release tax information, but most of the releases are to other departments and agencies of state government. Those other departments and agencies are subject to the basic prohibitions of G.S. 105-259, which apply throughout state government and not just to the Department of Revenue. But that doesn't answer the question about information shared with local governments. For one of the authorizations for local government sharing—the last one on the list set out above—another statute specifically provides that the shared information is not public but rather is subject to G.S. 153A-148.1 or G.S. 160A-208.1.[22] But there is no comparable provision for the other authorizations in the list. The answer to the question appears to be found in a subsection in G.S. 132-1.1. Subsection (b) of that section provides that "[t]ax information may not be disclosed except as provided in G.S. 105-259. As used in this subsection, 'tax information' has the same meaning as in G.S. 105-259." Although it is possible to understand this subsection as nothing more than a statutory cross-reference,[23] given the clear state policy of confidentiality for tax records and information it should be instead understood as an extension of the prohibitions of G.S. 105-259 to any governmental entity that receives tax information from the Department of Revenue pursuant to that statute.

---

22. *See* G.S. 105-164.14(f).

23. There are other subsections in G.S. 132-1.1 that appear to be cross-references rather than substantive provisions; for example, subsection (d), which appears to duplicate G.S. 15C-8(j), and subsection (e), which appears to duplicate G.S. 90-113.74.

Appendix 13A—Statutes

G.S. 153A-148.1 and G.S. 160A-208.1

§ 153A-148.1. Disclosure of certain information prohibited.

(a) Disclosure Prohibited.—Notwithstanding Chapter 132 of the General Statutes or any other law regarding access to public records, local tax records that contain information about a taxpayer's income or receipts are not public records. A current or former officer, employee, or agent of a county who in the course of service to or employment by the county has access to information about the amount of a taxpayer's income or receipts may not disclose the information to any other person unless the disclosure is made for one of the following purposes:

(1) To comply with a court order or a law.

(2) Review by the Attorney General or a representative of the Attorney General.

(3) To sort, process, or deliver tax information on behalf of the county, as necessary to administer a tax.

(4) To exchange information with a regional public transportation authority or a regional transportation authority created pursuant to Article 26 or Article 27 of Chapter 160A of the General Statutes, when the information is needed to fulfill a duty imposed on the authority or on the county.

(5) To exchange information with the Department of Revenue, when the information is needed to fulfill a duty imposed on the Department or on the county.

(6) To include on a property tax receipt the amount of property taxes due and the amount of property taxes deferred on a residence classified under G.S. 105-277.1B, the property tax homestead circuit breaker.

(b) Punishment.—A person who violates this section is guilty of a Class 1 misdemeanor. If the person committing the violation is an officer or employee, that person shall be dismissed from public office or public employment and may not hold any public office or public employment in this State for five years after the violation.

§ 160A-208.1. Disclosure of certain information prohibited.

(a) Disclosure Prohibited.—Notwithstanding Chapter 132 of the General Statutes or any other law regarding access to public records, local tax records that contain information about a taxpayer's income or receipts are not public records. A current or former officer, employee, or agent of a city who in the course of service to or employment by the city has access to information about the amount of a taxpayer's income or receipts may not disclose the information to any other person unless the disclosure is made for one of the following purposes:

(1) To comply with a court order or a law.

(2) Review by the Attorney General or a representative of the Attorney General.

(3) To sort, process, or deliver tax information on behalf of the city, as necessary to administer a tax.

(4) To include on a property tax receipt the amount of property taxes due and the amount of property taxes deferred on a residence classified under G.S. 105-277.1B, the property tax homestead circuit breaker.

(b) Punishment.—A person who violates this section is guilty of a Class 1 misdemeanor. If the person committing the violation is an officer or employee, that person shall be dismissed from public office or public employment and may not hold any public office or public employment in this State for five years after the violation.

G.S. 132-1.1

§ 132-1.1. Confidential communications by legal counsel to public board or agency; State tax information; public enterprise billing information; Address Confidentiality Program information.

. . .

(b) State and Local Tax Information.—Tax information may not be disclosed except as provided in G.S. 105-259. As used in this subsection, "tax information" has the same meaning as in G.S. 105-259. Local tax records that contain information about a taxpayer's income or receipts may not be disclosed except as provided in G.S. 153A-148.1 and G.S. 160A-208.1.

G.S. 105-259

§ 105-259. Secrecy required of officials; penalty for violation.

(a) Definitions.—The following definitions apply in this section:

(1) Employee or officer.—The term includes a former employee, a former officer, and a current or former member of a State board or commission.

(2) Tax information.—Any information from any source concerning the liability of a taxpayer for a tax, as defined in G.S. 105-228.90. The term includes the following:

a. Information contained on a tax return, a tax report, or an application for a license for which a tax is imposed.

b. Information obtained through an audit of a taxpayer or by correspondence with a taxpayer.

c. Information on whether a taxpayer has filed a tax return or a tax report.

d. A list or other compilation of the names, addresses, social security numbers, or similar information concerning taxpayers.

The term does not include (i) statistics classified so that information about specific taxpayers cannot be identified, (ii) an annual report required to be filed under G.S. 55-16-22 or (iii) the amount of tax refunds paid to a governmental entity listed in G.S. 105-164.14(c) or to a State agency.

(b) Disclosure Prohibited.—An officer, an employee, or an agent of the State who has access to tax information in the course of service to or employment by the State may not disclose the information to any other person unless the disclosure is made for one of the following purposes:

. . .

(4) To provide a governmental agency or an officer of an organized association of taxpayers with a list of taxpayers who have paid a privilege license tax under Article 2 of this Chapter.

(5) To furnish to the chair of a board of county commissioners information on the county sales and use tax.

(5a) Reserved.

(5b) To furnish to the finance officials of a city a list of the utility taxable gross receipts and piped natural gas tax revenues attributable to the city under G.S. 105-116.1 and G.S. 105-187.44 or under former G.S. 105-116 and G.S. 105-120.

(5c) To provide the following information to a regional public transportation authority or a regional transportation authority created pursuant to Article 26 or Article 27 of Chapter 160A of the General Statutes on an annual basis, when the information is needed to enable the authority to administer its tax laws:

a. The name, address, and identification number of retailers who collect the tax on leased vehicles imposed by G.S. 105-187.5.

b. The name, address, and identification number of a retailer audited by the Department of Revenue regarding the tax on leased vehicles imposed by G.S. 105-187.5, when the Department determines that the audit results may be of interest to the authority.

(5d) To provide the following information to a county or city on an annual basis, when the county or city needs the information for the administration of its local prepared food and beverages tax, room occupancy tax, vehicle rental tax, or heavy equipment rental tax:

a. The name, address, and identification number of retailers who collect the sales and use taxes imposed under Article 5 of this Chapter and may be engaged in a business subject to one or more of these local taxes.

b. The name, address, and identification number of a retailer audited by the Department regarding the sales and use taxes imposed under Article 5 of this Chapter, when the Department determines that the audit results may be of interest to the county or city in the administration of one or more of these local taxes.

. . .

(6a) To furnish the county or city official designated under G.S. 105-164.14(f) a list of claimants that have received a refund of the county sales or use tax to the extent authorized in G.S. 105-164.14(f).

. . .

(c) Punishment.—A person who violates this section is guilty of a Class 1 misdemeanor. If the person committing the violation is an officer or employee, that person shall be dismissed from public office or public employment and may not hold any public office or public employment in this State for five years after the violation.

Chapter 14—Medical and Patient Records

The Effect of HIPAA

Federal regulations adopted pursuant to the Health Insurance Portability and Accountability Act of 1996 (HIPAA)—the so-called HIPAA Privacy Rule[1]—establish a national standard for use and disclosure of health information by health care providers.[2] They do not, however, automatically override the provisions of a state's public records law. The Privacy Rule defines "health information" as any information that "[r]elates to the past, present, or future physical or mental health or condition of an individual; the provision of health care to an individual; or the past, present, or future payment for the provision of health care to an individual."[3] In general 45 C.F.R. § 164.502 prohibits disclosure of health information except as permitted by the Privacy Rule; and the rule does not contain a general authorization to disclose health information to the public. A later section of the Privacy Rule, however, specifically permits disclosure of health information when it is required by state or federal law,[4] and both the federal government and at least two state appellate courts have

1. The Privacy Rule is found in 45 C.F.R. Parts 160 and 164, especially Part 164, Subpart E.
2. The Privacy Rule applies to health care providers that conduct certain standardized electronic communications, so an occasional health care provider is not covered by the rule.
3. 45 C.F.R. § 160.103 (2008).
4. 45 C.F.R. § 164.512(a) (2008).

indicated that public records laws may furnish the necessary requirement. In August 2004 the federal Department of Health and Human Services posted the following question and answer about the HIPAA Privacy Rule and state public records laws:

> State public records laws, also known as open records or freedom of information laws, all provide for certain public access to government records. How does the HIPAA Privacy Rule relate to these state laws?
>
> Answer:
>
> If a state agency is not a "covered entity", as that term is defined at 45 CFR 160.103, it is not required to comply with the HIPAA Privacy Rule and, thus, any disclosure of information by the state agency pursuant to its state public records law would not be subject to the Privacy Rule.
>
> If a state agency is a covered entity, however, the Privacy Rule applies to its disclosures of protected health information. The Privacy Rule permits a covered entity to use and disclose protected health information as required by other law, including state law. See 45 CFR 164.512(a). Thus, where a state public records law mandates that a covered entity disclose protected health information, the covered entity is permitted by the Privacy Rule to make the disclosure, provided the disclosure complies with and is limited to the relevant requirements of the public records law.
>
> However, where a state public records law only permits, and does not mandate, the disclosure of protected health information, or where exceptions or other qualifications apply to exempt the protected health information from the state law's disclosure requirement, such disclosures are not "required by law" and thus, would not fall within § 164.512(a) of the Privacy Rule. For example, if a state public records law includes an exemption that affords a state agency discretion not to disclose medical or other information where such disclosure would constitute a clearly unwarranted invasion of personal privacy, the disclosure of such records is not required by the public records law, and therefore is not permissible under § 164.512(a). In such cases, a covered entity only would be able to make the disclosure if permitted by another provision of the Privacy Rule.
>
> As an example of how the Privacy Rule would apply in the case where an exemption exists in a freedom of information law, see the December 2000 Privacy Rule preamble discussion regarding the relationship of the Privacy Rule with the federal Freedom of Information Act (64 FR 82482).[5]

As chapter 1 of this book makes plain, the fundamental rule of the North Carolina public records law is that all government records are open to the public unless a North Carolina statute provides otherwise. That rule clearly creates a situation within which, in the absence of a North Carolina statute exempting the information, a local government would

---

5. The question and answer may be found on the Internet at www.hhs.gov/hipaafaq/permitted/require/506.html (created Aug. 24, 2004; last updated Aug. 8, 2005).

be obliged to provide public access to health information, and therefore HIPAA's own terms permit the disclosure.

This basic point, that the HIPAA Privacy Rule does not prohibit public access to records required to be open by state law, has been recognized by at least two state appellate courts. In *State ex rel. Cincinnati Enquirer v. Daniels,*[6] the newspaper sought copies of a local health department's lead-contamination notices issued to owners of residential property in which there were children whose blood tests had indicated elevated lead levels. The health department refused to provide the notices, claiming that it was prohibited from doing so by the HIPAA Privacy Rule. The Ohio Supreme Court first held that the notices were not covered by the Privacy Rule, deciding that they did not include protected health information.[7] The court then went on, as an alternate holding, to conclude that even if the notice did contain such information, and even if the health department was a covered entity, the department was still required to release the notices because it was required to do so under Ohio law. Ohio's public records law is like North Carolina's in that all government records are considered public unless a statute makes them not public, and there was no state statute that denied public access to these notices.

The second case is *Abbott v. Texas Department of Mental Health & Mental Retardation*, decided by the Texas Court of Appeals.[8] The records in the case, sought by a reporter, involved allegations of patient abuse at various facilities operated by the department, and in this case as well the department argued that the HIPAA Privacy Rule prohibited it from releasing the records. When the Texas state attorney general issued an opinion concluding that the reporter was entitled to the records, the department brought an action challenging the attorney general's opinion. Although the Texas court also doubted that the records at issue included protected health information, it assumed that they did for purposes of the appeal and then reached the same conclusion as the Ohio court, citing both that court and the posted question and answer set out at the beginning of this chapter. Again, the Texas public records law is like the North Carolina statute, making all records public unless a statute specifically exempts them.

Several North Carolina statutes do, however, exclude from public access health care information held by a number of different sorts of health care providers. To the extent that these statutes exclude records from public access, the health care providers subject to them are bound by the confidentiality provisions of the Privacy Rule. But to the extent that these statutes do not exclude records from public access, a health care provider must make them available to the public, if requested, and the Privacy Rule's own terms permit disclosure. Therefore, it is necessary to review these North Carolina statutes and compare their treatment of health information with that of the HIPAA Privacy Rule.

It must be noted that this chapter does not attempt a complete review of issues involving the confidentiality of medical records under state and federal law. Rather, it primarily

6. 844 N.E.2d 1181 (Ohio 2006).

7. There was only one sentence in the notice that made any reference to health information: "This unit has been reported to our department as the residence of a child whose blood test indicates an elevated lead level." *Id.* at 1185.

8. 212 S.W.3d 648 (Tex. App. 2006).

focuses on the availability of these records to the public under North Carolina's public records statutes.

Statutory Summary

There are five principal North Carolina statutes that exclude health information from public access, and a sixth that is not as comprehensive yet still deserves specific mention.[9] These statutes, and several more specialized statutes that are not discussed in this chapter,[10] evidence a consistent state legislative policy to exclude personal medical information from public access under the public records law. This body of statutes recognizes the intense privacy within which many people cloak personal medical information; it also probably reflects a legislative desire to encourage frankness between medical practitioners and their patients.[11] The five principal statutes discussed in this chapter approach the issue of medical records from different perspectives but with quite comparable consequences.

Section 131E-97 of the North Carolina General Statutes [hereinafter G.S.] excludes from the public records law two categories of records "compiled and maintained by health care facilities in connection with the admission, treatment, and discharge of individual patients": (1) medical records; and (2) "[c]harges, accounts, credit histories, and other personal financial records."

G.S. 130A-45.8 applies to public health authorities and is identical to G.S. 131E-97.

G.S. 130A-12 applies to local public health departments (and to the state Department of Health and Human Services and Department of Environment and Natural Resources). It excludes from the public records law (1) any records that contain "privileged patient medical information," (2) any information protected under the HIPAA Privacy Rule, and (3) information about lead poisoning in children.

---

9. These six statutes are set out in appendix 14A at the end of this chapter. N.C. Gen. Stat. [hereinafter G.S.] § 8-53 is another statute of general applicability. It exempts from public access information acquired by a physician within the physician–patient privilege when the "information was necessary to enable [the physician] to prescribe for such patient as a physician, or to do any act for him as a surgeon." It is hard to see how this statute creates any exemption from public access beyond those created by the five principal statutes discussed in this chapter, and for that reason it will not be addressed further; it is set out in the appendix, however.

10. Representative examples of specialized statutes include G.S. 15B-8.1 (makes confidential medical information about crime victims who are seeking compensation from the state); G.S. 20-27 (closes to public inspection a medical report furnished by an applicant for a driver's license); G.S. 58-2-105 (exempts from the public records law all patient medical records held by the Department of Insurance); G.S. 90-270.15(e) (permits the North Carolina Psychology Board to withhold from public access the identity of patients who have received psychological services); G.S. 130A-374 (exempts from the public records law individual medical records held by the State Center for Health Statistics); and G.S. 143B-139.6 (exempts from the public records law all privileged patient medical records held by the Department of Health and Human Services).

11. In 1962 the North Carolina Supreme Court stated that the purpose of G.S. 8-53, *see supra* note 9, was "to induce the patient to make full disclosure that proper treatment may be given, to prevent public disclosure of socially stigmatized diseases, and in some instances to protect patients from self-incrimination." Sims v. Charlotte Liberty Mut. Ins. Co., 257 N.C. 32, 36, 125 S.E.2d 326, 329 (1962).

G.S. 122C-52(a) applies to any agency or facility subject to G.S. Chapter 122C (collectively, *Chapter 122C facilities*), which deals with mental health, developmental disabilities, and substance abuse services. It excludes from the public records law "confidential information acquired in attending or treating a client" of any such facility. "Confidential information" is defined in G.S. 122C-3(9) as "any information . . . relating to an individual served by a facility that was received in connection with the performance of any function of the facility."

G.S. 143-518 excludes from the public records law two categories of records compiled and maintained by "emergency medical service" providers (as well as the Department of Health and Human Services): (1) records associated with "dispatch, response, treatment, or transport of individual patients"; and (2) "[c]harges, accounts, credit histories, and other personal financial records" associated "with the admission, treatment, and discharge of individual patients."

In addition to these five statutes, G.S. 130A-143 directs that any information or records, publicly or privately maintained, "that identify a person who has AIDS virus infection or who has or may have a disease or condition required to be reported pursuant to the provisions of this Article shall be strictly confidential." The article in question concerns communicable diseases and conditions. The section sets out the circumstances under which release of the information or record is permitted.

Discussion

The Interplay of the Five Principal Statutes

Local governments obtain medical and other patient records in at least two contexts. First, governments compile and maintain medical information about their own employees and about applicants for employment; this information is clearly part of the employee's (or applicant's) personnel file and will not be further considered in this chapter.[12] Second, a few local government agencies provide various forms of health care directly to citizens: public hospitals, county and district health departments, local management entities and some Chapter 122C facilities, and emergency medical services agencies. This section discusses how the statutes summarized above govern access by the public, under the public records law, to records in those agencies that provide health care to citizens.

Health Care Facility Records: G.S. 131E-97

G.S. 131E-97 excludes from public access two categories of records held by health care facilities. (It should be noted, however, that the statute does not prohibit all release of these records but simply denies public access. Any *prohibition* on release arises from other sources.) The first category is "medical records compiled and maintained . . . in connection with the admission, treatment, and discharge" of patients. G.S. 131E-97 does not itself define "medical records," nor does any other section in G.S. Chapter 131E. This records statute, however, is part of G.S. Chapter 131E, Article 5, the Hospital Licensure Act, and the

12. See *supra* chapter 7 on personnel records.

state regulations adopted pursuant to that act do set out minimum standards for hospital inpatient medical records. A minimum medical record must contain the following:

1. Identification data (name, address, age, sex)
2. Date and time of admission and discharge
3. Medical history
4. Diagnostic and therapeutic orders
5. Reports of procedures, tests, and their results
6. Provisional or admitting diagnosis
7. Evidence of appropriate informed consent
8. Clinical observations
9. Record of medication and treatment administration
10. Progress notes of all disciplines
11. Conclusions at end of hospitalization or evaluation and treatment
12. All relevant diagnoses
13. Consultation reports
14. Surgical record
15. In case of death, autopsy findings, if performed[13]

Hospitals often employ social workers or psychologists who may interview and otherwise work with patients. Sometimes the records of this work include information about persons other than the patient—for example, the patient's immediate family. Are these medical records within the meaning of G.S. 131E-97? Almost certainly they are. The statute does not require that the records subject to its exclusion concern a patient but only that they have been compiled in connection with a patient's treatment, and records such as these clearly meet that test.

The second category of records covered by the statute is financial information: "[c]harges, accounts, credit histories, and other personal financial records compiled . . . in connection with the admission, treatment, and discharge" of patients. This financial information often may be entirely free of medical references.[14]

When the two categories of information are considered together, it is apparent that the statute shields from public access at least the same information that is defined as health information in the HIPAA Privacy Rule. Health care facilities are not required by North Carolina law to disclose that information to the public. Therefore, they must abide by the HIPAA Privacy Rule restrictions on disclosure.

G.S. 131E-97 applies to records held by "health care facilities," a phrase that the section does not define. As noted above, the section is part of Article 5 of Chapter 131E, the Hospital Licensure Act, but the article does not define the phrase either. Clearly, given its location in the statutes, the phrase includes public hospitals; but because the statute does not refer to

---

13. N.C. Admin. Code tit. 10A, ch. 13B, § .3906(b) (June 2008) [hereinafter N.C.A.C.].

14. To the extent that financial records do include references to a patient's ailments and the treatment for those ailments, they would appear to qualify as medical records.

hospitals or public hospitals (while the other sections in the same part of Article 5 do use those terms),[15] G.S. 131E-97 appears to apply to other kinds of facilities as well. One possible interpretation looks to the succeeding article of G.S. Chapter 131E, Article 6, which is entitled the Health Care Facility Licensure Act and applies to nursing homes, home care agencies, ambulatory surgical facilities, and nursing pools. There is not a separate confidentiality statute that applies to all the agencies subject to Article 6, even though those agencies generate many health care records.[16] Perhaps G.S. 131E-97 uses the term health care facility in order to cover those agencies subject to Article 6 as well as those subject to Article 5.

Public Health Authority Records: G.S. 130A-45.8

As noted in the statutory summary, G.S. 130A-45.8 is identical to G.S. 131E-97, and therefore what is said above about the kinds of records subject to the latter statute also applies to the former.

Public Health Medical Records: G.S. 130A-12

G.S. 130A-12 is more specific in its coverage than G.S. 131E-97 and G.S. 130A-45.8, applying to records held by local health departments and the two state departments that supervise health department operations. It exempts from the public records law records held by a local health department that fall into either of two categories: (1) records containing "privileged patient medical information" or (2) records containing information protected under 45 C.F.R. Parts 160 and 164 (the HIPAA Privacy Rule).[17] Unlike G.S. 131E-97, G.S. 130A-12 does not simply deny public access to the records; it prohibits disclosure unless "authorized or required by State or federal law."

The first category—privileged patient medical information—was historically the only information protected under the statute, and it suffered from some limitations and ambiguities. These issues have disappeared, however, with the addition of the second category. This category—health information as defined in the HIPAA Privacy Rule—surely includes any information that might be included in the first category, and thus the first category is currently irrelevant. The information that is closed to public access under the health department statute is the identical information that is specifically protected by the HIPAA Privacy Rule. As a result, there is no state law that requires that the information be made public, and therefore local health departments must abide by the HIPAA Privacy Rule restrictions on disclosure of that information.

---

15. G.S. 131E-97.1 applies to independent contractor records of various "hospitals"; G.S. 131E-97.2 applies to credentialing information held by various "hospitals"; G.S. 131E-97.3 applies to information about competitive health care activities of "hospitals"; and G.S. 131E-98 applies to "hospital" medical records of patients who are inmates in the custody of the state Department of Correction.

16. There are confidentiality provisions for the "personal and medical records" of nursing home patients, G.S. 131E-117(5), and home care clients, G.S. 131E-144.3(5), but no comparable provisions for patients or clients of ambulatory surgical facilities or nursing pools. Furthermore, it is not clear that the confidentiality provisions that do exist apply to financial records associated with a particular patient or client.

17. The statute also applies to information collected under the authority of G.S. Ch. 130A, Art. 5, Pt. 4, which concerns lead poisoning affecting children.

Although G.S. 130A-12 does not itself contain any provision establishing penalties for improperly releasing protected information, G.S. 130A-25(a) makes it a misdemeanor to violate any provision of G.S. Chapter 130A. Because G.S. 130A-12 prohibits release of protected information unless the release is authorized or required by law, an improper release appears to fall within the misdemeanor statute. In addition, G.S. 130A-18 permits the North Carolina secretary of health and human services to bring actions to enjoin violations of Chapter 130A, and that remedy would be available as well to end improper releases of health information.

Chapter 122C Facility Records: G.S. 122C-52

G.S. 122C-52 is part of a comprehensive legislative treatment of client confidentiality for all the kinds of agencies and facilities subject to G.S. Chapter 122C. G.S. 122C-52 and the several following sections deal with the status of client records under the public records law and also with access to records by the client and by other government agencies and treatment facilities. In general the statute provides that confidential information acquired by a facility in attending or treating a client is not a public record and may not be released except as provided in the subsequent sections. Several points should be made about this statute.

First, although recent fundamental changes to the state's mental health system have generally taken local management entities out of the business of directly providing services, many still provide client screening and thereby generate client records. In addition, a local management entity may provide direct services if the secretary of health and human services grants it a waiver, and a few such waivers have been given. Finally, some local management entities have contracted to have services provided by county governments or by interlocal agencies, public entities generally subject to the public records laws.

Second, G.S. 122C-52 extends to records of clients who are not receiving health care as normally understood. Chapter 122C facilities provide services not only to persons with mental health or substance abuse problems but also to persons who are developmentally disabled. This latter group of people are clearly clients of Chapter 122C facilities, and therefore facility records concerning them are within the scope of G.S. 122C-52 and private. Often, though, a facility's services for developmentally disabled persons cannot be accurately described as medical in nature.[18]

Third, the statute appears to extend to at least some financial information about a client. At the least, if the financial information is "acquired" by the facility from some outside individual or entity— for example, a credit report on an individual acquired from a credit reporting agency—it appears to fit within the statutory definition of confidential information.[19] If the facility generates the information itself, however, it might be argued that the

---

18. Examples of nonmedical services include vocational training, personal and community living skills development, and consultations with clients' employers.

19. G.S. 122C-55 establishes exceptions to the confidentiality rules of G.S. 122C-52. One of these is for "confidential information necessary to establish financial benefits [through a governmental agency] for a client." G.S. 122C-55(g). The exception tends to prove the rule that confidential information includes at least some financial information. In addition, the rules adopted by the Commission for Mental Health, Developmental Disabilities, and Substance Abuse Services that implement G.S. 122C-52 make clear that

information has not been acquired, given the statute's use of that verb. This distinction, between information acquired by a facility and information generated by the facility itself, presents a difficulty, however. A good bit of clearly medical information about a client—such as a psychiatrist's notes detailing his or her own diagnosis of a client and treatment plans for that client—is generated rather than received, and clearly the statute does not exclude the medical information on that account. Therefore, it appears that confidential information includes the full range of financial information held by a facility about individual clients. If that is the case, the confidential information protected by G.S. 122C-52 is at least as broad as the health information protected by the HIPAA Privacy Rule, and Chapter 122C facilities are not required by North Carolina law to disclose that information to the public. As a result, they must abide by the HIPAA Privacy Rule restrictions on disclosure.

Fourth, G.S. 122C-52 makes it a misdemeanor to release confidential information except as provided in that and the succeeding sections.

It might also be noted that Chapter 122C facilities are probably health care facilities within the meaning of G.S. 131E-97, and therefore that statute provides a second source of exemption for many of the records of Chapter 122C facilities.

Emergency Medical Services Records: G.S. 143-518

G.S. 143-518 provides that two categories of records compiled and maintained by emergency medical services (EMS) providers are excluded from public access. The first is "[m]edical records compiled and maintained . . . in connection with dispatch, response, treatment, or transport of individual patients." The second is "[c]harges, accounts, credit histories, and other personal financial records compiled and maintained . . . in connection with the admission, treatment, and discharge of individual patients." With respect to both sorts of records, the statue prohibits their release (with certain listed exceptions for the medical records).

The statute clearly covers EMS call reports (sometimes called trip tickets), which set out the patient's name, his or her medical condition, and the treatment, if any, administered by EMS personnel. It also covers the billing records associated with particular services. What is not explicitly clear from the statute itself is whether it covers the information in 911 tapes that record calls for EMS assistance. When G.S. 143-518 is read in the context of the entire EMS regulatory system, however, it becomes clear that the 911 tapes are normally covered as well and therefore are not open to public access.

G.S. 143-518 applies to records of "EMS providers." G.S. 143-507, the opening section of the Emergency Medical Services Act, of which G.S. 143-518 is a part, defines emergency medical services to include "all services rendered by emergency medical services personnel as defined in G.S. 131E-155(7)," and that section in turn defines EMS personnel to include "emergency medical dispatchers," who are "emergency telecommunicator[s] who [have] completed an educational program approved by the Department [of Health and Human Services] and [who have] been credentialed as an emergency medical dispatcher by the

---

some financial information is to be covered by the statute; N.C. Admin. Code tit. 10A, ch. 26B, § .0103(b)(3) (June 2008) defines confidential information to include reimbursement records.

Department." Through these interrelated definitions, it is clear that an emergency medical dispatcher is an EMS provider within the meaning of the Emergency Medical Services Act. Therefore, assuming that a 911 center is staffed with credentialed dispatchers, the call records associated with EMS services are covered by G.S. 143-518.[20]

As with the other statutes considered in this chapter, the North Carolina statute exempts from public access a set of records at least as broad as those protected by the HIPAA Privacy Rule, and therefore those EMS agencies that are covered entities under HIPAA[21] are not required by North Carolina law to disclose that information to the public. They must abide by the HIPAA Privacy Rule restrictions on disclosure.

Summary

When each of these five North Carolina statutes is analyzed, it is clear that each exempts from public access a range of records that includes almost all health information as defined by the HIPAA Privacy Rule. Therefore, in regard to that information, the health care providers subject to the statutes must abide by the disclosure limitations imposed by the Privacy Rule. No state law requires otherwise. The Privacy Rule is extraordinarily broad, however, and there occasionally may be stray pieces of information held by an agency subject to the above statutes that is covered by the rule but not by the state statutes. If that is the case, state law would require release of the information regardless of the provisions of the Privacy Rule.

Communicable Disease Information: G.S. 130A-143

G.S. Chapter 130A, Article 6, concerns communicable diseases and requires various persons who suspect that another person has a communicable disease to report that fact to the local health director. G.S. 130A-143, a part of Article 6, directs that any information or record, publicly or privately maintained, "that identif[ies] a person who has AIDS virus infection or who has or may have a disease or condition required to be reported pursuant to the provisions of this Article shall be strictly confidential." The section goes on to specify the circumstances under which release of the information or record is permitted.

G.S. 130A-134 directs the Commission for Public Health to establish a list of communicable diseases and conditions that must be reported pursuant to the article, and the commission has promulgated a rule listing more than seventy such diseases and conditions.[22] The important point for this discussion is that it is entirely possible that agencies that are not health care providers might have communicable disease information covered by G.S. 130A-143. An animal control agency, for example, might have records about animal bites that identify persons who might have been exposed to rabies; or an environmental health agency might have records about outbreaks of food-borne disease that are covered

---

20. It is highly likely that a 911 center's dispatchers are appropriately credentialed. State regulations require each county to establish an EMS system that includes a "communications system operated by public safety telecommunicators with training in the management of calls for medical assistance available 24 hours per day." 10A N.C.A.C. [13P .0201(a)(10)(B)] (Mar. 2009).

21. Not all EMS dispatchers are covered under HIPAA, but if they are credentialed their records are still subject to G.S. 143-518.

22. 10A N.C.A.C. 41A .0101 (June 2008).

by the section. When the statute does apply, the custodial agency must be sure to redact any information in the record that might identify an individual before making the record public.

Records That Do Not Fall within the Six Statutes

Occasionally a local government will receive or generate medical records that do not fall within the six statutes discussed above. Here are some random examples:

- A law enforcement agency might serve an involuntary commitment order and take the person to the hospital, and the department's incident report would reflect those facts.[23]
- A city might undertake lead paint inspections and include in the inspection reports information about the occupants of buildings found with lead paint, including medical information about them.
- A county's claims department might receive a claim from a citizen, seeking compensation that includes medical information about the claimant.

In none of these cases (or others that might be listed) is the agency creating or maintaining the record a health care facility, a local health department, a Chapter 122C facility, or an EMS provider. Therefore, the various state statutes discussed in this chapter do not extend to these records, and they would be open to public access under state law. Because of that fact, even if the agencies holding the records are covered entities under the HIPAA Privacy Rule, they are required by state law to make the records public if a request is received.[24]

---

23. The law enforcement agency's incident report should be distinguished from the magistrate's custody and transportation order for the same event; the latter is a court record and is confidential pursuant to G.S. 122C-207.

24. It may be that some health information held by a local government and not subject to the statutes discussed in this chapter is protected by the constitutional right of privacy, discussed more fully *supra* in chapter 4.

Appendix 14A—Statutes

G.S. 131E-97

§ 131E-97. Confidentiality of patient information.

(a) Medical records compiled and maintained by health care facilities in connection with the admission, treatment, and discharge of individual patients are not public records as defined by Chapter 132 of the General Statutes.

(b) Charges, accounts, credit histories, and other personal financial records compiled and maintained by health care facilities in connection with the admission, treatment, and discharge of individual patients are not public records as defined by Chapter 132 of the General Statutes.

G.S. 130A-45.8

§ 130A-45.8. Confidentiality of patient information.

(a) Medical records compiled and maintained by public health authorities in connection with the admission, treatment, and discharge of individual patients are not public records as defined by Chapter 132 of the General Statutes.

(b) Charges, accounts, credit histories, and other personal financial records compiled and maintained by public health authorities in connection with the admission, treatment, and discharge of individual patients are not public records as defined by Chapter 132 of the General Statutes.

G.S. 130A-12

§ 130A-12. Confidentiality of records.

All records containing privileged patient medical information, information protected under 45 Code of Federal Regulations Parts 160 and 164, and information collected under the authority of Part 4 of Article 5 of this Chapter that are in the possession of the Department of Health and Human Services, the Department of Environment and Natural Resources, or local health departments shall be confidential and shall not be public records pursuant to G.S. 132-1. Information contained in the records may be disclosed only when disclosure is authorized or required by State or federal law. Notwithstanding G.S. 8-53 or G.S. 130A-143, the information contained in the records may be disclosed for purposes of treatment, payment, or health care operations. For purposes of this section, the terms "treatment," "payment," and "health care operations" have the meanings given those terms in 45 Code of Federal Regulations § 164.501.

G.S. 122C-52

§ 122C-52. Right to confidentiality.

(a) Except as provided in G.S. 132-5, confidential information acquired in attending or treating a client is not a public record under Chapter 132 of the General Statutes.

(b) Except as authorized by G.S. 122C-53 through G.S. 122C-56, no individual having access to confidential information may disclose this information.

(c) Except as provided by G.S. 122C-53 through G.S. 122C-56, each client has the right that no confidential information acquired be disclosed by the facility.

(d) No provision of G.S. 122C-205 and G.S. 122C-53 through G.S. 122C-56 permitting disclosure of confidential information may apply to the records of a client when federal statutes or regulations applicable to that client prohibit the disclosure of this information.

(e) Except as required or permitted by law, disclosure of confidential information to someone not authorized to receive the information is a Class 3 misdemeanor and is punishable only by a fine, not to exceed five hundred dollars ($500.00).

G.S. 143-518

§ 143-518. Confidentiality of patient information.

(a) Medical records compiled and maintained by the Department, hospitals participating in the statewide trauma system, or EMS providers in connection with dispatch, response, treatment, or transport of individual patients or in connection with the statewide trauma system pursuant to Article 7 of Chapter 131E of the General Statutes may contain patient identifiable data which will allow linkage to other health care-based data systems for the purposes of quality management, peer review, and public health initiatives.

These medical records and data shall be strictly confidential and shall not be considered public records within the meaning of G.S. 132-1 and shall not be released or made public except under any of the following conditions:

(1) Release is made of specific medical or epidemiological information for statistical purposes in a way that no person can be identified.

(2) Release is made of all or part of the medical record with the written consent of the person or persons identified or their guardians.

(3) Release is made to health care personnel providing medical care to the patient.

(4) Release is made pursuant to a court order. Upon request of the person identified in the record, the record shall be reviewed in camera. In the trial, the trial judge may, during the taking of testimony concerning such information, exclude from the courtroom all persons except the officers of the court, the parties, and those engaged in the trial of the case.

(5) Release is made to a Medical Review Committee as defined in G.S. 131E-95, 90-21.22A, or 130A-45.7 or to a peer review committee as defined in G.S. 131E-108, 131E-155, 131E-162, 122C-30, or 131D-21.1.

(6) Release is made for use in a health research project under rules adopted by the North Carolina Medical Care Commission. The Commission shall adopt rules that allow release of information when an institutional review board, as defined by the Commission, has determined that the health research project:

a. Is of sufficient scientific importance to outweigh the intrusion into the privacy of the patient that would result from the disclosure;

b. Is impracticable without the use or disclosure of identifying health information;

c. Contains safeguards to protect the information from redisclosure;

d. Contains safeguards against identifying, directly or indirectly, any patient in any report of the research project; and

e. Contains procedures to remove or destroy at the earliest opportunity, consistent with the purposes of the project, information that would enable the patient to be identified, unless an institutional review board authorizes retention of identifying information for purposes of another research project.

(7) Release is made to a statewide data processor, as defined in Article 11A of Chapter 131E of the General Statutes, in which case the data is deemed to have been submitted as if it were required to have been submitted under that Article.

(8) Release is made pursuant to any other law.

(b) Charges, accounts, credit histories, and other personal financial records compiled and maintained by the Department or EMS providers in connection with the admission, treatment, and discharge of individual patients are strictly confidential and shall not be released.

G.S. 130A-143

§ 130A-143. Confidentiality of records.

All information and records, whether publicly or privately maintained, that identify a person who has AIDS virus infection or who has or may have a disease or condition required to be reported pursuant to the provisions of this Article shall be strictly confidential. This information shall not be released or made public except under the following circumstances:

(1) Release is made of specific medical or epidemiological information for statistical purposes in a way that no person can be identified;

(2) Release is made of all or part of the medical record with the written consent of the person or persons identified or their guardian;

(3) Release is made to health care personnel providing medical care to the patient;

(4) Release is necessary to protect the public health and is made as provided by the Commission in its rules regarding control measures for communicable diseases and conditions;

(5) Release is made pursuant to other provisions of this Article;

(6) Release is made pursuant to subpoena or court order. Upon request of the person identified in the record, the record shall be reviewed in camera. In the trial, the trial judge may, during the taking of testimony concerning such information, exclude from the courtroom all persons except the officers of the court, the parties and those engaged in the trial of the case;

(7) Release is made by the Department or a local health department to a court or a law enforcement official for the purpose of enforcing this Article or Article 22 of this Chapter, or investigating a terrorist incident using nuclear, biological, or chemical agents. A law enforcement official who receives the information shall not disclose it further, except (i) when necessary to enforce this Article or Article 22 of this Chapter, or when necessary to conduct an investigation of a terrorist incident using nuclear, biological, or chemical agents, or (ii) when the Department or a local health department seeks the assistance of the law enforcement official in preventing or controlling the spread of the disease or condition and expressly authorizes the disclosure as necessary for that purpose;

(8) Release is made by the Department or a local health department to another federal, state or local public health agency for the purpose of preventing or controlling the spread of a communicable disease or communicable condition;
(9) Release is made by the Department for bona fide research purposes. The Commission shall adopt rules providing for the use of the information for research purposes;
(10) Release is made pursuant to G.S. 130A-144(b); or
(11) Release is made pursuant to any other provisions of law that specifically authorize or require the release of information or records related to AIDS.

G.S. 8-53

§ 8–53. Communications between physician and patient.

No person, duly authorized to practice physic or surgery, shall be required to disclose any information which he may have acquired in attending a patient in a professional character, and which information was necessary to enable him to prescribe for such patient as a physician, or to do any act for him as a surgeon, and no such information shall be considered public records under G.S. 132-1. Confidential information obtained in medical records shall be furnished only on the authorization of the patient, or if deceased, the executor, administrator, or, in the case of unadministered estates, the next of kin. Any resident or presiding judge in the district, either at the trial or prior thereto, or the Industrial Commission pursuant to law may, subject to G.S. 8-53.6, compel disclosure if in his opinion disclosure is necessary to a proper administration of justice. If the case is in district court the judge shall be a district court judge, and if the case is in superior court the judge shall be a superior court judge.

Chapter 15—Social Security Numbers and Other Identifying Information

Statutory Summary

Congress created the Social Security retirement system in 1935, and the next year the Social Security Board, the predecessor of the Social Security Administration created to administer the retirement system, invented the Social Security number (SSN) to assist in that administration. The original purpose of the SSN, which is still applicable, was to allow the federal agency administering Social Security to track individuals' personal earnings and thereby compute the Social Security benefits they were entitled to. Early on, though, Congress recognized the universal nature of the SSN and began requiring use of the numbers in other government programs.[1] In addition, private sector actors and state and local

1. The Social Security Administration has published a Social Security Number Chronology, which details the various uses to which the legislative and executive branches of the federal government have put the numbers since the advent of the Social Security system in 1935. The chronology, which in March 2009 continued through 2005, is available at www.ssa.gov/history/ssn/ssnchron.html.

governments frequently have used—and continue to use—SSNs to help manage programs in a variety of ways. This expanding use of the SSN has caused concern for many Americans, although the cause of the concern has perhaps changed over time.

The initial concern was grounded in the fear that any number that became a universal identifier could allow much greater governmental control of citizens. One privacy organization summarized the matter this way:

> The issuance of a single, unique number to Americans raises the risk that the SSN will become a de jure or de facto national identifier. This risk is not new; it was voiced at the creation of the SSN and has since been raised repeatedly. The SSN was created in 1936 for the sole purpose of accurately recording [an] individual worker's contributions to the social security fund. The public and legislators were immediately suspicious and distrustful of this tracking system fearing that the SSN would quickly become a system containing vast amounts of personal information, such as race, religion and family history, that could be used by the government to track down and control the action of citizens. Public concern over the potential for abuse inherent in the SSN tracking system was so high, that in an effort to dispel public concern the first regulation issued by the Social Security Board declared that the SSN was for the exclusive use of the Social Security system.[2]

More recently, concern has shifted to the SSN's role in identity theft, where the potential abuse comes from other individuals rather than from government.[3]

Although—perhaps surprisingly—no single federal statute regulates the overall use of the SSN, both Congress and the North Carolina General Assembly have reacted to these public concerns by enacting a patchwork of statutes that regulate local (and other) governments' ability to collect, use, and release Social Security numbers. (In addition, the principal state statute discussed in this chapter also regulates governments' ability to release certain other information, characterized as "identifying information.") The earliest statute discussed, the federal Privacy Act of 1974, emerged from a congressional concern that the Social Security number was becoming more and more a universal identifier, a trend that Congress wanted to halt (even though it had contributed to the trend). As the title of the legislation indicated, the primary legislative focus was on individual privacy, particularly in relation to various governmental entities. The Senate committee that drafted the legislation wrote that the widespread use of the SSN was "one of the most serious manifestations of privacy concerns in the Nation. . . . [If the SSN becomes a universal identifier, it] may become a means of violating civil liberties by easing the way for intelligence and surveillance uses of the number for indexing or locating the person."[4] The most recent statute

---

2. Electronic Privacy Information Center, Social Security Numbers (last updated Aug. 19, 2008), http://epic.org/privacy/ssn.

3. "The widespread use of the SSN as an identifier and authenticator has lead [sic] to an increase in identity theft. According to the Privacy Rights Clearinghouse, identity theft now affects between 500,000 and 700,000 people annually. . . . Identity theft litigation also shows that the SSN is central to committing fraud." *Id.*

4. S. Rep. No. 93-1183 (1974), *reprinted in* 1974 U.S.C.C.A.N. 6916, 6943–44.

discussed, however—the 2005 North Carolina legislation that enacted Section 132-1.10 of the North Carolina General Statutes [hereinafter G.S.]—was motivated not so much by concerns about privacy as by concerns about identity theft.

The primary state statute considered in this chapter is G.S. 132-1.10, enacted, as noted just above, in 2005.[5] Its primary concern is the collection, use, and public release of Social Security numbers, as well as the release of other so-called identifying information. It prohibits collection of SSNs unless their collection is required or authorized by federal or state law or unless the collecting government determines that collection is imperative to its operations. It requires the collecting government to prepare a notice, to be given to individuals upon their request, setting out the use or uses it will make of the SSN, and it limits the government's use of the numbers to the use or uses set out in the notice. The statute provides that the number (as well as other identifying information) is not open to public access and establishes a number of other requirements intended to avoid unintentional public release of the number. It also includes special protections when a register of deeds posts records that include SSNs on the Internet.

The primary federal statute considered is Section 7 of the Privacy Act of 1974, codified as a note to 5 U.S.C. § 552a. (The federal statute's provisions are repeated, almost word for word, in the State Privacy Act, G.S. 143-64.60.)[6] This statute deals only with collection and use of SSNs. It prohibits any state or local government agency from denying any person a right, benefit, or privilege provided by law simply because that person refuses to disclose his or her SSN to the government agency, unless the disclosure is required by a federal statute or unless the agency was requiring disclosure of the number prior to January 1, 1975, under a statute or regulation adopted before that date. In addition, the federal Privacy Act provision requires any government agency that requests persons' SSNs to prepare a notice that (1) informs an individual whether disclosure is mandatory or voluntary, (2) gives the statutory authority for soliciting the number, and (3) sets out the uses that the agency will make of the number.

The other general federal statute considered here is 42 U.S.C. § 405(c)(2)(C)(viii), enacted in 1990. It provides that if state or local government officers or employees obtain SSNs pursuant to legislation enacted after October 1, 1990, those officers or employees may not release the numbers to the public, and the statute makes it a federal felony to do so. (A number of other federal and state statutes prohibit release of SSNs by specific agencies in specific circumstances. They are not addressed in this chapter.)

Discussion

Most of the statutory provisions discussed in this chapter deal with the collection and use of SSNs obtained from the persons who have been assigned the numbers. Some local governments, however, obtain SSNs by purchasing them from private suppliers, generally

---

5. This statute and others summarized in this section are set out in appendix 15A at the end of this chapter.

6. All but two of the wording differences are stylistic. The first substantive difference is that the federal statute regulates federal actions as well as state and local government actions, and obviously the state statute does not attempt that. The second substantive difference is noted infra in note 23.

known as information brokers. The statutory limitations on collection and use of the numbers do not apply to purchased SSNs. The statutory restrictions on public release of the numbers, however, do apply. Social Security numbers are not open to public access, regardless of how the government obtains them.

Why Do Governments Obtain Social Security Numbers?

In 2002 the federal General Accounting Office prepared a report on the use of SSNs by all levels of government.[7] The report summarized governmental use of the numbers in this way:

> When federal, state, and county government agencies administer programs that deliver services and benefits to the public, they rely extensively on the SSNs of those receiving the benefits and services. Because SSNs are unique identifiers and do not change, the numbers provide a convenient and efficient means of managing records. They are also particularly useful for data sharing and data matching because agencies can use them to check or compare their information quickly and accurately with that from other agencies. In so doing, these agencies can better ensure that they pay benefits or provide services only to eligible individuals and can more readily recover delinquent debts individuals may owe. . . . Moreover, all government departments or agencies use their employees' SSNs to varying extents to perform some of their responsibilities as employers, such as paying their employees and providing health and other insurance benefits.[8]

There are many contexts within which North Carolina local governments seek to obtain SSNs. Sometimes collecting the numbers is a requirement of federal or state law; often it is not, but the collecting government finds that it needs the numbers for some purpose or another, or at least finds them useful. Here is a somewhat haphazard, and undoubtedly incomplete, list of the various reasons and circumstances for and in which local governments obtain Social Security numbers. What these various uses have in common is that they either use the number as an identifier within the government or they allow the government to obtain information from or submit information to others about specific individuals.

Reporting Social Security Earnings and Withholdings

Governments, like all employers, must withhold Social Security taxes from their employees' wages and remit those taxes to the U.S. Department of the Treasury. At the end of the year employers transmit a copy of each employee's W-2 form to the Social Security Administration, which uses each employee's SSN to give the employee credit for his or her work—the original purpose of the Social Security number.

Compiling Various Income Tax Reports

Governments, again as employers, send a second copy of each employee's W-2 form to the North Carolina Department of Revenue, which uses the SSN to track an employee's

---

7. U.S. Gen. Accounting Office, Report No. GAO-02-352, Social Security Numbers: Government Benefits from SSN Use but Could Provide Better Safeguards (2002).

8. *Id.* at 3.

wages. (At the federal level, the Social Security Administration shares with the Internal Revenue Service the W-2 copy sent to it.) In addition, governments as businesses need Social Security numbers (or, alternatively, tax identification numbers) from individuals and companies with which they do business in order to file a variety of Form 1099s with the Internal Revenue Service.

Conducting Criminal Records Checks

Local governments sometimes wish to obtain criminal records checks of prospective or current employees or certain kinds of volunteers, and the individual's SSN is normally necessary to be sure the records check is about the appropriate person.

Conducting Credit Checks

Local governments sometimes wish to obtain credit histories for prospective employees, new utility customers, or persons who have made application for government loans. In addition, economic or community development agencies might include a credit check as part of their due diligence concerning persons or businesses seeking assistance or incentives. The individual's SSN is normally necessary to ensure that the correct history is obtained.

Conducting Drug Tests

Local governments require drug tests for certain classes of employees, and the laboratories that conduct the tests often use the person's SSN in the chain of custody process.

Using the Debt Setoff Program

Local governments often seek to collect moneys due them through the debt setoff program, which subtracts the moneys from state income tax refunds otherwise due the debtor and remits the moneys to the creditor government.[9] The government needs the debtor's SSN in order to use the debt setoff program.

Administering the Property Tax and Other Local Taxes

Certain property tax exclusions or classifications are available only to persons with household incomes below, or sometimes above, a certain level.[10] Tax assessors often seek to verify income information through the Department of Revenue and need the applicant's SSN in order to do so. In addition, tax collectors who wish to use garnishment or attachment to collect property and other taxes find doing so much easier if they have the taxpayer's SSN.[11]

---

9. The debt setoff program is authorized by N.C. Gen. Stat. [hereinafter G.S.] Ch. 105A.

10. For example, G.S. 105-277.1 establishes the property tax homestead exclusion, which is available only to persons whose annual income is below a specific threshold; G.S. 105-277.1B establishes the property tax homestead circuit breaker, which is available only to persons whose annual income is below a different specific threshold; and G.S. 105-277.3 establishes a special class of property for land that is used for agricultural or horticultural purposes and requires that the owner produce a stated minimum of annual gross income from the property.

11. G.S. 105-368(b) sets out the information required to be in the notice served by a tax collector when using attachment or garnishment, which may include the taxpayer's SSN.

Collecting from Insurance Companies

Agencies that can seek reimbursement from insurance companies—most often, various health care providers—use SSNs in making claims with the companies.

Identifying Individuals

Local governments have made use of SSNs as identifiers in a variety of settings—for employees, for students, for utility account customers, for patients or clients of human services agencies, for library patrons, and so on.

Collecting Social Security Numbers—Authority to Collect and to Require Disclosure

No Constitutional Right to Refuse Release of the Number

If a governmental agency is permitted by law to require a person to give to the agency the person's SSN, there is no constitutional right that supports the person's refusal to reveal the number. A few plaintiffs have argued that giving up the number somehow violates their right to freely exercise their religion, but the courts have uniformly rejected the argument.[12] At least one plaintiff also argued that revealing the number would violate his constitutional right of privacy, but again the court rejected the argument.[13] Therefore, the remainder of this section will discuss the statutory framework within which a North Carolina local government may either request or demand that a person give his or her SSN to the government.

G.S. 132-1.10: When Collection Is Authorized by Law or Imperative to the Government's Operation

G.S. 132-1.10(b)(1) sets out two circumstances under which a North Carolina local government may collect a Social Security number from the person whose number it is:

1. When the government is "authorized by law to do so"
2. When collection of the number is "imperative for the performance of [the government's] duties and responsibilities"

Here is a list of federal or state statutes or regulations that either authorize or require a local government to collect an SSN:

- *For Social Security Act administration.* 26 C.F.R. § 31.6011(b)-2 requires an individual to release his or her SSN to his or her employer.
- *For income tax reporting.* 26 U.S.C. § 6109 requires persons submitting statements or other documents to the Internal Revenue Service to include in the statement or other documents an identifying number for the person who is the subject of the statement. The statute specifies that the SSN is to be that identifying number for individuals.[14] The requirement applies to reports about employees and also to reports about various sorts of contractors.

---

12. *E.g.*, Bowen v. Roy, 476 U.S. 693 (1986); Mefford v. White, 770 N.E.2d 1251 (Ill. App. Ct. 2002).

13. North Carolina *ex rel.* Kasler v. Howard, 323 F. Supp. 2d 675 (W.D.N.C. 2003), *aff'd*, 78 Fed. App'x 231 (4th Cir. 2003).

14. See also 26 C.F.R. § 301.6109-1(a)(1)(ii)(A), which repeats the requirement that the SSN is to be the taxpayer identifying number used by an individual.

- *For other employee reporting.* 42 U.S.C. § 653a requires that each state establish a State Directory of New Hires and directs that each employer in that state furnish to the directory the name, address, and SSN of each newly hired employee. G.S. 110-129.2 implements this requirement in North Carolina law. In addition, federal regulations require all employers to prepare and retain for inspection by the federal government a Form I-9 (Employment Eligibility Verification Form) for each new employee,[15] and the required form includes the employee's SSN.[16]
- *For state tax reporting.* G.S. 105-163.7 requires each employer to send a copy of each employee's W-2 form to the Department of Revenue and to include on the form the employee's SSN.
- *For administering taxes and general public assistance.* 42 U.S.C. § 405(c)(2)(C)(i) permits state or local government agencies to require SSNs from individuals as part of "the administration of any tax, general public assistance, driver's license, or motor vehicle registration law."
- *For certain social services programs.* 42 U.S.C. § 1320b-7 requires a person applying for Temporary Assistance for Needy Families (TANF), Medicaid, or food stamps to provide his or her SSN to the social services agency administering the program.[17]
- *For child support enforcement.* 42 U.S.C. § 666(a) requires states to put into effect laws requiring use of a variety of procedures to improve the collection of child support payments. One requirement, found in 42 U.S.C. § 666(a)(13)(A), mandates that state and local governments collect an SSN from any applicant for a professional license, driver's license, occupational license, recreational license, or marriage license.
- *For school lunch programs.* 42 U.S.C. § 1758(d) requires that the application for a child to receive free or reduced price school lunches include the SSN of the child's parent or guardian or of some other appropriate adult member of the household.
- *For debt setoff.* G.S. 105A-3(c) requires that local agencies wishing to make claims under the debt setoff program "whenever possible obtain the . . . social security number" of any person who is likely to become a debtor under the program.
- *For collection of vital records.* G.S. 130A-101(g) requires that parents of a newborn child provide their SSNs to the person responsible for preparing and filing the child's birth certificate.[18] In addition, G.S. 51-8 and G.S. 51-8.2 require that applicants for a marriage license include their SSNs on the application. Finally, G.S. 130A-116 requires that North Carolina death certificates include "those items prescribed and specified on the standard certificate of death as prepared

15. 8 C.F.R. § 274a.2 (2008).

16. The I-9 form can be found at www.uscis.gov/files/form/i-9.pdf. It should be noted that the form's instructions state that "[p]roviding the Social Security Number is voluntary, except for employees hired by employers participating in the USCIS Electronic Employment Eligibility Verification Program (E-Verify.)"

17. 7 U.S.C. § 2025(e) requires the Secretary of Agriculture and appropriate state agencies to require SSNs from food stamp applicants.

18. 42 U.S.C. § 405(c)(2)(C)(ii) requires states to require parents to provide their SSNs as part of the process of issuing birth certificates.

by the federal agency responsible for national vital statistics," and the referenced standard death certificate includes the deceased's SSN.[19]

- *As part of law enforcement citations.* Some of the forms promulgated by the Administrative Office of the Courts include a space for an individual's SSN. A good example is the basic arrest warrant form, form AOC-CR-100. In addition, G.S. 15A-831(c) requires a law enforcement agency to transmit an accused person's SSN to the district attorney's office, which implies that the agency has collected the number from the person arrested.
- *For concealed weapon permits.* G.S. 14-415.14 requires an applicant for a concealed weapon permit to include his or her SSN on the application.
- *For blood donation programs.* 42 U.S.C. § 405(c)(2)(D) permits state and local governments to require blood donors to provide their SSNs for identification purposes.
- *For jury selection.* 42 U.S.C. § 405(c)(2)(E) permits state and local governments to use SSNs that have been legally collected in order to identify duplicate names on master lists used for jury selection. In turn, G.S. 20-43.4 directs the Commissioner of Motor Vehicles to provide each county jury commission with a list of licensed drivers resident in the county, including each person's SSN.

When no federal or state law requires or permits a governmental agency to collect Social Security numbers, G.S. 132-1.10(b)(1) requires the agency to make a written determination that the numbers are "imperative" to performing some duty or responsibility.[20] It appears that some common uses of SSNs can meet this test while others cannot. Among those uses for which a number may well be imperative are criminal records checks and credit checks. It is surely reasonable to conduct criminal records checks of new employees and credit checks of utility account applicants and loan applicants; indeed, it might be unreasonable not to do so. That being the case, if the entities that perform such checks require an SSN in order to provide the desired information, collecting the number satisfies the requirement that doing so is imperative. Similarly, if an insurance company requires the client's SSN before reimbursing a government health care provider, collecting the number is clearly imperative to the provider's operations. On the other hand, there is much less likelihood that collection of SSNs can be justified when the agency's intended use is as some sort of internal identifier. There are computer-based generators of alternative numbering systems that can replace the SSN as an identifier. In addition, G.S. 132-1.10(c)(4) expressly permits the use of redacted SSNs—as noted later in this chapter, the last four digits of the full SSN—and almost any agency can use an identifier system that combines a person's name with the redacted version of his or her SSN as a suitable replacement for the SSN itself.[21] Basically,

19. The U.S. standard death certificate is promulgated by the National Center for Health Statistics, a part of the Centers for Disease Control and Prevention. The certificate can be found at www.cdc.gov/nchs/data/dvs/DEATH11-03final-ACC.pdf.

20. G.S. 132-1.10(b)(1) requires that the need for a Social Security number must be "clearly documented." That seems to imply that the determination of imperativeness must be in writing.

21. When G.S. 132-1.10 was passed the state personnel system stopped using the SSN as an identifier for employment applicants and instead asked only for the final four digits of the applicant's SSN. *See*

the statute requires any agency that wishes to collect SSNs without a statutory or regulatory authorization to seriously consider the use or uses it will make of the numbers and the alternatives to the SSN. Only if there is no alternative, or the alternative is significantly worse—because of cost, efficiency, or other factors—should an agency determine that collection of the number is imperative.

It should be noted that the standard for obtaining an SSN from another government agency that already has the number may be slightly lower than for obtaining it from the individual whose number it is. As noted above, unless there is clear statutory authority to collect the number from the individual, the agency must find that collection of the number is "imperative." Under G.S. 132-1.10(c)(1), however, a government already possessing an SSN may share it with another governmental entity if the number "is necessary for the receiving entity to perform its duties and responsibilities." Both words are strong, but "imperative" seems to imply a slightly stricter standard than "necessary."

The Privacy Acts: Improper to Condition Rights, Privileges, or Benefits on Collecting an SSN

G.S. 132-1.10, as just described, limits a North Carolina local government's authority to collect SSNs. That statute, however, does not determine whether a local government can *require* a person to disclose his or her SSN or merely *request* that he or she do so. To make that determination, we must turn to the federal Privacy Act of 1974. That act establishes a general rule that governments *may not* require individuals to disclose their SSNs. It prohibits any state or local government agency from denying "any individual any right, benefit, or privilege provided by law" because that individual refuses to disclose his or her SSN to the agency.[22] There are two exceptions to this basic prohibition:

1. When the disclosure of the SSN is required or permitted[23] by *federal* statute
2. When the disclosure is within a system that the state or local agency was maintaining before January 1, 1975, and in addition the disclosure was required under a statute or regulation (state or federal) that had been adopted before that date

---

Memorandum from Thomas H. Wright, N.C. State Personnel Director, to Agency and University HR Directors (Nov. 23, 2005) (on file with the author).

22. 5 U.S.C. § 552a note (2006). The State Privacy Act, G.S. 143-64.60, has essentially identical provisions. In *Schmitt v. City of Detroit*, 395 F.3d 327 (6th Cir. 2005), the court held that the federal Privacy Act does not apply to state or local governments. Two years earlier the Eleventh Circuit had reached an opposite conclusion, Schwier v. Cox, 340 F.3d 1284 (11th Cir. 2003), and its reasoning is more persuasive than the Sixth Circuit's. After all, Section 7 of the Privacy Act does *explicitly* apply to state and local government agencies.

23. The federal Privacy Act itself limits this exception to circumstances when collection of an SSN is *required* by federal law. Later federal legislation, however, has created further exceptions to the Privacy Act provision, even though the later legislation only permits, rather than requires, collection of the number. See, for example, 42 U.S.C. § 405(c)(2)(C)(i), enacted in 1976, which *permits* states and local governments to collect SSNs as part of the administration of any tax, general public assistance, driver's license, or motor vehicle registration law. For that reason the text uses the phrase "required or permitted." That is also the phrase used in the State Privacy Act, G.S. 143-64.60.

There are very few instances of disclosures that fit within the second exception (an obvious one is the requirement to use an employee's SSN in making reports to the Social Security Administration), so the only exceptions, as a practical matter, are those that fit within the first exception: disclosure is required or permitted by some federal statute. Here is a list of such statutory exceptions:[24]

1. Income tax administration
2. Administration of a tax, general public assistance, or motor vehicle law
3. Administration of certain social services programs: TANF, Medicaid, or food stamps
4. Child support enforcement
5. Immigration enforcement
6. Vital records registration
7. School lunch programs
8. Blood donation programs

If a program is included in the long list set out above in the discussion of G.S. 132-1.10(b)(1) but is not included in the summary list directly above, a local government may not require a person to disclose to the government his or her SSN in order to participate in that program and may not deny a person a right, privilege, or benefit because the person refuses to disclose the number. What does the statute mean by "right, benefit, or privilege"?

None of the cases that have been decided under the Privacy Act deal directly with this question. Rather, they assume that what the government has denied is a right, privilege, or benefit under the act and focus instead on whether the government's demand for the SSN fits within one of the two exceptions. Nevertheless, a list of the sorts of things that have been denied is useful, because the parties to these cases and the courts have assumed they are rights, privileges, or benefits within the meaning of the Privacy Act:

- The right to register to vote[25]
- Entitlement to government benefit programs, such as public assistance or workers compensation[26]
- Employee benefits[27]
- Government licenses and permits[28]

---

24. This list is partially redundant in light of the list set out above in the section discussing the collection provision in G.S. 132-1.10. Because that earlier listing includes the statutory and regulatory citations, they are omitted in this one. It should be noted that there is no express *statutory* requirement of using SSNs in the I-9 reports required for immigration enforcement; the only mention of SSNs is in the cited regulation.

25. McKay v. Thompson, 226 F.3d 752 (6th Cir. 2000).

26. Doe v. Sharp, 491 F. Supp. 346 (D. Mass. 1980) (Aid to Families with Dependent Children); Florida Div. of Workers' Comp. v. Cagnoli, 914 So. 2d 950 (Fla. 2005) (workers' compensation).

27. Brookens v. United States, 627 F.2d 494 (D.C. Cir. 1980) (travel advances).

28. North Carolina *ex rel.* Kasler v. Howard, 323 F. Supp. 2d 675 (W.D.N.C. 2003), *aff'd*, 78 Fed. App'x 231 (4th Cir. 2003) (driver's license); Kentucky Rest. Concepts, Inc. v. City of Louisville, 209 F. Supp. 2d 672 (W.D. Ky. 2002) (business license); Russell v. Bd. of Plumbing Exam'rs, 74 F. Supp. 2d 339 (S.D.N.Y.) (occupational license), *adhered to on reargument*, 74 F. Supp. 2d 349 (S.D.N.Y. 1999), *aff'd on other grounds*, 1 Fed. App'x 38 (2d Cir. 2001).

- Refunds of moneys improperly paid to a government[29]
- Employment (perhaps)[30]

The list suggests other potential rights, privileges, or benefits:

- Reception of government services, such as medical services or utility services
- Participation in government programs, such as loan programs
- Acting as government volunteers, such as citizen board members, recreation volunteers, and public safety auxiliaries
- Applying for government employment (perhaps)

The second list raises a number of practical issues. Let's look at specific programs and services.

Medical services. Government health providers sometimes seek SSNs from patients or clients in order to seek reimbursement from third-party payers, such as insurance companies. The Privacy Act seems to prohibit a government from refusing to provide health services because a patient or client refuses to disclose his or her SSN.

Utility services. Government utility providers sometimes seek SSNs from applicants for service in order to run a credit check or to be able to use debt setoff to collect unpaid bills. The Privacy Act seems to prohibit a government from denying service to a person who refuses to disclose his or her SSN. Perhaps, however, the government could impose a deposit requirement or a higher deposit amount on someone for whom it is unable to obtain a credit check.

Loan programs. A government that offers loans, perhaps as part of its community development program, needs to be able to run credit checks on potential borrowers. Not doing so would be a failure of due diligence. Although the Privacy Act would forbid denying someone the right to apply for a loan because the person refuses to disclose his or her SSN, it probably does not entitle anyone to actually receive a loan. If the government is unable to complete a reasonable application process, including a credit check, because it doesn't have necessary information, it is unlikely that it has violated the Privacy Act.

Volunteers. Governments sometimes run criminal records checks on certain categories of volunteers, especially those who work with children or serve as public safety auxiliaries. It seems hard, however, to characterize service as a government volunteer as a right, privilege, or benefit, and for that reason the Privacy Act may not prohibit requiring such persons to submit SSNs before being appointed to such volunteer positions.

Applicants for employment. Many governments run criminal records or credit checks on potential employees and require applicants for certain types of jobs to undergo drug tests. Each of these is a reasonable precaution. Although the Privacy Act probably forbids denying someone the right to apply for a government job because the person refuses to disclose

---

29. Doyle v. Wilson, 529 F. Supp. 1343 (D. Del. 1982) (refund of court fine).

30. In *Sutton v. Providence St. Joseph Medical Center*, 192 F.3d 826 (9th Cir. 1999), the plaintiff was offered a position at the defendant hospital; he would not provide his SSN, however, and therefore was not hired. The court rejected his Privacy Act claim because the hospital was a private entity rather than a governmental one, but the case suggests that employment might be a right, benefit, or privilege under the Privacy Act for a governmental employer.

his or her SSN, it probably does not entitle anyone to actually get a job. If the government is unable to complete a reasonable application process—including a credit check, criminal records check, or drug test—because it doesn't have necessary information, it seems unlikely that it has violated the Privacy Act.

Collecting Social Security Numbers—Required Notice

G.S. 132-1.10 includes a requirement that a government that requests SSNs provide an individual, upon that person's request, with a statement setting out the use or uses the government will make of the SSNs. With one exception, however, this provision is legally irrelevant, because its substantive requirements are subsumed within the broader requirements of the Privacy Act of 1974 (and the essentially identical State Privacy Act). (The exception has to do with the effect of a failure to comply with the notice requirements and is discussed at the end of this section.) The federal statute requires that such a statement, or notice, be given to an individual whether he or she requests it or not; in addition, it requires more information than a statement of planned use or uses. Therefore, the remainder of this discussion focuses on the Privacy Act provision.

Here is the relevant Privacy Act provision, found in subsection (b) of the statute:

> Any Federal, State, or local government agency which requests an individual to disclose his social security account number shall inform that individual whether that disclosure is mandatory or voluntary, by what statutory or other authority such number is solicited, and what uses will be made of it.

Thus, the Privacy Act requires a notice—generically known as the Privacy Act Notice—that includes three components:

1. Whether the individual's disclosure of his or her SSN is required by law or is voluntary
2. The statutory or other authority under which the governmental agency is soliciting the SSN
3. The use or uses that the governmental agency will make of the number[31]

There have been a number of cases involving these Privacy Act Notices, and the lessons drawn from them are set out below.

---

31. Although this notice requirement has been part of federal law for more than thirty years, it has been widely ignored by state and local governments. In 1982 a federal district court in Delaware was asked to hold state court officials liable under 42 U.S.C. § 1983 for failure to comply with a federal statute, the notice provisions of the Privacy Act. In *Doyle v. Wilson*, 529 F. Supp. 1343 (D. Del. 1982), the court refused, even though the statutory violation was clear, because "[t]he requirements of section 7 of the Privacy Act have not been so widely disseminated . . . as to become an integral part of the public [or governmental officials'] consciousness." *Doyle*, 529 F. Supp. at 1351. Twenty years later the Government Accounting Office reported that there was still widespread failure to provide the notice required by the Privacy Act. *See* U.S. Gen. Accounting Office, *supra* note 7, at 3, 23.

The Notice Must Be Given before Soliciting the SSN

The purpose of the Privacy Act Notice, as summarized by the General Accounting Office, is to "[allow] SSN holders to make informed decisions about whether to provide their SSN to obtain the services in question."[32] As a result, the notice must be given to an individual *before or at the time the SSN is solicited.* Doing so after the fact (and in response to a court challenge) does not serve the statutory purpose.[33]

The Notice Must Be Given Even When Disclosure Is Required by Law

Some government agencies have argued that the Privacy Act Notice is irrelevant when the individual has no choice as to whether to disclose his or her SSN and therefore need not be given in that situation. That position seems inconsistent with the provision in the Privacy Act that requires the notice to specify whether disclosure of the number is mandatory or voluntary—if the notice is never required when disclosure is mandatory, that specification seems nonsensical—and the courts agree. Even if disclosure is mandatory, the government soliciting the number must still prepare and disseminate the Privacy Act Notice.[34]

The Notice Must Be Detailed and Complete

Because a primary purpose of the notice is to allow an individual to decide whether to disclose his or her SSN, the courts have held that the notice must be sufficiently detailed to permit that decision to be informed. For example, in *Greater Cleveland Welfare Rights Organization v. Bauer*,[35] the plaintiffs attacked a Privacy Act statement prepared by a state welfare department. The statement read as follows:

> Your social security number will be used as a means of identification in the administration of the ADC or Medicaid programs. It will be used to determine your initial or continuing eligibility when contacting other people or agencies in order to obtain or verify information necessary to determine your eligibility and to determine that all public assistance regulations have been met.

The district court held that the statement was inadequate. The court held that in addition to the information included in the statement, the agency must inform recipients that (1) their Social Security numbers will be used to verify with the Social Security Administration employment information supplied on the application, and (2) the recipient might be subject to prosecution for fraud if the records of the Social Security Administration reveal that the recipient supplied inaccurate information on the application. Basically, the court said, a meaningful disclosure must show not only the uses to which the number will be put but also the consequences of those uses.

---

32. *See* U.S. Gen. Accounting Office, *supra* note 7, at 3.
33. Doe v. Sharp, 491 F. Supp. 346 (D. Mass. 1980).
34. *In re* Crawford, 194 F.3d 954, 961 (9th Cir. 1999) ("A close reading of § 7 makes it clear that § 7(a)(2)(A)'s exclusion for federal statutes only pertains to the limitation recited in § 7(a)(1)—that no right, benefit, or privilege be denied to any individual for refusing to disclose her SSN."). *See* Doe v. Sharp, 491 F. Supp. 346 (D. Mass. 1980) (holding that notice was required even though the government was entitled to mandate disclosure of the SSN).
35. 462 F. Supp. 1313 (N.D. Ohio 1978).

In addition, the notice must include all the uses to which the agency will put the number. In *Schwier v. Cox*, the Eleventh Circuit was presented with a case brought by persons who refused to provide their SSNs to elections officials and therefore were denied their right to register to vote. The plaintiffs argued that the Privacy Act Notice was inaccurate because it

> promises confidentiality and "internal" use only. [The defendant] admits that state law allows the ssns to be disclosed to other Georgia state agencies if requested by those agencies. . . . [The defendant] also states that the other modification to the [notice] is that it will now explain that "internal use only" "means to identify and verify the identity of voters." If it is true that other state agencies in Georgia will have access to Georgia voters' ssns, this modification would seem insufficient to bring the [notice] into compliance with section 7(b) of the Privacy Act.[36]

Thus, if the agency soliciting the SSN expects to share the number with other agencies, its Privacy Act Notice must say so.[37]

Uses Not Included in the Privacy Act Notice May Be Prohibited

The appellate courts have not particularly penalized governmental agencies that have failed to provide adequate, or even any, notice under the Privacy Act. The one court that was asked to allow damages under 42 U.S.C. § 1983 refused to do so;[38] and the one court that

---

36. 340 F.3d 1284, 1293–94 (11th Cir. 2003).

Here is an example of another Privacy Act Notice, which is set out in a relatively early federal case and which no party to the case suggested was inadequate. The plaintiff was a federal employee who resisted providing his agency with his SSN in order to receive a travel advance. The Notice read:

> Disclosure by you of your social security number (SSN) is mandatory to obtain the services, benefits or processes that you are seeking. Solicitation of the SSN by the United States Civil Service Commission is authorized under provisions of Executive Order 9397, dated November 22, 1943. The SSN is used as an identifier throughout your Federal career from the time of application through retirement. It will be used primarily to identify your records that you file with the Civil Service Commission or agencies. The SSN also will be used by the Civil Service Commission and other Federal agencies in connection with lawful requests for information about you from your former employers, educational institutions and financial or other organizations. The information gathered through the use of the number will be used only as necessary in personnel administration processes carried out in accordance with established regulations and published notices of systems of records. The SSN also will be used for the selection of persons to be included in statistical studies of personnel management matters. The use of the SSN is made necessary because of the large number of present and former Federal employees, and applicants who have identical names and birth dates, and whose identities can only be distinguished by the SSN.

Brookens v. United States, 627 F.2d 494, 496–97 (D.C. Cir. 1980).

37. G.S. 132-1.10(c)(1) provides that subsection (b) of that section, which includes the requirement that a government soliciting SSNs prepare a statement setting out the uses it will make of the numbers, "does not apply" when the collecting government shares the number with "another governmental entity or its agents, employees, or contractors if disclosure is necessary for the receiving entity to perform its duties and responsibilities." This seems to mean that, as a matter of state law, the statement of uses need not reveal that the number might be shared with other governmental entities. The case law set out above, however, demonstrates that the Privacy Act Notice required by federal law does require including such potential uses.

38. Doyle v. Wilson, 529 F. Supp. 1343 (D. Del. 1982).

was asked to enjoin use of the SSNs collected under a faulty notice also refused to do so.[39] Rather, these courts have essentially limited their remedies to (1) enjoining governments from requiring SSNs when the Privacy Act prohibits them from doing so and (2) requiring governments to provide notice, or more complete notice, in the future.[40]

It may be, though, that North Carolina's Social Security number statute, G.S. 132-1.10, provides a broader and more effective remedy. As was noted at the beginning of this section, this North Carolina statute mirrors the Privacy Act by requiring a notice that sets out the use or uses to which the government will put the SSN. It then goes on, unlike the federal statute, to specifically prohibit using the number for "any purpose other than the purpose stated" in the notice.[41] The statute further goes on, in subsection (h), to allow "[a]ny affected person [to] petition the court for an order directing compliance with this section." This seems to allow a person who has disclosed his or her SSN to a North Carolina government agency to seek a court order prohibiting the agency from using the number for any purpose not set out in the relevant Privacy Act Notice.[42]

Using Social Security Numbers

The Basic Limitation

There is no federal statute that generally governs the use that state or local governments make of SSNs. As noted just above, however, G.S. 132-1.10 prohibits a state agency or local government in North Carolina from using SSNs for some purpose other than those set out in the agency's or government's Privacy Act Notice. The one apparent exception to this limitation on use without notice is the permission in G.S. 132-1.10(c)(1) to disclose SSNs to "another governmental entity or its agents, employees, or contractors if disclosure is necessary for the receiving entity to perform its duties and responsibilities."

Sharing SSNs Internally and with Agents and Contractors

G.S. 132-1.10(c)(1) expressly permits sharing SSNs not only with other governments but with the agents and contractors of those other governments. Oddly, though, there is no provision in G.S. 132-1.10 that permits the collecting government to share its SSNs with its own agents and contractors or within the government itself. It seems unlikely that the legislation would intend to permit sharing with other governments' agents and contractors and not

---

39. Greater Cleveland Welfare Rights Org. v. Bauer, 462 F. Supp. 1313, 1320 (N.D. Ohio 1978) ("The only purpose that could possibly be served by this Court forbidding defendants from making further use of [the SSNs] is the deterrence of future requests for social security numbers without compliance with Section 7(b). The Court is confident that the granting of prospective relief alone will accomplish the same result without the huge waste of effort and funds that would result from an Order forbidding further use of [the numbers]." (footnote omitted)).

40. *E.g.*, Russell v. Bd. of Plumbing Exam'rs, 74 F. Supp. 2d 339 (S.D.N.Y. 1999) (requiring adequate Privacy Act Notice), *adhered to on reargument*, 74 F. Supp. 2d 349 (S.D.N.Y. 1999), *aff'd on other grounds*, 1 Fed. App'x 38 (2d Cir. 2001); Florida Div. of Workers' Comp. v. Cagnoli, 914 So. 2d 950 (Fla. 2005) (enjoining mandatory disclosure of SSN).

41. G.S. 132-1.10(b)(4).

42. Note 37, *supra*, explains that as a matter of state law the Privacy Act Notice need not disclose that an agency might share SSNs with other governmental entities. It seems to follow, therefore, that the remedy provision discussed in this paragraph could not be used to enjoin such use even though the use was not included in the Privacy Act Notice.

with the collecting government's own, so the probable interpretation is that the second sort of sharing is implicitly permitted. Because there is no mention of such sharing in subsection (c), however, it may mean that intended sharing within the collecting government or with its agents and contractors must be mentioned in the Privacy Act Notice and that such sharing is impermissible unless mentioned in the notice.

Redaction

G.S. 132-1.10(c)(4) provides that all of subsection (b) of the section—the rules on collecting SSNs, giving notice, using, and releasing to the public—does not apply to "social security numbers . . . that have been redacted." Although the section does not define "redaction," there is a fairly clear notion of the word's meaning. The statute was enacted as part of a session law that also enacted the Identity Theft Protection Act, codified as Article 2A of G.S. Chapter 75. This companion legislation, which applies to the private sector, contains a number of provisions that mirror provisions in G.S. 132-1.10, including a general exception for Social Security numbers that have been redacted. The companion legislation, though, does define redaction. Under G.S. 75-61(13), redaction constitutes "[t]he rendering of data so that it is unreadable or is truncated so that no more than the last four digits of the identification number is accessible as part of the data." Although this definition strictly only applies to the Chapter 75 legislation, it is certainly reasonable to extend it to the public records section as well. Indeed, G.S. 132-1.10(g)(1) seems to assume that the definition applies within the public records statute as well. Thus, a government adequately redacts a Social Security number when it blocks out all but the last four digits.

Release of Social Security Numbers

G.S. 132-1.10(b)(5) prohibits a government that has obtained a Social Security number from intentionally communicating or making the number available to the general public.[43] This restriction applies whether the number was collected from the individual, obtained from another governmental agency, purchased from an information broker, or acquired in some other manner. Social Security numbers are not public records. An SSN's presence within a record does not, though, make the record itself confidential. Rather, the government's responsibility is to remove or redact the SSN and then make the adjusted record public (assuming it does not fall within some other exception to the right of access).

The section also includes a number of other requirements that are intended to reinforce the confidentiality of an SSN.

Separate Page

G.S. 132-1.10(b)(2) directs a state agency or local government that has collected an SSN from an individual to "segregate that number on a separate page from the rest of the record . . . in

43. A number of cases have considered whether federal or state constitutional rights of privacy prohibit a government from releasing a person's Social Security number to the public. For the most part the courts have ruled that release of an SSN is not prohibited by either the federal or state constitution. *E.g., In re* Crawford, 194 F.3d 954 (9th Cir. 1999). *Contra* State *ex rel.* Beacon Journal Publ'g Co. v. City of Akron, 640 N.E.2d 164 (Ohio 1994). Given the North Carolina statute discussed below, the issue is no longer important.

order that the social security number can be more easily redacted pursuant to a valid public records request." This direction is probably more hortatory than mandatory. Many records—perhaps most records with SSNs—are electronic databases, and the records are organized by rows and columns rather than pages. Clearly the SSN should be in a separate column and one that can be easily deleted from any response to a request for a copy of the database. Even with paper records, any segregation must include enough information on the separate page to be able to connect the number to the individual. One method that is used for some records, such as marriage licenses, is to have a form that is filled out in duplicate or triplicate, with only one copy including the SSN. That copy, then, is not shared with the public.

Benefits Card

G.S. 132-1.10(b)(6) prohibits a state agency or local government from intentionally printing or imbedding a person's SSN "on any card required for the individual to access government services." Because the most likely number to have printed on such a card is the person's identifier number for the government program in question, this prohibition appears to have the effect of prohibiting programs using such cards from using the SSN as the identifier for the patient, client, or customer.

Internet Access or Transmission

G.S. 132-1.10(b)(8) prohibits a state agency or local government from requiring a person to use his or her SSN to access an Internet website, unless the agency or government also requires some authentication device or number, other than the SSN, to access the website. In addition, G.S. 132-1.10(b)(7) prohibits an agency or government from requiring a person to transmit his or her SSN over the Internet, unless the Internet connection is secure or the SSN is encrypted.

Mailings

G.S. 132-1.10(b)(9) prohibits a state agency or local government from printing a person's SSN on materials that it mails to the person unless either federal or state law requires the materials to be mailed with the number on them. Even if a mailing including an SSN is permitted, the paragraph goes on to prohibit allowing the number to be in any way visible. That is,

- The number may not be printed on a postcard
- The number may not be printed on any other mailer not requiring an envelope
- The number may not be visible on the envelope
- The number may not be visible in any way without the envelope being opened

Release of Other Identifying Information

G.S. 132-1.10(b)(5), which prohibits intentionally communicating or making SSNs available to the general public, also applies to "other identifying information." (None of the provisions in G.S. 132-1.10 that regulate collecting or using SSNs apply to this other information.) The list of other identifying information is drawn from G.S. 14-113.20(b) and is as follows:

- Employer taxpayer identification numbers
- Driver's license numbers, except any that appear on law enforcement records
- State identification card numbers
- Passport numbers
- Checking account numbers
- Savings account numbers
- Credit card account numbers
- Debit card account numbers
- Personal identification codes, which are "numeric and/or alphabetical code[s] assigned to the cardholder of a financial transaction card [FTC] by the issuer to permit authorized electronic use of that FTC"[44]
- Digital signatures
- Any other numbers or information that can be used to access a person's financial resources
- Biometric data
- Fingerprints
- Passwords

G.S. 132-1.10(b)(5) specifically provides that the following information (which is included in the listing in G.S. 14-113.20[b]), is not identifying information for purposes of the public records law:

- Electronic identification numbers
- Electronic mail names and addresses
- Internet account numbers
- Internet identification names
- The maiden name of a person's mother

Apparently this additional information is public record, unless it is part of a record—such as a personnel file—that is independently excepted from the right of public access.

The Effect of G.S. 132-1.2(2)

G.S. 132-1.2(2) is an earlier statute that governs some of the same identifying information subject to G.S. 132-1.10.[45] It excludes from the public records law—and prohibits disclosure of—any information that reveals an account number used for electronic payments

- as defined in G.S. 147-86.20, and
- obtained pursuant to G.S. 159-32.1.

If we look at the two cross-references, we discover that G.S. 147-86.20 defines "electronic payment" as "payment by charge card, credit card, debit card, or by electronic funds transfer as defined in this subsection." Actually there is no definition of "electronic funds transfer"

44. The definition of a "Personal Identification Code" is found in G.S. 14-113.8(6).
45. The statute is set out in appendix 15A at the end of this chapter.

in the subsection or the entire section, but it would presumably include such transactions as automatically drawing on a customer's bank account to pay a monthly utility charge. G.S. 159-32.1 permits a local government, public authority, or public hospital to, "in lieu of payment by cash or check, accept payment by electronic payment . . . for any tax, assessment, rate, fee, charge, rent, interest, penalty, or other receivable owed to it."

Thus, under G.S. 132-1.2(2) bank account numbers and credit and debit card account numbers are not public records if they have been obtained through electronic transactions. Under G.S. 132-1.2(2), however, a government is prohibited from releasing this account number information under any circumstances, while G.S. 132-1.10(c) permits release in certain narrow circumstances, particularly to other governments. Because G.S. 132-1.10 is the later-enacted statute, perhaps it controls in case of conflict, but there does remain some uncertainty about the ability of a local government to share account numbers that have been obtained through electronic transactions.

Penalties for Improper Release of an SSN or Other Identifying Information

State law does not impose any liability for improper release of an SSN or other identifying information, nor does it make improper release a crime. Rather, G.S. 132-1.10(h) simply permits any "affected person," which presumably means the person whose number or information is involved, to petition a court for an order directing compliance with the section. Federal law, however, is different, at least with respect to SSNs.

Although there is no federal statute that comprehensively prohibits or restricts governmental agencies from releasing SSNs,[46] one federal statute does require that many such numbers held by local governments be kept confidential, with the requirement depending on the enactment date of the law under which the SSNs were obtained. Furthermore, violation of the statute is a felony. The basic federal provision reads as follows:

> Social security account numbers and related records that are obtained or maintained by authorized persons pursuant to any provision of law enacted on or after October 1, 1990, shall be confidential, and no authorized person shall disclose any such social security account number or related record.[47]

"Authorized person" in this statute is defined to include officers and employees of state or local governments. The subsection goes on to make violation of the provision a federal felony, punishable by a fine of up to $5,000, imprisonment for up to five years, or both. Given the seriousness placed upon violation of this statute, it is unfortunate that it is somewhat ambiguous.[48] Primarily, it is not clear whether the reference to "provision of law" means a federal statute or regulation or whether it also includes state laws, local ordinances, and so on. It is probable, however, that it is limited to federal statutes or federal regulations. There has been a good bit of other federal legislation, listed earlier in this chapter, that expressly permits or requires the collection of SSNs for specific programs, and

---

46. *See* American Fed'n of State, County, & Mun. Employees, Council 75 v. City of Albany, 725 P.2d 381 (Or. Ct. App. 1986).

47. 42 U.S.C. § 405(c)(2)(C)(viii) (2006).

48. The quoted provision was added to the enacted statute in a conference committee, and there is no published legislative history to explain its meaning.

it is reasonable to conclude that Congress was thinking of that body of legislation when it referred to "provision[s] of law." Furthermore, if it included state laws or local ordinances, the application of the statute would be different in different states, as some state or local governments might have enacted or adopted their enabling laws before October 1, 1990, and some afterward. That kind of interstate variability would be unusual for a federal criminal statute. Fortunately, because North Carolina law now prohibits the public release of SSNs, regardless of the statute under which they have been collected, these nuances under the federal law will probably not need to be resolved. But the federal statute does stand as a reminder of the serious need to maintain the confidentiality of SSNs.

Security Breaches

G.S. 132-1.10(c1) provides that if a state agency or local government has suffered a "security breach," as that term is defined in Article 2A of G.S. Chapter 75, the agency or government must take the steps set out in G.S. 75-65. Article 2A is the Identity Theft Protection Act, which was enacted in the same session law as G.S. 132-1.10; it applies to the private sector and contains several provisions concerning SSNs that parallel those in the public records statute. It included provisions about security breaches when it was enacted in 2005, but the security breach provision was not added to G.S. 132-1.10 until the next year. That is probably why the latter statute's security breach provisions are referenced to Chapter 75 rather than being set out in the public records statute.

G.S. 75-61(14) defines a security breach as follows:

> An incident of unauthorized access to and acquisition of unencrypted and unredacted records or data containing personal information where illegal use of the personal information has occurred or is reasonably likely to occur or that creates a material risk of harm to a consumer. Any incident of unauthorized access to and acquisition of encrypted records or data containing personal information along with the confidential process or key shall constitute a security breach.

The section, in paragraph (10), defines "personal information," used in the definition of security breach, as "[a] person's first name or first initial and last name in combination with identifying information as defined in G.S. 14-113.20(b)." That is the information set out in the first list in the section on Release of Other Identifying Information.[49] Personal information also includes SSNs.

G.S. 75-65 details what a local government must do if it has suffered a security breach as defined above. Essentially, it must notify each person whose information may have been included in the material subject to the breach. Unless the government has been notified by a law enforcement agency that providing notice would impede a criminal investigation into

---

49. There are two minor differences between the lists of personal identifying information in G.S. 132-1.10 and G.S. 75-65(a). First, passwords are identifying information in the public records section but are not so treated in the security breach statute, "unless this information would permit access to a person's financial account or resources." Second, the public records statute, in G.S. 132-1.10(b)(5), provides that driver's license numbers appearing in law enforcement records are not identifying information, but there is no comparable exemption in the security breach statute. The effect of these differences is not clear.

the breach or jeopardize national or homeland security, the notice must be made "without unreasonable delay." Subsection (d) sets out the required content of the notice:

- A general description of the incident
- The type of information involved
- What is being done to prevent further unauthorized access
- A telephone number a person can call for further information
- Advice to the person to "remain vigilant by reviewing account statements and monitoring free credit reports"

Giving the notice can be expensive. Except in extraordinary circumstances, unlikely to often apply to a local government, the notice must be given in one of three ways:

1. In writing, presumably sent by U.S. mail
2. Electronically, to those for whom the government has an e-mail address and who have agreed to receive communications electronically
3. By telephone, as long as the government makes direct contact with the affected person

The extraordinary circumstances that justify a form of notice other than the three set out just above are either (1) that the total cost of notice would exceed $250,000, (2) that the affected class of persons to be notified exceeds 500,000, or (3) that the government does not have sufficient information to be able to use any of the three standard methods of notice. If any of these justifications apply, the government may use substitute notice that includes all three of these components:

1. E-mail when the government has an e-mail address for an affected person
2. A conspicuous placing of notice on the government's website
3. Notification of major statewide news media

Finally, if the government must give notice to more than 1,000 persons, it must also notify the Attorney General's Consumer Protection Division and all national consumer reporting agencies that compile and maintain files on consumers.

It is important for a local government that has suffered a security breach to comply with the requirements of G.S. 75-65. Subsection (i) of the section provides that a violation is also a violation of G.S. 75-1.1, and G.S. 75-16 permits a person who can show damages from such a violation to obtain treble damages from the person or entity responsible for the violation.

Social Security Numbers and Other Identifying Information in Land Records

In the past, SSNs frequently were included in land records, especially deeds of trust. G.S. 132-1.10 now prohibits inclusion of these numbers in records that are to be filed with a register of deeds (as well as with the secretary of state or a clerk of court). It also prohibits inclusion of the following personal identifying information: a person's employer taxpayer identification number, driver's license number, state identification number, passport number, checking account or savings account number, credit card or debit card account number, or any personal identification code or password. The statute, however, only became effective December 1, 2005, and these numbers remain in many older records.

For many years, these records containing identifying information could only be found in the register of deeds' office and therefore required a personal visit to access; this provided some protection against improper collection or use of the information. In recent years, however, many registers of deeds have placed land records on the Internet, which made the records and any identifying information in them much more widely accessible. The General Assembly recognized this trend and included a provision in G.S. 132-1.10 to protect against this form of release of the numbers. G.S. 132-1.10(f) permits any person to demand that a register of deeds (or clerk of court) remove the person's SSN or any of the other listed identifying information from any document that is or will be placed on the Internet by the register (or clerk). The usual way of doing this is to delete the number or other identifying information from the online version of the record, leaving it on the original paper record in the public office. The statute, however, seems to recognize the possibility of deleting the number or information from the original, inasmuch as it states that the register or clerk has no duty to reinstate the number, if requested to do so, if reinstating is "impossible."

Appendix 15A—Statutes

G.S. 132-1.10

§ 132-1.10. Social security numbers and other personal identifying information.

(a) The General Assembly finds the following:

(1) The social security number can be used as a tool to perpetuate fraud against a person and to acquire sensitive personal, financial, medical, and familial information, the release of which could cause great financial or personal harm to an individual. While the social security number was intended to be used solely for the administration of the federal Social Security System, over time this unique numeric identifier has been used extensively for identity verification purposes and other legitimate consensual purposes.

(2) Although there are legitimate reasons for State and local government agencies to collect social security numbers and other personal identifying information from individuals, government should collect the information only for legitimate purposes or when required by law.

(3) When State and local government agencies possess social security numbers or other personal identifying information, the governments should minimize the instances this information is disseminated either internally within government or externally with the general public.

(b) Except as provided in subsections (c) and (d) of this section, no agency of the State or its political subdivisions, or any agent or employee of a government agency, shall do any of the following:

(1) Collect a social security number from an individual unless authorized by law to do so or unless the collection of the social security number is otherwise imperative for the performance of that agency's duties and responsibilities as prescribed by law. Social security numbers collected by an agency must be relevant to the purpose for which collected and shall not be collected until and unless the need for social security numbers has been clearly documented.

(2) Fail, when collecting a social security number from an individual, to segregate that number on a separate page from the rest of the record, or as otherwise appropriate, in order that the social security number can be more easily redacted pursuant to a valid public records request.

(3) Fail, when collecting a social security number from an individual, to provide, at the time of or prior to the actual collection of the social security number by that agency, that individual, upon request, with a statement of the purpose or purposes for which the social security number is being collected and used.

(4) Use the social security number for any purpose other than the purpose stated.

(5) Intentionally communicate or otherwise make available to the general public a person's social security number or other identifying information. "Identifying information", as used in this subdivision, shall have the same meaning as in G.S. 14-113.20(b), except it shall not include electronic identification numbers, electronic mail names or addresses, Internet account numbers, Internet identification

names, parent's legal surname prior to marriage, or drivers license numbers appearing on law enforcement records. Identifying information shall be confidential and not be a public record under this Chapter. A record, with identifying information removed or redacted, is a public record if it would otherwise be a public record under this Chapter but for the identifying information. The presence of identifying information in a public record does not change the nature of the public record. If all other public records requirements are met under this Chapter, the agency of the State or its political subdivisions shall respond to a public records request, even if the records contain identifying information, as promptly as possible, by providing the public record with the identifying information removed or redacted.

(6) Intentionally print or imbed an individual's social security number on any card required for the individual to access government services.

(7) Require an individual to transmit the individual's social security number over the Internet, unless the connection is secure or the social security number is encrypted.

(8) Require an individual to use the individual's social security number to access an Internet Web site, unless a password or unique personal identification number or other authentication device is also required to access the Internet Web site.

(9) Print an individual's social security number on any materials that are mailed to the individual, unless state or federal law required that the social security number be on the document to be mailed. A social security number that is permitted to be mailed under this subdivision may not be printed, in whole or in part, on a postcard or other mailer not requiring an envelope, or visible on the envelope or without the envelope having been opened.

(c) Subsection (b) of this section does not apply in the following circumstances:

(1) To social security numbers or other identifying information disclosed to another governmental entity or its agents, employees, or contractors if disclosure is necessary for the receiving entity to perform its duties and responsibilities. The receiving governmental entity and its agents, employees, and contractors shall maintain the confidential and exempt status of such numbers.

(2) To social security numbers or other identifying information disclosed pursuant to a court order, warrant, or subpoena.

(3) To social security numbers or other identifying information disclosed for public health purposes pursuant to and in compliance with Chapter 130A of the General Statutes.

(4) To social security numbers or other identifying information that have been redacted.

(5) To certified copies of vital records issued by the State Registrar and other authorized officials pursuant to G.S. 130A-93(c). The State Registrar may disclose any identifying information other than social security numbers on any uncertified vital record.

(6) To any recorded document in the official records of the register of deeds of the county.

(7) To any document filed in the official records of the courts.

(c1) If an agency of the State or its political subdivisions, or any agent or employee of a government agency, experiences a security breach, as defined in Article 2A of Chapter 75 of the General Statutes, the agency shall comply with the requirements of G.S. 75-65.

(d) No person preparing or filing a document to be recorded or filed in the official records of the register of deeds, the Department of the Secretary of State, or of the courts may include any person's social security, employer taxpayer identification, drivers license, state identification, passport, checking account, savings account, credit card, or debit card number, or personal identification (PIN) code or passwords in that document, unless otherwise expressly required by law or court order, adopted by the State Registrar on records of vital events, or redacted. Any loan closing instruction that requires the inclusion of a person's social security number on a document to be recorded shall be void. Any person who violates this subsection shall be guilty of an infraction, punishable by a fine not to exceed five hundred dollars ($500.00) for each violation.

(e) The validity of an instrument as between the parties to the instrument is not affected by the inclusion of personal information on a document recorded or filed with the official records of the register of deeds or the Department of the Secretary of State. The register of deeds or the Department of the Secretary of State may not reject an instrument presented for recording because the instrument contains an individual's personal information.

(f) Any person has the right to request that a register of deeds or clerk of court remove, from an image or copy of an official record placed on a register of deeds' or court's Internet Web site available to the general public or an Internet Web site available to the general public used by a register of deeds or court to display public records by the register of deeds or clerk of court, the person's social security, employer taxpayer identification, drivers license, state identification, passport, checking account, savings account, credit card, or debit card number, or personal identification (PIN) code or passwords contained in that official record. The request must be made in writing, legibly signed by the requester, and delivered by mail, facsimile, or electronic transmission, or delivered in person to the register of deeds or clerk of court. The request must specify the personal information to be redacted, information that identifies the document that contains the personal information and unique information that identifies the location within the document that contains the social security, employer taxpayer identification, drivers license, state identification, passport, checking account, savings account, credit card, or debit card number, or personal identification (PIN) code or passwords to be redacted. The request for redaction shall be considered a public record with access restricted to the register of deeds, the clerk of court, their staff, or upon order of the court. The register of deeds or clerk of court shall have no duty to inquire beyond the written request to verify the identity of a person requesting redaction and shall have no duty to remove redaction for any reason upon subsequent request by an individual or by order of the court, if impossible to do so. No fee will be charged for the redaction pursuant to such request. Any person who requests a redaction without proper authority to do so shall be guilty of an infraction, punishable by a fine not to exceed five hundred dollars ($500.00) for each violation.

(g) A register of deeds or clerk of court shall immediately and conspicuously post signs throughout his or her offices for public viewing and shall immediately and conspicuously post a notice on any Internet Web site available to the general public used by a register of deeds or clerk of court a notice stating, in substantially similar form, the following:

(1) Any person preparing or filing a document for recordation or filing in the official records may not include a social security, employer taxpayer identification, drivers license, state identification, passport, checking account, savings account, credit card, or debit card number, or personal identification (PIN) code or passwords in the document, unless expressly required by law or court order, adopted by the State Registrar on records of vital events, or redacted so that no more than the last four digits of the identification number is included.

(2) Any person has a right to request a register of deeds or clerk of court to remove, from an image or copy of an official record placed on a register of deeds' or clerk of court's Internet Web site available to the general public or on an Internet Web site available to the general public used by a register of deeds or clerk of court to display public records, any social security, employer taxpayer identification, drivers license, state identification, passport, checking account, savings account, credit card, or debit card number, or personal identification (PIN) code or passwords contained in an official record. The request must be made in writing and delivered by mail, facsimile, or electronic transmission, or delivered in person, to the register of deeds or clerk of court. The request must specify the personal information to be redacted, information that identifies the document that contains the personal information and unique information that identifies the location within the document that contains the social security, employer taxpayer identification, drivers license, state identification, passport, checking account, savings account, credit card, or debit card number, or personal identification (PIN) code or passwords to be redacted. No fee will be charged for the redaction pursuant to such a request. Any person who requests a redaction without proper authority to do so shall be guilty of an infraction, punishable by a fine not to exceed five hundred dollars ($500.00) for each violation.

(h) Any affected person may petition the court for an order directing compliance with this section. No liability shall accrue to a register of deeds or clerk of court or to his or her agent for any action related to provisions of this section or for any claims or damages that might result from a social security number or other identifying information on the public record or on a register of deeds' or clerk of court's Internet website available to the general public or an Internet Web site available to the general public used by a register of deeds or clerk of court.

Federal Privacy Act of 1974 (Pub. L. No. 93-579), Section 7—5 U.S.C. § 552a note

(a)(1) It shall be unlawful for any Federal, State or local government agency to deny to any individual any right, benefit, or privilege provided by law because of such individual's refusal to disclose his social security account number.

(2) [The] provisions of paragraph (1) of this subsection shall not apply with respect to—

(A) any disclosure which is required by Federal statute, or

(B) the disclosure of a social security number to any Federal, State, or local agency maintaining a system of records in existence and operating before January 1, 1975, if such disclosure was required under statute or regulation adopted prior to such date to verify the identity of an individual.

(b) Any Federal, State, or local government agency which requests an individual to disclose his social security account number shall inform that individual whether that disclosure is mandatory or voluntary, by what statutory or other authority such number is solicited, and what uses will be made of it.

State Privacy Act—G.S. 143-64.60

§ 143-64.60. State Privacy Act.

(a) It is unlawful for any State or local government agency to deny to any individual any right, benefit, or privilege provided by law because of such individual's refusal to disclose his social security account number.

The provisions of this subsection shall not apply with respect to:

(1) Any disclosure which is required or permitted by federal statute, or

(2) The disclosure of a social security number to any State or local agency maintaining a system of records in existence and operating before January 1, 1975, if such disclosure was required under statute or regulation adopted prior to such date to verify the identity of an individual.

(b) Any State or local government agency which requests an individual to disclose his social security account number shall inform that individual whether that disclosure is mandatory or voluntary, by what statutory or other authority such number is solicited, and what uses will be made of it.

42 U.S.C. § 405(c)(2)(C)(viii)

(viii)(I) Social security account numbers and related records that are obtained or maintained by authorized persons pursuant to any provision of law enacted on or after October 1, 1990, shall be confidential, and no authorized person shall disclose any such social security account number or related record.

(II) Paragraphs (1), (2), and (3) of section 7213(a) of the Internal Revenue Code of 1986 shall apply with respect to the unauthorized willful disclosure to any person of social security account numbers and related records obtained or maintained by an authorized person pursuant to a provision of law enacted on or after October 1, 1990, in the same manner and to the same extent as such paragraphs apply with respect to unauthorized disclosures of return and return information described in such paragraphs. Paragraph (4) of section 7213(a) of such Code shall apply with respect to the willful offer of any item of material value in exchange for any such social security account number or related record in the same manner and to the same extent as such paragraph applies with respect to offers (in exchange for any return or return information) described in such paragraph.

(III) For purposes of this clause, the term "authorized person" means an officer or employee of the United States, an officer or employee of any State, political subdivision of a State, or agency of a State or political subdivision of a State, and any other person (or officer or employee thereof), who has or had access to social security account numbers or related records pursuant to any provision of law enacted on or after October 1, 1990. For purposes of this subclause, the term "officer or employee" includes a former officer or employee.

(IV) For purposes of this clause, the term "related record" means any record, list, or compilation that indicates, directly or indirectly, the identity of any individual with respect to whom a social security account number or a request for a social security account number is maintained pursuant to this clause.

G.S. 132-1.2(2)

§ 132-1.2. Confidential information.

Nothing in this Chapter shall be construed to require or authorize a public agency or its subdivision to disclose any information that:

. . .

(2) Reveals an account number for electronic payment as defined in G.S. 147-86.20 and obtained pursuant to Articles 6A or 6B of Chapter 147 of the General Statutes or G.S. 159-32.1.

Chapter 16—Public Enterprise Billing Information

Statutory Summary

Section 132-1.1(c) of the North Carolina General Statutes[1] [hereinafter G.S.] excludes from public access customer billing information held by counties, cities, and other local government entities that provide public enterprise services. Billing records often include information about specific customers that might be thought private in nature, such as credit histories, forwarding addresses, information about a customer's property or habits (to facilitate access to meters), and information about the customer's relatives. In addition, if the enterprise itself competes with other providers of such services, billing records might include information whose release would disadvantage the governmental provider in relation to its competitors.

Although the statute is drafted in a somewhat confusing manner, it does not prohibit a government from releasing customer billing information. Rather, it simply denies automatic public access to the information. In fact, there are a number of situations in which governmental providers of public enterprise services routinely release some of the information protected by this provision of the statute.

Discussion

Functions and Entities Covered

Counties and Cities

The exemption from the right of public access provided by G.S. 132-1.1(c) extends to counties and cities with respect to the records of any "public enterprise, as defined in G.S. 160A-311

1. The statute is set out in appendix 16A at the end of this chapter.

[for cities] . . . and G.S. 153A-274 [for counties]," except airports. The city and county functions to which the statute applies are listed in the two cited statutes, as follows:

- electric power generation, transmission, and distribution (cities only);
- water supply and distribution;
- wastewater collection, treatment, and disposal;
- gas production, storage, transmission, and distribution (cities only);
- public transportation;
- solid waste collection and disposal;
- cable television (cities only);
- off-street parking; and
- stormwater management.

The statute applies to the listed functions regardless of whether the city or county operates the function as an enterprise. For example, many cities operate solid waste collection services out of their general funds, paying for most of the service with property taxes and other general fund revenues. Such a city might, however, provide some of its collection services—such as collecting yard waste or collecting containers from a customer's back yard rather than from the street—for a fee. The customer records for those isolated fees would be subject to the statute, even though the solid waste activity itself was not operated as an enterprise through a separate enterprise fund.

Special Purpose Governments

In addition to applying to the expressly listed city and county functions, G.S. 132-1.1(c) extends to any other "public entity providing utility services, excluding airports." The quoted language is somewhat problematic. For counties and cities, the statute extends to all the public enterprises listed in the two cited statutes. For special purpose governmental entities, the statute applies to any "public entity providing utility services." It is not clear whether the General Assembly used the word "utility" as a synonym for "public enterprise" or intended the word in a more technical sense, which would omit some of the listed enterprises. That is, does the statute extend to any public enterprise listed above, regardless of the kind of local government entity involved; or, for entities other than counties and cities, does it apply only to activities traditionally recognized as public utilities? In the latter case, the statute would not extend to solid waste services and parking, which are not normally considered public utilities, nor would it likely extend to stormwater management.

It seems more reasonable to understand "utility" as a synonym for "public enterprise," despite the normally narrower meaning the word carries. First, the specific exclusion of airports from the phrase "utility services" supports the broader meaning. If the narrower meaning were intended, the exclusion would be unnecessary; airports are not utilities. Second, there seems to be no good reason to enact a policy that exempts from public access the records of solid waste collection entities operated by a city or county but not those of entities operated by a sanitary district, or that exempts a city's stormwater management records but not those of a water and sewer authority. The privacy and competitive concerns are identical and do not differ simply because of the kind of local government entity involved. Based on that conclusion, here is a list of the kinds of local government entities, besides counties and cities, whose records might include customer billing information:

- water and sewer authorities (water, sewer, stormwater management);[2]
- metropolitan water districts (water, sewer);[3]
- metropolitan sewerage districts (sewer);[4]
- county water and sewerage districts (water, sewer);[5]
- sanitary districts (water, sewer, solid waste);[6]
- regional solid waste management authorities (solid waste);[7]
- regional public transportation authorities (public transportation);[8]
- regional transportation authorities (public transportation);[9]
- public transportation authorities (public transportation);[10]
- parking authorities (parking);[11] and
- regional natural gas districts.[12]

Functions That Are Not Covered

There are a number of local government functions that are not public enterprises but nevertheless charge fees and produce customer billing records. These functions are not covered by the statute, and their billing records are open to the public unless some other statute provides an exemption. Here are some important examples:

Airports. G.S. 132-1.1(c) itself provides that it does not extend to airport operations, even though that function is included in the listing of public enterprises in G.S. 153A-274 and G.S. 160A-311. Thus, records of hangar leases, for example, remain open to public access.

Public housing. Both public housing authorities and some cities operate public housing programs, and their billing records concern tenants of public housing. Those records remain open to public access.

Recreation programs. Some local government recreation programs operate facilities that offer memberships, such as golf courses or fitness centers. Those records are not covered by this statute.

What Is Billing Information?

The statute defines "billing information" as "any record or information, in whatever form, compiled or maintained with respect to individual customers." Clearly the category

---

2. N.C. GEN. STAT. [hereinafter G.S.] Ch. 162A, Art. 1.
3. G.S. Ch. 162A, Art. 4.
4. G.S. Ch. 162A, Art. 5.
5. G.S. Ch. 162A, Art. 6.
6. G.S. Ch. 130A, Art. 2, Pt. 2.
7. G.S. Ch. 153A, Art. 22.
8. G.S. Ch. 160A, Art. 26.
9. G.S. Ch. 160A, Art. 27.
10. G.S. Ch. 160A, Art. 25.
11. G.S. Ch. 160A, Art. 24.
12. G.S. Ch. 160A, Art. 28.

includes records that a local government operating an enterprise maintains separately for each enterprise customer, starting with information as basic as the customer's name and address. These records would include the following:

- information a customer or entity provides when applying for and being accepted for service;
- information generated by the enterprise as a result of the application, such as a credit check;
- the amount of enterprise services used by a customer;
- the customer's payment history;
- information about the customer's bank account or credit card account;[13]
- records of special services provided to a customer, such as a lead pipe inspection conducted by a water utility;
- records of complaints or inquiries made by the customer and the government's response to them;
- information a customer provides when terminating service, such as a forwarding address.

If a local government generates a list from the protected information, such as a list of new customers or a cutoff list, the list is also covered by the statutory exemption. If the covered information is used, however, to generate statistical records, and those statistics do not reveal individual customers, the statistical record would remain open to public access. Thus, for example, if a water utility generated a record showing the number or percentage of customers who were more than 120 days delinquent in their accounts, that record would not be covered by the exemption as long as no individual customers were identified.

Penalty Records

Some public enterprises impose monetary penalties on customers who break operating rules. For example, a city water system might impose monetary penalties on customers who violate usage restrictions during a drought. Whether the records showing such penalties are covered by this exemption depends upon the method the city uses to establish the penalty system. If the penalty was established as part of the operating rules of the system, so that the method of collection is to include the penalty on the customer's water bill, the amount of the penalty would be covered as billing information. If, on the other hand, the city established the penalty under a police power ordinance and enforces it in the manner of other ordinances—for example, through suit before a magistrate—it is no longer billing information but rather an ordinance enforcement record, and the amount of any penalty would be open to public access.

---

13. A customer's bank account or credit card account number is independently exempted from public access by G.S. 132-1.10, discussed *supra* in chapter 15.

Release of Billing Information

The statute provides that nothing in its terms is intended to limit a governmental entity from releasing billing information in three specified circumstances:

1. In connection with bond financing associated with the enterprise
2. When necessary to maintain the integrity and quality of enterprise services
3. When necessary to assist public safety, emergency management, or judicial officers with their duties

The issue then arises, may a local government release billing information in circumstances other than those specified in the statute? The answer is probably yes.

It is useful to begin by recalling a point made in chapter 6: some exceptions to public access are mandatory and some are merely permissive.[14] Several statutes exclude one or more categories of records from the right of public access and specifically prohibit a government or official with custody of those records from making them public. In contrast, other statutes exclude certain categories of records from the right of public access but do not prohibit their custodians from making them public. Rather, these statutes leave the decision about public access to these categories of records within the custodians' discretion, thus allowing permissive exceptions to access. How does the billing information statute fit within this dichotomy?

G.S. 132-1.1(c) was enacted by Session Law 2001-473, which began as Senate Bill 774.[15] It was introduced in the Senate as a blank bill—that is, it carried no substantive provisions when it was introduced and referred to a committee. The substantive provisions first emerged as a Senate committee substitute that proposed to exclude billing information from public access by amending G.S. 132-1.2. This section is an example of a statute that creates a mandatory exclusion from public access; its introductory language provides that nothing in the public records law "shall be construed to . . . authorize a public agency . . . to disclose" the information specified in the section. (Originally enacted to exclude business trade secrets from public access, the section has been amended over time to exclude other types of information as well.) The bill passed the Senate in that form. If it had been enacted as an amendment to G.S. 132-1.2, the circumstances listed in the subsection would clearly be the only ones in which billing information could be made public. The House, however, prepared its own committee substitute, one of the features of which was to shift the proposed statute's codification from G.S. 132-1.2 to G.S. 132-1.1. This change was significant because the latter statute includes a permissive, rather than a mandatory, exception to the right of access: subsection (a) excludes from public access letters written from a governmental agency's attorney to its governing board but permits the governing board to make such

14. *See supra* chapter 6, text accompanying note 10.

15. The following account of the progress of Senate Bill 774 through the 2001 General Assembly is based on copies of the original bill and each modification to it found in the library of the School of Government, The University of North Carolina at Chapel Hill. The various versions of the bill are also available on the General Assembly's website at www.ncga.state.nc.us/gascripts/BillLookUp/BillLookUp.pl?Session=2001&BillID=S774. The exclusion of airport records from the subsection was made by S.L. 2003-287.

a letter public if it wishes.[16] Furthermore, the House committee substitute also explicitly stated that "[n]othing contained herein shall limit disclosure by a city or county of billing information." The House passed the bill in the form the committee presented to it, but the Senate then refused to concur in the House changes. The final language was agreed upon in a conference committee. Significantly, the conference committee's version retained the House's codification of the statute in G.S. 132-1.1, which is not a wholly mandatory exclusion statute. In addition to this legislative history, the statute itself contains no language expressly prohibiting a local government from disclosing billing information; it is cast in permissive rather than mandatory form.

Therefore, it seems a better reading of the sentence referenced at the beginning of this section and of the three circumstances listed in the statute to assume that the General Assembly wanted to make it clear that local governments could disclose billing information in the three listed circumstances but that the listing does not exhaust the circumstances under which public disclosure might be made.

This conclusion is reinforced by the number of circumstances in which many would think it appropriate to disclose certain sorts of billing information but which do not fit easily within the specific listed circumstances. Here are some examples:

- The government's auditor may need billing information in order to carry out the testing of financial systems required by generally accepted auditing standards.
- A rate consultant may need billing information in order to propose modifications in the enterprise's rate structure.
- A landlord of federally subsidized housing may need billing information in order to calculate allowable rents.
- An adult child may want access to billing information to assure herself that her elderly parent is continuing to keep current on utility and other bills.

Perhaps a government could argue that each of these examples already fits within the three listed circumstances—particularly the one referencing the integrity and quality of the enterprise's service—but if that were the case, it is hard to imagine a legitimate disclosure that does not fit within the list. The following sections provide some specific comments on release of billing information.

Establish Specific Policies

It is greatly preferable that any release of billing information that does not fit neatly within the three listed circumstances be done pursuant to policies that have been appropriately adopted by the governing board or the administration rather than on an ad hoc basis. Chapter 6 discusses the possibility of waiver of exceptions to the right of access to public

---

16. Subsection (a) of G.S. 132-1.1 is discussed *supra* in chapter 9. Subsection (b) of the section is a cross-reference to the statutes excluding from public access certain categories of local tax information, while subsections (d) and (e) are cross-references to other, specialized exclusions; all of these cross-referenced statutes are mandatory in nature. Finally, subsection (f) creates a mandatory exclusion from access for certain admissions information in the university and community college systems.

records,[17] and a series of ad hoc—and potentially inconsistent—releases of billing information might be grounds for finding a waiver of the exception.

Customer Consent

The statute does not create any right on the part of the customer to have to consent to a release of billing information. The decision is solely in the discretion of the government providing the enterprisory service.

Postcard Billing

A number of local governments use postcard billing for enterprise services, and they have wondered whether such a billing system in some fashion violates this statute. As has just been discussed, the statute does not appear to restrict release of the information to the three listed circumstances; but even if it did, postcard billing fits easily within that framework. The usual reason for that form of billing is to save on mailing costs, and it is quite clear that measures taken to reduce enterprise expenses have the effect of maintaining the quality of enterprise services.

Sharing within the Government

The statute does not bar sharing billing information within the local government providing the enterprise service. The statute at most restricts "public disclosure" of billing information, and sharing among government departments is not public disclosure. Therefore, for example, a water department could share billing information with the unit's tax department, in order to facilitate collection of taxes.

---

17. Chapter 6, *supra,* text accompanying notes 39 through 42.

Appendix 16A—Statute

G.S. 132-1.1

§ 132-1.1. Confidential communications by legal counsel to public board or agency; State tax information; public enterprise billing information; Address Confidentiality Program information.

. . .

(c) Public Enterprise Billing Information.—Billing information compiled and maintained by a city or county or other public entity providing utility services in connection with the ownership or operation of a public enterprise, excluding airports, is not a public record as defined in G.S. 132-1. Nothing contained herein is intended to limit public disclosure by a city or county of billing information:

(1) That the city or county determines will be useful or necessary to assist bond counsel, bond underwriters, underwriters' counsel, rating agencies or investors or potential investors in making informed decisions regarding bonds or other obligations incurred or to be incurred with respect to the public enterprise;

(2) That is necessary to assist the city, county, State, or public enterprise to maintain the integrity and quality of services it provides; or

(3) That is necessary to assist law enforcement, public safety, fire protection, rescue, emergency management, or judicial officers in the performance of their duties.

As used herein, "billing information" means any record or information, in whatever form, compiled or maintained with respect to individual customers by any owner or operator of a public enterprise, as defined in G.S. 160A-311, excluding subdivision (9), and G.S. 153A-274, excluding subdivision (4), or other public entity providing utility services, excluding airports, relating to services it provides or will provide to the customer.

Chapter 17—Personal Information from Motor Vehicle Records

Statutory Summary

In 1994 the United States Congress enacted the Driver's Privacy Protection Act (DPPA) to regulate the release by state departments of motor vehicles (DMVs) of "personal information . . . about any individual obtained by the department in connection with a motor vehicle record."[1] The statute defines "personal information" as information that identifies a person, including the person's

- name,
- address,
- photograph,
- Social Security number,
- driver identification number,
- telephone number, and
- medical or disability information.[2]

Personal information does not, however, include information on vehicular accidents, driving violations, or driver's status.

The DPPA includes a long list of exceptions to its basic ban on disclosing personal information, and the first of these permits a state DMV to disclose such information "[f]or use

1. The Driver's Privacy Protection Act (DPPA) is codified at 18 U.S.C. §§ 2721 through 2725 and is set out in appendix 17A at the end of this chapter; the quotation in the text is from 18 U.S.C. § 2721(a)(1). The U.S. Supreme Court upheld the constitutionality of the statute and its regulation of state government in *Reno v. Condon*, 528 U.S. 141 (2000). The North Carolina Division of Motor Vehicles is directed to comply with the federal statute by N.C. Gen. Stat. [hereinafter G.S.] § 20-43.1.

2. 18 U.S.C. § 2725(3) (2006).

by any government agency, including any court or law enforcement agency, in carrying out its functions."[3] Once a government agency has received this information, the federal statute restricts the recipient agency's own disclosure of the information to the same list that is applicable to a state DMV.

Discussion

Federal Rules Not Applicable to Personal Information Gathered by a Local Government

The DPPA applies only to personal information gathered by a state DMV. If a local government independently gathers some of the same information, even from motor vehicle records, the federal statute does not apply. For example, say a local police officer stops a car because of a traffic violation. The officer will be able to obtain the car's license plate number from the vehicle itself and will be able to learn the driver's name, address, and driver's license number from the license, which will be shown to the officer by the driver. When the officer enters this information on the traffic citation, the information is not protected by the DPPA, because the officer did not obtain the information from the North Carolina DMV.[4] (The citation would, of course, be subject to the provisions concerning criminal investigation information enacted in Section 132-1.4 of the North Carolina General Statutes [hereinafter G.S.] and discussed *supra* in chapter 8.)

The Status of Personal Information Obtained from the DMV under the Public Records Law

There are at least two sorts of local government agencies that routinely obtain personal information from the North Carolina DMV. First, the structure of North Carolina's system for collecting property taxes on motor vehicles currently requires the DMV to disclose to county tax officials certain information about the owners of taxed vehicles that is gathered from motor vehicle records.[5] Some of this information is personal, such as the name and address of the owner of the vehicle, the owner's Social Security number, and the owner's driver's license number. Second, there are a variety of circumstances under which a local law enforcement agency might request personal information from the North Carolina DMV. For example, when an officer places a parking ticket on a vehicle, the only information the ticketing officer has about the vehicle is its license plate number. If the government needs to proceed with some sort of enforcement mechanism against the driver, it must first identify that person, and it will need the help of the DMV to do so. Or, if a city is utilizing a red light camera program, in which the camera photographs only the license plate of the vehicle running the red light, once again the city will need the help of the DMV to identify the driver of the vehicle. Once the local government agency has received personal

---

3. 18 U.S.C. § 2721(b)(1) (2006).
4. *See* Atlas Transit, Inc. v. Korte, 638 N.W.2d 625 (Wis. Ct. App. 2001).
5. *See* G.S. 105-330.5(a).

information from the North Carolina DMV, is that information subject to the normal rules on public access or is access to it restricted under the federal DPPA?

At first blush, it might appear that the DPPA restricts public access to the information once it is in the hands of the local government. As noted in the statutory summary, 18 U.S.C. § 2721(c) specifies that an entity that has received personal information pursuant to the federal statute "may resell or redisclose the information" only in the same ways that are available to the DMV under the federal statute. General disclosure to the public, pursuant to a state public records law, is not on the federal statutory list; indeed, the entire purpose of the federal statute was to preempt the applicability of state public records laws to this kind of information.[6] The matter is not that simple, however.

As was noted in the statutory summary, the DPPA permits a state DMV to release personal information to a governmental entity for the latter's use "in carrying out its functions." This seems to mean that if a governmental entity must release the information in order to carry out its functions, doing so is permitted under the federal scheme. For example, if a law enforcement agency is investigating a hit-and-run accident in which it knows only the license plate number of the vehicle, it might obtain the name and address of the driver from the DMV, as well as a photograph of the driver. It might then make the name, address, and photograph public in order to apprehend the suspect.

In addition, some government agencies gather or generate information for the purpose of making that information public. In the Connecticut case of *Davis v. Freedom of Information Commission*,[7] an insurance investigator had gone to the Bridgeport tax assessor's office and asked to inspect the motor vehicle grand list books. The assessor refused to allow the inspection, on the ground that the information in the books had come from the state DMV and that therefore the DPPA prohibited public access to the information. The investigator appealed to the state's Freedom of Information Commission, which directed the assessor to allow the inspection, and this order was affirmed by the superior court. In its opinion (which, as indicated in note 7, was adopted by the state supreme court), the superior court pointed out that state law required the tax assessor to compile the information received from the DMV and then make it available for public inspection; that opportunity for public inspection was an integral part of the statutory scheme. As a result, the superior court affirmed the order of the Freedom of Information Commission. Although the Connecticut court did not elaborate on this point, the fact that the federal statute permits disclosure of personal information to government agencies to carry out their functions seems to permit public release of the information, at least when an agency's functions specifically call for such release.

The North Carolina attorney general's office reached a similar conclusion about information supplied to local tax officials by the North Carolina DMV. In a February 2005 opinion issued to the state's commissioner of motor vehicles, the chief deputy attorney general

---

6. *See* Electronic Privacy Information Center, *History of the DPPA*, The Drivers Privacy Protection Act (DPPA) and the Privacy of Your State Motor Vehicle Record (last updated Aug. 26, 2005), http://epic.org/privacy/drivers/.

7. 787 A.2d 530 (Conn. 2002). The Connecticut Supreme Court issued a per curiam opinion, affirming and adopting the opinion of the superior court. That lower court decision is found at 790 A.2d 1188 (Conn. Super. Ct. 2001).

pointed out several provisions in the Machinery Act (the statute regulating property tax listing, assessing, and collecting) that required publication and distribution of tax information, including information obtained by the DMV. Noting that "[t]his well-established statutory process would be substantially impeded if motor vehicle registration information obtained from DMV was required to be kept confidential," the author concluded that "[w]e do not believe it was the intent of Congress in enacting the DPPA to prohibit local taxing authorities from releasing such generic information when required by state tax laws."[8]

Similarly, if a law enforcement agency receives basic information from the DMV that it enters into the public portion of an incident report, G.S. 132-1.4 specifically makes that information public, and the same considerations would seem to apply to that statute as apply to the tax statutes.

The Connecticut case and the attorney general's opinion each involved information that the appropriate statutes specifically directed be made public, and that is also true of any information that becomes part of a law enforcement incident report. What about information, though, that is not subject to such a specific direction but that is simply open to public access under North Carolina's basic public records law? Does making the information public pursuant to the public records law amount to carrying out the governmental entity's functions, so that it is permissible under the DPPA? There does not appear to be any case law involving that issue, but the situation differs enough from *Davis* and the situation that was addressed by the attorney general to at least make possible a different answer.[9] There is some risk in releasing the information. The DPPA creates a private right of action for damages against anyone who knowingly and improperly discloses personal information from a motor vehicle record in favor of the person whose information was disclosed.[10] Unfortunately, we will have to await further legislative or judicial action to be certain about the answer to this last question.[11]

---

8. Letter to George Tatum, 9 February 2005, Advisory Opinion No. 574, *available at* www.ncdoj.gov/About-DOJ/Legal-Services/Legal-Opinions.aspx.

9. State legal officers have reached opposing conclusions on this point. The Wisconsin attorney general has issued an informal opinion arguing that local law enforcement agencies have a duty to allow public access to their public records, and therefore they are carrying out their functions when they allow public access to records including personal information obtained from that state's DMV. Letter to Robert J. Dreps & Jennifer L. Peterson, 29 April 2008, *available at* www.ncdoj.gov/About-DOJ/Legal-Services/Legal-Opinions.aspx. On the other hand, the Office of Open Records Counsel of the Tennessee State Comptroller of the Treasury has concluded that protected personal information must be redacted from an otherwise public local law enforcement document because of the provisions of the DPPA. Letter to Charles T. Ziegler & Melissa Ashburn, 6 March 2009, Opinion No. 09-03, *available at* www.tn.gov/comptroller/openrecords/opinions.htm.

10. 18 U.S.C. § 2724 (2006).

11. The question may be more rhetorical than real, in that it appears to be rare for the DMV to share information with local agencies except for tax offices and law enforcement agencies.

Appendix 17A—Statute

The Driver's Privacy Protection Act

TITLE 18—CRIMES AND CRIMINAL PROCEDURE

PART I—CRIMES

CHAPTER 123—PROHIBITION ON RELEASE AND USE OF CERTAIN PERSONAL INFORMATION FROM STATE MOTOR VEHICLE RECORDS

Sec. 2721. Prohibition on release and use of certain personal information from State motor vehicle records

(a) In General.—A State department of motor vehicles, and any officer, employee, or contractor thereof, shall not knowingly disclose or otherwise make available to any person or entity:

(1) personal information, as defined in 18 U.S.C. 2725(3), about any individual obtained by the department in connection with a motor vehicle record, except as provided in subsection (b) of this section; or

(2) highly restricted personal information, as defined in 18 U.S.C. 2725(4), about any individual obtained by the department in connection with a motor vehicle record, without the express consent of the person to whom such information applies, except uses permitted in subsections (b)(1), (b)(4), (b)(6), and (b)(9):

Provided, That subsection (a)(2) shall not in any way affect the use of organ donation information on an individual's driver's license or affect the administration of organ donation initiatives in the States.

(b) Permissible Uses.—Personal information referred to in subsection (a) shall be disclosed for use in connection with matters of motor vehicle or driver safety and theft, motor vehicle emissions, motor vehicle product alterations, recalls, or advisories, performance monitoring of motor vehicles and dealers by motor vehicle manufacturers, and removal of non-owner records from the original owner records of motor vehicle manufacturers to carry out the purposes of titles I and IV of the Anti Car Theft Act of 1992, the Automobile Information Disclosure Act (15 U.S.C. 1231 et seq.), the Clean Air Act (42 U.S.C. 7401 et seq.), and chapters 301, 305, and 321-331 of title 49, and, subject to subsection (a)(2), may be disclosed as follows:

(1) For use by any government agency, including any court or law enforcement agency, in carrying out its functions, or any private person or entity acting on behalf of a Federal, State, or local agency in carrying out its functions.

(2) For use in connection with matters of motor vehicle or driver safety and theft; motor vehicle emissions; motor vehicle product alterations, recalls, or advisories; performance monitoring of motor vehicles, motor vehicle parts and dealers; motor vehicle market research activities, including survey research; and removal of non-owner records from the original owner records of motor vehicle manufacturers.

(3) For use in the normal course of business by a legitimate business or its agents, employees, or contractors, but only—

(A) to verify the accuracy of personal information submitted by the individual to the business or its agents, employees, or contractors; and
(B) if such information as so submitted is not correct or is no longer correct, to obtain the correct information, but only for the purposes of preventing fraud by, pursuing legal remedies against, or recovering on a debt or security interest against, the individual.

(4) For use in connection with any civil, criminal, administrative, or arbitral proceeding in any Federal, State, or local court or agency or before any self-regulatory body, including the service of process, investigation in anticipation of litigation, and the execution or enforcement of judgments and orders, or pursuant to an order of a Federal, State, or local court.

(5) For use in research activities, and for use in producing statistical reports, so long as the personal information is not published, redisclosed, or used to contact individuals.

(6) For use by any insurer or insurance support organization, or by a self-insured entity, or its agents, employees, or contractors, in connection with claims investigation activities, antifraud activities, rating or underwriting.

(7) For use in providing notice to the owners of towed or impounded vehicles.

(8) For use by any licensed private investigative agency or licensed security service for any purpose permitted under this subsection.

(9) For use by an employer or its agent or insurer to obtain or verify information relating to a holder of a commercial driver's license that is required under chapter 313 of title 49.

(10) For use in connection with the operation of private toll transportation facilities.

(11) For any other use in response to requests for individual motor vehicle records if the State has obtained the express consent of the person to whom such personal information pertains.

(12) For bulk distribution for surveys, marketing or solicitations if the State has obtained the express consent of the person to whom such personal information pertains.

(13) For use by any requester, if the requester demonstrates it has obtained the written consent of the individual to whom the information pertains.

(14) For any other use specifically authorized under the law of the State that holds the record, if such use is related to the operation of a motor vehicle or public safety.

(c) Resale or Redisclosure.—An authorized recipient of personal information (except a recipient under subsection (b)(11) or (12)) may resell or redisclose the information only for a use permitted under subsection (b) (but not for uses under subsection (b)(11) or (12)). An authorized recipient under subsection (b)(11) may resell or redisclose personal information for any purpose. An authorized recipient under subsection (b)(12) may resell or redisclose personal information pursuant to subsection (b)(12). Any authorized recipient (except a recipient under subsection (b)(11)) that resells or rediscloses personal information covered by this chapter must keep for a period of 5 years records identifying each person or entity that receives information and the permitted purpose for which the information will be used and must make such records available to the motor vehicle department upon request.

(d) Waiver Procedures.—A State motor vehicle department may establish and carry out procedures under which the department or its agents, upon receiving a request for personal information that does not fall within one of the exceptions in subsection (b), may mail a copy of the request to the individual about whom the information was requested, informing such individual of the request, together with a statement to the effect that the information will not be released unless the individual waives such individual's right to privacy under this section.

(e) Prohibition on Conditions.—No State may condition or burden in any way the issuance of an individual's motor vehicle record as defined in 18 U.S.C. 2725(1) to obtain express consent. Nothing in this paragraph shall be construed to prohibit a State from charging an administrative fee for issuance of a motor vehicle record.

Sec. 2722. Additional unlawful acts

(a) Procurement for Unlawful Purpose.—It shall be unlawful for any person knowingly to obtain or disclose personal information, from a motor vehicle record, for any use not permitted under section 2721(b) of this title.

(b) False Representation.—It shall be unlawful for any person to make false representation to obtain any personal information from an individual's motor vehicle record.

Sec. 2723. Penalties

(a) Criminal Fine.—A person who knowingly violates this chapter shall be fined under this title.

(b) Violations by State Department of Motor Vehicles.—Any State department of motor vehicles that has a policy or practice of substantial noncompliance with this chapter shall be subject to a civil penalty imposed by the Attorney General of not more than $5,000 a day for each day of substantial noncompliance.

Sec. 2724. Civil action

(a) Cause of Action.—A person who knowingly obtains, discloses or uses personal information, from a motor vehicle record, for a purpose not permitted under this chapter shall be liable to the individual to whom the information pertains, who may bring a civil action in a United States district court.

(b) Remedies.—The court may award—

(1) actual damages, but not less than liquidated damages in the amount of $2,500;
(2) punitive damages upon proof of willful or reckless disregard of the law;
(3) reasonable attorneys' fees and other litigation costs reasonably incurred; and
(4) such other preliminary and equitable relief as the court determines to be appropriate.

Sec. 2725. Definitions

In this chapter—

(1) "motor vehicle record" means any record that pertains to a motor vehicle operator's permit, motor vehicle title, motor vehicle registration, or identification card issued by a department of motor vehicles;

(2) "person" means an individual, organization or entity, but does not include a State or agency thereof;
(3) "personal information" means information that identifies an individual, including an individual's photograph, social security number, driver identification number, name, address (but not the 5-digit zip code), telephone number, and medical or disability information, but does not include information on vehicular accidents, driving violations, and driver's status.\1\

\1\ So in original. The period probably should be a semicolon.

----

(4) "highly restricted personal information" means an individual's photograph or image, social security number, medical or disability information; and
(5) "express consent" means consent in writing, including consent conveyed electronically that bears an electronic signature as defined in section 106(5) of Public Law 106-229.

Chapter 18—Minutes and General Accounts of Closed Sessions

Statutory Summary

The open meetings law imposes two requirements for making records of closed sessions.[1] First, the law requires that each public body (an entity subject to the open meetings law) prepare "full and accurate minutes" of all meetings subject to the open meetings law, including all closed sessions. Second, the law requires that each public body prepare a "general account" of each closed session, so that someone who was not present may gain a "reasonable understanding" of what happened during the session. Both the minutes and the general account may take written form, or the public body may meet these two requirements by making a video or audio recording. Although normally minutes of a meeting are public record, the open meetings law permits a public body to seal both the minutes and the general account if public inspection of them would "frustrate the purpose" of the closed session. The public body may withhold sealed minutes and general accounts from public inspection for as long as is necessary to avoid the frustration.

Discussion

The Distinction between Minutes and the General Account

Full and Accurate Minutes

In *Maready v. City of Winston-Salem*[2] the North Carolina Supreme Court discussed the meaning of "full and accurate minutes" for a closed session. The defendant board of county

1. *See* N.C. Gen. Stat. [hereinafter G.S.] § 143-318.10(e). The subsection is set out in appendix 18A at the end of this chapter.
2. 342 N.C. 708, 467 S.E.2d 615 (1996).

commissioners had held closed sessions to discuss economic development matters, and the minutes, in their entirety, read "discussion." Because the board took no action in the closed sessions, the court held that the minutes met the statutory requirement. The court argued that the purpose of minutes was to record what was done at a meeting and not what was said, and therefore when no action was taken, "the cursory reference to 'discussion' in the minutes sufficed."[3]

This holding is consistent with earlier decisions. That the purpose of a public body's minutes is to provide the official record, or proof, of what that body has done has long been recognized by the North Carolina courts. In *Norfolk Southern Railroad Co. v. Reid*,[4] for example, the court wrote that "[t]he object [of minutes] is to preserve a memorial of official transactions, which shall serve both as a record and as a guide."[5] By a record, the court means that the minutes are the best evidence for proving in court what a board has done;[6] by a guide, the court means that the minutes are the best direction to the board's staff to carry out its wishes.[7] Given those purposes, it is the actions that are taken that are important, not the conversation leading up to the actions.

In addition, local government statutes have used the phrase full and accurate minutes (or journal) since at least 1917, and the phrase has been consistently interpreted in this narrower fashion. The state's Municipal Corporation Act of 1917 required that cities and towns keep "[a] full and accurate journal of the proceedings" of their governing bodies.[8] When the local government statutes were modernized in the early 1970s, this phrase was brought forward only slightly modified: both city councils and boards of county commissioners were required to keep full and accurate minutes of their proceedings.[9] These earlier statutes were the obvious source for the phrase set out in the open meetings law.

A 1942 decision of the North Carolina Supreme Court addressing the requirement that city governing bodies keep full and accurate journals of their proceedings evidenced the court's continuing acceptance of the purpose of minutes and the consequent interpretation of the statutory requirement. The court explained that

> "[t]he law requires a record of municipal proceedings to the end that those who may be called to act under it may have no occasion to look beyond it, and to avoid the mischief of leaving municipal corporate action to be proved by parol evidence. The record made by the Clerk of a town meeting, board of supervisors, city council, school district or similar organization is conclusive of the facts therein stated. . . . So long as it is in existence, and can be produced, it is the only competent evidence of the *action of the town or county*."[10]

---

3. *Id.* at 734, 467 S.E.2d at 631.
4. 187 N.C. 320, 121 S.E. 534 (1924).
5. *Id.* at 326, 121 S.E. at 537.
6. *E.g.*, State v. Baynes, 222 N.C. 425, 23 S.E.2d 344 (1942).
7. *Id.*
8. 1917 N.C. Pub. Laws ch. 136, subch. 13, § 1(b). This language was first codified in § 2822 of the Consolidated Statutes (1919) and then in G.S. 160-269.
9. See G.S. 160A-72 for cities (enacted in 1971) and G.S. 153A-42 for counties (enacted in 1973).
10. *Baynes*, 222 N.C. at 427, 23 S.E.2d at 345–46 (quoting 23 Ruling Case Law *Records* § 9, at 159 (1919)) (emphasis added).

A final point supporting the court's decision is the General Assembly's own practice with its "minutes," the journals of each house. Each house of the General Assembly is a public body under the open meetings law, and presumably their own journals meet the requirement for full and accurate minutes that they have imposed on themselves and all other public bodies. The legislative journals have long been limited to setting out motions made, committee reports submitted, the results of each vote, other actions taken by each house, and comparable matters. They do not contain any record of debate nor of subjects about which no action is taken.

Therefore, minutes are full and accurate if they set out any actions taken by the public body, any other information that is necessary to prove that those actions were validly taken, and perhaps a listing of the general topic or topics discussed.

Can Action Be Taken in Closed Session?

A possible source of confusion about the meaning of full and accurate minutes is the misunderstanding about whether a public body can even take official action in closed session. Some think that no action can be taken and therefore, given the *Maready* court's reading of the statutory requirement, question the necessity of recording the minutes of a closed session at all. A careful review of the authorizations for closed sessions, however, makes clear that this premise is incorrect. The law permits a number of actions to be taken in closed session and does not require the fact or substance of such actions to be made immediately public. Here are three examples:

Litigation decisions. Section 143-318.11(a)(3) of the North Carolina General Statutes [hereinafter G.S.] permits a closed session so that a public body may "consider and give instructions to an attorney" concerning anticipated or current litigation. Giving instructions to an attorney constitutes action, and the public body may need to decide (perhaps even by voting) among alternative courses of action before instructing its attorney.

Real property acquisition. G.S. 143-318.11(a)(5) permits a closed session "[t]o establish, or to instruct the public body's staff" concerning the price and other terms of a contract to acquire real property. Establishing a negotiating position constitutes action, as does instructing staff to act in accordance with that position.

Student discipline. G.S. 143-318.11(a)(1) broadly permits closed sessions "[t]o prevent the disclosure of information that is privileged or confidential . . . or not considered a public record." Among the sorts of records that might occasion a closed session under this provision are student records. For example, only a board of education may expel a student;[11] in addition, G.S. 115C-45(c) creates a right to appeal to a school board various decisions made by school personnel, and many such appeals and resulting board decisions involve students. Any actions taken by a school board under these statutes become part of the confidential student record, and the only way to protect the record's confidentiality is to take those actions in closed session.

---

11. G.S. 115C-391(d).

The Nature of the General Account

After the *Maready* decision and its interpretation of full and accurate minutes, the General Assembly responded by adding the requirement of the general account. Obviously the addition of the general account requirement indicates a legislative intention that a public body prepare a fuller narrative of closed sessions than *Maready* required. But how much fuller?

The legislative history. The general account requirement was added to the open meetings law in 1997. The bill, Senate Bill 844, underwent a number of changes as it worked its way through the 1997 General Assembly, and some attention to those changes will help in understanding the requirement.

As introduced, the proposed requirement read as follows:[12]

> When a public body meets in closed session, it shall keep an account of the closed session in a written narrative form such that a person not in attendance would have a reasonable understanding of what transpired, including a record of positions taken by public officials during discussion by the public body. Such accounts, at the option of the public body, may be in the form of sound or video recordings.

The enacted version, however, reads as follows:

> When a public body meets in closed session, it shall keep a general account of the closed session so that a person not in attendance would have a reasonable understanding of what transpired. Such accounts may be a written narrative, or video or audio recordings.

Apart from some reorganizing of the language, two significant modifications were made to the original language in the course of the legislative process. First, and most important, the original requirement that the account include "a record of positions taken by public officials during discussion by the public body" was deleted. It seems reasonable, therefore, to conclude that the final statutory requirement of a general account does not require inclusion of such a record of positions. A general account need not be that specific. Second, the word "general" was placed before account. One must be careful not to place too much emphasis on this change, but it does reinforce the conclusion that the final language contemplates a less-particularized, less-specific account than did the original.

The* Multimedia *case. A 2001 decision of the North Carolina Court of Appeals confirms this understanding of the statutory requirement and gives important guidance in preparing general accounts. *Multimedia Publishing of North Carolina, Inc. v. Henderson County*[13] concerned a closed session held by the county commissioners to receive legal advice about a proposed noise ordinance and a proposed moratorium on construction or operation of race tracks (the particular noise leading to consideration of the ordinance). One of the issues in the case was whether the county's general account of the session met the statute's

---

12. The developing versions of this legislation are found in the original bill file, found in the School of Government library, and are also available on the General Assembly's website at www.ncga.state.nc.us/gascripts/BillLookUp/BillLookUp.pl?Session=1997&BillID=S844.

13. 145 N.C. App. 365, 550 S.E.2d 846 (2001).

requirements; the court held that it did. To discuss and fully understand the court's holding, it will be useful to set out the county's general account in full:

> **CONSULT WITH ATTORNEY**
>
> Staff Attorney, Jennifer Jackson informed the Board that we have already been informed that action on a moratorium will be challenged. She briefly explained the difference between a "Land Use Ordinance" and a "Police Power Ordinance."
>
> There was discussion about the legality of making the term longer than 90 days. It was decided that 90 days would be enough time to give staff time to complete the Noise Ordinance.
>
> The County Attorney then suggested some wording changes to the Ordinance as follows:
>
>> under Moratorium paragraph it will now read "There is hereby imposed a moratorium on the construction or operation of racetracks within the County of Henderson. No permits may be issued by any County department under the control of the Board of Commissioners during the moratorium. This moratorium shall continue in full force and effect for ninety (90) days expiring at midnight on February 9, 1999." (The underlined sentence was the added verbiage.) Also an additional paragraph was suggested entitled Enforcement which read "This Ordinance may be enforced by any legal and equitable remedies including but not limited to injunctive relief."
>
> After conferring with the County Attorney, it was the consensus of the Board to amend the Moratorium Ordinance as recommended by the County Attorney.[14]

This general account includes two sorts of material. First, it lists the legal subjects presented or discussed in the closed session—the difference between land use and police power ordinances and the permissible length of a moratorium. The general account does not, however, set out the substance of either the presentation or the discussion; it merely sets out the subject matter. Second, it lists each consensus agreed to by the board in the closed session—the length of the moratorium (ninety days) and the new language of the moratorium ordinance. Even though these were not board actions of the kind that had to be included in the minutes, they were sufficiently like such actions to justify their inclusion in the general account. Many closed sessions, of course, do not result in any board action or consensus; in such cases, the account need only include the first sort of material. (Of course, any public body is free to prepare more detailed general accounts should it wish to.)

Combining the Minutes and the General Account

Although the minutes and the general account are listed in the open meetings law as two separate documents, as a practical matter most public bodies combine them into a single

14. *Id.* at 366–67, 550 S.E.2d at 848 (emphasis omitted).

document, the general account. This practice reflects the fact that any general account is likely to include any specific actions taken by the public body in a closed session, and therefore having a separate set of minutes is redundant.

Sealing the Minutes and General Account

The Mechanics

The open meetings law specifies that both minutes and general accounts are public records but then goes on to permit either or both to be sealed—that is, shut off from public inspection—in order to avoid frustrating the purpose of the closed session. The implication of the language is that openness is the norm and sealing the exception, but the widespread practice is in fact the opposite. That is, most public bodies and their staffs assume that their closed session records are sealed and only consider opening them when a request for access is made.

If that is to be a public body's practice, it is preferable that it be regularized. That is, the public body should adopt a general policy that all closed session minutes and general accounts are initially sealed and opened only upon action by the public body or pursuant to its policies. A number of public bodies have delegated the decision about opening their closed session records to a staff person—their attorney or perhaps their chief administrator—with instructions to such a person to review the records periodically and remove the seal as appropriate.

For How Long

The period for which minutes or general account (hereinafter, together, the "closed session record") may remain sealed depends in the first instance on the level of detail with which they are prepared. For example, suppose a city or county governing board holds a closed session to discuss the performance of the unit's manager. If the closed session record is only as detailed as the statute requires, and if the closed session was limited to the board's discussion and to communicating to the manager any concerns that the board had about his or her performance, the record might simply state that the board discussed the manager's performance. In such a case, there seems little reason to seal the closed session record. But if the board preferred a more detailed record, it might spell out the members' specific concerns with the manager or include an agreed-upon plan to deal with those concerns. The remainder of this section's discussion assumes that the closed session record is sufficiently detailed so that opening it to public inspection would in fact risk frustrating the purpose of the closed session.

The other factor that will determine the appropriate period for sealing a closed session record is the purpose of the closed session. In some instances the record should be sealed for only a short time. For example, if a board in closed session instructs its attorney to bring a lawsuit and he or she does so shortly thereafter, at that point the closed session record should be unsealed. In other instances, though, the record should be sealed permanently. For example, if a school board in closed session expels a student, the closed session record would become part of the student's record, and G.S. 115C-402(e) makes such a record permanently confidential. The remainder of this section sets out each of the permissible reasons for a closed session and suggests for how long it would be appropriate to seal the record of such a closed session.

To discuss confidential records.[15] This closed session authorization covers a myriad of possible subjects—records that are not open to public inspection under the public records laws. It seems most sensible to treat the closed session record in the same way as the record that was discussed in the closed session. Thus, if the record is one that is permanently confidential, so would the closed session record be permanently confidential. On the other hand, if the record under discussion at some point becomes available for public access, then the closed session record should become available at the same time.

To decide on honorary degrees or other prizes or awards.[16] The purpose of this closed session authorization is to "prevent the premature disclosure" of an honorary degree or comparable prize or award. Clearly, once the degree or prize is awarded or announced, the closed session record should be unsealed.

To meet with an attorney representing the public body.[17] The purpose of this closed session authorization is "to preserve the attorney–client privilege between the attorney and the public body." The attorney–client privilege technically is never lost unless released by the client; it even survives the client's death.[18] Therefore, it might be argued that the record of such a closed session need never be made public. It seems more likely, however, that a court would require unsealing such a record once the particular legal issue or issues that occasioned the closed session have been resolved.[19] Thus, if the public body was discussing particular litigation, the closed session record would be unsealed once the litigation was over; or if the discussion involved a particular ordinance, as in Henderson County in the *Multimedia* case, the closed session record would be unsealed once the ordinance was adopted.

To consider economic development matters.[20] Public bodies use this closed session authorization to consider possible economic development incentives and to otherwise discuss negotiations with companies considering locating to or expanding within the community served by the public body. As is discussed *supra* in chapter 12, G.S. 132-6(d) requires that records "relating to the proposed expansion or location of specific business or industrial projects" be made public once the project has either been announced or abandoned. It is likely that any closed session records related to such a project are covered by the statute and should be made public pursuant to its direction.

To consider acquisition of real property.[21] This closed session authorization permits a public body to consider its negotiating position in acquiring real property and to give instructions to its bargaining agent. Once the property has been acquired, or the government decides not to pursue it any further, the closed session record should be made public.

---

15. G.S. 143-318.11(a)(1).

16. G.S. 143-318.11(a)(2).

17. G.S. 143-318.11(a)(3).

18. In *In re Investigation of Death of Eric Miller*, 357 N.C. 316, 584 S.E.2d 772 (2003), the North Carolina Supreme Court held "that the attorney–client privilege does survive the death of the client." 357 N.C. at 323, 584 S.E.2d at 779.

19. There has been no appellate discussion of this issue, but the only trial court known to the author to have addressed it rejected the public body's argument that the closed session record could remain sealed once the legal issue was resolved. *See* Fayetteville Publ'g Co. v. Cumberland County, No. 01-CVS-9134 (N.C. Super. Ct., Cumberland County, June 7, 2002).

20. G.S. 143-318.11(a)(4).

21. G.S. 143-318.11(a)(5).

To consider an employment contract.[22] This closed session authorization permits a public body to consider its negotiating position in regard to an employment contract and to give instructions to its bargaining agent. Once such a contract is entered into, it is a public record,[23] and therefore the closed session record should be made public at that time.

To consider a personnel matter.[24] This closed session authorization permits a public body to consider an employee's performance, to review and discuss applicants for employment, or to hear and investigate complaints by or against public employees. In each case the closed session record is part of the employee's personnel file[25] and therefore should be made public only pursuant to the relevant personnel privacy statute.

To consider criminal investigations.[26] This closed session authorization permits a public body to plan, conduct, or hear reports about investigations into alleged criminal misconduct. It seems appropriate to consider the resulting closed session record as a criminal investigation record, discussed *supra* in chapter 8, which would permit keeping the record sealed permanently.

To consider school violence response plans.[27] This closed session authorization permits a local school board to formulate plans for responding to school violence. The purpose of the closed session is to permit the school board's plans to remain confidential, and for that reason it appears that the closed session record can remain permanently sealed.

To consider terrorism prevention or response plans.[28] This closed session authorization permits a public body to discuss and approve plans to prevent or respond to terrorist activity or to receive briefings about possible terrorist activity. Under G.S. 132-1.7, discussed *infra* in chapter 20, these plans need never be made public, and therefore it appears that the closed session record can be sealed permanently as well.

Miscellaneous Matters

Notes Taken at Closed Sessions

It may often be that participants in a closed session take notes at the session in order to guide their actions afterwards. For example, in a closed session with the public body's attorney at which the public body gives instructions to the attorney as to the handling of litigation, the attorney may take notes on the board's instructions. Assuming that those notes are public records in the broad sense,[29] are they closed to public inspection? They are not part of the minutes or general account of the closed session, but to require their release would certainly frustrate the purpose of holding the closed session as much as would premature release of minutes or general account. This situation arose in Maine, where a local school board held a closed session and two board members and the board's attorney each took notes of the board's deliberations. Neither the Maine open meetings law nor the Maine

---

22. *Id.*
23. *See supra* chapter 7, notes 41 through 45 and accompanying text.
24. G.S. 143-318.11(a)(6).
25. *See supra* chapter 7, notes 57 through 58 and accompanying text.
26. G.S. 143-318.11(a)(7).
27. G.S. 143-318.11(a)(8).
28. G.S. 143-318.11(a)(9).
29. See the discussion of the status of personal notes as public records in chapter 1, *supra*, in the text accompanying notes 64 through 76.

public records law addressed the status of such notes, and therefore the local newspaper sought copies of the notes. Despite the statutory silence, the Maine Supreme Judicial Court held that such notes were not open to the public.[30] That result seems sensible and should be adopted by the North Carolina courts as well.

Minutes of Groups Not Subject to the Open Meetings Law

Not all government groups that exist are public bodies under the open meetings law. The group might be self-selected or otherwise so informal in its creation that it does not meet the statutory definition of public body, or it might be a staff group that is specifically exempted from the definition.[31] Such a group is not subject to the requirements of the open meetings law, but neither is it eligible for the benefits of that statute. In *News & Observer Publishing Co. v. Poole,* the so-called Poole Commission was not a public body under the then-current definition in the open meetings law.[32] When the commission attempted to shield minutes of its meetings from public access because the meetings were legally closed to the public, the North Carolina Supreme Court would not allow it to do so. The court stated:

> The Public Records Act and the Open Meetings Law are discrete statutes, each designed to promote in a different way openness in government. There is no suggestion in either statute that an agency not subject to one is, *ipso facto*, exempt from the other.[33]

As a result, the minutes of such a group are public record. It may be that some other exception to the right of public access might occasionally apply to minutes of such a group, but the group cannot use the exception for closed session minutes applicable to public bodies under the open meetings law.

Tapes of Closed Sessions

Many public bodies do not tape their closed sessions. Even when they do, they are more likely to use the tapes to help prepare a written general account and minutes rather than accept the statute's invitation to use the tape recording as the general account and minutes. As long as the closed session record is sealed, it seems apparent that the tape is also sealed. Once the closed session record has been made available to the public, however, the tape, if it still exists, is probably open to public access as well.

The Importance of Complying with Closed Session Procedures

Under G.S. 143-318.11(c), a public body planning to go into closed session may do so only upon a motion made and voted upon in open session, and the statute sets out certain specifications as to the content of the motion. If a public body holds a closed session without complying with these procedural requirements, it jeopardizes its ability to seal the

---

30. Blethen Maine Newspapers, Inc. v. Portland Sch. Comm., 947 A.2d 479 (Me. 2008). The court also held that materials prepared for the closed session were not open to public inspection. Such materials could be made part of the minutes of a closed session, however, and therefore their status is not as ambiguous under North Carolina's public records law.

31. *See* G.S. 143-318.10(b), (c).

32. 330 N.C. 465, 412 S.E.2d 7 (1992).

33. *Id.* at 478, 412 S.E.2d at 15.

records of the closed session. In *Gumina v. City of Sterling*,[34] a 2004 case from Colorado, a city council held a pair of closed sessions to discuss the performance of an assistant city manager and subsequently terminated her. Colorado law requires that a public body holding a closed session for that purpose give notice of its intention to the employee, who can then demand that the discussion take place in open session. The council did not give the required notice to the assistant city manager, and the Colorado appellate court held that the closed session was therefore illegal. Because the session was not legally closed, the court held that the minutes could not be sealed.

34. 119 P.3d 527 (Colo. App. 2004).

Appendix 18A—Statute

G.S. 143-318.10

§ 143-318.10. All official meetings of public bodies open to the public.

. . .

(e) Every public body shall keep full and accurate minutes of all official meetings, including any closed sessions held pursuant to G.S. 143-318.11. Such minutes may be in written form or, at the option of the public body, may be in the form of sound or video and sound recordings. When a public body meets in closed session, it shall keep a general account of the closed session so that a person not in attendance would have a reasonable understanding of what transpired. Such accounts may be a written narrative, or video or audio recordings. Such minutes and accounts shall be public records within the meaning of the Public Records Law, G.S. 132-1 et seq.; provided, however, that minutes or an account of a closed session conducted in compliance with G.S. 143-318.11 may be withheld from public inspection so long as public inspection would frustrate the purpose of a closed session.

Chapter 19—Construction and Procurement Records

Public agencies in North Carolina solicit bids and award contracts for purchases, for construction or repair services, and for a variety of other services; they also manage contracts for construction or repair. A number of statutes, scattered throughout the North Carolina General Statutes [hereinafter G.S.], affect some of the local government records received or generated as part of the procurement or construction process, and these are discussed in this chapter. There is a second group of statutes, applicable only to state government, that sometimes establish different rules, and when relevant they are referenced in this chapter as well.

Cost Estimates, Bidders' Lists, and Related Information

G.S. 133-33, unlike some of the other statutes discussed in this chapter, applies to both state and local government, permitting both to exclude limited project information from public inspection.[1] The statute permits any public agency to adopt rules that make confidential

1. The statute is set out in appendix 19A at the end of this chapter.

both the agency's cost estimates for a project and any list of contractors who have obtained proposals for bid purposes. The statute itself does not make this information confidential; rather, each public agency must first adopt regulations to that end.

Formal Bids

G.S. 143-129 governs formal contracts for local government agencies, including school administrative units. Currently, the statute defines such contracts as purchase contracts of $90,000 or more and construction or repair contracts of $500,000 or more. The statute requires that bids, which are sealed when submitted, be opened in public.[2] G.S. 143-129 contains no provision justifying a denial of public access to the bids at any time after they have been opened.

Informal Bids

G.S. 143-131 governs informal contracts for local government agencies, including school administrative units. Currently, the statute defines such contracts as purchase contracts and construction and repair contracts of $30,000 or more, up to the minimum thresholds for formal contracts. The statute requires the local government to maintain a record of the bids and specifies that this record "shall not be subject to public inspection until the contract has been awarded."[3]

If a local government submits informal bids to its governing board for award, purchasing officials might want to make the bids public at that time, before the actual awarding of the contract. Because the statute does not prohibit such a release but simply does not require it, it is entirely appropriate for purchasing officials to make the bids public when they are considered by the board.

It is common for local governments to follow the informal bid procedure for contracts that are smaller than $30,000, as a matter of local policy. It should be noted that the exception to public access enacted in G.S. 143-131 applies only to contracts in the statutorily defined informal range. If the amount of a contract will be less than $30,000, there is no exception that applies to the bids once received, and therefore they are public once received, without regard for when the contract is awarded.

Request for Proposal Processes

Local governments often procure services through a request for proposal (RFP) process. In addition, the statutes permit using such a process occasionally as an exception to the usual requirement of formal or informal bidding. The question then arises, at what point

2. The relevant provision is set out in appendix 19A at the end of this chapter.
3. The relevant provision is set out in appendix 19A at the end of this chapter.

do any proposals received as part of such a process become public record? For two sorts of processes, each a specific statutory exception to formal bid requirements, the statute provides an answer. For other RFP processes, the statutes are silent.

Information Technology Goods and Services

G.S. 143-129.8 permits local governments to use an RFP procedure to acquire information technology. Subsection (d) of the statute specifically provides that proposals submitted under such a procedure "shall not be subject to public inspection until a contract is awarded."[4] This exception to the right of inspection probably applies as well to any analysis of the proposals prepared by the local government, because release of such an analysis would probably reveal many of the details of the proposals that had been received. The statute defines "information technology" by reference to G.S. 147-33.81, which in turn defines the term as follows:

> "Information technology" means electronic data processing goods and services, telecommunications goods and services, security goods and services, microprocessors, software, information processing, office systems, any services related to the foregoing, and consulting or other services for design or redesign of information technology supporting business processes.

Regional Transportation Agency Procurement

G.S. 143-129(h) creates an exception to the formal bid process for procurement contracts for two sorts of regional transportation agencies: regional public transportation authorities and regional transportation authorities.[5] Instead of formal or informal bids, the subsection permits such an agency to enter into procurement contracts through an RFP procedure described in the statute. The subsection concludes by declaring that the contents of any proposal are not open to public inspection "until 14 days before the award of the contract." As with information technology proposals, this exception to the right of inspection probably applies as well to any evaluation of the proposals prepared by the transportation agency, because release of such an evaluation would probably reveal many of the details of the proposals that had been received.

Other RFP Processes

If a local government seeks to procure other services through an RFP procedure, no statute excepts the proposals that have been received from public inspection, and therefore they are open to such inspection from the time that they are opened by the procuring local government.

---

4. The relevant provision of the statute is set out in appendix 19A.
5. The relevant provision in the statute is set out in appendix 19A.

Bid Analyses and Construction and Repair Diaries

G.S. 136-28.5(b), which applies only to contracts awarded by the state Department of Transportation, specifies that bid analyses prepared by the department are permanently confidential and not public record. No statute establishes comparable confidentiality for any analysis made of bids received by a local government, and therefore they are open to public inspection once prepared.

Similarly, G.S. 136-28.5(a), which applies only to construction or repair projects under contract with the state Department of Transportation, provides that any diaries on the project kept by the department are excluded from public inspection until the final estimate on the contract has been paid. Again, there is no statute that establishes a comparable exclusion for such a diary kept on a construction or repair project by a local government, and therefore any such diary is open to public inspection.

Appendix 19A—Statutes

G.S. 133-33 (Cost Estimates and Bidders' Lists)

§ 133-33. Cost estimates; bidders' lists.

Any governmental agency responsible for letting public contracts may promulgate rules concerning the confidentiality of:

(1) The agency's cost estimate for any public contracts prior to bidding; and
(2) The identity of contractors who have obtained proposals for bid purposes for a public contract.

If the agency's rules require that such information be kept confidential, an employee or officer of the agency who divulges such information to any unauthorized person shall be subject to disciplinary action. This section shall not be construed to require that cost estimates or bidders' lists be kept confidential.

G.S. 143-129 (Formal Bids)

§ 143-129. Procedure for letting of public contracts.

. . .

(b) Advertisement and Letting of Contracts.—. . .

All proposals shall be opened in public and the board or governing body shall award the contract to the lowest responsible bidder or bidders, taking into consideration quality, performance and the time specified in the proposals for the performance of the contract.

G.S. 143-131 (Informal Bids)

§ 143-131. When counties, cities, towns and other subdivisions may let contracts on informal bids.

(a) All contracts for construction or repair work or for the purchase of apparatus, supplies, materials, or equipment, involving the expenditure of public money in the amount of thirty thousand dollars ($30,000) or more, but less than the limits prescribed in G.S. 143-129, made by any officer, department, board, local school administrative unit, or commission of any county, city, town, or other subdivision of this State shall be made after informal bids have been secured. All such contracts shall be awarded to the lowest responsible, responsive bidder, taking into consideration quality, performance, and the time specified in the bids for the performance of the contract. **It shall be the duty of any officer, department, board, local school administrative unit, or commission entering into such contract to keep a record of all bids submitted, and such record shall not be subject to public inspection until the contract has been awarded.**

G.S. 143-129.8 (Information Technology Contracts)

§ 143-129.8. Purchase of information technology goods and services.

(a) In recognition of the complex and innovative nature of information technology goods and services and of the desirability of a single point of responsibility for contracts that include combinations of purchase of goods, design, installation, training, operation, maintenance, and related services, a political subdivision of the State may contract for information technology, as defined in G.S. 147-33.81(2), using the procedure set forth in this section, in addition to or instead of any other procedure available under North Carolina law.

(b) Contracts for information technology may be entered into under a request for proposals procedure that satisfies the following minimum requirements:

(1) Notice of the request for proposals shall be given in accordance with G.S. 143-129(b).

(2) Contracts shall be awarded to the person or entity that submits the best overall proposal as determined by the awarding authority. Factors to be considered in awarding contracts shall be identified in the request for proposals.

(c) The awarding authority may use procurement methods set forth in G.S. 143-135.9 in developing and evaluating requests for proposals under this section. The awarding authority may negotiate with any proposer in order to obtain a final contract that best meets the needs of the awarding authority. Negotiations allowed under this section shall not alter the contract beyond the scope of the original request for proposals in a manner that: (i) deprives the proposers or potential proposers of a fair opportunity to compete for the contract; and (ii) would have resulted in the award of the contract to a different person or entity if the alterations had been included in the request for proposals.

(d) Proposals submitted under this section shall not be subject to public inspection until a contract is awarded.

G.S. 143-129(h) (Regional Transportation Agency Contracts)

§ 143-129. Procedure for letting of public contracts.

. . .

(h) Transportation Authority Purchases.—Notwithstanding any other provision of this section, any board or governing body of any regional public transportation authority, hereafter referred to as a "RPTA," created pursuant to Article 26 of Chapter 160A of the General Statutes, or a regional transportation authority, hereafter referred to as a "RTA," created pursuant to Article 27 of Chapter 160A of the General Statutes, may approve the entering into of any contract for the purchase, lease, or other acquisition of any apparatus, supplies, materials, or equipment without competitive bidding and without meeting the requirements of subsection (b) of this section if the following procurement by competitive proposal (Request for Proposal) method is followed.

The competitive proposal method of procurement is normally conducted with more than one source submitting an offer or proposal. Either a fixed price or cost reimbursement type contract is awarded. This method of procurement is generally used when conditions are not appropriate for the use of sealed bids. If this procurement method is used, all of the following requirements apply:

(1) Requests for proposals shall be publicized. All evaluation factors shall be identified along with their relative importance.

(2) Proposals shall be solicited from an adequate number of qualified sources.

(3) RPTAs or RTAs shall have a method in place for conducting technical evaluations of proposals received and selecting awardees, with the goal of promoting fairness and competition without requiring strict adherence to specifications or price in determining the most advantageous proposal.

(4) The award may be based upon initial proposals without further discussion or negotiation or, in the discretion of the evaluators, discussions or negotiations may be conducted either with all offerors or with those offerors determined to be within the competitive range, and one or more revised proposals or a best and final offer may be requested of all remaining offerors. The details and deficiencies of an offeror's proposal may not be disclosed to other offerors during any period of negotiation or discussion.
(5) The award shall be made to the responsible firm whose proposal is most advantageous to the RPTA's or the RTA's program with price and other factors considered.

The contents of the proposals shall not be public records until 14 days before the award of the contract.

The board or governing body of the RPTA or the RTA shall, at the regularly scheduled meeting, by formal motion make findings of fact that the procurement by competitive proposal (Request for Proposals) method of procuring the particular apparatus, supplies, materials, or equipment is the most appropriate acquisition method prior to the issuance of the requests for proposals and shall by formal motion certify that the requirements of this subsection have been followed before approving the contract.

Nothing in this subsection subjects a procurement by competitive proposal under this subsection to G.S. 143-49, 143-52, or 143-53.

RPTAs and RTAs may adopt regulations to implement this subsection.

Chapter 20—Public Security Records

Statutory Summary

Sections 132-1.6, 132-1.7, and 132-6.1(c) of the North Carolina General Statutes [hereinafter G.S.] address public security issues.[1] Combined, the three sections exempt from public access the following sorts of materials:

- Emergency response plans (this exemption only applies to such plans when adopted by an institution of the University of North Carolina, a community college, or a public hospital)
- Public security plans and arrangements
- Detailed plans and drawings of public buildings and infrastructure facilities
- Plans to prevent or respond to terrorist activity, to the extent disclosure would jeopardize human safety or the security of government structures or information storage systems

The first two sections were enacted in response to the terrorist attacks of September 11, 2001. The third statute was enacted before the September 11 attacks and exempts from public access a myriad of security features of government information technology systems, telecommunication networks, and electronic security systems.

1. The statutes are set out in appendix 20A at the end of this chapter.

Discussion

The provisions codified as G.S. 132-1.6 and G.S. 132-1.7 resulted from three separate session laws, enacted in two separate sessions of the General Assembly. The information technology security provisions in G.S. 132-6.1 were enacted through a fourth session law, in a third session of the General Assembly. As a result, there is some overlap among the various statutes, but there are also gaps in their coverage that might seem puzzling. The discussion below is intended to give some sense of the substance of the three statutes, point out some of the overlaps, and suggest certain categories of records that are comparable to those included in the statutes but that are not in fact included in them and therefore remain open to public access.

Plans for Dealing with Terrorist Acts and Other Emergencies

The last enacted provision, and in some ways the broadest, is found in G.S. 132-1.7(b). This subsection exempts from public access a range of materials associated with preventing and responding to terrorist activities and attacks. A local government might assess the ways in which the community or the government's personnel or facilities might be vulnerable to terrorist attack, determine steps needed to deter or prevent such an attack, and establish procedures for responding to an attempted or successful attack. The records associated with all these activities clearly fall within the exemption created in the statute. Examples include a health department's plans for responding to a bioterrorism attack, a police department's plans for guarding VIPs who might be visiting the community, and a utility department's vulnerability assessment prepared in compliance with federal law.[2] As part of its plans for coordinating its activities with other entities, a government might also possess records from those entities spelling out their plans for preventing or responding to terrorist attacks; these records also fall within the statutory exemption. For example, a town or county that includes or is near a power generation facility might have received this sort of information from the utility that owns the facility.

G.S. 132-1.6 exempts from public access "emergency response plans" and related material for constituent institutions of the University of North Carolina, community colleges, or public hospitals. Many such plans and other materials are probably also exempt from public inspection under G.S. 132-1.7(b); that is, they are materials associated with preventing or responding to terrorist activities and attacks. It is certainly possible, however, for such institutions to have plans for responding to a variety of emergencies that have nothing to do with terrorism—for example, a university's plans for dealing with student unrest that is clearly not terrorist in nature or a public hospital's plans for dealing with the aftermath of a natural disaster. To the extent this is true, G.S. 132-1.6 is broader in coverage than 132-1.7(b), although it might lead to an odd situation in which some agencies have plans that are exempt from public access while other agencies' comparable plans are not exempt. For example, a public hospital might have an emergency response plan for dealing with a hur-

---

2. 42 U.S.C. § 300i-2 requires each community water system serving a population of more than 3,300 persons to prepare a vulnerability assessment and submit a copy to the administrator of the federal Environmental Protection Agency. The statute also requires each such system to prepare an emergency response plan incorporating the results of the vulnerability assessment.

ricane or tornado, and a public health department might have a comparable and complementary plan. Because a health department is not a public hospital, however, its plan would not be exempt from public inspection under G.S. 132-1.6. Some emergency response plans not covered by G.S. 132-1.6 might, however, qualify as public security plans and arrangements and be exempt from public access under G.S. 132-1.7(a), which is discussed in the next paragraph.

G.S. 132-1.7(a) exempts from public access "public security plans and arrangements." To the extent that such plans are related to terrorism, this provision appears to be entirely redundant given the antiterrorism assessments and plans exempted in subsection (b) of the same section. (Subsection (a) was enacted in 2002 and subsection (b) in 2003, so some redundancy might be expected.) To the extent, however, that a local government prepares public security plans for situations not involving terrorism, subsection (a) provides an additional exemption from public access. Law enforcement agencies, for example, may have a number of plans or procedures in place that protect public security in nonterrorist situations—plans to deal with large-scale jail breaks, parades by controversial organizations such as the Ku Klux Klan, student riots in a university town after athletic contests, and so on. All of these plans clearly involve *public security* but none involves terrorist acts in the normal sense. (It would be difficult, however, to characterize the health department plan for dealing with a natural disaster, mentioned in the preceding paragraph, as a public security plan, and so it would not be exempt from access under G.S. 132-1.7(a).)

Plans for Public Buildings and Infrastructure

The final relevant provision in G.S. 132-1.7(a) exempts from public access "the detailed plans and drawings of public buildings and infrastructure facilities." There are a number of definitional questions about some of the terms in the subsection and a couple of practical issues related to handling such plans and drawings.

First, the term "public buildings" clearly includes buildings owned and used by governmental entities. At the local level, it includes county courthouses, city halls, local government office buildings, public schools, auditoriums, convention centers, police or fire stations, public works garages, and so on. It probably also includes sports facilities, although a narrow view of the word "building" might cause some to quibble about, for example, an outdoor stadium. It probably also includes buildings that are leased and used by local governments—for example, a building leased for city offices or a clinical space leased by a local health department. The statute does not limit the exemption to *publicly owned* buildings but applies to "public" buildings, easily accommodating any building used by a governmental entity. Similarly, the term probably also includes any building owned by a governmental entity, even if leased to a nongovernmental user or users, such as a city-owned sports facility leased to a private team. After all, the New York World Trade Center itself was owned by a governmental entity but most of its space was leased to private companies. Such a broad interpretation of the statute's terminology promotes the apparent purpose of the statute: protecting buildings associated with government from attack.

More problematic is whether the term also includes facilities that are privately owned and occupied but open in some broad fashion to the public. A football stadium owned by a private university, for example, is public neither in ownership nor governmental use, but it is a facility crowded with the general public several times a year. Nevertheless, it is difficult to push the term to include a facility that is neither owned nor used by some sort of governmental entity. After all, some portion of almost any facility is open to the public during business hours, whether it is a stadium that holds forty thousand people on a Saturday afternoon or a restaurant that serves forty patrons that same evening. It makes no sense to call them both "public" buildings, and the statute offers no logical way to distinguish between them.

The second issue concerns the term "infrastructure facilities." This most obviously includes utility facilities owned by local governments, such as water or sewer lines, treatment plants, or water supply reservoirs. It almost certainly also includes airport facilities, streets and highways, parking structures, dams, and communication lines that are owned or used by local governments. Does it also, though, include infrastructure facilities owned by private entities, or does the word "public" modify both "buildings" and "infrastructure"? If the infrastructure facilities covered by the statute include only those owned or used by governmental entities, then the exemption does not cover most of the state's electric power generating facilities, nor most of the natural gas lines or rail facilities, nor many of the dams. Yet a local government might well possess detailed plans and drawings of such privately owned infrastructure. The purposes of the statute are much better met by reading it in a way that does not limit the exemption to publicly owned or publicly used infrastructure, and such a reading is well within the natural meaning of the statutory language.

The final ambiguity concerns the term "detailed plans and drawings." A building project of any complexity will have construction plans and drawings prepared before construction commences, and these are typically modified during the construction period. Often, once the project is complete, "as-built" drawings will be prepared to reflect the finished structure. Clearly the statute applies to the as-built drawings, but it almost certainly applies as well to those plans and drawings prepared before construction and modified during construction. Release of the earlier plans would negate most of the benefit of denying access to as-built drawings, and so fulfillment of the statutory purpose argues strongly for inclusion of both preliminary and final plans and drawings.

There are at least two practical issues that arise under this provision. The first involves how a government that is seeking to deny general public access to the detailed plans for a new public building, as permitted by the statute,[3] can square that goal with the need to allow access to those same plans by companies interested in bidding on the construction contract. One commonly used method is to distribute the plans to companies that have expressed interest in bidding and require those companies, by contract, to keep the plans confidential and return them once their bid has been prepared and submitted. Obviously, a terrorist interested in destroying a public building is not likely to be deterred by a contractual obligation to the building's owner, but such a contract might cause potential bidders to more tightly control access to the plans. An alternative possibility is to place the plans in a secure location under the control of the local government and require bidders to inspect the drawings only in that location.

---

3. Each of these exemptions denies public access to the described records and materials but does not prohibit the custodial government from releasing the records.

A second practical issue involves making plans and drawings available to persons and entities whose everyday business requires that availability, such as engineering companies or planning consultants. Some governments have developed access systems that accord automatic access to such companies if they register themselves with the government and agree to abide by the government's restrictions on use and distribution of the plans and drawings.

Information Technology Systems and Telecommunications Systems

The provision in G.S. 132-6.1(c), which is expressed as a proviso rather than a direct exemption from public access, is somewhat roundabout, but its intention is plain. It exempts from public access security features in information technology systems, telecommunications systems, and electronic security systems. The term "security features" includes "hardware or software security, passwords, or security standards, procedures, processes, configurations, software, and codes."

Radio Frequency Codes

One question that has arisen is whether this provision covers the codes programmed into modern public safety radio systems that reveal the frequencies used by public safety officers and units. Many public safety agencies use radio systems that change frequency every few seconds, so that scanning such systems is almost impossible. Revealing the codes would make it possible for knowledgeable listeners to modify their scanners and listen to over-the-air conversations. This might seem unimportant for the routine car-to-car or dispatcher-to-car communications, but such a scanner might also pick up conversations among vice squad members preparing for a raid, swat team members responding to an emergency, street crime units covering an undercover operation, and so on. These codes appear to be covered by this statutory provision, which would permit a local government to deny access to them, and doing so is certainly consistent with the policy of G.S. 132-6.1(c) and the other statutes discussed in this chapter.

Appendix 20A—Statutes

G.S. 132-1.6

§ 132-1.6. Emergency response plans.

Emergency response plans adopted by a constituent institution of The University of North Carolina, a community college, or a public hospital as defined in G.S. 159-39 and the records related to the planning and development of these emergency response plans are not public records as defined by G.S. 132-1 and shall not be subject to inspection and examination under G.S. 132-6.

G.S. 132-1.7

§ 132-1.7. Sensitive public security information.

(a) Public records, as defined in G.S. 132-1, shall not include information containing specific details of public security plans and arrangements or the detailed plans and drawings of public buildings and infrastructure facilities.

(b) Public records as defined in G.S. 132-1 do not include plans to prevent or respond to terrorist activity, to the extent such records set forth vulnerability and risk assessments, potential targets, specific tactics, or specific security or emergency procedures, the disclosure of which would jeopardize the safety of governmental personnel or the general public or the security of any governmental facility, building, structure, or information storage system.

(c) Information relating to the general adoption of public security plans and arrangements, and budgetary information concerning the authorization or expenditure of public funds to implement public security plans and arrangements, or for the construction, renovation, or repair of public buildings and infrastructure facilities shall be public records.

G.S. 132-6.1(c)

§ 132-6.1. Electronic data-processing records.

. . .

(c) Nothing in this section shall require a public agency to create a computer database that the public agency has not otherwise created or is not otherwise required to be created. Nothing in this section requires a public agency to disclose security features of its electronic data processing systems, information technology systems, telecommunications networks, or electronic security systems, including hardware or software security, passwords, or security standards, procedures, processes, configurations, software, and codes.

Chapter 21—Geographic Information System Records

Statutory Summary

Geographic information systems (GIS) are computerized mapping systems in which a wide variety of information is digitized and entered into the system with precise locational coordinates. Such a system permits users to research locational questions. For example, a user could ask the system to produce a list of prospective landfill sites within a county that meet a range of requirements, such as soil type, relation to flood plains, distance from population centers, and so on. Or a user could ask for the precise location and nature of all utility wires and pipes at a particular spot. Section 132-10 of the North Carolina General Statutes [hereinafter G.S.] addresses the public records status of GIS databases.[1] The statute begins by affirming that GIS records are public records, and it directs local governments to provide mechanisms, such as dumb terminals, for public access to system records and to provide copies of GIS records at reasonable cost.

Geographic information systems are costly to develop, often requiring a public investment of several million dollars. Local officials involved in developing such systems objected to the ability of a private company, under the general public records law, to gain a copy of a GIS database for the price of a computer tape and then use the database in its private business, often at considerable profit. From the government's perspective, such a practice meant that the government was creating a record with significant commercial value without being able to recoup any of its cost from the commercial use of the record. These objections have been recognized in G.S. 132-10. The statute permits a local government to refuse to provide an electronic copy of a GIS database to any person or entity who refuses to enter into a written commitment that the copy will not be used for trade or commercial

1. The statute is set out in appendix 21A at the end of this chapter.

purposes. The statute declares, however, that three activities are not to be considered use for trade or commercial purposes:

1. Publishing or broadcasting of GIS data by the news media
2. Use of the data by a licensed professional in his or her profession
3. Resale at cost by a real estate trade association or a Multiple Listing Service operated by such an association

Thus, the news media, licensed professionals, and real estate trade associations are entitled to electronic copies of GIS records without having to enter into the written commitment noted above, as long as they use the records for the purposes set out in the statute.[2]

Discussion

The Cost for a Copy of a GIS Database

Reasonable Cost

If a person or entity enters into a written commitment not to use GIS records for trade or commercial purposes (or if the local government decides not to require such a commitment from those seeking electronic copies of GIS records), the local government may charge a copying fee of reasonable cost. What is the meaning of "reasonable cost"? G.S. 132-6.2 permits a local government generally to impose copying charges to recoup "actual cost," according to that statute's somewhat restrictive definition of actual cost.[3] Is the phrase reasonable cost simply a cross-reference to G.S. 132-6.2, or does it permit a somewhat higher fee than is normally possible under the public records law?

The legislative history suggests that reasonable cost has a different meaning than actual cost. G.S. 132-6.2, the actual cost section, and G.S. 132-10, the GIS records statute, were enacted as part of the same session law.[4] Presumably, then, the General Assembly was aware of the juxtaposition of the two sections and of the slightly different phrases used to authorize copying charges. If the General Assembly had intended that G.S. 132-6.2 govern charges for GIS records, it could have easily stated that governments were to furnish copies "pursuant to G.S. 132-6.2" rather than stating that they were to do so at reasonable cost. The failure to cross-reference the general rule, or to use the phrase actual cost, suggests that something else was intended.

---

2. During the 1990s there were a number of cases, mostly in the federal courts, that successfully challenged statutes that restricted the commercial use of public records. In *Rhode Island Ass'n of Realtors, Inc. v. Whitehouse*, 51 F. Supp. 2d 107 (D.R.I.), *aff'd*, 199 F.3d 26 (1st Cir. 1999), for example, the federal district court invalidated a state statute that prohibited using information from public records to solicit for commercial purposes; the plaintiff association wished to use the records to solicit newly licensed real estate agents for membership in the association. These cases generally stopped after the U.S. Supreme Court upheld such a statute against a facial attack in *Los Angeles Police Department v. United Reporting Publishing Corp.*, 528 U.S. 32 (1999). Although the court left open the possibility of an attack on such a statute as applied, there have been few such challenges and none that were successful.

3. See the discussion of copying fees *supra* in chapter 2 in the text accompanying notes 61 through 65.

4. 1995 N.C. Sess. Laws ch. 388.

If so, what is that something else? What cost components might a local government seek to recover with a copying charge for GIS records that it could not recover under G.S. 132-6.2? The most likely components are those direct costs of making a copy that G.S. 132-6.2 prohibits including in the copying charge: costs that the government would have incurred whether the copy was made or not. As the discussion in chapter 2 points out, the effect of the G.S. 132-6.2 prohibition is usually to disallow including personnel costs in the copying charge and often to disallow including fixed costs such as equipment depreciation in the charge.[5] Nevertheless, these are costs directly associated with making a copy and therefore seem appropriately part of a charge based on reasonable costs. On the other hand, a local government probably cannot attempt, through its charges for copies of GIS records, to recoup any of the costs of developing the GIS database itself. It is a general principle of public records laws nationally that the charges for copies of public records may not include the cost of creating the record itself, and it would take stronger language than "reasonable cost" to work an exception to that general principle.

Charges for Copies Intended for Commercial Use

If a person or entity wishes to use an electronic copy of GIS records for trade or commercial purposes, the local government maintaining the GIS has no legal obligation to provide the copy. But it may do so if it wishes. If it does, however, the reasonable cost provision does not apply. Rather, the local government may set whatever price it wishes for electronic copies that will be used for trade or commercial purposes, or it may negotiate a price with the person or entity seeking the copy. If the negotiations are unsuccessful, no copy need be made.

Trade or Commercial Purposes

The Meaning of "Trade or Commercial Purposes"

One issue that has arisen in interpretation of G.S. 132-10 is whether the phrase "trade or commercial purposes" means all private business uses of GIS databases or whether some narrower meaning is intended. Does the phrase, for example, extend to manufacturing activities? The answer is probably yes.

The local governments that sought this provision of law were concerned in a general way about private companies receiving electronic copies of GIS databases, at nominal cost, and then using the databases to make money. There is no evidence that the local governments distinguished among different ways of profiting from the databases. The North Carolina courts have long understood that the word "trade" is often used as a shorthand for any private economic activity,[6] and it is likely that they would understand the word in that broader way in this context. This interpretation is reinforced by the special provision for

---

5. *See supra* note 3.

6. See, for example, *State v. Worth*, 116 N.C. 1007, 21 S.E. 204 (1895), in which the court held that constitutional and statutory authority to levy taxes on "trades" included authority to tax manufacturers; and *Orange Speedway, Inc. v. Clayton*, 247 N.C. 528, 533, 101 S.E.2d 406, 410 (1958), in which the court held that the state constitutional ban on local acts relating to trade included an act limiting Sunday car racing in a single county, saying that "[a] trade . . . includes any employment or business embarked in for gain or profit."

use by licensed professionals. When "trade" or "commerce" is understood narrowly, it is usually distinguished from *professional* activities.[7] Therefore, if the narrow meaning of trade was intended, it would have been unnecessary to make special provision for professional use of a database.

Licensed Professional

As the summary notes, G.S. 132-10 provides that "use of [GIS] information without resale by a licensed professional in the course of practicing the professional's profession" is not use for a commercial purpose. What does the statute mean by "licensed professional"?

Preferably, readers develop the meaning of a statutory term or phrase by reference to the policy underlying the statutory provision; unfortunately, the policy behind the special provision for professional services is unintelligible. Why should a licensed professional, such as a licensed engineer helping to locate a landfill, be allowed to use GIS data while someone who is not licensed, such as a consulting planner doing the same task, is not? Because the policy behind the provision is obscure, we must proceed to develop the meaning of the language in something of a vacuum.[8]

One possibility is that licensed professional means no more than a person who is subject to a North Carolina occupational licensing board and holds a license or certificate from such a board. In a different context, for example, the Georgia Court of Appeals equated "profession" with the holding of a state occupational license, in that case a license as a pest controller.[9] Most courts, however, have rejected such an equation, holding that a profession is more than a licensed occupation.[10] Courts have noted that many licensed occupations are not normally thought of as professions and sought to define the term "professional" in a way that distinguishes licensed professions as a subset of licensed occupations. This narrower interpretation is the more likely meaning of the language in G.S. 132-10. The section uses the words "professional" or "profession" three times within a nine-word stretch, which indicates a conscious choice in using that term, when "occupation" could have been used.

---

7. See, for example, *Short v. Demopolis,* 691 P.2d 163 (Wash. 1984), in which the court held that Washington's unfair competition statute, which applies to acts in "trade or commerce," did not extend to the substantive aspects of law practice. North Carolina's unfair competition statute, N.C. GEN. STAT. [hereinafter G.S.] § 75-1.1, at one time extended to "acts or practices in the conduct of any trade or commerce," which the North Carolina Supreme Court defined to include only transactions involving the sale of goods. State *ex rel.* Edmisten v. J.C. Penney Co., 292 N.C. 311, 233 S.E.2d 895 (1977). The General Assembly responded by amending the statute to add a broad definition of "commerce" but then specifically excluded professional services from the statute. 1977 N.C. SESS. LAWS ch. 747.

8. It should be repeated that the subject of this discussion is which occupational groups are entitled to an electronic copy of a GIS database, at reasonable cost, even if the groups' members use the database in their work. Anyone, of course, is entitled to make use of the database at the public office in which it is kept, without any charge whatsoever.

9. Colston v. Fred's Pest Control, Inc., 436 S.E.2d 23 (Ga. Ct. App. 1993) (holding that an action against a pest control company was subject to a statute requiring the filing of an expert affidavit with the complaint in cases of *professional* negligence).

10. *E.g.*, Pierce v. AALL Ins. Inc., 531 So. 2d 84 (Fla. 1988) (professional negligence statute of limitations does not apply to insurance agents), *receded from in part on other grounds by* Garden v. Frier, 602 So. 2d 1273 (Fla. 1992); Tylle v. Zoucha, 412 N.W.2d 438 (Neb. 1987) (professional negligence statute of limitations does not apply to real estate broker); Jilek v. Berger Elec., Inc., 441 N.W.2d 660 (N.D. 1989) (professional negligence statute of limitations does not apply to electrician).

If not all licensed occupations are professions, what characteristics cause a business activity to be termed a profession? Although the North Carolina courts have had little occasion to define profession, courts in other states have done so in a number of contexts. The two most frequent contexts in which this issue has become determinative have been the application of special statutes of limitation for professional malpractice[11] and the interpretation of zoning provisions that limit home offices to professional services. By and large, the courts of different states have developed comparable definitions of professional activities. They have emphasized the specialized knowledge that is characteristic of a profession and the long and difficult process of study that is necessary to acquire that knowledge.[12] At least one state has refined the need for significant study into a requirement of a college degree,[13] but it is doubtful that North Carolina would impose such a requirement. This is because in this state, too many occupational licensing statutes that regulate activities that are clearly professional in nature permit licensing to be granted to those who can show considerable practice experience, in lieu of a specialized four-year degree. G.S. 89C-13(a), for example, permits a person without an engineering degree to qualify for registration as a professional engineer if that person has had at least twenty years of progressive engineering experience. Therefore, our courts are likely to use a definition that emphasizes special knowledge and long and intense study but that does not require a four-year degree to be a condition of licensing. Under such a definition, architects[14] and engineers[15] clearly qualify as licensed professionals, as do licensed occupations such as soil scientists[16] and geologists.[17] Landscape architects[18] probably do so as well. On the other hand, it appears equally clear that real

11. North Carolina has a special statute of repose for professional malpractice, G.S. 1-15(c). The state's appellate courts have not been asked to determine what is a profession under that statute.

12. *E.g.*, Georgetowne Ltd. P'ship v. Geotechnical Servs., Inc., 430 N.W.2d 34 (Neb. 1988) (engineer is a professional); Willett v. Chu, 507 N.Y.S.2d 318 (App. Div. 1986) (unlicensed consultant is not a professional because, in part, neither a college degree nor a license is required to engage in the occupation).

13. Jilek v. Berger Elec., Inc., 441 N.W.2d 660 (N.D. 1989) (electrician is not a professional because no college degree is required).

14. G.S. 83A-7(a)(1) requires that a person have a "professional education," have at least three years of practical training and experience, and pass an examination as conditions of licensing.

15. G.S. 89C-13(a) requires, as a condition of licensing, graduation from an engineering or related curriculum and several years of engineering experience or a substantial number of years of progressive engineering experience alone, plus passage of licensing examinations.

16. G.S. 89F-10(a) requires a bachelor of science degree with certain science coursework, three years of work experience as a soil scientist or an advanced degree or teaching or research experience, and passage of an examination as conditions of licensing for a soil scientist.

17. G.S. 89E-9 requires a licensee to hold a college degree in geology or have completed a significant number of geology courses, pass a licensing examination, and have five years of geological work experience, a requirement that can be met in part by further education or research.

18. G.S. 89A-4 requires a licensee to be a graduate of an accredited collegiate curriculum in landscape architecture and to have four years' experience in landscape architecture (or have a combination of ten years' education and experience), and pass a licensing examination.

estate brokers[19] do not qualify and that real estate appraisers[20] and registered foresters[21] probably do not qualify.

One licensed occupation whose members would probably be able to make effective use of GIS databases has a more uncertain status under this definition of licensed professional. That occupation is licensed land surveyor. The difficulty for this occupational group is that its licensing statute allows a person with a high school diploma and seven years of supervised experience to be licensed;[22] and it simply is not clear whether such a relatively short experience alternative to formal training is consonant with the notion of intense study associated with a profession. There must remain some uncertainty about the status of this important potential group of users of GIS databases.[23]

A State License

Finally, when the statute speaks of a "licensed" professional, it is clear that it is speaking of a North Carolina state occupational license. It is not speaking of a certification from some national organization when there is no corresponding state occupational license.[24]

---

19. G.S. 93A-4 permits a person to be licensed as a broker upon completion of a number of short courses, or the equivalent in education and experience, and passage of a licensing examination.

20. G.S. 93E-1-6 permits a person to be certified as an appraiser upon completion of an associate's degree or specified college credit hours, a number of short courses, and 2,500 hours of appraising experience, or education and experience equivalent to the preceding requirements, plus passage of a licensing examination.

21. G.S. 89B-9 requires, as a condition of registration, either a bachelor's degree or higher in forestry or six years of professional experience.

22. G.S. 89C-13(b).

23. GIS operators are likely to offer GIS database records to licensed land surveyors even if they do not qualify as licensed professionals. Many GIS operators rely on surveyors to confirm the reliability of the coordinates in the GIS database and to provide corrections; that kind of cooperation is less likely if the surveyors are charged a high fee for a copy of the database.

24. Thus, for example, it is not speaking of a person certified as a planner by the American Institute of Certified Planners.

Appendix 21A—Statute

G.S. 132-10

§ 132-10. Qualified exception for geographical information systems.

Geographical information systems databases and data files developed and operated by counties and cities are public records within the meaning of this Chapter. The county or city shall provide public access to such systems by public access terminals or other output devices. Upon request, the county or city shall furnish copies, in documentary or electronic form, to anyone requesting them at reasonable cost. As a condition of furnishing an electronic copy, whether on magnetic tape, magnetic disk, compact disk, or photo-optical device, a county or city may require that the person obtaining the copy agree in writing that the copy will not be resold or otherwise used for trade or commercial purposes. For purposes of this section, publication or broadcast by the news media, real estate trade associations, or Multiple Listing Services operated by real estate trade associations shall not constitute a resale or use of the data for trade or commercial purposes and use of information without resale by a licensed professional in the course of practicing the professional's profession shall not constitute use for a commercial purpose. For purposes of this section, resale at cost by a real estate trade association or Multiple Listing Services operated by a real estate trade association shall not constitute a resale or use of the data for trade or commercial purposes.

Chapter 22—Miscellaneous Records

This chapter briefly discusses issues that might arise under two statutes—one dealing with library records, and the second dealing with recreation records that identify minors.

PART 1—Library Records

Statutory Summary

The confidentiality of library use is an important ethical principle for public libraries,[1] and Sections 125-18 and 125-19 of the North Carolina General Statutes [hereinafter G.S.] have

1. The American Library Association has written:

> What people read, research or access remains a fundamental matter of privacy. One should be able to access all constitutionally protected information and at the same time feel secure that what one reads, researches or finds through our Nation's libraries is no one's business but their own.

codified the principle into North Carolina law.[2] G.S. 125-19 generally prohibits a library from disclosing "any library record that identifies a person as having requested or obtained specific materials, information, or services" from the library. The only statutory exceptions to this prohibition are when

- disclosure is "necessary for the reasonable operation of the library,"
- the patron has given written consent, or
- the library has received a subpoena or court order or is otherwise required by law to disclose the information.

Discussion

Records to Which the Statute Applies

Although this statute appears at first blush to be straightforward, it is in fact somewhat confusing at the edges. To understand the confusion, let's begin with the statutory language. G.S. 125-19(a), which is the basic prohibition on disclosure, reads as follows:

> Disclosure—A library shall not disclose any library record that identifies a person as having requested or obtained specific materials, information, or services, *or as otherwise having used the library*, except as provided for in subsection (b).

The confusion arises from the language italicized for purposes of this discussion: *or as otherwise having used the library.* To further understand the issue, let's posit the sorts of records that a library might hold:

- Circulation records, showing the books and other materials checked out by a patron
- Equipment use records, listing the persons who have signed up to use computers, microfilm readers, or other equipment
- Membership lists of library-sponsored book clubs
- Registration records, showing the names and addresses of persons receiving library cards
- Security videos that show persons who are in the library facility

Several of the listed records clearly reveal the specific library materials or services that have been used by individuals. All of the records reveal that the persons listed or shown have used the library. Are all the listed records therefore covered by the statute's prohibition on disclosure?

Probably not. The reason is that G.S. 125-18, which accompanies G.S. 125-19, includes a definition of "library records." Under G.S. 125-18(2), a library record is one "that identifies a person as having requested or obtained specific information or materials from a library."

American Library Association, Privacy (last updated July 28, 2008), www.ala.org/ala/aboutala/offices/wo/woissues/civilliberties/privacy/privacy.cfm.

2. The statutes are set out in appendix 22A at the end of this chapter.

Therefore, the threshold question for the list of records set out above is whether each of them is a library record as so defined, and in fact most of them are not. Let's look at each of them in turn.

Circulation Records

Circulation records identify the specific books, videos, or other materials that have been checked out by a library patron. They clearly are library records under the statutory definition.

Equipment Use Records

Equipment use records show only that a person has used a library computer, microfilm machine, or other equipment. They do not reveal any specific information or materials the person might have accessed through the computer or read on the microfilm reader. Therefore, by themselves they are not library records under the statutory definition.[3]

Book Club Membership Lists

A book club membership list obviously reveals that those listed have used a specific library *service*, sponsored book clubs. But the list does not reveal any specific information or materials that each person listed has either requested or obtained. Therefore, the membership lists are not library records under the statutory definition.

Registration Records

A listing of persons with library cards obviously shows library use, at least enough to obtain the card. But it does not reveal what specific information or materials a person may have obtained with the card and therefore is not a library record under the statutory definition.

Security Videos

In general a security video will show that someone was present in a library facility, but it will not show what information or materials a person was using. Therefore, such a video is not a library record under the statutory definition. (In rare cases the video might show a book in a patron's hands with enough clarity that the title can be read; in such a case it apparently would qualify as a library record.)

In summary, it appears that many records held by a library may well show that a person has used a library or specific services of the library, but those records would not be covered by this statute. That is because they do not meet the statutory definition of library record, which is only a subset of the larger group of records held by a library.

---

3. It might be possible to combine equipment use records with other information to determine what websites, for example, a person visited on a library computer. In that case, the equipment use record, when combined with the other information, would be a library record under the statutory definition.

Permitted Releases of Records

Release to Bill Collectors

One issue that arises under the statute is whether a library can release to a bill collector the names of persons who have significant amounts of unpaid library fines. Although a list of such persons would not normally reveal the specific books they had checked out (and perhaps never returned), it would show that they had used the library, and because the list would have been created from circulation records, it may be covered by the statute. But the statute, in G.S. 125-19(b), permits disclosure of library records "[w]hen necessary for the reasonable operation of the library." Just about all libraries administer a system of small fines for the late return of library materials and larger fines to replace materials that are never returned, and so such a system of fines is clearly part of the reasonable operation of any library. If a system of fines is reasonable, then it is also reasonable to attempt to collect those fines and to contract with a bill collector to do so when the library's own efforts are unavailing. Therefore, releasing such a list to a bill collector is permitted under the statute.

Release Pursuant to a Subpoena or Court Order

Chapter 6 discusses the meaning of "court order" in a variety of statutes that permit the release of records otherwise closed to the public and concludes that the term does not include a subpoena.[4] That is not an issue under G.S. 125-19, inasmuch as this statute permits release pursuant to either a court order or a subpoena.

PART 2—Recreation Records That Identify Minors

Statutory Summary

G.S. 132-1.12 states that certain information about minors participating in parks or recreation programs is not public record under G.S. Chapter 132. The listed information is as follows:

- The minor's name
- The minor's address
- The minor's age and date of birth
- The minor's telephone number
- The name and address of the minor's parent or legal guardian
- "[A]ny other identifying information on an application to participate in [a recreation] program or other records related to that program."

4. The text is *supra* in chapter 6, accompanying notes 53 through 64.

Despite the above list, the statute goes on to specify that the county, municipality, and zip code of each participating minor is in fact a public record and therefore open to the public.

The statute concludes by making clear that it does not create a prohibition against disclosure but simply denies automatic public access to these records.

Discussion

Below are a couple of minor interpretive issues that have arisen under this statute, and one suggestion for good practice.

Who Is a Minor?

The statute does not define the term "minor," so we must look elsewhere for the meaning of the term. G.S. Chapter 48A is titled "Minors," and G.S. 48A-2 defines the word, apparently for the General Statutes generally: "A minor is any person who has not reached the age of 18 years."

What Is Other Identifying Information?

Although the statute uses the term "identifying information," the term probably does not have the same meaning in the recreation statute that it does in G.S. 132-1.10, which deals with Social Security numbers and other identifying information. In G.S. 132-1.10 the term references a statutory list that is certainly not a complete list of all information that might lead to a person's identity; such a complete list does not appear to be intended. But it might well be intended in G.S. 132-1.12. Given what is not public record—the minor's name, address, parents, etc.—the term probably includes any information a recreation department might have that would facilitate identifying a minor who is participating in that department's programs. Among the sorts of information that one finds on recreation department applications that might be characterized as indentifying information would be

- a minor's gender;
- a minor's e-mail address;
- the name of a person, other than parents, to reach in an emergency;
- the school attended by the minor; and
- any physical limitations or medical conditions that might affect participation in the recreation program.

Notice of Policies

As was noted in the statutory summary, this is not a mandatory exception to the right of access: a local government may release some or all of the covered information if it wishes to. Indeed, many recreation departments do so routinely; for example, by releasing results of league games that include individual statistics. This practice suggests that it might be helpful to citizens for a recreation department to attempt to codify and explain to the public its policies concerning release of information about minors participating in the department's programs.

Appendix 22A—Statutes

Library Records

Article 3—Library Records.

§ 125-18. Definitions.

As used in this Article, unless the context requires otherwise:

(1) "Library" means a library established by the State; a county, city, township, village, school district, or other local unit of government or authority or combination of local units of governments and authorities; community college or university; or any private library open to the public.

(2) "Library record" means a document, record, or other method of storing information retained by a library that identifies a person as having requested or obtained specific information or materials from a library. "Library record" does not include nonidentifying material that may be retained for the purpose of studying or evaluating the circulation of library materials in general.

§ 125-19. Confidentiality of library user records.

(a) Disclosure.—A library shall not disclose any library record that identifies a person as having requested or obtained specific materials, information, or services, or as otherwise having used the library, except as provided for in subsection (b).

(b) Exceptions.—Library records may be disclosed in the following instances:

(1) When necessary for the reasonable operation of the library;

(2) Upon written consent of the user; or

(3) Pursuant to subpoena, court order, or where otherwise required by law.

Recreation Records about Minors

§ 132-1.12. Limited access to identifying information of minors participating in local government parks and recreation programs.

(a) A public record, as defined by G.S. 132-1, does not include, as to any minor participating in a park or recreation program sponsored by a local government or combination of local governments, any of the following information as to that minor participant: (i) name, (ii) address, (iii) age, (iv) date of birth, (v) telephone number, (vi) the name or address of that minor participant's parent or legal guardian, or (vii) any other identifying information on an application to participate in such program or other records related to that program.

(b) The county, municipality, and zip code of residence of each participating minor covered by subsection (a) of this section is a public record, with the information listed in subsection (a) of this section redacted.

(c) Nothing in this section makes the information listed in subsection (a) of this section confidential information.

Index

A

B

C

D

E

F

G

H

M

N

O

Q

R

S

T

U

V

W

Z

CPSIA information can be obtained
at www.ICGtesting.com
Printed in the USA
LVHW060042150223
739555LV00010B/583

9 781560 116141